Religious and Spiritual Issues in Counseling

Religious and Spiritual Issues in Counseling

Applications Across Diverse Populations

Mary Thomas Burke
Jane C. Chauvin
Judith G. Miranti

Brunner-Routledge
Taylor & Francis Group

NEW YORK AND HOVE

Published in 2005 by
Brunner-Routledge
270 Madison Avenue
New York, NY 10016
www.brunner-routledge.com

Published in Great Britain by
Brunner-Routledge
27 Church Road
Hove
East Sussex   BN3 2FA
www.brunner-routledge.co.uk

10 9 8 7 6 5 4 3 2 1

Library of Congress Cataloging-in-Publication Data
    Burke, Mary Thomas.
        Religious and spiritual issues in counseling : applications across diverse
    populations / Mary Thomas Burke, Jane C. Chauvin, Judith G. Miranti.
            p. ; cm.
        Includes bibliographical references and index.
        ISBN 1-58391-372-6 (pbk. : alk. paper)
        1. Counseling—Religious aspects. 2. Spirituality—Psychology.
        [DNLM: 1. Counseling—methods. 2. Religion. 3. Spirituality. 4.
    Cultural Diversity. WM 55 B959r 2005] I. Chauvin, Jane C., 1941- II.
    Miranti, Judith G. III. Title.

    BF637.C6B815 2005
    158'.3—dc22   2004009403

Table of Contents

A Tribute to the Life of Mary Thomas Burke

Samuel T. Gladding
Wake Forest University

Mary Thomas Burke was already a legend in the field of counseling when I entered the profession. I first met her in a receiving line for newcomers at the North Carolina Counseling Association's annual conference in Greensboro in the early 1970s. I do not know what position she held in counseling at the time; most probably she was president. What stands out in my mind then and now is her presence. It was powerful, kind, and pervasive. After shaking her hand for the first time I thought, "I've met a good and important person." I was right.

Mary Thomas held numerous and significant posts during her life. She did so in a productive and gracious way. Yet it is her presence that I remember most and have never stopped experiencing. I interacted numerous times with her, especially upon returning to North Carolina in 1990 after a nine-year departure for academic appointments elsewhere. She was always personable, purposeful, persuasive, and to-the-point. Once she convinced me to give a three-hour workshop on spirituality and counseling. It was not a subject on which I considered myself an expert. In fact, I literally and metaphorically sweated to find enough material to construct my presentation so that my novice status would not be noticeable, because I was sure she would be in the audience (which she was). I think that that assignment and others like it were Mary Thomas's way of helping me grow and get beyond my comfort zones. For that I will always be grateful and I will always be glad that I found it difficult, if not impossible, to say "no" to her requests.

I am aware that my life was not the only one Mary Thomas's presence and personality touched. She was always doing for others less fortunate than herself, challenging those who were privileged and insensitive, teaching in simple but elegant ways, and in the process of it all promoting counseling. I know she sensed that everyone is born for a reason. Because of her active involvement in many of our lives, that reason is more discernable now. Some of us may have even experienced a rebirth personally or professionally because of Mary Thomas.

The following poem is my attempt to capture part of the essence of Mary Thomas Burke's life. Hopefully, part of the poem will speak to you about your own life and the importance of spirituality in it. A less modest wish is that these words will describe to you who Mary Thomas Burke was and why she made such a positive difference in the world. From either source of knowledge, or both, may come inspiration and energy to grow and carry forth in the spirit of this wonderful woman. That is why this poem is entitled "Spirit."

Spirit
Your spirit lives among us
quietly, modestly, almost unnoticed,
yet instilling life into our lives
like the heart pumps blood into the body.
You have left our lives
richer, fuller, more compassionate,
a phenomenon we cannot explain
but a presence we can feel
      like the wind upon our faces.
We hear your voice sometimes in the silence
urging us to reach out
to those oppressed and forgotten
to souls in the midst of turmoil and fright
to people who differ from us
      in color, creed, or circumstance,
        to brothers and sisters without a light
          a hope, a direction, a dream, or a prayer.
We cannot ignore the call
lest we not aspire to be who we are and can be.
And so at the end of daylight
we enter the darkness of those less fortunate
preparing, sharing, caring
      in the spirit of your life

that now intertwines with ours
and gives us strength
beyond what we had imagined.
Thus you continue to be among us
as we go ever onward, even when scared,
in the realization that
        light follows night
        right follows wrong
               peace follows war
                     and in love we are strong.
From you, through us,
can come a touch, a word, a wish, and a hope,
that leads us onward and with a vision that goes
past mortal expectations
so that in transformation
        a sense of grace is created
               that helps us discover ever anew
                     that we are one with one another
                         and with that which is divine.

Acknowledgments

We would like to thank the following people without whom we would not have reached the point of submission of this text. We have been blessed with the capable assistance of Emily Epstein, our editor, and her understanding and patience in allowing the additional time as a result of Mary Thomas's cancer diagnosis as well as the timely review of the manuscript. We are grateful to our reviewers whose careful and insightful remarks helped to clarify and refine the intent of the manuscript.

We are indebted to the Sisters of Mercy at Belmont for their love and support throughout this project. They nourished our bodies and souls, and continuously encouraged us by their prayers. We could not have met the timeline for submission of the draft without the capable assistance of our graduate assistants, Lauren Farrell, Brandy Tant, Marti LeBourgeois, and Jennifer Creel, research assistant, whose research, editing, and technological skills expedited the process. And finally, we are grateful to our spouses, Vincent Miranti and Elmore Chauvin for their undying love, support, and encouragement during the challenging times while working on the manuscript.

Foreword

ELLIOT INGERSOLL

It is an honor and a pleasure to write this foreword. I have had the privilege of knowing the authors in different contexts for over 10 years and they have each had a profound influence on me. During my time as a struggling and cantankerous doctoral student, the authors reached out to me, helped me refine my thinking on counseling and spirituality, and involved me in the community of people who make up the Association for Spiritual, Ethical, and Value Issues in Counseling. Anyone who knew me as a doctoral student will appreciate the tolerance, equanimity, and good humor that this took. The thing that stands out for me in knowing the authors has consistently been their contagious excitement and enthusiasm for the counseling field and their vision of human potential. I believe it is this vision that qualifies them to tackle the cumbersome topic of spirituality in counseling. Their earlier published works mark them as pioneers in this area and communicate an inspired vision that spirituality is not just a component of being human but a keystone that supports the core of our highest potential.

Of course, these three wise women do not pretend to tell us what our highest potential is. They do, however, engage us in a journey toward the horizon of that potential and encourage us to look beyond it to what we may be as counselors and human beings. This book is a journey well worth taking. It makes an important contribution to the growing literature on counseling and spirituality. In undertaking a daunting topic, these authors have placed themselves in a crucible. Recall that the crucible (apart from being a severe test or a metal vessel in which elements are heated) is a metaphor for the spiritual journey that burns off the impurities we are prone to collect throughout the course of our lives. The authors placed themselves in the crucible of writing a peer-reviewed book on what is still a controversial topic.

Counseling and spirituality are still controversial because spirituality itself cannot be concretely defined in any manner that all parties agree upon. Special interests battle daily over preferred definitions of spirituality that are partial to their own belief systems and create contentious "in-groups" and "out-groups." In the health sciences, many researchers believe that spirituality is nothing more than the hopeful figment of weak minds and prefer to turn to the latest psychotropic medication for even the most existential pain. Even within the counseling field there are those who would reduce spirituality to nothing more than a cultural variable. Psychometric researchers across the helping professions who fancy themselves "tough-minded" have for years tried to make the case that because no objective test has confirmed the spiritual domain then such a domain does not exist. In addition, a continued debate wages on regarding what spiritual development means for children and adolescents. Many take a strictly stage-development position that maintains (despite contrary evidence) that spiritual experiences are not possible for children until they reach concrete and formal operational thinking. Controversial indeed!

Drs. Burke, Chauvin, and Miranti have risen to a difficult task and produced a book that addresses many of these issues head-on. Through their own brand of tough-minded logic they not only support the contention that spirituality is a robust construct but they also illustrate the place for it in the counseling process. In terms of understanding how diversity issues are included in and transcended by spirituality, the chapters on special populations cover the elements unique to each population and yet illustrate the universal aspects of people in each group. Regarding the topic of counseling, spirituality, and working with children and adolescents, the authors have produced a chapter that provides a broad overview of the kind of development that contributes to spiritual growth as well as how children and adolescents may respond to spiritual issues at different levels of development.

Finally, I am painfully aware that I have no idea what it must be like to begin a project as three friends and colleagues only to lose one before she could see the final fruit of these labors. This is an entirely different type of crucible—one that burns you with the existential pain of loss, grief, and finitude. And yet, if anything, this book reads as a testament to the potential we all have for abundance, joy, and a timeless sense of grace—the potential that is our spiritual birthright and that can be partially actualized in the counseling process. That is what stands out clearly from the vision these three authors have forged through their collaboration, a vision that allows us to peer further beyond the horizon of our own potential as counselors and human beings.

Preface

Introduction

Counseling and spirituality are important topics that are evolving at an exponential pace. Resources and suggestions for application are proving to be helpful to mental health professionals who seek holistically to address the spiritual and religious concerns and issues of their clients. As the literature continues to expand, the resources may also serve as a roadmap and will help to keep clinicians centered in order to be able to work effectively with clients. Many practitioners have hesitated to address spiritual and religious issues either for fear that they do not have the competencies or expertise needed or because they fear imposing their own values and beliefs on the client. They also fear they may violate ethical principles. Practitioners who think that they lack the formal training or expertise to help clients resolve religious and/or spiritual issues will often refer such clients to their priest, rabbi, or minister.

Today the mental health professionals are acknowledging a need for training to address religious and spiritual issues. Several authors have documented their successes in dealing with these issues and have provided methods, strategies, examples, and case studies for incorporating spirituality into the therapeutic process (Chandler, Holden, & Kolander, 1992; Curtis & Davis, 1999; Frame & Williams, 1996; Hinterkopf, 1994; Ingersoll, 1994: Kelly, 1995; Prest & Keller, 1993; Richards & Bergin, 1997; Shafranske & Malony, 1990; Smith, 1993; Wiggins-Frame, 2003).

Counselors and other mental health professionals whose training did not include the exploration of spirituality in the therapeutic process could benefit from this book. Also, counselors, psychologists, social workers, and pastoral counselors who teach graduate-level courses will find this text to be valuable in their training programs.

This book is intended as one of many resources for trainers, trainees, and practitioners to use in addressing the spiritual and/or religious dimensions as an integral component of the therapeutic relationship. In order to assist in this process, each chapter will cover the various topics and issues surrounding spirituality, the unique characteristics and needs of a specific population, case studies, interactive exercises, approaches and strategies, and a bibliography. The major intent of this book is to provide a practical guide for mental health professionals and to fill a void that exists in the available resources for addressing clients' spiritual needs. Major religious traditions will also be discussed, along with the significance that these faith traditions may have in the lives of clients.

Organization of the Text

The text is divided into two sections. Section I focuses on the counselor or health care professional and provides guidelines for examining the basic philosophical, religious, and/or spiritual beliefs and values prevalent in society today. Section II targets specific populations, outlining the unique characteristics and needs of each population. It will also address spirituality and religion from a multicultural perspective, provide an overview of the major faith traditions, and highlight transitional issues such as grief and loss, death and dying. Specific guidelines to be used during these critical periods will also be provided. The case studies and interactive exercises will provide opportunities to apply the necessary skills in addressing the spiritual and/or religious concerns of the clients.

Training Standards and Codes of Ethics

This book is timely insofar as the topic of spirituality, long neglected in the literature, is receiving serious attention in the practice of mental health. Recent interest in the topic has provided the impetus for the development of training standards and competencies to aid beginning practitioners in addressing the spiritual and/or religious needs of clients. Also, the codes of ethics of the various professional organizations have provided guidelines for addressing clients from a diversity perspective to include the clients' religious values and beliefs.

The Person of the Counselor

Part of training to be a counselor includes opportunities for personal growth and the evaluation of personal values and beliefs. Before counselors can effectively deal with client issues, they must begin to address the unresolved issues in their own lives and come to terms with their own spiritual and religious issues. Mapping out their own spiritual development and understanding their own yearning for a fulfilling and rewarding life is an ongoing process.

The authors have engaged in a similar process, taking advantage of opportunities to discuss their spiritual journeys with other counselors, educators, and supervisors. Also, by reflecting on feedback from workshops and seminars on the topics of spirituality and religion, they were able to incorporate the suggestions into future papers and presentations. The most personal, rewarding, and difficult times for Judy and Jane were spent with Mary Thomas as she struggled with the diagnosis of pancreatic cancer. If ever there is a time for personal reflection and renewal, it is during the process of watching one die daily and lose independence and control. In order to make this a time of healing, lasting friendship that endures beyond the grave, and renewed purpose in life, the subject of death and dying was not avoided. In fact, both Judy and Jane gained a lot from this experience, and both had an opportunity to say goodbye to a treasured friend and colleague. This book is a testament to the fact that one can overcome even the bitterness of death and leave a legacy of hope to those who follow. Mary Thomas Burke was living proof that a life spent in spiritual reflection and helping others to find meaning and purpose in life was its own great reward.

As three white, Christian women, we realized early on our limitations in taking on this daunting task. Having searched the literature for ways to address the topics contained in this book and launching out into uncharted territory, the idea of being pioneers never really crossed our minds. We knew that in order to be fully present to our students and clients, we had to first be true to ourselves. Herein lies the passion and commitment that, to be fully human, one must deal with at the core of our being. That core is and will always be the deep spirituality and connectedness to others that makes life worth living.

SECTION I

CHAPTER 1
Introduction

It is generally agreed that the total person consists of several dimensions, namely the physical, intellectual, emotional, social, and spiritual. Accepted definitions exist for each component, with the exception of the spiritual dimension. One may argue that the spiritual dimension of personhood is not defined because one cannot quantitatively measure the spiritual or prove that it exists. Yet much has been written about psychological constructs even though they are not concrete or measurable (Bergin, 1991; Ingersoll, 1994). So the argument that mental health professionals must ignore the spiritual because of lack of proof or concreteness is a moot point. Perhaps the spiritual dimension is ignored because many researchers are afraid to address this component, either for fear of violating professional ethics or because spirituality is still considered to be synonymous with religion and as such is still primarily the domain of religion (Chandler et al., 1992). Other writers agree that even though the spiritual dimension is recognized as an important and valued component of the total person, its structure makes it difficult to define. Further, it is difficult to validate the subcomponents or parameters of any definition (Chapman, 1986). Many contributors to the literature recognize the difficulties associated with the definition of spirituality as a component of health. Most mental health professionals acknowledge the historical separation of church and state and the difficulties and misconceptions that occur regarding the recognition of the spiritual dimension of personhood.

In twentieth-century America, religion and psychotherapy were generally accepted as separate and distinct disciplines. Freud's (1927) view of religion as a "mere illusion" strongly influenced the separation of religion and mental health practice. Despite the influence of Jung (1933) and a number of other leading voices, the scientific paradigm emerged as the dominant modus operandi in the mental health profession. As the twenty-first century dawns, some mental health professionals see a growing interest in spirituality as a shift in the pendulum away from strictly empirical science. There seems to be an increasing interest in reopening mental health practice to the integration of religion and spirituality (Kelly, 1995; Richards & Bergin, 1997; Shafranske, 1996; Steere, 1997;). Mental health professionals and institutions of higher education are asking for resources to help them explore and develop the spiritual and religious dimensions of psychotherapy (Summit on Spirituality, 1995).

Most agree that many definitions and interpretations exist regarding the terms *religion* and *spirituality*. For some, they could be defined in relation to spiritual or peak experiences that anyone may have at any point in his or her life. Spirituality can also be viewed as the highest level of any line of development. For example, emotional development expressed as universal compassion and patience is typically the highest level of emotional development, just as the ability to see networks of relationships among competing worldviews is an upper level of expression of cognitive development. Spirituality may be defined as its own development. Perhaps a combination of all three would be appropriate for purposes of applying strategies for addressing spiritual and religious issues in counseling. Although some authors concur that there have been many challenges in defining and/or describing the terms religion and spirituality, it is necessary to agree on a definition or description if an application is to be effective.

Most agree that the terms religion and spirituality have many definitions and interpretations. Wilber (2000) offered several definitions of spirituality:

- "Spirituality involves the highest levels of any of the developmental lines" (p. 129)
- "Spirituality is the sum total of the highest levels of the developmental lines" (p. 30)
- "Spirituality is itself a separate developmental line" (p. 130)
- "Spirituality is an attitude (such as openness or love) that you can have at whatever stage you are at" (p. 133)
- "Spirituality basically involves peak experiences" (p. 134)

Although spirituality may be experienced and expressed through religion, which is defined as an organized system of faith, worship, cumulative traditions, and prescribed rituals (Ingersoll, 1994), spiritual issues that arise in counseling may or may not be associated with a religious belief system. Just as mental health professionals have recognized the importance of inquiring about ethnicity and other aspects of culture, they should routinely explore the spiritual dimension of clients' lives. It is essential to clarify whether spiritual beliefs are based in deeply held convictions or merely followed meaninglessly. The following questions suggest some lines of inquiry that can be useful:

- How important are spiritual beliefs and practices in the clients' lives?
- To what extent do the clients identify with a spiritual orientation?
- How do past or present spiritual beliefs and practices contribute to presenting problems or block healing and growth?
- How has adversity or trauma wounded the spirit?
- How might a spiritual void or disconnectedness from religious roots exacerbate suffering or alienation?
- How can past, current, or potential spiritual resources be identified or drawn upon to ease distress, support problem-solving, help clients to accept what cannot be changed, and foster healing? (Adopted from Walsh, 1999).

A more comprehensive definition is necessary in order to explore the issues. A distinction between spirituality and religion must first be established. *The American Heritage Dictionary of the English Language* (1992) defined spirituality as "of concern with or affecting the soul in relation to God" (p. 1238). Spirituality refers to a way of being in the world that acknowledges the existence of and the desire to be in relationship with a transcendent dimension of God. This spiritual tendency is believed to move the individual toward knowledge, hope, love, transcendence, connectedness, and compassion. "Spirituality includes one's capacity for creativity, growth, and the development of a value system" (Summit on Spirituality, 1995, p. 30).

The American Heritage Dictionary (1992) defined religion as "having or showing belief in and reverence for God or a deity and of, concern with, or teaching religion" (p. 1525). Religion refers to the social or organized means by which a person expresses spirituality. In this sense, religion is expressed through a faith tradition such as Christianity, Judaism, Islam, Hinduism, Buddhism, Taoism, or one of the many institutionalized variations within each of these traditions (Kelly, 1995).

Thus, the terms religion and spiritual are interrelated, but they can be distinguished from each other along several dimensions. Maher and Hunt (1993) had this to say about spirituality: "If only there were a more concrete, value-universal, and easily understood definition of this rich and sometimes mystifying word, the public might be able to hold a clear line over the counseling profession and say 'Aha, we trust in what we see here.

We can understand this part of what might take place in the name of help-ing us'" (p. 21). Religious expressions tend to be denominational, external, cognitive, behavioral, realistic, and public. Spiritual experiences tend to be universal, internal, spontaneous, ecumenical, and private. It is possible to be religious without being spiritual and spiritual without being religious (Richards & Bergin, 1997). Spiritual and religious belief systems provide faith explanations of past history and present experiences; for many, they offer pathways toward understanding the ultimate meanings of life and ex-istence (Campbell, 1988). Coles (1997) believed that a moral awareness evolves out of such spiritual belief systems. Moral or ethical values spur the individual to respond to the suffering of others, to feel an obligation to ded-icate efforts to help others, and to alleviate pain or injustice in society (Walsh, 1999).

Background for the Inclusion of Spirituality in the Counseling Process

Hickson et al. (2000) investigated attitudes of licensed professional coun-selors (LPCs) concerning spirituality in the therapeutic process and found that LPCs recognize the importance of being aware of their own spiritual beliefs. Spirituality was also viewed as a universal phenomenon that can act as a powerful psychological change agent.

Addressing spirituality in counseling means using various approaches directed at assisting clients in exploring meaning and purpose in life. As clients express their issues and concerns, counselors must listen actively to themes and narratives that will facilitate the exploration of the client's choices. Consideration of the spiritual influences in a person's life will as-sist the counselor in understanding the client more fully, in responding to his or her needs, and providing resources and options compatible with the client's interest and aptitudes.

Emphasis on the spiritual dimension in all specialties within the coun-seling profession has received national recognition over the past decade, as evidenced by the numerous publications on the topic (Burke & Miranti, 1995; Kelly, 1995; Richards & Bergin, 1997). Yet most feel ill equipped, from a training perspective, to explore this most significant dimension of human experience with their clients. Several influences have contributed to this omission in the training of mental health professionals:

- Our nation's founding principle of separation of church and state, the sacred from the secular, has contributed to the segregation of reli-gious beliefs and practices from the professional mental health field.

- Like the larger society, secular mental health professionals adopted a hands-off attitude, wanting to be "value-free" so as not to intrude into client's spirituality or to impose personal values on the client.
- Rigid boundaries were drawn and issues of religion and spirituality have been viewed as the province of ministers, priests, and rabbis.
- Spiritual issues were seen as existing in a separate realm from psychological and physical distress and therefore were to be ignored.
- Professionals were taught to adopt a stance of neutrality and remain objective and unbiased.

Critics have expressed concern that mental health professionals who incorporate a spiritual dimension into their clinical work may be likely to violate ethical guidelines by imposing their values on clients (Richards & Potts, 1995). However, no professional ethical guidelines prohibit a clinician from discussing the religious traditions or using the spiritual beliefs of their clients as part of the therapeutic practice. Rather, ethical standards encourage members to respect the individual differences in belief and value systems (American Counseling Association, 1995; American Association for Marriage and Family Therapy, 1985; American Psychological Association, 1992). The clinician who incorporates the spiritual and/or religious dimensions, if that therapist is well trained, is no more likely to violate a client's value autonomy than any other therapist. Clearly, sensitivity and respect for the diversity of religious and spiritual traditions, as well as for the multicultural dimensions, are ethical behaviors expected of all mental health professionals (Lee & Sirch, 1994). To act otherwise clearly violates the ethical codes of their profession.

Importance of Addressing All Needs in a Person's Life

Most counselor education programs, and all Council for Accreditation of Counseling and Related Educational Programs (CACREP) accredited counselor education programs, require that human growth and development be included as an integral part of every student's program. Thus, the physical, emotional, intellectual, and social needs of the person are fully explored and studied. The interrelationships among these needs are illustrated in Figure 1.1 by using a Venn diagram of four circles representing the (a) physical, (b) emotional, (c) social, and (d) intellectual dimensions of every human being.

Figure 1.1 shows the spiritual essence of the person, integrating and uniting all parts with equal force and bringing meaning and depth to human behavior. Emphasis on the holistic, integrated model allows counselors to acknowledge that the spiritual and religious dimensions of clients'

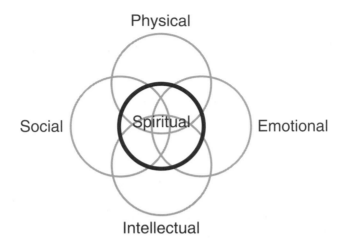

Figure 1.1 Human Growth and Development Model.

needs are at the core of wellness (Witmer & Sweeney, 1992). Wellness may be defined as the level of functioning at which individuals feel comfortable and are considered healthy for themselves and for society (Theodore, 1984). Nowhere in a client's life is this more poignant than in the therapeutic relationship.

Because of the interrelationships among the physical, emotional, social, and intellectual dimensions of every human being, it is imperative that mental health professionals address all the dimensions, including the spiritual. Research states that an individual spends at least one third of each day at work. Because interpersonal relationships in the workplace can determine the level of satisfaction and feelings of fulfillment, the practitioner can explore with the client just how productive and happy he or she reports to be. If, on the contrary, the person's work lacks meaning and purpose, the individual may risk his or her health and mental wellness. Counselors who do not address the spiritual dimension could possibly be omitting an essential aspect that could contribute to the client's overall well-being.

Several authors suggest practical reasons for incorporating the spiritual dimension into the counseling process:

- Incorporating the spiritual dimension provides the counselor with a type of metaphor or roadmap for better understanding the worldview of the client (Miranti, 1998).
- Religious identity is often seen as strongly influencing racial and/or cultural identity (Worthington, 1991).

- The multicultural perspective includes variables such as religion, ethnicity, language, gender, age, and locality, as well as social, economic, and educational factors and affiliations (Pedersen, 1990).
- Sensitivity to client diversity necessitates that all aspects of a client's worldview are important in the exploration and facilitation of the counseling process.

Training programs would be remiss if they fail to train professionals to explore effectively and to facilitate with clients the spiritual and religious influences in a person's life. The counseling profession and counselor educators need to engage more deeply in professional dialogue about ways to incorporate the spiritual dimension of the client into the counseling program. Counselors need the means to acquire the necessary competencies in order to facilitate the exploration and selection process.

Advantages of Incorporating the Spirituality Dimension into Counseling

Integrating the spirituality of the client into the counseling process has many advantages. In comparing counseling and spirituality, one becomes aware that both attempt to help the client to:

- learn to accept one's self.
- forgive others and one's self.
- acknowledge one's shortcomings.
- accept personal responsibility.
- let go of hurts and resentments.
- deal with guilt.
- modify self-destructing patterns of thinking, feeling, and acting (Gladding, 1995).

In the past decade, a majority of Americans reported that active religious beliefs and/or a spiritual awareness is integral to their lives (Gallup, 1993). The data from the Gallup poll suggest that many of these individuals will seek mental health professionals to help them resolve their deep spiritual and/or religious issues. The common denominator of spirituality and counseling is human suffering. Few clients come for counseling when everything is going well, and many, if not all, turn to their spiritual and/or religious beliefs when things go wrong. In dealing with these clients, counselors must recognize the importance of the issues and communicate a willingness to explore them in an empathic and understanding manner. In addition, the counselor must be skillful in discerning healthy from unhealthy practices in the client's belief system. For example, a client's description of a personal problem may focus excessively on guilt-oriented thoughts or depression, which may be directly related to his or her belief system. In cases such as this, it is imperative for the counselor to conceptualize these feelings and behaviors in an effective manner in order to select the appropriate therapeutic approach (Faiver & O'Brien, 1993).

Frequently, the issues presented initially may not be at the root of the expressed concerns. They may surface later in subsequent sessions. A clinical assessment or structured intake may facilitate the acknowledgment of the root problem much sooner. If the counselor is skilled in interpreting the unexpressed concerns, the intervention selected may help the client to express the concerns that brought him or her into counseling.

Thyne, in a research study conducted in 1997, investigated the potential positive and negative consequences and concluded that evidence supported the possibility that the client could benefit from perceived support from his or her God or higher power, as well as social support from the members of his or her church or religious group (Wolf & Stevens, 2001).

Competencies Needed

Counselor educators have begun to give serious attention to training counselors in the spiritual dimension by providing opportunities to apply the necessary competencies and by outlining the advantages of incorporating spirituality into the counseling process. The participants in the Summit on Spirituality held in Charlotte, North Carolina, in the fall of 1995 developed a listing of competencies needed to effectively assist clients in dealing with their spiritual and/or religious concerns (*Counseling Today*, 1995, p. 30).

The first Invitational Summit on Spirituality was convened by the authors in 1995 for the purpose of providing a forum for those who contributed to the literature and practice of incorporating spirituality into the counseling process. During the summit, a description of spirituality and a listing of competencies to address the spiritual and/or religious concerns of clients were developed. Subsequent to the summit, a second edited volume on the topic was published. The authors have been active in presenting, publishing, and providing leadership in the development of resources on the topic of spirituality.

CACREP has included in the standards for the accreditation of counseling programs the spiritual and/or religious dimensions in the practice of counseling. Professional counselors, in order to assist clients with spiritual and/or religious issues, must be able to:

- Explain the relationship between spirituality and religion.
- Describe religious and spiritual beliefs and practices in a cultural context.

- Engage in self-exploration of one's religious and spiritual beliefs in order to increase sensitivity, understanding, and acceptance of one's belief system.
- Demonstrate sensitivity and acceptance of a variety of religious and/or spiritual expressions in client communication.
- Identify the limits of one's understanding of a client's religious and/or spiritual expressions. Demonstrate appropriate referral skills and possible referral sources.
- Assess the relevance of the religious and/or spiritual themes in the counseling process as befits each client's expressed preference.
- Use a client's religious and/or spiritual beliefs in the pursuit of the client's therapeutic goals as befits the client's expressed preference.

Hickson, Housley, and Wages (2000) investigated the attitudes of 147 LPCs in two southeastern states concerning the integration of religion and spirituality in the therapeutic process. They concluded that the LPCs recognized the importance of being aware of their own religious and spiritual beliefs and the need to develop the appropriate skills and competencies. They concurred that tapping into the client's religious and spiritual beliefs and resources could serve as a change agent.

It is becoming increasingly recognized that that mental health professionals cannot be totally neutral in regard to spirituality and religion in the counseling process (Walsh, 1993). Inescapably, the practice of counseling involves the interaction of counselors' and clients' value systems. Just as other aspects of culture, such as ethnicity, social class, and gender, influence clients' and therapists' constructs of norms, problems, and solutions, so too does the spiritual dimension of experience. What clinicians ask and pursue may or may not influence the therapeutic relationship, course, and outcome. Counselors respect clients not by avoiding a discussion of spirituality altogether but by demonstrating an active interest in exploring and understanding their values and behaviors. It is most critical to understand constraining beliefs and to affirm and encourage those that foster well-being. At times, specific beliefs and values are to be challenged when they contribute to distress or are harmful to others, such as when violence toward wives is rationalized by citing fundamental religious precepts.

Conversely, concerns about mental health professionals' persuasion and clients' susceptibility stem largely from recognition of the power of the therapist and the vulnerability of the clients. In many ways, mental health professionals have assumed the role of shamans and priests in more traditional cultures but have lacked the training in how to use such power constructively (Harner, 1980). Many professionals, uncomfortable with this power differential, may deny their influence. Nevertheless, power is projected onto the therapists by clients who, in their distress, are vulnerable to adapting to their therapists' beliefs and practices. Therapists should recognize this influence and work collaboratively with their clients. At times, mental health professionals can help clients therapeutically by appropriate self-disclosure, such as sharing aspects of a crisis from their own lives. Such disclosure must be done with great sensitivity to its appropriateness and potential value to the client's needs. Whenever sharing is done in this manner, the healing relationship is deepened.

The inclusion of spiritual issues in the latest revision of the *Diagnostic and Statistical Manual of Mental Disorders (DSM-IV)* is indicative of a growing recognition of the importance of spirituality in mental health assessment and treatment. In the DSM-IV, the Religion or Spiritual Problem category (V Code 62.89) can be used "when the focus of clinical attention is a religious or spiritual problem. Examples include distressing experiences that involve loss or questioning of spiritual values that may not necessarily be related to an organized church or religious institution" (American Psychiatric Association, 1994, p. 685).

The general public is clearly indicating a need for mental health and health care professionals to address the spiritual dimension in their work. Bergin and Jensen (1990) found that 81% of respondents preferred to have their spiritual practices and beliefs integrated into any counseling process; 75% wanted physicians as well as therapists to address spiritual issues in their care. Yet those authors noted that therapists tend to be less religious than most clients and may underestimate the importance of spirituality in their work. Mental health professionals who neglect the potential relevance of clients' spiritual beliefs and practices are likely to be at odds with the needs of their clients (Bergin, 1991).

Incorporating Spirituality in the Counseling Process

Just as mental health professionals must recognize the importance of inquiring about ethnicity and other aspects of culture, they should routinely explore the spiritual dimension of clients' lives. It is essential to clarify whether spiritual beliefs are based on deeply held convictions or are merely followed meaninglessly. The following questions suggest some lines of inquiry that can be useful:

- How important are spiritual beliefs and practices in the clients' lives?
- To what extent do the clients identify with a spiritual orientation?
- How do past or present spiritual beliefs and practices contribute to presenting problems or block healing and growth?
- How has adversity or trauma wounded the spirit?

- How might a spiritual void or disconnectedness from religious roots exacerbate suffering or alienation?
- How can past, current, or potential spiritual resources be identified or drawn upon to ease distress, support problem-solving, help clients to accept what cannot be changed, and foster healing? (Walsh, 1999)

In assessing these issues with the clients, therapists can ascertain how spiritual belief systems can be a positive, sustaining force for the client. Conversely, therapists can also determine how religious precepts may be used to justify abusive patterns in relationships. For example, a husband's controlling, demeaning, or violent behavior toward his spouse may be grounded in religious tenets that a wife should be submissive to her husband. Mental health professionals have an ethical responsibility to challenge abuses of power and harmful behavior, even when it is supported by cultural or religious traditions. It is important for therapists to know that every major religion upholds the core principles of respect for others and the dignity and worth of human beings. Furthermore, the healing power of compassion and forgiveness is central to the teachings of all major religions, as well as to many approaches in therapy (Hargrave, 1994).

It is crucial to explore how religious ideations or experiences may have had a destructive or dispiriting effect, fostering guilt, shame, or worthlessness in clients. Spiritual distress, an inability to invest life with meaning, impedes coping and the ability to face challenges in life with courage and hope. Seligman (1990), who introduced the concept of "learned helplessness," believed that the soul, which is deep within the personality, is the key to change and that any change proposed needs to take into account the human spirit.

Spirituality at Time of Loss
Facing death and the loss of a loved one are the most difficult challenges of life. For mental health professionals, it is essential to understand the various conceptions of death and the afterlife. As an example, it is in the face of death that Native American tribal religions demonstrate their magnificence (Deloria, 1994). Although death is saddening, it is viewed as an event that each person must face, not as an arbitrary, capricious exercise of divine intervention. The tribespeople view death in the larger context of life. They believe that human beings are an integral part of the natural world; as such, human beings contribute their bodies to become the dust that nourishes the plants and animals, which in turn feed people during their lifetimes. Native Americans see death as simply another transitional event in a much larger human life cycle.

As mental health professionals trained to help clients solve problems and bring about healing, counselors may feel helpless at times when clients experience the sadness from the loss of a loved one. What therapists can do is be fully present to the client's suffering and offer compassion for a full range of feelings in their grief. These feelings may include anger, sadness, remorse, and so on. The most important roles a therapist has in such a situation are to be a listener and a witness to others' suffering. Counselors need to acknowledge the suffering and perhaps raise some issues that will help clients experience a spiritual connection with their counselor. Thus, through this higher privileged exchange of spirituality and suffering, a new meaning is created in the midst of sorrow for client and therapist.

Training Standards and Codes of Ethics

Counselors may miss critical aspects of a client's problem if they lack training in addressing religious and spiritual issues. It is vital for counselors to understand that a person's religious beliefs and spiritual values are aspects of client diversity (Souza, 2002). The *Code of Ethics and Standards of Practice* (1995) of the American Counseling Association addresses the religious and spiritual needs of clients. Counselors who choose to ignore these dimensions may be in violation of the *Code*, which regulates the counseling profession, and they may fail to promote the growth and development of their clients. Section A on the Counseling Relationship, A.2., "Respecting diversity," specifically mentions that "counselors do not condone or engage in discrimination based on . . . religion . . . ," they must "actively attempt to understand diverse cultural backgrounds of the clients with whom they work," and they must also learn "how the counselor's own cultural/ethnic/racial identity impacts his or her values and beliefs about the counseling process." Ignoring spiritual and religious issues in counselor preparation runs the risk of inadvertently fostering some degree of insensitivity to clients' spiritual and religious concerns, as these are relevant to counseling (Hinterkopf, 1994).

Although not specifically recommending an extensive treatment of spirituality and religion, accreditation standards do refer to the spiritual/religious dimensions by including "religious preference" in curricular standards in the core area of social and cultural foundations (Council for Accreditation of Counseling and Related Educational Programs, 1994). An article published in the *Journal of Counseling and Development*, "Spirituality, Religion, and CACREP Curriculum Standards" (1999, pp. 251–257) by Burke, Hackney, Hudson, Miranti, Watts, and Epp provides methods and examples for including spirituality and religion for each of the CACREP core curriculum areas. The authors recommended that including

spiritual and religious topics at appropriate points in the CACREP curriculum is a reasonable method for teaching counselor trainees how to incorporate these aspects into the counseling process. For a convenient review of the specific codes of ethics and standards of practice for the various professional associations, please see the appendixes at the end of the book.

Despite the heightened awareness in the mental health fields, relatively little literature has been written on the integration of religion and spirituality in marriage and family counseling (Wolf & Stevens, 2001). Richards and Bergin in 1997 outlined several potentially ethical challenges that counselors could face. Dual relationships could be present if the counselor who is also a religious leader is in a position of leadership in a religious affiliated church or agency and is seeing members of the congregation for counseling. Richards and Bergin also discussed potential value imposition when the therapist uses a religious or spiritually based intervention without the client's consent (Wolf et al., 2001, p. 70). A further caution by Richards and Bergin is to avoid practicing outside the boundaries of competence. Before integrating religion or spirituality into the process, the counselor should possess the skills necessary for this type of intervention (Wolf et al., 2001). These cautions do not imply that spiritual and religious issues should not be addressed but rather that the counselor respect the client's religious or spiritual autonomy and remain free to discuss these issues if the client is so inclined.

References

American Association for Marriage and Family Therapy. (1985). *Code of ethical principles for marriage and family therapists.* Washington, D.C.: Author.

American Counseling Association. (1995). *Code of ethics and standard of practice.* Alexandria, VA: Author.

American heritage dictionary of the English language. (1992). P 1238, 1525.

American Psychiatric Association. (1994). *Diagnostic and statistical manual of mental disorders* (4th ed.). Washington, D.C.: Author.

American Psychological Association. (1992). *Ethical principles of psychologists and code of conduct.* Washington, D.C.: Author.

Bergin, A. E. (1991). Values and religious issues in psychotherapy and mental health. *American Psychologist, 46,* 394–403.

Bergin, A. E., & Jensen, J. P. (1990). Religiosity of psychotherapists: A national survey. *Psychotherapy, 27,* 32–39.

Burke, M. T., & Miranti, J. G. (1995). *Counseling: The spiritual dimension.* Alexandria, VA: American Counseling Association.

Campbell, J. (1988). *The power of myth.* New York: Doubleday.

Chandler, C. K., Holden, J. M., & Kolander, C. A. (1992). Counseling for spiritual wellness: Theory and practice. *Journal of counseling and development, 71,* 168–175.

Chapman, L. (1986). Spiritual health: A component missing from health promotion. *American Journal of Health Promotion, 1*(1), 38–41.

Coles, R. (1997). *The moral obligation of children.* New York: Random House.

Curtis, R. C., & Davis, K. M. (1999). Spirituality and multimodal therapy: A practical approach to incorporating spirituality in counseling. *Counseling and Values, 43,* 199–210.

Deloria, V., Jr. (1994). *God is red: A native view of religion* (2nd ed.). Golden, CO: Fulcrum.

Faiver, C. M., & O'Brien, E. M. (1993). Assessment of religious beliefs form. *Journal of Counseling and Values, 37*(3), 176–178.

Frame, M. W., & Williams, C. B. (1996). Counseling African-Americans: Integrating spirituality in therapy. *Counseling and Values, 41,* 16–28.

Freud, S. (1961). The future of an illusion. In J. Strachey (Ed. & Trans.), *The standard edition of the complete psychological works of Sigmund Freud* (Vol. 21, pp. 1–56). London: Hogarth Press. (Original work published in 1927)

Gallup. (1993). *Report on Trends, 331*(4), 36–38.

Gladding, S. T. (1995). Creativity in counseling. *Counseling and Human Development, 28,* 1–12.

Hargrave, T. D. (1994). *Families and forgiveness: Healing wounds in the intergenerational family.* New York: Brunner/Mazel.

Harner, M. (1980). *The ways of the shaman: A guide to power and healing.* New York: Harper and Row.

Hickson, J., Housley, W., & Wages, D. (2000). Counselors' perceptions of spirituality in the therapeutic process. *Counseling and Values, 45,* 58–66.

Hinterkopf, E. (1994). Integrating spiritual experiences in counseling. *Counseling and Values, 38,* 165–175.

Ingersoll, R. E. (1994). Spirituality, religion, and counseling: Dimensions and relationships. *Counseling and Values, 38,* 98–111.

Jung, C. G. (1933). *Modern man in search of a soul.* New York: Harcourt Brace.

Kelly, E. W. (1995). *Spirituality and religion in counseling and psychotherapy: Diversity in theory and practice.* Alexandria, VA: American Counseling Association.

Lee, C. C., & Sirch, M. L. (1994). Counseling in an enlightened society: Values for a new millennium. *Counseling and Values, 38,* 90–97.

Maher, M. F., & Hunt, T. K. (1993). Spirituality reconsidered. *Journal of Counseling and Values, 38*(1), 21–28.

Miranti, J. G. (1998). The spiritual/religious dimension of counseling: A multicultural perspective. In P. B. Pedersen & D. C. Locke (Eds.), *Cultural and diversity issues in counseling* (pp. 117–120). Alexandria, VA: American Counseling Association.

Pedersen, P. (1990). The multicultural perspective as a fourth force in counseling. *Journal of Mental Health Counseling, 12,* 93–95.

Prest, L. A., & Keller, J. F. (1993). Spirituality and family therapy: Spiritual beliefs, myths, and metaphors. *Journal of Marital and Family Therapy, 19,* 137–148.

Richards, P. S., & Bergin, A. E. (1997). *A spiritual strategy for counseling and psychotherapy.* Washington, D.C.: American Psychological Association.

Richards, P. S., & Potts, R. W. (1995). Using spiritual interventions in psychotherapy: Practices, successes, failures, and ethical concerns of Mormon psychotherapists. *Professional Psychology: Research and Practice, 26*(2), 163–170.

Seligman, M. (1990). *Learned optimism.* New York: Random House.

Shafranske, E. P. (Ed.). (1996). *Religion and the clinical practice of psychology.* Washington, D.C.: American Psychological Association.

Shafranske, E. P., & Malony, H. N. (1990). Clinical psychologists' religious and spiritual orientations and their practice of psychotherapy. *Psychotherapy, 27,* 72–78.

Smith, D. C. (1993). Exploring the religious-spiritual needs of the dying. *Counseling and Values, 37,* 71-77.

Souza, K. Z. (2002). Spirituality in counseling: What do counseling students think? *Counseling and Values, 46,* 213–218.

Steere, D. A. (1997). *Spiritual practice in psychotherapy: A guide for caregivers.* New York: Brunner/Mazel.

Summit on Spirituality. (1995). *Counseling today.* Alexandria, VA: American Counseling Association.

Theodore, R. M. (1984). Utilization of spiritual values and counseling: An ignored dimension. *Counseling and Values,* 162–198.

Walsh, F. (1993). *Conceptualization of normal family processes.* New York: Guilford Press.

Walsh, F. (1999). Opening family therapy to spirituality. In F. Walsh (Ed.), *Spiritual resources in family therapy.* New York: Guilford Press.

Wilber, K. (2000). *Integral psychology: Consciousness, spirit, psychology, therapy.* Boston: Shambhala Publications.

Witmer, J. M., & Sweeney, T. J. (1992). A holistic model for wellness and prevention over lifespan. *Journal of Counseling and Development, 71,* 140–148.

Wolf, C. T., & Stevens, P. (2001). Integrating religion and spirituality in marriage and family counseling. *Counseling and Values, 46,* 66–75.

Worthington, E. L. (1991). A primer on intake interviews with couples. *American Journal of Family Therapy, 19,* 344–350.

CHAPTER 2

Children and Adolescents

Children

A 5-year-old child wonders who made the flowers and the grass. A 10-year-old child begins to question some of the beliefs his parents hold. A 12-year-old becomes absorbed with thoughts of death and dying and whether there is life beyond death. These are common occurrences of childhood, yet few research studies have focused on the spiritual concerns of children or on developmental issues regarding children and spirituality. Lovecky (1997) describes a "spiritual sensitivity" that she uses to denote the spiritual concerns of children. She further describes this sensitivity as having both cognitive and emotional aspects. She explains that spiritual sensitivity does not necessarily mean that the child or family belong to a religion or even believe in a Supreme Being. "The seeking of the transcendent may be an experience of connection to something larger than oneself, to nature, to the universe, or as an inner experience of wonder and awe" (Lovecky, p.179).

A debate is taking place on the age at which spiritual or religious development begins. Most theories begin with late adolescence because this age group presupposes a differentiated and autonomous self that can reason abstractly. Many disregard younger children as being incapable of spiritual development because they are seen as still in the process of forming identities and learning to think abstractly. They are viewed as incapable of the type of self-transformation upon which the highest stages of spiritual development depend. This is not, however, a universally held belief. Others perceive children as being very spiritually "aware." These same authorities view spirituality in more of a developmental schema with age-appropriate tasks.

Coles (1990), after numerous interviews with various children, saw these young people as pilgrims on life's journey, starting spiritual development at an early age and growing in experience over time. Lovecky (1997) reported that young children were by no means seen as spiritually inferior or less developed than their older peers. Like Matthews's (1994) exploration of moral development, Coles (1990) and Lovecky (1997) viewed spirituality as a process in which paradigms develop over time, dependant on what came before, but not supplanting earlier stages.

Population Characteristics and Issues

Understanding the stages of child development is a necessity for any professional counselor who aspires to work with this population, especially in light of what has been said in the previous section. This chapter will focus on the school-age child because this is the age when most counselors accept children as clients.

One of the hallmarks of the school-age child is the growing ability to put him- or herself in someone else's place. This ability to think as another would think, or feel what another person might feel, or even anticipate what that person might actually do is referred to as *social role-taking ability* (Schickedanz, Schickedanz, Forsyth, & Forsyth, 1998). This trait gives school-age children more sophistication and a greater sensitivity to friendships and peer group reactions than they had at an earlier age. Social role-taking ability is but one facet of social cognition, but it tends to be an important one because it often governs whether or not a person is accepted into any social grouping.

Even in the very early stages of infancy, a baby learns to read facial expressions and respond to voice variations. As children approach the stages of middle childhood, they begin to understand that an individual can have two very different emotions about any given situation and that the feelings can exist simultaneously. Children in this age group also begin to understand that any given situation can elicit different emotions from different people. These new insights into other people help school-age children better understand themselves and their own emotions as well. As children develop, they become more sophisticated in recognizing feelings and emotions, as well as in their ability to distinguish positive and negative reactions in themselves and others.

A key to this type of social maturity is the child's ability to understand not only people but also situations and how they differ. Children begin to see that some situations are very straightforward and predictable, whereas others are rather ambiguous. With this knowledge comes the realization that things are not always what they appear to be on the surface. One of the most important discoveries at this age is that discrepancies can, and sometimes *should*, exist between feelings and the expression of those feelings. This added sophistication is referred to as *emotional literacy* (Schickedanz et al., 1998). This facet of development is very important to moral development.

Another developmental task for the school-age child is that of understanding intentions. This can be a challenging job for the middle-school-age child, but a necessary step in self-protection. A failure to recognize and understand the motives behind an action leaves the individual defenseless whether they occur in a social situation or relationship or whether they come from propaganda and advertising. Adults can teach children to read and understand *intention cues* from facial expressions, tone of voice, or situational factors, but it is usually difficult for younger children in this age group to distinguish between "deliberate" and "accidental."

Researchers (Dixon and Moore, 1990) have investigated the ability of school-age children to think about their own thinking and the thinking of other people. Researchers have also attempted to measure children's ability to estimate how much knowledge another person may possess. These skills are important if one wishes to understand another's point of view. It also enables one to truly understand his or her own value system and that of another.

All the research that was reviewed showed that these skills that make up social role-taking ability are developmental in nature and represent growing emotional and cognitive maturity. Older children are almost always better able to deal with these concepts than younger children. The ability to understand how people think, know, and understand appears to increase with age in most individuals.

It is important to understand the developing emotional and cognitive abilities of a child if we are to explore the role of spirituality in the lives of children or to understand the moral development of an individual. Both of these entities require a certain level of maturity that most often increases with age and is linked to the attributes described in the previous paragraphs. Papalia and Olds (1990) maintained that moral thinking is an outgrowth of personality, emotional attitudes, and cultural influences. Modern researchers (Rheingold, 1982) have also reported that even toddlers can and do express prosocial concerns, or as it is called by others, *social perspective-taking*.

Prosocial behavior is defined as:

> Any action that benefits other people, such as sharing with someone less fortunate than oneself, comforting or rescuing a distressed person, cooperating with someone or helping him or her to achieve an objective, or even simply making others feel good by complimenting them on their appearance or accomplishments. (Shaffer, 1999, p. 306)

With the ability to discern values and consequences comes the beginning of spiritual growth. *Spiritual* is not the same thing as the creedal formulations of any faith tradition, as much as they may be respected. What is meant instead is "the ancient and abiding human quest for connectedness with something larger and more trustworthy than our egos—with our own souls, with one another, with the worlds of history and nature, with the invisible winds of the spirit, with the mystery of being alive" (Palmer, 1998/1999, p. 6). Belief in a higher power is often the basis for what developmentalists term *altruism*, although this is not necessarily so in very young children.

Before very young children have even comprehended a notion of a "God-like" entity, they are capable of sharing, expressing sympathy, and behaving compassionately toward their companions—in other words, engaging in altruistic acts. Cognitive theories of altruism are linked with the ability to recognize and appreciate the factors that contribute to another person's distress and misfortune.

The motivational or intentional definition of altruism focuses on the motives or intentions that underlie prosocial acts. An act can be considered altruistic only if the person's primary motive or intent is to provide positive consequences for another person. The true altruist acts solely out of concern for others with no thought of reward or self-enhancement. Some skeptics maintain that a human being is virtually incapable of such extreme virtue. They believe that altruism is more behavioral than motivational.

From the behaviorist's perspective, an altruistic act is one that benefits another person, regardless of the doer's motives. Peterson and Gelfand (1984) surveyed first-, fourth-, and sixth-graders, as well as college students, and found that all the school-age children seemed to favor a more behavioral approach to altruism when judging scenarios. The college students and other adults in this study, however, were definitely more inclined to see the motivational or intentional side of issues.

Also, biological, psychoanalytic, and social-learning theories have been put forth regarding altruism and its development in the middle-age child. What none of these theories truly account for, however, is the spiritual basis of mankind's actions. A six- or seven-year-old child is usually capable of reasoning that certain actions are value laden and even fit into one's moral construct of the world. Being capable of love and sacrifice links one with the divine. This perspective sees the cognitive and the social-learning theories as complimentary rather than contradictory.

A genuine concern for the welfare of others and a willingness to act on this concern form the basis for the spiritual or inner life of the middle-age child. Must this child also internalize a higher power as the motivating force of his or her actions? No, but most do as they mature. Older elementary-age children are definitely capable of a strong, well-thought-out belief system.

Unique Needs of Children

Children are capable of spiritual awareness and spiritual soul-searching. As they struggle to figure out the world they confront, they also become aware of the complex, ironic, inconsistent, contradictory nature of human character, and they also begin to fathom faith and doubt (Coles, 1990). Children attempt to understand not only what is happening to them but why it happens. In doing this, they call upon the religious life they have experienced, the spiritual values they have received, and the other sources of potential explanation. Robert Coles, a well-respected researcher of the spiritual life of children, said that he first became aware of religious and spiritual reflection in children's development when he was a young doctor working with children who had contracted polio. He observed their search for an explanation for why they had been so unfortunate as to be confined to an iron lung:

> As I go over the interviews I've done with children, I find certain psychological themes recurring. I hear children talking about their desires, their ambitions, their hopes, and also their worries, their fears, their moments of deep and terrible despair—all connected in idiosyncratic ways, sometimes, with biological stories, or with religiously sanctioned notions of right and wrong, or with rituals such as prayer or meditation. Indeed, the entire range of children's mental life can and does connect with their religious and spiritual thinking. Moral attitudes, including emotions such as shame and guilt, are a major psychological side of young spirituality. (Coles, 1990)

Accidents, illness, bad luck—such moments of danger and pain prompt reflection in children as well as adults. A boy's vulnerability becomes an occasion for prayer and the scrutiny of the mind and soul. Religions are known, of course, for upholding various moral principles and standards. But less obvious are the strategies both boys and girls desire in order to accommodate a secular and familiar morality they hear espoused in churches, mosques, and synagogues. The task for these boys and girls is to weave together a particular version of a morality both personal and yet tied to a religious tradition, to ponder their moral successes and failures (the essence of the spiritual life), and consequently to reflect on their prospects as human beings who will someday die.

For children, even those quite healthy who have never been seriously sick, death has a powerful and continuing meaning. They hear what their elders hear in sermons, stories, songs, and scriptural warnings. They also experience death personally when grandparents and other older adults depart.

In some homes where religion is more explicitly and constantly evoked, practiced rituals, enforced mandates and rules, and spiritual values become for children part and parcel of the emotional life they struggle to consolidate for themselves. In American families that are committed to the evangelical tradition or to fundamentalist religion (and of course in Orthodox Jewish families and passionately Muslim families), religion and psychology in a sense merge. For instance, those children have to contend not merely with teachers, parents, and other authority figures but with the full, everyday force of their families' beliefs. These children are rewarded, punished, and are told what to do and when, all in the name of God. Such a child's passions, ardent and angry, will engage with that parent of all parents, God. The child will love God, spurn God, fight for God, obey God, and angrily disobey God. It is hard for those of us whose religious life is merely a part of what we do, one of many commitments, to put ourselves in the shoes of people for whom the phrase "God's presence" has an utter rock-bottom psychological reality that gives meaning to the phrase "my parents' parent and mine, too." In such people, spirituality makes up the warp and woof of psychology; the integration of religion and everyday life is complete.

Children try to coalesce what they have observed, learned, read, and heard from others to make their own "system," their own set of principles. They have an urgent desire and determination to define God, to locate him in time and place, to know Him as precisely as possible, to explain (to themselves and others) who and what He is. Children appear to have a keen desire to be in touch with the eternal.

The notion of God as a moral guide and, just as important, a demanding judge is shared by children of many religions. A righteousness clearly outlined certainly speaks to a sense of order, but with attendant dangers: the envy, shame, guilt, and rage of many, as well as the admiration and applause of a few. Yet righteousness can certainly get out of bounds, a major danger for any of us, whether we've been told we have a special body of truth to protect or whether we are simply left to our own moral resources. Vanity, the constant temptation to self-importance and self-aggrandizement, often accompanies righteousness. Covenantal and prophetic religions become an ethical endowment for many children. Such religions have an emphasis not only on moral exposition and analysis but on the sacrament of the family's life, one in which metaphors are not only spoken but connected to the everyday rhythms of existence. We constantly use metaphors to explain life and justify our thought processes. In people who are "constantly mindful" of God's presence these metaphors rule their every waking moment, for example "God's will."

Other children are also drawn to soul-searching, even though religion is not a great part of their lives. Many such children have spiritual thoughts, and much of their soul-searching partakes less of religious reflection than of an individual's struggle to make some persisting sense of life. Children will proclaim their conventional faith one day and on the next talk about how difficult it is to believe in anything.

As young and middle-age children engage in such soul-searching for the meaning or even existence of the divine, they may look to a school counselor with whom to discuss their many questions. Counselors should be open to listening without judging and to understanding the great inner struggle such dilemmas possess for the young.

Adolescence

The adolescent period of development has its own unique set of challenges and issues, which frequently are not understood by the adolescent. For him or her, it is a time to experience life and to test limits. Impulsive and reckless behavior may contribute to the adolescent finding him- or herself in dangerous and life-threatening situations. The epidemic of suicide is but one example of impulsivity. Balk (1997) suggested that crises may provide a catalyst for enhanced spirituality defined as a quest for understanding life's meaning.

Developmental Context

All adolescents struggle with change as new developmental capacities emerge. Young adolescents deal with changes in their physical development and the emotional impact this has on their mental psyche. As the adolescent develops new cognitive capacities, such as the ability think abstractly, experiences and events take on new and different meanings.

An adolescent who has experienced a crisis, such as the death of a sibling either through an accident or suicide, could begin to question why. Death to the adolescent is no longer an event, as it is for a younger child, but rather a process. This death crisis could provide a catalyst for spiritual growth. Balk (1997) noted that such growth is limited to those crises that (a) include time for reflection, (b) impact the life of the individual permanently, and (c) create a psychological imbalance that resists quickly being stabilized. Butnam suggested that "spiritual development will often take place when an individual must examine, assess, and reconstruct his or her values and beliefs and then act autonomously on those new values and beliefs" (Butnam, 1990, p.14).

Another aspect of the developmental context, allowing for spiritual growth during adolescence, is related to the religious development of the adolescent. Religion refers to the way an individual expresses his or her relationship to a higher force, being, power, or God (Mahrer, 1996). It is expressed through either belief systems or communal rituals such as prayer and worship, and it is not limited to organized religions (Mahrer). The adolescent, because of his or her emerging cognitive abilities, is also able to consider religious beliefs in new ways. It is during adolescence that religious values and beliefs begin to be clarified (Balk, 1983). Fowler (1996) suggested that because adolescents are able to think abstractly, they are able to construct an image of God in new ways. The new God image may include personal qualities of accepting love, understanding, loyalty, and support during crisis. This would seem to emphasize the importance of peer support groups in junior and senior high school.

Addressing developmental concerns can be the best means of supporting the quest of adolescents for answers to profound questions about the meaning of life. For more than a decade, newspaper headlines have highlighted "a generation at risk." The void of spiritual guidance and the lack of opportunities to interact with each other on a deeper level regarding life's meaning and purpose are still rarely noticed factors contributing to violence in schools. Gangs, drugs, sex, and suicide may be a search for a connection and meaning, as well as an escape from the pain of not having a genuine source of spiritual fulfillment (Kessler, 1998–1999).

The Passage Program at Crossroads School for Arts and Sciences in Santa Monica, California, is a curriculum for adolescents that "integrates heart, spirit, and community with strong academics. This curriculum of the heart is a response to the 'mysteries' of teenagers: their usually unspoken questions and concerns are at the center"(Kessler, 1998–1999, p. 49). Like other holistic and comprehensive programs, Passage deals with a broad range of issues:, communication skills, diversity, friendship, study skills, problem-solving, health, personal and social responsibility, and stress management. Unlike most programs, however, it also addresses spiritual development.

In the lives of adolescents, the search for meaning and purpose can take many detours, with many burning questions being asked, such as (a) Does my life have a purpose? (b) Is there life after death? (c) Is there a God? (d) Why was I born? Such questions must have an opportunity for expression if teenagers are to believe in themselves. Counselors, in collaboration with educators, must also help create a safe, nonthreatening environment where adolescents can explore these existential questions. However, counselors and teachers may be uncomfortable dealing with these types of questions and may need additional training in order to facilitate these types of discussions. Ron Miller (1995–1996), the historian of holistic education, observes that spirituality is nourished not through formal rituals that students practice in school but by *the quality of relationship* that is developed between the person and the world. "We can, and must, cultivate an attitude of caring, respect, and contemplation to replace the narrow modernist view that the world is a resource to be exploited" (Miller, p. 5).

Religious beliefs change as children enter and pass through adolescence as a consequence of maturation and of becoming more global in their thinking. Teens, for example, are less likely than younger children to believe in an absolutely literal translation of the Holy Bible. Children are more likely to report that they believe in God because of what their parents tell them. On the other hand, adolescents rely more on rational or logical thinking in determining their faith, rather than on choices their parents might make and espouse. They believe in God because, for example, the universe is orderly, because they believe there must have been a beginning to all things.

Among the more extensive studies on how faith changes as people age is the work of James Fowler (1996). After interviewing youth of all ages from a variety of backgrounds, Fowler delineated six stages of adolescent faith development of adolescent spirituality that have come to be accepted by many. The first stage, according to Fowler, is termed *mythical-literal faith*, the beginning of adolescents' spiritual journey. Still operating in a some-what concrete stage, adolescents respond to religion according to their cognitive or intellectual capacity. Because of the differences in maturational levels, no definite chronological age can be placed on this stage. Persons at this stage view almost all stories, particularly religious ones, in literal, concrete ways. God is a spirit being who sometimes takes a human form and resides somewhere in the sky. Many adolescents accept the religious faith traditions of their parents or household with little or no questions asked.

The next stage, according to Fowler, is termed *synthetic-conventional faith*. As adolescents age and mature, they increase their capacity to think abstractly, or as Swiss psychologist Jean Piaget termed it, they enter the stage of "formal operations." The primary task at this stage of cognitive operations is for the adolescent to relate his or her religious views with those of others, even though these views may be quite different. God, at this stage of development, is usually viewed as a personal advisor, friend, or guide, but sometimes it is not as necessary to personify this figure in a concrete or formal manner.

The last and final stage in Fowler's model of the development of adolescent spirituality is *individual-reflective faith*. This is obviously the highest level and may not be attained by everyone. Those individuals who have the capacity for such advanced development, however, engage in critical self-reflection and the examination of their personal beliefs and values. This is a crucial stage in the development of the individual as such questioning leads to making personal religious beliefs one's own. Adolescents who are capable of attaining this level of advancement view God in more abstract ways—not just as a personal advisor but also as a spirit embodying moral truths and personal presence. God or "Spirit" becomes a standard whereby moral certitude is measured. Adolescent spirituality, as defined by Fowler, is different from both a child's and an adult's spirituality. In order to understand it, we must have the capacity to think like a teenager and understand that every adolescent is in a singular phase of faith development.

Developing empathy for the adolescent quest for spiritual meaning requires knowing what *not to do* as well as what needs to be done. Parrott (1995) enumerates four "traps" or mistakes that should be avoided at all costs if the adolescent is to emerge healthy and whole from his or her quest for the spiritual. They consist of the following:

- *Motivating by guilt.* The teen years are a prime time for the acquisition of guilt as these young people struggle with unrealistic self-expectations and a relentless, sometimes overdemanding conscience. So why would someone use guilt to motivate the already self-punishing? Because, Parrott asserts, it works! Guilt gets results and often rather fast—but it is almost never long-lasting. Guilt fails to instill qualities that are good for the long run. Adolescents can be prompted to donate to charity by a sense of guilt because they have more than others. "More" is a relative term, however, and if the real gift of sharing is not instilled the gesture becomes self-serving and meaningless. What is created is a desire to clear one's conscience and to please those who are watching. Guilt eventually engenders anger and will sabotage a true effort to instill the virtue of charity or selflessness in a young person.
- *Equating spirituality with youth group activity.* Churches sometimes confuse activity with spirituality. Keeping adolescents "busy" does not make them "holy!" In today's world, there are simply too many activities that demand a young person's time, leaving them little space to simply "be" and "think." Parrott warns us that it is simply inaccurate and insensitive to gauge youth's spiritual maturity by how dedicated they are to our programming.
- *Setting our expectations for teenagers too high.* Our own high self-expectations often cause us to set the bar too high for others. Having the same expectations of adolescents as that of adults is simply unrealistic. Placing such expectations on adolescents about their spiritual development or religious maturity ensures failure and compounds guilt.
- *Setting our expectations for teenagers too low.* It is just as easy to err on the other side also. Setting expectations of adolescent spirituality too low can be as detrimental as setting them too high. In communicating lower expectations to an adolescent, we are in effect saying, "You really are not capable." Adolescence is often a very idealistic time and

youth aspire to lofty goals by nature. To hold them back is to stunt their spiritual growth. The hardest thing in the world is to let people learn by their mistakes and their sometimes too-lofty ambitions, material or spiritual.

Are young people today less religious than a decade or a generation ago? A recent Gallup Youth Survey (Parrott, 1995) reports that a majority of American young people continue to consider religion important in their lives. About 7 teenagers in 10 according to this poll say they agree with the statement that they are religious, including 19% who agree very strongly. Among the remaining 3 in 10 who disagree, only 5% strongly assert they are not religious.

Another important characteristic to remember is that spiritual development does not progress at a steady direction toward a pinnacle of maturity. Adolescents experience the feelings of emptiness that are part of human existence even on their spiritual journey, possibly especially during this time. An emotional rush or emotional "high" is common during the days, weeks, or even months following new spiritual commitments, but eventually this energy dissipates and questions arise that may cause doubt or even depression. This process is natural. It is all a predictable part of spiritual growth. Some theologians see doubting as a dynamic stage that is necessary to true belief, and not necessarily in opposition to it. A strong faith is not the result of avoiding questions, but of working with and within one's doubts. There can be no answers without questions.

Piaget, the world's most noted authority on the development of the intellect, explained that people come to understand new information in two different ways. He labeled these *assimilation* and *accommodation*. Assimilation is the effort that a person makes to incorporate new information into their existing body of knowledge. The new experience either fits easily or may require minor adjustments.

Accommodation, on the other hand, is necessary when the new experience does not fit within the current beliefs or knowledge base and goes beyond the accepted structure of thought. An example of this would be an adolescent's completely new insight or way of thinking about God. New ways of thinking about spiritual matters, whether radical or mainstream, can launch adolescents into an unsettling spiritual phase in their young lives.

One of the most essential needs of the emerging adolescent, especially in spiritual matters, is good role models. Teenagers need to see faith lived out in the lives of the adults who surround them. Unhealthy models, especially in the guise of spiritual authorities, only compound the angst of adolescents. Besides adults who can serve as role models, young adolescents yearn for a peer group who shares a common faith. Without this spiritual support system from individuals in their age group, they may have a difficult time developing a religious commitment. Most sociologists believe that faith is kept alive by a human support system as well as by divine faith in a Supreme Being. It's hard to maintain your belief in something when almost all of those around you think in an opposite manner.

One roadblock in the development of adolescent spirituality is the fact that idealistic thinking often leads to criticism. Because of their predisposition to idealism, adolescents can easily suffer disillusion with and disappointment in organized religion. Yet no organization, spiritual or otherwise, can adequately fulfill every ideal of every person. Disappointed and disillusioned young people can be fiercely critical of everyone and everything that they once held sacred. Their own difficulty in living up to their self-expectations further contributes to their disillusionment. They may begin to think that life, as they feel it should be lived within a religious context, is quite impossible, and therefore their only recourse is to abandon organized religion.

Adolescents tend to be more emotional than cognitive or intellectual in their interplay with the abstract. They remember feelings more readily than facts. Concerning their spiritual or religious beliefs, they know exactly how they feel about their last religious service even when they cannot remember what was said or the lesson to be learned. A young person's unpleasant feelings at religious events may exert more influence than the content of the service when it comes to whether or not he or she is drawn to a religious way of life.

Contrary to popular belief, youth today want to know right from wrong. The large majority (92%) of youth, according to Coles (1990), want to learn more about values. Young people intuitively understand that serious problems like violence, sexual promiscuity, drug use, and teen pregnancy can become less formidable if values that they can reason out intellectually are taught and believed. According to William Kilpatrick (1992), author of *Why Johnny Can't Tell Right from Wrong*, young people seem to understand that if they do not learn self-discipline and respect for others, they'll continue to exploit each other sexually, no matter how many health clinics and condom-distribution plans are created (Parrott, 1995). Confronted by the ills of today's society, many adolescents yearn for a place of safety and security, just as their elders do, even if it exists only in their hearts. The heroes of these young people are similar to the firefighters of New York City after the September 11, 2001 tragedies. These brave men put their own lives on the line for others when they could just as easily have run for shelter or headed for home. This is morality in action, a powerful lesson for an adolescent. Justice is not an easy concept, but social justice is the embodiment of the concept of right and wrong for the young people of today. A religious sect that does not emphasize these concepts holds little appeal for the youth of today or the adult of tomorrow.

Teenagers have a powerful psychological need to belong—a longing that, for adolescents with a developing faith, can be channeled into a church or a specific religious denomination. Although all sorts of demands compete for teenagers' time, most youth respect a call of commitment to a group. Being held accountable by a group of caring peers and adults is, in fact, exactly what many teens are looking for in their daily lives. A structure that affords an outlet for spiritual longing only adds to their desire to be part of something that really matters. The "belonging" that a church or religious group can provide represents stability to an adolescent struggling with feelings of "fitting in." These aren't always the most lofty reasons for membership, but they are real and should be nurtured.

Novelists from Walker Percy to J. D. Salinger have described in poignant detail the adolescent's search for truth, genuineness, and something to believe in. The adolescent's laborious search for a genuine faith or belief system is not a single, emotional decision made in the fervor of a retreat of some type or in a blinding moment of conversion. A teenager's quest for faith must be bolstered by deliberate actions that move him or her along the path to spiritual maturity. Adolescents can understand the importance of discipline in sports and schoolwork, even if they do not always live up to these ideals. They can also understand that the nurturing of an inner life depends upon discipline, inner strength, and fortitude. Teenagers need to be challenged to climb that high mountain we call maturity. Without challenge, and the discipline that it entails, there would be no sense of accomplishment or commitment.

In their fervor to embrace prayer, worship, and other activities that keep them focused on God, the danger exists of committing to what some call a vertical Christianity—that is, an absorption with self that may not be totally healthy. Obsessiveness is sometimes the earmark of too much focus on self. Youth seeking a realistic spiritual or religious emphasis in their lives, however, are highly capable of a horizontal dimension to their beliefs that impels them to reach out and care for other people. Again, a sense of social justice acts as a balance to religious worship and ritual. Reaching out to others keeps religious practice from being strictly self-absorbing. For the spiritual person, it is necessary to also see and feel the needs of others.

Exercises

1. Design a children's group that gathers weekly to discuss spirituality and what it means to them. What questions might they need to

address? What do they need to learn? What have they already learned from their families?

2. Design a teen group that will gather weekly to discuss spirituality and what it means to them. What questions might they need to address? What do they need to learn? What have they already learned from their families? What are some considerations that will be different in discussing spirituality with children versus teens?

Case of Ben

Ben is a mature fifteen-year-old who ran away from home. His older peers were able to convince him that by staying with his family he wouldn't experience the thrills of being free. Ben's parents practiced Orthodox Judaism, which caused Ben to feel stifled and unable to take part in many of his peers' activities. The older teens had access to drugs, credit cards, and the freedom Ben could only hope for. Only after crossing state lines did Ben realize that his mother must have been frantic, so he decided to call to tell her where he was. She implored him to return home, and by promising to allow him some additional freedom Ben's parents were able to convince him to return.

Case Discussion

- Discuss how Ben's parents were still an influence in Ben's life and how Ben's actions were developmentally appropriate while transgressing family values.
- How were Ben's older peers able to convince him to temporarily reject his family system?
- How did the family's religious values influence Ben to reconsider and return home?
- Developmentally, was this age-appropriate behavior for Ben?

References

Balk, D. (1983). How teenagers cope with sibling death: Some implications for school counselors. *The School Counselor, 31*(2), 150–158.

Balk, D. E. (1997, December). *Spirituality and bereavement: Contextual and developmental considerations.* Paper presented at Colorado State University by invitation of the Department of Human Development and Family Studies in the College of Applied Human Science, Fort Collins, CO.

Butnam, R. E. (1990). The assessment of religious development: Some possible options. *Journal of Psychology and Christianity, 9*(2), 14–26.

Coles, R. (1990). *The spiritual life of children.* Boston: Houghton Mifflin.

Dixon, J. A., & Moore, C. F. (1990). The development of perspective taking: Understanding information and perspective differences. *Child Development, 62,* 441–459.

Fowler, J. W. (1981). *Stages of faith: The psychology of human development and the quest for meaning.* San Francisco: Harper & Row.

Fowler, J. W. (1996). Pluralism and oneness in religious experience: William James, faith-development theory, and clinical practice. In E. P. Shafranske (Ed.), *Religion and the clinical practice of psychology* (pp. 165–186). Washington, D.C.: American Psychological Association.

Kessler, R. (1998–1999). Nourishing students in secular schools. *Educational Leadership, 56*(4), 49–52.

Kilpatrick, W. (1992). *Why Johnny Can't Tell Right from Wrong.* New York: Simon and Schuster

Lovecky, D. V. (1997). Spiritual sensitivity in gifted children. *Roeper Review, 20,* 178–183.

Mahrer, A. R. (1996). Existential-humanistic psychotherapy and the religious person. In E. P. Shafranske (Ed.), *Religion and the clinical practice of psychology* (pp. 433–460). Washington, D.C.: American Psychological Association.

Matthews, G. B. (1994). *The philosophy of childhood.* Cambridge, MA: Harvard University Press.

Miller, R. (1995–1996, Winter). The renewal of education and culture: A multifaceted task. *Great Ideas in Education, 7,* 5.

Palmer, P. J. (1998/1999). *The active life: A spirituality of work, creativity and caring.* San Francisco: Jossey-Bass.

Papalia, D. E., & Olds, S. W. (1990). *A child's world: Infancy through adolescence.* New York: McGraw-Hill.

Parrott, F. (1995). Normative expectations and exchanges of help and support between adult children and their parents. Unpublished dissertation.

Peterson & Gelfand (1984). Causal attributions of helping as a function of age and incentives. *Child Development, 55,* 504–511.

Rheingold, H. L. (1982). Little children's participation in the work of adults: A nascent behavior. *Child Development, 53,* 114–125.

Schickedanz, J. A., Schickedanz, D. I., Forsyth, P. D., & Forsyth, G. A. (1998). *Understanding children and adolescents* (3rd ed.). Boston, MA: Allyn and Bacon.

Shaffer, D. A. (1999). *Developmental psychology: Childhood and adolescence* (5th ed.). Pacific Grove, CA: Brooks/Cole.

http://ifcl.com/links/childrenandspirituality.shtml

www.susankramer.com/spirituality.html#Introduction

CHAPTER 3
Men and Spiritual Development

Why a chapter on men and spirituality? Are a man's religious or spiritual beliefs different from those of a woman? Research tells us that it is not in the belief system that the differences in male and female spirituality occur but rather in how that belief system is formed. Although some women chafe under the all-encompassing patriarchal context of most organized religions, men often suffer from the idea that faith-related beliefs and practices are too "feminine" for "real men." Ian Harris (1997) maintained that spirituality plays an important role in how a man feels about himself. Harris asserts that belief in a higher power helps men choose the moral "high road." Other writers see the masculine quest for a higher power as a search for the "Great Warrior" or the "Supreme Being." What most writers agree upon, however, is that the path to spirituality is a journey that is often fraught with uncertainty and even pain. However, it can also be a powerful force for good and a source of much inner peace and joy.

Pestalozzi (1951) stated, "there is in us a sacred and Divine presence, which a man can cherish and foster on his own, thus rising to the inner dignity of his nature, the only means by which he can truly become a man" (p. 4). Although all would not completely agree with this statement, it is true that for many men this search for the "divine" does serve as a powerful motivational force for the majority of their lives. The continuum of spirituality and/or religious beliefs ranges from spiritual practices observed in isolation to sharing in a faith community where most observances take on a communal nature. Whether spirituality leads to attendance in a particular church, temple, synagogue, or mosque and following a particular religious doctrine, faith in a higher power can exert a strong influence upon human behavior.

In studies that seek to describe masculine gender identity formation, the spiritual side of the male psyche has virtually been ignored (Harris, 1997). This may be in large part because many social scientists ignore or severely minimize the impact of religious training upon human behavior. Other facets of development such as gender role stereotypes in the media, parental influence, and peer associations are more often the subjects of research. Man is viewed by many social scientists as strictly a secular being without a soul or spiritual domain. In preserving this secularist viewpoint, researchers and theorists lose sight of a very important dimension of humanity that can be a driving force in moral and ethical decision-making, as well as in the acquisition of guilt. To ignore this dimension of manhood is to deny an essential element of humanity.

A Gallup Poll taken in 1989 reported that 60% of all men in the United States said that they were members of a church or synagogue, and that 36% attended the church or synagogue frequently. Muslims tend to be present in their mosques more often because their religion is a part of their daily lives. Statistics for other Asian religions were not obtainable.

This same research also claims that men become more spiritual as they grow older, but the same tendency was also observed in the female population. Adults over 50 years of age are the most frequent churchgoers, whereas those between 18 and 29 are the least faithful in attendance. Statistics that claim that men are not faithful about church attendance are usually based on Christian populations only. The Islamic and Jewish faiths usually count more men in attendance than women. This is accounted for in part by the special role accorded to men in both of these religions. Most researchers agree, however, that in the Western countries of the world, faith has lost some of its "manly appeal" (Mathewes-Green, 1999).

Several reasons have been given for the reluctance of men to embrace religious, doctrine-driven organizations, and among them is the emphasis in most Christian faiths in a personal, passionate relationship with the "bridegroom" of the Old Testament. Bill McCartney of Promise Keepers asserts that men should be in a love affair with Jesus. As Frederica Mathewes-Green maintains, "the church's mystical bond was now imagined as me-and-Jesus-alone, and as swooning and passionate" (1999, p. 1). This type of emotional, sensual approach to God is often alien to men who want more of a "hero" or even "action figure" type of deity.

European and American men report that they still see the need for transcendent meaning in their lives, but if all they see in churches is a sappy, passive, and soft approach to belief and worship, they will continue to leave organized forms of religion in record numbers. Even in churches that were created with a very patriarchal, masculine-based leadership, women actually run things in the daily life of the church. This "feminizing" of religion has left many men to see their quest for a powerful "god-image" as a lonely journey without too many familiar guideposts.

Unique Characteristics of the Population

Ian M. Harris (1997) undertook a fairly thorough study of several hundred men in order to ascertain the particular spiritual beliefs of the masculine gender. From the surveys and interviews he conducted with these men, he was able to cull 10 categories of tenets or beliefs that had a commonality among the respondents. His research isolated the following themes: (a) finding inner wisdom, (b) searching for truth, (c) speaking from the heart, (d) confronting the dark side, (e) loving, (f) working for a better world, (g) passing a test, (h) belonging to something great, (i) following scripture, and (j) believing in destiny.

In looking at this list gleaned from an important research study, a counselor can see that the average European or American man does not appear to be looking for a spirituality that is overly feminine or that contains the romanticism portrayed in many religious texts. In moving from a belief in the avenging, wrathful God of the Old Testament to a more merciful and loving God of the New Testament, many religious sects lost their appeal to men. Although many women would argue that this transition was sorely needed because it also brought about an improvement in the way that men viewed women, many men felt lost in this "new church." In the Roman Catholic faith, many of the same types of masculine identity crises occurred after Vatican II and the changes in the Church at that time.

In analyzing the 10 tenets proposed by Harris, a counselor can come to a better understanding of exactly what a western male client may be searching for in the pursuit of a spiritual dimension to his life. These 10 themes appear to sum up and categorize many of the unique characteristics of the European or western masculine population. One does not want to overgeneralize about all men, but neither would we want to lose the opportunity to explore this proposed delineation of the inner psyche of men. This inner psyche consists of ideas and dreams, as well as thoughts of death, dying, and the spiritual realm, even though these thoughts may be present only to deny the existence of any power higher than the individual.

Finding inner wisdom: This powerful belief ranked number one in the survey and interviews conducted by Harris (1997). The belief that an individual contains the divine within himself is powerful and self-actualizing. Although not putting man on the same level as the God-figure, it does make man the chosen one of the deity. This inner spiritual belief is seen as the source of all wisdom, and from wisdom comes discernment, judgment, and inner peace. It implies that a man will spend a lifetime in some type of spiritual introspection or self-discovery. Meditation, reflection, and inner stillness are requirements for someone seeking this type of relationship in his life. Taking this path does not always imply a belief in a personal god or deity but simply in a power higher than oneself. Individuals who are comfortable with a life guided by intellect will often choose this path. However, for any type of belief system, the type of depth, intellectual honesty, and curiosity implied in this tenet is a necessity.

Searching for truth: As men resolve to lead a more inner-focused life, the search for truth must accompany their journey into the realm of the spiritual. The examination of the very essence of existence is the force that guides the spiritual being. The search for truth is the journey to find the answers to life's greatest questions and riddles. Famous figures in both history and literature have wrestled with the answers to the "unanswerable." According to Gandhi, the search for truth is what provides a divine dimension to human existence (Brown, 1989). Mohammed, Buddha, and Confucius all extolled the search for truth. Truth is not an entity that is directly perceived but rather is found through metaphor and paradox. Men are often driven to this quest for truth by the hypocrisy and unethical behavior they perceive in the world in which they live. Many males come into therapy because of the stress that working in a business world that is not centered in truth and moral conviction exerts upon them. Because historically men have spent most of their lives outside the home, the paradoxes of the secular world have often haunted them more than has been the case with women. With western women entering the workforce in almost equal numbers, however, these same types of dilemmas now face both genders.

Speaking from the heart: In literature and movies, the heart is the seat of love, compassion, and lust. It is often equated with the soul, because of the "feelings" associated with it. Western men are not usually socialized to deal with issues of the heart but rather to think of everything in rational, precise terms. Issues of the heart are perceived as belonging more to the feminine side of one's nature. In the modern era of the 1990s, western men were called upon to demonstrate that their thoughts and actions were derived more from the heart than from the intellect. They were asked to show their "sensitive" sides more and to make themselves as comfortable in the world of feelings as they were in the world of the intellect. For some men, this was a welcome relief from the constraints of an overmasculine identity and for others this was pure agony. Many European and American men need to be taught how to think and feel simultaneously. The search for "heart" leads one to rely more on intuition and to become more "childlike" and trusting. Many men are currently on a spiritual journey to discover their "heart" just like the Tin Man in the *Wizard of Oz*. No journey can be more painful for a man who has been socialized to think that matters of the "heart" are emasculating and inferior. However, in terms of what this dimension of spirituality can bring to human relationships, no journey can be more rewarding.

Confronting the dark side: According to Jungian psychology, man always has a dark, or shadow side, to his personality. To many, this is seen as a side of the personality with which one must do battle; however, to the more enlightened, this facet of spirituality is actually very freeing and hopeful. Instead of running away from aspects of oneself that are least desirable, one confronts and conquers them. It is a matter of maximizing the positive in one's life and coming to understand the negative sides of one's personality. It is the age-old battle of good versus evil, humanity versus godliness. "Spirituality helps a man come to grips with his shadow side, accepting the contradictions of good and evil" (Harris, 1997, p. 20). Sometimes this is seen as the fear of going to hell rather than to the rewards of heaven. However it is defined, men of all ages have had to deal with the good and the evil that exists first within themselves and then in the world in which they live.

Spirituality gives one hope in this lifelong quest and dispels the dread that death sometimes engenders. Sin is the primary evil that most men face, and spirituality serves to take away the fear that surrounds this issue, yet at the same time it makes a person realize the seriousness of the offense. Some men seek counseling when this fight within themselves to reconcile the positive and negative sides of their humanity becomes too great for them, as is often the case with substance abuse when it becomes apparent that it cannot be conquered alone. It is through the realization that, as humans, we can so easily despair at all the sorrow the world holds and that men are brought to the realization of the divine. Hope, compassion, forgiveness, and faith can all come from the search for the reconciliation of good and evil.

Many men somehow find this journey more difficult than their feminine counterparts. Men of all nationalities have been socialized to see forgiveness as weak, compassion as soft, and hope in anything other than themselves as foolhardy. How transforming this spiritual journey can be for any man courageous enough to undertake it! Individuals who were changed by this battle with good and evil include St. Augustine, St. Paul, Confucius, Lao Tse, Buddha, Gandhi, and Francis of Assisi.

Loving: To give without thought of self has been immortalized not just in the death of Jesus Christ, or in the fastings and prayers of Gandhi, but in the immortal words of a Dickens character: "It is a far, far, better thing that I do, than I have ever done." The realization that love comes from giving rather than from possessing is a life-changing experience that is also very alien to men to whom success and material possessions have been held up as the true measures of an individual's worth. Many men are socialized to be rather selfish and to think first of themselves, as these are felt to be traits that any one who really succeeds in business must have. The idea of unconditional love often comes much later in life. Yet in order to be a successful friend, husband, companion, or father, a man must learn to love in this way. Western men are encouraged to be ego-driven and self-assertive, yet it is primarily in service to others and in nurturing and caring for others that these same men truly mature. Often it takes a spiritual type of enlightenment to allow a European or American male to embrace the "softer," more caring side of his nature. This type of spiritual journey allows a man to experience another's reality and in so doing to identify with the pain and suffering of others. It is often only through therapy that a man can have the type of enlightenment that is necessary to change his behavior. The spiritual man is usually more willing to embrace this type of behavior because he sees in the God-figure or higher self a model of love and nonviolence, as well as a reason to develop his own capacity to nurture and enhance living systems, such as his family, his work, his community. M. Scott Peck (1978) defines love as "The will to extend one's self for the purpose of nurturing one's own or another's spiritual growth" (p. 81).

Working for a better world: As a result of the many steps described previously, a man usually comes to the realization that the universe is basically good and that he must constantly search for evidence of this. Spirituality is what allows him to embrace the good that exists even when its presence is masked in the evil that appears to be all around us. Charity toward others is a natural offspring of recognizing the good in all things and the acceptance that all mankind must work to improve social institutions. This is quite a journey from the competitive world of one-upmanship and caring solely for oneself. It is only in working for a better world that a man sanctifies the present and gains hope for a life hereafter. "Spiritual men believe that good will eventually conquer evil" (Harris, 1997, p. 24). History is replete with the stories of great men who have made service to others their hallmark: Albert Schweitzer, Mahatma Gandhi, Ignatius Loyola, Siddhartha Gautama (Buddha), and so on. Most men are not prepared to go to quite the extreme of these role models, but they can embrace a spirituality that prompts them to participate more actively in civic organizations, youth organizations, sports leagues, and so on. The idea of giving back is an earmark of a mature adult.

Passing a test: Two different kinds of "tests" occur in life. The first of these consists of events over which we have little or no control: illness, accidents, crime, loss of loved ones, loss of employment, natural disasters, and war. The second category consists of mistakes or actions we take that may cause us pain: divorce, unwise decisions, difficult relationships, and mistakes we make in general. Life is fraught with pitfalls and these are often accompanied by pain and worry. Most men have been socialized to think that they must be the ultimate problem-solver who is not afraid of anything. This is the tremendous burden under which many men labor, and it may ultimately cause them to cut off all feelings in an effort to appear "strong" and to protect themselves from emotions that are too overwhelming to handle. Spirituality may give a man the strength that is needed to face the hardships and trials of life. It can help a man define for himself the code of conduct upon which he chooses to build his life. Spirituality also allows an individual to forgive himself for the mistakes he has made in life or when he fails to live up to his high ideals. In a word, spirituality provides a balance in life that is hard to attain almost anywhere else.

Belonging to something great: Believing in something more powerful than oneself is a great comfort. When a man faces himself and realizes how vulnerable he is, the thought of a power greater than himself is very reassuring. Most individuals call this higher power God or Allah. "This aspect of spirituality implies a connection with creation, with the spirit that links all beings in the universe, with the flow of life" (Harris, 1997, p. 26). Belief in such a spirit force gives meaning to life and allows one to share life's burdens. Men contact this greater power through prayer, meditation, dreams, rituals, and so on. A personal relationship with a greater power is an outcome of embracing spirituality. All of this does not, however, imply that man totally understands the God-figure or all of His powers. Faith is the word used to describe the belief in a higher power without totally comprehending who or what that power is. It is in the surrender to a force greater than his own that a man acquires true strength and a relief from always having to be an all-knowing, all-powerful person. The highest step in the acquisition of spirituality is the ability to surrender one's will to that of the Supreme Being and to accept in faith all that befalls him in this life. Taoists refer to it as "nonaction." Out of such surrender, true faith and true freedom are found. God, Allah, or Yahweh is seen in the entire universe and His majesty provides meaning for life. In acknowledging the higher power and His control over the universe, man develops true intimacy with the Creator. It also implies the obligation of passing on this belief to future generations through worship and, for some, a definite liturgy. It means never being truly alone again. It means that suffering has a deeper meaning and purpose. For those whose spirituality also includes belief in the Resurrection, it means that life's journey is only a preparation for the hereafter.

Following scripture: The Bible, the Koran (Qur'an), the Book of Mormon, the Tao Te Ching, the Veda, the Bhagavad Gita, the Dhammapada, and other religious texts or scriptures are believed to be divinely inspired words and they form the basis of spirituality for many people. These texts provide a blueprint for how men ought to lead their lives. In every religious text, certain "commandments" or basic tenets are there to provide a pathway or guide through the journey of life. Conservative, more fundamentalist sects believe in a more literal interpretation of the holy scriptures of all faiths. More liberal individuals believe that a lot of allegory is contained in these texts and that the words are open to many interpretations. They also believe that religion must change as the world changes where outward practices are concerned, yet strict adherents do not allow for any change.

Believing in destiny: If one believes in a higher power and that this entity is all wise and all knowing, then there must be a divine plan that is revealed to us day by day. "Spirituality implies destiny, that life has a higher purpose completely outside of mortal control" (Harris, 1997, p. 28). Belief in a higher power implies that this being has control over us, possesses superior knowledge, and is able to see all of life at once and not just in small segments as man does. It implies that past, present, and future are all one to this being. The faith that leads one to belief in such a God or higher source of being also leads one to see him- or herself as part of the divine destiny. Far from fatalism, one sees oneself as an active participant in carrying out the will of God. Rather than feeling constricted, people who live according to a spiritual code feel that they are freer to enjoy life and experience happiness because their life has purpose and meaning. They have established a reason for being. Research has shown that such individuals may experience less stress in their lives because they see a reason for most things that happen in life. Men who are guided by a belief in destiny feel that their lives are part of a divine plan and that each day gives them a further glance into this spiritual blueprint. Holding this belief, each moment becomes a sacrament.

Kyle's Story (Taken from the Counseling Files
of One of the Authors)

In the summer of 2000, a man in his late thirties came to my office because he was feeling depressed and unhappy with his life, but he could not quite identify what was causing his problems. His wife was instrumental in getting him to come to see me, as was his physician. Kyle presented himself as an intelligent man who was successful in most areas of his life.

Kyle had been married for seven years to Jean who was three years his junior. He reported that he loved his wife and their two children, a boy of 4 and a little girl who was almost a year old. He was a salesman who worked for a large national home-building supply company. Kyle appeared to like his job, although he did not always like the hours that retail required or the mandatory work on some weekends and holidays.

At his first session, Kyle reported that he had not been sleeping well and that he felt anxious and tense most of the time. He also reported that he had recently sustained the death of his father, which left him feeling depressed and somewhat isolated. His physician had recommended counseling after tests revealed no serious medical condition.

As we went through the story of his life, Kyle revealed that he had been raised in a very conservative Protestant sect to which both of his parents belonged. While residing in their home, Kyle went to church every Sunday and often in the middle of the week. Many of his friends both in elementary school and high school belonged to the same church and going to church was an opportunity to see them as well. He reported that he did not really question the subject of religion while in high school. In his words, "it was just something that you did."

Kyle left his hometown in order to attend college on a basketball scholarship, although he left before obtaining his degree. While he was attending college, he began to make a wide circle of friends and observed that their belief systems were very different from his. Initially, this made him nervous and unsure of himself, but it also intrigued him and made him want to learn more. He attended several different types of church services, but that only seemed to add to his confusion. In time, he simply stopped going to church altogether.

After he met Jean and they decided to get married, he was not opposed to the marriage taking place in a church of her choice. Secretly, he also knew this would please his parents. Once they were married, Jean went to church almost every Sunday, but Kyle usually stayed home alone, played golf, or later babysat the children. For a while he seemed content with this arrangement. However, with the death of his father, Kyle suddenly felt nervous and unsure, but did not really know why.

Because other areas of his life seemed rather stable, and because Kyle had introduced the topic, we began to explore the importance of spirituality and religion in his life. Kyle was able to go back to his childhood and relate his earliest conceptions of God. He remembered feeling a great deal of fear about a God who on one hand was presented as loving and merciful, yet at the same time was one who counted sins and condemned people to hell. He remembered having nightmares in which God spoke to him harshly and turned His back on Kyle because he was judged to be unworthy. At the same time, however, Kyle related that church had seemed familiar and even comforting at times. It gave him a sense of belonging.

I asked Kyle what was the most comforting thing his church attendance had provided for him. After thinking about this for a rather long time, he responded thoughtfully, "I think that it was a sense of hope. A belief that there was another world that was better than this one. The hope that death was not really final, but that one day I would be reunited with family members and friends who had died." I asked Kyle if he still believed in that, to which he replied, "Yes, of course, but maybe I don't think about it often enough."

In another session, as we discussed Kyle's marriage, he suddenly appeared quite thoughtful. "Jean and I share many things and we are really very close, but I think I am not happy about the fact that we really don't share the same faith," mused Kyle. He went on to say that although they were both Christians, their belief systems seemed different. However, he added, "We really don't talk about this a whole lot." I ventured to ask Kyle who in his family of origin had been the most fervent and faithful in terms of religious observances. He thought for a while and said that it was probably his mother, although his father had been a frequent church attendee also. He felt that it was his mother who talked about God more often and who seemed in some ways to live her beliefs more openly—helping others, volunteering at church events, teaching Sunday school, and so on. He also remembered that usually more women than men were at church services and gatherings.

On another occasion I questioned Kyle about his work situation and his degree of job satisfaction. Kyle reported that he really liked what he did for a living but that he didn't feel completely fulfilled in that either. He spoke about the difficulty he sometimes felt when money and sales were the constant indicators of success. He also felt an immense amount of stress in constantly dealing with quotas, sales projections, and competition. All in all, he sometimes experienced a sense of hopeless, a feeling of "Is this all there is?"

As time went on and we explored other areas of Kyle's life, he began to reveal his hopes and dreams for the future. Kyle wanted to be a good husband and father but felt that something was holding him back in both cases. He wanted to make a good life for his family in all respects. He looked forward to doing family-type things with his two children as they grew older and were able to participate in activities like sports, Scouts, and family vacations. Especially, he wanted a strong, loving, and meaningful relationship with Jean. At times he doubted that he had the strength to accomplish all of this.

As we explored steps that Kyle could take to lift some of the depression and anxiety he was feeling, Kyle began to gain an insight into some of his struggles. He came in one day and wanted to discuss some thoughts he had had during the previous week. "I find myself puzzling over many of these things all during the day," he explained. "They keep revolving around in my mind. I think that a lot of my anxiety may come from the uncertainty of the world around me. I want to be a good husband and father, but I don't really feel in control of my own destiny. I feel as though everything that I have worked so hard for could vanish in a moment. We have seen the collapse of so many businesses recently, and we know that the job market is awful out there. I have no sense of security and this frightens me!" he proclaimed.

As he talked, Kyle became more agitated and at one point even began to pace back and forth. He was obviously emotionally distraught. As we talked, he began to calm down a little. Kyle began to see that it was foolhardy to place all of his hope in any job or work situation, or to think that doing so was the answer to all of his problems.

From a practical standpoint, we explored some possibilities to calm his fears. He could try to save more by restructuring some of his investments and spending habits, so that he would have a cushion to fall back on in case of an emergency. Kyle acknowledged that he possessed very good health and could always find some kind of work if he really had to do so. Jean was currently staying at home with their two young children but in a couple of years, or even sooner if need be, she could go back to work and contribute to the family's finances. We even looked at the remote possibility that even if a major catastrophe occurred, they could sell their home and move into an apartment that would be less expensive and have less upkeep. Kyle looked hard at all these possibilities, and as he let himself accept each one, he became calmer and calmer. It was a case of imagining the worst-case scenario, and by accepting it he freed himself of the fear that it held for him. The future began to appear more manageable.

However, Kyle was still dealing with other restlessness that we had not yet touched upon in any significant way. One day Kyle came in and said, "I think that I have begun to truly understand myself and what I am going through. It occurred to me this week that I keep trying to find some kind of permanence in this world, when in reality I need to accept that the only permanent thing is 'impermanence.' I am in a constant state of anxiety because

I feel I must be in control of all things while at the same time feeling so helpless to control almost anything. I think that I am looking in the wrong place for an answer to my problem. I keep focusing on things outside of myself for answers without being willing to look more within myself."

This was certainly a major breakthrough. As Kyle and I began to explore his inner self, he came to the realization that he needed to cultivate more of an inner life based on some kind of spiritual principle. He had been reacting in the typical American fashion of trying to physically work harder to solve his problems, when what he really needed was to slow down and get in touch with his feelings and personal needs. Kyle had turned into a human "doing" instead of a human "being." Kyle did not like the idea of taking anti-anxiety medication so we did not explore this option, although I did suggest that he get a complete physical as soon as possible.

Kyle himself brought up the idea of meditation as a way to relieve some of the stress he was currently undergoing. Together we explored some of the Eastern faiths and their practices. Kyle was not thinking about converting to any of these sects, but their emphasis on peace, harmony, and serenity was very appealing to him. He also began to take Tai Chi lessons and reported that he really enjoyed this activity. Kyle liked the combination of movement along with the meditative practice.

He also began to read stories about famous and powerful men who meditated daily as a means of increasing their inner peace and centering themselves. After a couple of months, Kyle reported some very optimistic results, but still something appeared to be lacking. Kyle and Jean came together to a counseling session and the three of us discussed Kyle's concerns. Jean seemed quite willing to make concessions as far as the choice of a church that they might attend was concerned. Together they settled on a nondenominational Christian church close to their home. The doctrine that it preached was based on the Bible but did not follow any of the mainline Protestant sects as far as tradition went. Kyle and Jean were particularly anxious to affiliate with a church before their children started school because they wanted them to attend Sunday school and belong to a religious group as they grew up. If they later wanted to choose a different denomination, Jean and Kyle both felt that they could be comfortable with their children's decisions.

The positive changes that Kyle made in his life from a spiritual standpoint seemed to relieve some of his anxiety. Although prayer and meditation will not work for everyone, in Kyle's case they seemed to provide something he had been searching for. A presence of the divine in his life gave purpose to it, yet he was not pulled back into the fear and negativism that had surrounded some of the religious practices from his youth. He felt more centered and definitely more hopeful, as he expressed it. Kyle's journey had taken a while, but it had proven to be fruitful.

Implications for Counselors

Kyle was a willing client and a thoughtful and introspective man who wanted to better his life. By looking at Ingersoll's seven factors (1994) for integrating spirituality into one's life, one can analyze Kyle's receptivity to developing spiritual or religious practices into his life:

1. One's conception of the divine, absolute, or "force greater than oneself"
2. One's sense of meaning of what is beautiful or worthwhile
3. One's relationship with the divine and other human beings
4. One's tolerance or negative capability for mystery
5. Peak ordinary experiences that enhance spirituality (which may include rituals or spiritual disciplines)
6. Seeing spirituality as play
7. Viewing spirituality as a systemic force that acts to integrate all the dimensions of one's life (p. 11)

Kyle experienced a sense of the divine as a child and was accepting of this concept. He believed in a God or higher power who was the creator of all things. As an adult, he yearned for this same centering belief in his life, and he took steps to integrate it into his daily existence. Kyle was successful as a human being and did not turn to God as an "answer" to his problems as much as a companion and guide on life's journey.

Kyle was not looking for a counselor to tell him what he should believe but rather to help him clarify his thoughts about what was going on in his life and his psyche. He was missing "meaning" in his life by his own definition. In this hurried and hectic world, it is easy to lose sight of life's deeper meanings. Kyle needed something more and was willing to do what was necessary in order to acquire it.

The relationships in Kyle's life gave meaning and focus to his inner longing. He valued his relationship with his wife Jean and was proud of their two children. Kyle was not coming from a sense of unhappiness in his personal life, but he wanted to share something with Jean on a deeper level. He also wanted to be able to pass down to his children a belief system based on hope and faith in a creator. Not everyone has these same needs or envisions them to the same extent as Kyle did. Not to acknowledge them when they are present, however, leads to the restlessness and anxiety that Kyle was experiencing.

Kyle was able to tolerate the ambiguity and mystery that belief in a higher power entails, as the effects of a creative force that supercedes humanity can be felt but not seen or touched. Kyle credited his early background with imbuing him with a sense of faith that was very strong, even though at times it seemed remote. Kyle also profited from examining Eastern religious or spiritual practices because of their mystical properties. They also suited his temperament and current disposition. Kyle was simply at an age where he was questioning what his true values really were. He wanted his life centered on more than work, competition, and material things.

In addition, Kyle missed a sense of ritual or religious ceremony in his life. Although not drawn to churches where elaborate celebrations were the norm, he did enjoy music, the Scriptures, and a sense of community prayer. Earlier experiences with an "angry God" had not all been pleasant, but as an adult Kyle could transcend this and carve out a place for himself in a religious community of his choice. People who fixate on negative experiences from the past and are not able to move on seriously limit their own personal growth and development as human beings.

Kyle was forced to go to church as a youngster, but now as an adult he was choosing to attend services. Spirituality or religious practice was no longer perceived as strictly a duty but rather as something to look forward to and enjoy. It enriched Kyle's life rather than making him feel guilty. Sometimes it is necessary for an individual to lose something or at least do without it for a while in order to really appreciate it.

As a result of going deep within himself to explore what he was lacking and what was making him restless and uncomfortable, Kyle was able to sort out his feelings and desires. This is an important step, but a meaningless one if actions do not result or some plan does not evolve. In Kyle's case, he began to meditate and practice Tai Chi for inner peace, and he and his wife discussed their religious differences. Together they made a plan for the family to join a nondenominational church that suited both of them. Kyle improved his inner personal life through research and experimentation with different belief systems. He made positive steps to live out his need to belong to a faith community. Kyle's spiritual and religious beliefs were acted upon and integrated into his personal life in a meaningful and conscious manner.

Darren's Case

Darren is a 40-year-old of Irish decent whose family is Protestant. Darren came to America at the age of 3 and lives in Miami, Florida. He worked his way through college and law school and excelled sufficiently to be asked to join a prestigious law firm. The firm is well known for its practice of maritime law. Darren, assigned to this department, was given a big case involving the smuggling of drugs from South America. While meeting with the principal litigants, Darren discovered that a member of his law firm was connected with this particular cartel and had received kickbacks unknown to the firm's president. This colleague approached Darren to offer his services informally in the case. Darren was conflicted but was aware that this case could put him in a position to become a junior partner, so he accepted the offer of assistance.

Darren, who recently returned to his Protestant faith, had been attending a professional men's church group on a monthly basis. The discussion at the last session concerned the tradeoffs in the workplace and how each of the participants had been handling the situation. Darren, unable to discuss the case, began to realize he had placed himself in a compromised position by accepting the assistance of his colleague. Darren wanted to approach his immediate senior partner to discuss the implications, but this would put the position of his colleague in jeopardy. Darren's conscious was saying one thing and his practice another.

Case Discussion

- Discuss the dilemma that Darren is experiencing and how his religious values could be called upon to resolve the complexities of this case.
- How does Darren's pursuit of the truth cause conflict in his practice of the law?
- What religious influences in Darren's life could be useful in the resolution of his dilemma?
- As a counselor, how would you use Darren's conversion to his Protestant faith to help him consider alternatives that would allow him to practice his profession and adhere to his values?

References

Brown. J. M. (1989). *Gandhi. Prisoner of hope.* New Haven: Yale University Press.

Harris, I. (1997). The ten tenets of male spirituality. *Journal of Men's Studies* 6, (1), 29

Ingersoll, R. E. (1994). Spirituality, religion, and counseling: Dimensions and relationships. *Counseling and Values* 38, 98–112

Mathewes-Green, F. (1999). *At the corner of east and now: a modern life in ancient Christian Orthodoxy.* New York: Jeremy P. Tarcher/Putnam.

Peck, M. S. (1978). *The road less traveled.* New York: Simon & Schuster.

Pestalozzi, J. H. (1951). *The education of man.* New York: Philosophical Library.

www.spiritualsanctuary.com/men's_spirituality.htm

CHAPTER 4

The Elderly Population

The "graying of America" is a subject often written and spoken about in contemporary society. McFadden (1995) stated, "Among the many changes in the human self-concept produced by developments in the twentieth century has been the emergence of the expectation that a long life is normative" (p. 161). The elderly population itself is aging, and at the turn of the recent century nearly half of this population was 75 or older.

In a book on spirituality and mental health, why would the elderly be a population that is targeted? Many studies cited in the sections that follow show a positive link among religion, spirituality, and well-being. The reader's attention will also be drawn to the fact that most elderly African-American and other minority groups are reported to have higher levels of religious commitment and participation than younger counterparts. The most positive outcome of this research is that a strong inner belief system, founded upon trust in a higher power, is not confined to organized religion but also encompasses spirituality, which is broader in meaning. Such a spiritual belief system, whether practiced in an organized or nonorganized manner, usually also contains reflections on an afterlife, which brings meaning to everyday life for the elderly, and this belief system serves to counteract the popular negative stereotypes of older people being bitter or depressed that sometimes pervade our society.

Society has come a long way from Freud's contention that religion or spirituality is an "obsessional neurosis." A respected researcher in the area of aging, Harold G. Koenig (1993) cited positive evidence that not only is the person who practices his or her spiritual beliefs less likely to engage in irrational thinking or neuroticism but that the practice of a faith tradition actually enhances health and well-being. It serves to protect against anxiety and depression in later life. In short, spirituality gives meaning to one's everyday existence. Clinicians must be aware of these research findings and be trained to work with older clients on issues of spirituality and/or religion. A knowledge of the characteristics and needs of this unique population is mandatory for all mental health professionals.

Unique Characteristics

The elderly population has definite characteristics that make this age group a particularly interesting one to study. Not only are their numbers increasing rapidly but it is a time of life when spiritual and religious issues form a large part of most senior citizens' consciousness. The 1990s have seen a plethora of research devoted to the significance of spirituality and religion on aging well. People are living longer because of better health care and modern wonder drugs. Although at one time 60 was considered "old," most 70-year-olds today are active, engaged in life, and enjoying their leisure years, as are some 80- and 90-year-olds.

Age is just a number; quality of life is the determining factor of aging. Research has suggested three factors as being the biggest sources of life-quality for people over 65 years of age: health, financial security, and social support (Campbell, 1975; George, 1981; Larson, 1978; McFadden, 1995). However, other research maintains that a person could have a reverse of these—poor health, a reduction of income, and a shrinking social network —yet that person could still have a perfectly adequate sense of well-being and a deep conviction that life had meaning for them (George & Clipp, 1991, McFadden, 1995).

Individuals in the older age groups are inclined to have more health problems and frequently suffer sensory loss, such as sight, hearing, and so on. These losses affect them personally, socially, and economically. Health status, according to Levin (1994), should be viewed as multidimensional, incorporating clinical, subjective, and functional elements.

The positive aspects of religious/spiritual involvement have been found to be prevalent for adults of all ages (Levin & Vanderpool, 1992). Among the characteristics that Idler (1987) discovered in the elderly population was the fact that, for women, public religiosity was associated with lower levels of functional disability and depression, whereas among men, private religiousness was associated with less disability and depression. Gender made a significant difference in this sample. A sense of isolation is often experienced by the elderly, as they lose some of their mobility and experience the deaths of family and close friends. Koenig, George, and Siegler (1988) reported that religion or spirituality was the coping resource most frequently cited by older persons when experiencing sadness, loneliness, and loss. Another charactcristic of this age group may be the loss of self-esteem due to feelings of lessened competence. Krause and Tran (1989) found that religious or spiritual beliefs served as a buffer to relieve this type of stress. Strong religious or spiritual beliefs act as an anchor to keep the individual grounded during loss.

Other problems facing people at this stage of life are emotional and psychological dissatisfaction linked to the regrets of past life experiences or depression following the death of a spouse, significant other, child, or friend. Another stress characteristic of older age may be that of an involuntary change of residence, such as institutionalization, and the sense of loss that comes from fear of being cut off from social support systems such as family and community (Mehta, 1997). Coping with this sense of loss requires inner resources that Mehta believes are closely linked with spiritual beliefs, which in turn are linked with religious beliefs, though not necessarily so.

Another characteristic of aging is a change in the relationship between partners, whether they are married or not, heterosexual or homosexual. This change comes about because of illness, the more rapid aging of one of the partners, or a shift in finanacial situations. Mental health counselors can play a significant role in assisting the elderly to maintain and strengthen their relationships. A shared spirituality or at least an abiding respect for the differences in belief systems is a starting place for couples counseling. Johnson (1999) identified six essential components of a truly healthy relationship: (1) mutuality, (2) respect, (3) positive communication, (4) intimacy, (5) trust, and (6) staying power. Each of these components will be discussed.

1. *Mutuality:* At younger stages in a relationship, loving partners perceive themselves as equals and share a conviction of togetherness. As partners age, one of the pair may suffer a debilitating illness such as Alzheimer's disease, which severely disrupts the equality they once shared. Suddenly, one partner becomes extremely dependent on the other and the relationship suffers a dramatic shift. Belief in a higher power and a spiritual faith that accepts such events as a part of life's journey can be a powerful force to support and sustain the partner who assumes the role of caregiver. Many churches provide support groups and other means of assistance for persons experiencing these types of distress.

2. *Respect:* As couples age, one partner may become impatient and even angry at the other person because of diminished competence in some areas of functioning. Consequently, respect begins to erode. Fear is usually the motivating factor here. The basic tenets of honoring the self and others, which is a major component of all faiths, can

be the basis for restoring the respect the two persons once shared. Prayer and a rich inner life can be the means of acceptance that may be needed to embrace the changes that the aging process may cause.

3. *Positive communication:* Sensory loss, especially in hearing and sight, may make communication more difficult for the elderly. Anger and frustration may result when one partner has to make special accommodations because of the other person's diminishing abilities. The impaired individual is usually also angry and frustrated at not being able to communicate as well as he or she once did. Many churches or religious groups offer counseling for couples to help them survive these difficult times in what was once a healthy relationship. Many such counseling centers operate on a sliding fee schedule or are offered as a ministry of the church.

4. *Intimacy:* Of all the six areas cited, intimacy can sometimes produce the deepest anxiety for the aging. As Johnson observed, "[t]he human relationship is a feeling condition created by a strong and positive emotional bond, an almost mystical bond, that produces devotion, attachment, and affection between relationship partners and which sometimes requires sacrifice" (1999, pp. 107–108). Fear of diminished sexual activity, health issues, sensory loss, and lessened mobility all work to erode the intimacy in a relationship. However, spiritual fortitude and a deep inner core of faith, particularly when shared by the partners, can provide solace, comfort, and an acceptance of the infirmities that life may bring. An actual deeper intimacy often accompanies the senior years when the age-related changes are accepted and partners explore other avenues of intimacy open to them. The added time together, without the distractions of their earlier working years, may also strengthen the "mystical bond" they share. Many couples devote time to volunteering and engaging in efforts that bring spiritual rewards and other benefits to society. A shared value system is one of the deepest intimacies known.

5. *Trust:* Couples come to rely on each other for certain things in the evolution of a relationship. Each looks to the other for help and assistance in their personal growth and development as a dynamic human being of intrinsic worth. The aging process may diminish the mental competency and physical capabilities of one or both of the partners. Because of these changes, the shared feelings of complete trust in each other are lessened, and fear and doubt may set in. Trust is based on love in most relationships. Spiritually aware individuals use this love, which deepens with age, to maintain trust in the partner's ability to negotiate change. Gratitude is present for what used to be, and a greater acceptance of the inability to be all that one once

was is present in an older individual who attributes all of life to a divine plan.

6. *Staying power:* The change that aging brings is not all unpleasant, but it does require an adaptability to change and an acceptance of one's current status in life. Perseverance, steadfastness, and patience are all spiritual values that most elders desire. An inner life based on prayer and meditation results in a courageous commitment that only grows stronger over time. The mental health counselor can help couples to recognize strengths in this area and provide positive reinforcement to those who are struggling to "stay the course."

Many researchers (Erickson, 1963; Mehta, 1997; Reker & Wong, 1988; Roscow, 1967; Sherman, 1991) cite the importance of the integrative process in old age. This process entails all of life's experiences coming together like threads in a tapestry to create a picture of the entirety of one's life. The individual with strong inner beliefs and values attributes this to a higher power and accepts with satisfaction the journey of life. The older individual who cannot find some meaning in his or her life creates the "despair" attributed to this group by Erickson (1963).

Older adults have been found to have higher levels of religious commitment and participation than any other age group (McFadden, 1995). Most researchers cited in this section would agree that organized and nonorganized religious activities have a positive effect on the well-being of older adults. Many spiritual and/or religious traditions encompass reflections on the meaning of a long life and such ideas serve to counterbalance the many negative stereotypes about older people. Lastly, many faith traditions have historically provided services to older persons in order to improve their overall well-being (Koenig, 1993).

The most popular spiritual or religious activities that have been cited by older persons, particularly women and minorities, are prayer, Bible reading, and watching religious television. The importance attached to religious faith (religious meaning) has been a stronger predictor of life satisfaction than one's number of friends or marital status (Hadaway & Roof, 1978).

In characterizing the elderly and the concept of spirituality, McFadden (1995) cited some of the benefits of a rich inner life and membership in a faith community:

- Inner and emotional calm produced by prayer and meditation
- Pleasure and feelings of belonging derived from attending worship services
- Caring and concerned response of some clergy
- Social and personal support offered by a caring community
- Provision of opportunities to interact with people of all ages

• Feelings of inner security, especially if the person has been a member of this spiritual or religious community for some time

Spirituality and/or a faith community offers an individual a patterned way of comprehending the world as meaningful. Being grounded in a fundamental sense of the meaningfulness of life can affect one's decision-making ability in regard to other activities and attitudes that affect well-being.

Several excellent books summarize much of the current research on the relation between religiosity and physical and mental health in later life (Ellor, McFadden, & Seeber, 1995; Koenig, 1994; Koenig, Smiley, & Gonzales, 1988; Levin, 1994). The majority of these authors assert that, compared to nonreligious elders, older persons who are religious have better functional health and higher levels of adjustment as indexed by lower levels of depression, fewer suicides, less anxiety, and lower rates of alcohol abuse.

Idler and Kasl (1992) examined the relationship among disability, depression, and mortality in an important study affirming the interrelationship of physical and mental health. Their findings revealed that for men religion had a buffering effect, reducing the probability that they would become depressed following an accident or incident that would render them disabled. These same researchers studied people across three major religious groups, Catholic, Protestant, and Jewish, and discovered a pattern in the timing of death with significantly fewer deaths occurring in the month preceding important religious holidays. The researchers readily acknowledged that this may be attributed to social reasons rather than religious ones, but in interviews conducted with the elderly subjects, they talked about years of memories associated with their various faiths and the holidays. These stored memories could be a factor in this phenomenon.

The previous example is but one study of many now beginning to appear in the literature that focuses on the effects of religious faith and practices on older adults' lives. Some behavioral scientists who have studied the typical objective indicators of health, financial security, and social support in the lives of the elderly are beginning to discover how important a sense of spirituality is to overall satisfaction. Through their discovery and utilization of spiritual resources, older persons may experience their lives as meaningful even in the face of multiple, serious challenges to their satisfaction with life (Wong, 1989). Spirituality has not always received the attention it deserves in studies of the aging population because of the difficulty of measuring its effects on overall well-being.

Frankl (1963) maintained that the drive to locate meaning and purpose in life is the essence of spirituality. A variety of experiences can give meaning to life, and religious experiences for some elders promote positive emotions that in turn enhance a sense of well-being. Beliefs, symbols, rituals, traditions, and institutions all provide individuals with avenues that help articulate how meaning is found in relation to God. This is not true for all individuals in later life, however, because of negative experiences they may have had in their earlier years.

Ingersoll (1994), McFadden (1995), and others have attempted to discuss the differences between religion and spirituality, especially as they exist in persons over 60. Some individuals experience a sense of spiritual connectedness within themselves that is not dependent on thoughts of a god. These same persons also experience the integrative powers of spirituality in their relationships with others and with the rest of the world. Their peace comes from reflections on the memories and satisfaction with the life they have led and not from communion with a higher power. Still others feel bitterness towards organized religion but describe themselves as being very spiritual in their private lives.

Bianchi (1994), after interviewing 100 creative elders, concluded that they had experienced the inward turn of spirituality signaled by their feelings of ego integration. For some, this deepened sense of spirituality directed them away from earlier religious convictions, whereas others connected their emergent spiritual awareness with religious traditions that sustained them earlier in life. Other individuals expressed their spirituality in their later years with a heightened response to others. Rubinstein (1994), in his interviews with older women who appeared to be aging well, observed that these women expressed caring, empathic concern for the well-being of others as they conducted their daily lives. He postulated that their generative responses to others had a spiritual component, and preferring not to associate this love of the other with religion, he called this generativity a form of "pragmatic spirituality" (p. 170). Although Rubinstein indicated no specific religious motivation operating in the activities of the women he studied, for many older persons religious commitments activate meaningful relationships with others that are infused with helpfulness and compassion (McFadden, 1995).

According to McFadden (1995), many older persons derive a sense of meaning in life through their sense of connectedness to their homes, their neighborhoods, and the natural environment. A spiritual quality resounds in the interviews conducted by Rubinstein (1990) in which he inquired about older persons' environmental attachments and their significance. Nature takes on a meaning for some elderly individuals akin to the connection Native Americans have with the earth and nature . Thus, nature becomes a means of spirituality in and of itself. Their ecological environment can promote a positive sense of self that helps to stave off depression and other signs of aging.

Psychologists have not found conclusive evidence about whether any differential outcomes occur in well-being for persons who demonstrate religious versus nonreligious spirituality. In addition, considerable work remains to be done to understand the influences of a spiritual sense of meaning and purpose in life for all human beings. The only effect that has been noted is that older persons with a sense of spirituality express more contentment with life than do those who claim no interest in the spiritual realm.

Practitioners, according to McFadden (1995), need to understand the urgency of finding answers to these questions. Researchers have observed the fact that some elders feel spiritually deprived if they are unable to attend religious services, whereas others feel a spiritual loss if prevented from being able to go outdoors. Those who design programs of all varieties for older persons are beginning to recognize the importance of paying attention to meeting spiritual needs as well as physical, psychological, and social needs. Practitioners need to work with researchers to find ways to adequately assess these individual spiritual needs and to evaluate assiduously whether programs are effective in meeting them.

Much exciting work is yet to be done by psychotherapists who believe in the importance of examining religion and spirituality in order to understand the parameters of aging well. Mental health professionals cannot undertake this work alone. They need to coordinate their efforts with those in sociology, medicine, education, the humanities, and theology. This work is multidisciplinary by its very nature and must include both academicians and practitioners in order to derive meaningful data and outcomes.

Unique Needs of the Aging

Living life to the fullest at any age requires an integration of the whole person, including the physical, social, emotional, intellectual, and spiritual. Older adults face a diminishment of certain facets of their lives, including the economic, social, cognitive, and physical dimensions. Their general conditions tend to spiral downward accompanied by a decrease in vitality and an increase in vulnerability. Even though physical functions decline with aging, the spiritual dimension of life does not succumb to the effects of aging even in the presence of debilitating physical and mental illness. The aging process can be considered a spiritual rather than a biological process. Older adults may experience a loss of spirit when they experience a loss of their sense of identity, and their world is threatened as a result of their functional decline and dependency (Blazer, 1991). The spirit is the dimension of the whole person that unifies, permeates, and deepens all of life. A spirituality is essential for older adults who choose to accept the fact that meaning and purpose in life are achievable despite the decline that may be taking place as a result of the aging process (Fisher, 1985). A spiritual awakening helps older adults acknowledge that aging can be both a time for growth and a time for letting go. Pilch (1988) described this as "a way of living, a lifestyle that views and lives life as purposeful and pleasurable, that seeks out life-sustaining and life-enriching options to be chosen freely at every opportunity and that seeks its roots deeply into spiritual values or specific religious beliefs" (p. 84).

Older adults may experience numerous difficulties, such as ill health, a reduction of income, loneliness, a lack of transportation, limited health insurance, and a shrinking social network. Among all of these, health is considered the most chronic problem. Varying degrees of arthritis, hypertension, heart conditions, hearing impairments, and sight impairments are the most common conditions of the elderly. Because these conditions interfere with performing daily activities, functional health must be considered as one of the most unique needs of older adults. Although a spiritual dimension of personhood is beginning to be accepted as an integral part of life, little attention is given by mental health providers to nurturing the spirit. What are the reasons for this reluctance?

Resistances from Within

Research in the health care field shows that feelings of discomfort and inadequacy on the part of health care providers are often cited as reasons why they neglect giving attention to the spiritual well-being of their clients (Carson, 1989). Unfortunately, such feelings of inadequacy are prominent in those individuals who care for clients most at risk or who are experiencing a sense of meaninglessness in their life. Conversely, resistance is often evident in the client who is not willing to confront suffering, loss, anger, issues of meaning and forgiveness, and ultimately death. The challenge to the mental health worker is to help the client realize that he or she must undergo a conversion, an experience of losing their song in order to be able to sing it again in a new key. Even though the melodies of their life will not be played again in the same way they must not close the piano and allow it to gather dust (Coward, 1995, p. 314).

There is a building up as well as a destroying, a changing, and a creating based on the learned experiences and wisdom of the older adult. Unfortunately, not all clients make the decision to enjoy or participate in the opportunity for self-fulfillment and spiritual growth (Heriot, 1992).

Mattie's Story (An Interview Conducted by One of the Authors)

In conducting research for an article on aging and spirituality, I encountered Mattie D., an elderly African-American female who was a resident at a church-owned and -operated nursing home. When inquiring about her age, all Mattie would say is that she "passed" 90. Whether this was a case of her not knowing her exact age, or not wanting to reveal it, was never known. However, with Mattie, her age was irrelevant because her wisdom was timeless. Mattie was a sage with the enthusiasm of the young and the wisdom of the old. Mattie was a force to be reckoned with at any age.

When I met her, Mattie was bedridden for most of the day. Nurses would sit her up in a chair on her good days, for an hour at a time twice a day, but some days even this was too much for her. When I went into her room on most occasions, I would find Mattie lying on her left side clutching her pillow and humming to herself. Sometimes her mouth would be moving, but no sound would be coming forth, as though she were having a conversation that only her ears could hear. In the beginning, Mattie was a little reluctant to talk to me very much, yet she had not refused to be interviewed. I would later come to realize that this was only one of the paradoxes that surrounded Mattie. Although definitely not unsocial, Mattie dealt with people on her own terms and when she wished to do so. There was no question about who had the upper hand in any encounter.

Shortly after meeting Mattie, I asked her if there was something I could bring to her that she might enjoy. A smile crossed her face and she began to talk about "Bubble Mints" that came in a can and were so soft that they just melted in your mouth. I searched high and low for this confection, vaguely remembering from my childhood that they were often found in drugstores. Alas, none were to be found, which prompted me to start sampling peppermints of all kinds to find one that was soft enough to just "melt in your mouth." I brought several different varieties to Mattie for her to try. Somehow none of them evoked the same kind of gustatory experience that the famed "Bubble Mints" of long ago had. She looked at me one day and said, "I just know that when I gets to heaven, Jesus is going to greet me with one of those green cans of Bubble Mints!" This summed up Mattie's true belief—God can and will do anything for those who believe in His love.

I went to the nursing home full of enthusiasm for my research project and filled with the importance of my mission. I was conducting interviews for a qualitative research project and thought that my time with these elderly individuals might be a comfort to them. In the end, the one who was comforted was me. I came away touched by the profoundness of their faith, wisdom, and love that most of them manifested in what for many was the most trying phase of their lives. None touched me more deeply than Mattie.

As Mattie gradually grew to trust me, she began to open up more and seemed to enjoy talking about her youth, her life as an adult, and her many experiences that had brought her to the age she now was. Mattie had been born on a sugarcane plantation in a southern coastal state and had remained there until her late teens. Mattie's mother was "ailing" most of the time, and Mattie and her sister Lilly ran the house from the time they were very little. She described to me how she would roll out biscuits and knead bread while standing on a wooden box that allowed her to reach the table. She cooked, cleaned, and washed clothes for her mother, father, and her younger sister, skills she would later use when she sought work as a domestic in the homes of the wealthier families that lived "to town." When I met Mattie, she was still rather tall, but her body was thin and frail. She told me that she had never been "downright fat" but that she had been very strong and could outwork any "ole man." She had a pair of the largest hands, with some of the longest fingers, I had ever seen on a woman. As I looked at those strong brown hands, I could easily visualize them handling bread, cleaning, and doing laundry. The touch of those hands on mine will remain with me forever.

Mattie didn't really know if her mother and father had ever been formally married, but they were God-fearing people as Mattie described them. In her youth, they attended a small church built by the servants on the large plantation where she had been born. This little frame church was located in a clearing in the woods, next to a cane field, in the "quarters" where the black families had two-room cabins in which to live. Mattie's earliest memories of God and religion revolved around this simple little building and the services that were conducted there. Work on the plantation went on six and even seven days a week, especially during "grinding," but the families living in the quarters managed to find time to worship. She described Sunday services that lasted for hours and even included lunch on the church grounds. Wednesday was "prayer night" and the women and children, though not too many men, often attended this service as well. To Mattie, this time was precious and meaningful. It revealed to her a world that was so much better than what she experienced on a day-to-day basis. The preacher talked of an afterlife where there was no more work, pain, or suffering, only happiness. Mattie dreamed of this beautiful world where she would have everything her heart desired.

Mattie loved music and the Sunday and Wednesday services gave her an opportunity to sing, clap, and release this part of her soul. These were the highlights of her week. When I asked Mattie if she minded the long hours spent in church, she replied that, no, these were happy times for her and the time just "flew away" when she was singing and praying. Even "past 90," Mattie was still singing.

When I asked her where the preacher came from and where he was trained, she replied that at that time anyone could be a preacher if he felt God's word in his heart and the church members accepted him as their leader. She related that members of the congregation were often preachers for a day. One requirement was a knowledge of the scriptures, and Mattie always admired and liked those preachers who could quote from the Bible. Mattie confessed that she could neither read nor write, having never been to school and living "in the country" most of her life. She had, however, committed many scriptural passages to memory during her lifetime. I was amazed at how many she remembered and how clearly she seemed to speak them, citing author, passage, and verse. This was an obvious source of pride for her and always evoked a smile as she "preached forth" the Word of her Lord.

As time went on, Mattie and I talked about all kinds of things, most often with Mattie doing most of the talking. She loved to roam the sugarcane fields and the roads that surrounded her childhood home, even if only in conversation. Although she spoke fondly of many experiences she had had as a child, Mattie never sought to gloss over the harsh realities of her up-bringing. Besides taking care of her immediate family, Mattie also worked for the plantation owners from the time she was about 6 or 7. Schooling was just not something available to her at that time. She mostly worked in the kitchen, gradually moving from washing dishes and sweeping floors to becoming a cook in her teens. This was something of which she was very proud. She proclaimed herself the best cook in the entire county, if not the entire state. Mattie was no shrinking violet.

I asked her once how she knew there was a God. Rising up on her pillows, she gave me a look usually reserved for someone who has just uttered the stupidest statement imaginable. "Lordy, woman, just look around you! Who else could have made all this! I ain't talking 'bout furniture and clothes. I'm talking about the sky and the earth and all the flowers. Have you ever really looked at a flower, like a rose? Now who else could have thought that up?" Mattie's faith in a Supreme Being was unwavering.

As I grew bolder, I asked Mattie if she was ever angry about the fact that she had been born into a race that had to struggle so hard. After thinking for a moment, she looked at me through her deep brown eyes and replied, "I have gone through lots of anger in my life over many things, but I didn't see none of them as something that God wanted to happen, but rather as something that some people done. I don't blame God for what people does, and neither should you."

One day as we were talking, the subject of forgiveness arose and I asked Mattie if it was hard for her to forgive. For one of the few times I was with her, I saw a look of sadness cross her face. In a low voice she began to relate a story from her life to me. When she was a young girl of about 15 or 16, she was raped by a man who lived on the plantation. She was afraid to tell anyone for fear that he would hurt her. After a few months, she began to suspect that she might be pregnant, and she worried about telling her parents. She described her mother as a very loving woman, but, as she had already told me, one who was ill a lot. She hoped that after the tears and anger were over, her mother would forgive her and take care of her. Her father was a more distant figure to her, and Mattie had no idea how he would take the news. Other girls in the quarters had gotten pregnant without the benefit of marriage, but her parents had always held Mattie and her sister to a higher standard. She agonized over how much this might hurt them. Never once though did she blame the man who raped her. To her at the time, it was all her fault somehow and the baby was her problem and hers alone.

When she finally could not hide her pregnancy any longer, she confided in her mother, but she still withheld the name of the man who had done this to her. Her mother also was a bit afraid to tell the father about this since Mattie would not name who the man was. Mattie also confided her pregnancy to her sister Lilly, who by this time was married to a man named Al. Finally, one day her father confronted her as her condition became more and more obvious. When she confirmed that his suspicions were true, he struck her. She had never really "gone with a boy" that he knew of, so his only conclusion was that she had been sneaking around behind his back. For days, he would not talk to her and treated her as though she were a shameful, dirty person. She could hear him ranting and raving at her mother and blaming her for not watching Mattie more closely.

Eventually, when she could take it no longer, Mattie told both of them about the rape and the name of the man who had done it. At first she doubted that her father really believed her because her confession had been met with stony silence. Later she came to realize that this was merely a way for him to contain his anger at the perpetrator. The man who had raped her was several years older than Mattie, and she found out later she was just one of his victims. It seemed that he had fathered several children in the quarters. Her father felt almost as helpless as Mattie did. The man was an overseer on the plantation, and short of killing him, there was really no way he could be punished. To the owner of the plantation, he was a valuable worker and thus he was protected. No one was going to believe Mattie or her father if they tried to press charges, and it would mean the end of her father's job if he tried to report someone in such a position of authority. Furthermore, it would be difficult to find work on another plantation once he was branded a "troublemaker." There was also the fear that the rapist might harm all of them. Mattie described seeing her father age before her eyes and her mother begin to weaken even more. The hopelessness of their situation weighed heavily on all of them.

A decision was made that once the child was born it would be given to her sister and her husband to raise. Mattie would be kept out of sight with an imaginary illness until the child arrived to avoid further suspicion. Neither she nor her parents ever wanted the overseer to know that he was the father of the child. Mattie wanted nothing more to do with him, ever. He had hurt her physically beyond belief, robbed her of her innocence, and she was helpless to defend herself. As she described it, she hurt "all the way down to my soul."

The labor was long and intensive, and her mother and sister helped her as much as they could during the birthing process. Finally, after Mattie had been in labor "all night," the baby was born close to dawn the next morning. Mattie was exhausted but conscious that her son had been born. I asked her how she felt about the baby. She said that her feelings were mixed. She longed for this little baby that had grown inside her, but she was afraid that if he resembled his father, she might not be able to love him as he grew older. She felt "sad" and "alone" after the birth and cried a lot.

It was during this time after the birth, when she was confined to bed because of the amount of blood she had lost and the physical trauma she had sustained, that she began to formulate a plan. She would leave her home and seek employment in a town some 50 miles away. That way she would not have to see the man who raped her and would not be in daily contact with a son who would never call her mother. Lilly and Al had took the child soon after his birth and were telling people he had come to them from a cousin who died in childbirth. I asked Mattie if she felt that most people in the quarters believed this story and she replied, "Maybe yes, and maybe no." But even if they did not, they would never question it in public for fear of repercussion. Mattie found out later that such pregnancies were somewhat common and that the rapists were both white and black men. Women were usually powerless against either group.

I asked Mattie if she had been angry with God for any of this. She looked sad again and said no, she hadn't been angry, but she had felt lost and abandoned by her God. After thinking about this for many years, Mattie said she realized that the reason she felt God had forsaken her was because she felt so bad about herself at the time. She felt it was all her fault and didn't think that anyone, including God, could love her. It was many years before she could rid herself of these feelings of unworthiness.

After she recovered, Mattie related that she moved to a neighboring town and found work at the home of a prominent family. The husband was a judge and the wife was a kind woman who treated her servants well. Mattie learned many things while working in their home and one of the things she cherished the most was something the lady of the house had taught her. Whenever anything required Mattie's signature, she could only "make her mark," a large X. This was an embarrassment to her and made her feel ignorant. She said this to the lady of the house one day and the woman took the time to teach her to write her name out in full, which became a source of pride for Mattie. Whenever one of those "ole men" would say, "Make your mark, Mattie," she would draw herself up to her full height and say in a loud voice, "I don't makes my mark; I can sign my name, thank you, sir." Mattie would always chuckle out loud when she related this story. It was an obvious source of pride for her and a memory she cherished.

During Mattie's time in the "city," she began to attend an African-American Baptist church. She soon felt at home there and once again began to enjoy the singing and the Bible stories and verses. She spoke enthusiastically about some of the preachers who had either served or visited her church. She would relate stories about people being overcome with emotion as they shouted out the Lord's name. She also liked the baptisms a lot and was always glad when people "found the Lord." Much like life on the plantation, weekdays were full of hard work and Sunday was full of church, but Mattie liked it that way.

It was also during this time that Mattie found a preacher she could talk to and a woman in the church membership "who took a shine to her." In time, she related to both of them what had happened to her as a teenager and about the baby boy she had left in her sister's keeping. Both of these people from her religious faith were very instrumental in her life because they were able to convince Mattie that the rape had not been her fault and that in no way did God hold her responsible or love her less because of it. Mattie said that when she could finally accept the truth of this it was like "a big metal collar" had been lifted from her shoulders. She could remember exactly what she was wearing and exactly what the preacher had said on that day when his words had released her soul from its agony.

After Mattie had told me all of these things, I asked her if she had ever been able to forgive the man who had raped her. She answered with a thoughtful voice that she had prayed for forgiveness, because she knew that only when she could reconcile these feelings within herself would she truly be free. As Mattie put it, "I asked the Lord to help me to let go of my hatred for what that man done to me, but I kinda wished for a while that something bad would happen to him. As time went on though, I realized that just having to live with his sorry self was punishment enough for him. I had to let it go because it was eating out my insides. I really prayed a lot over this, and the Lord helped me to put those memories away where they couldn't hurt anyone." Mattie paused and didn't speak for a while. Finally, she looked up and said, "Forgiveness ain't no one-day event. You gotta work on forgiveness every day of your life, in one way or the other. You got to just keep on working, till you get it right!"

Mattie died about a year after I first began to visit her. I asked the director of the nursing home to let me know if Mattie's condition became critical. When I heard this woman's voice on the phone one March afternoon, I feared for the worse. She related that Mattie had had a peaceful death. She went to sleep one night and just didn't wake up. Mattie had gone home. Now she could sing to her heart's content, and I sincerely hoped that God had met her with that green can of "Bubble Mints."

Implications for Counselors

Mattie was not a client of the interviewer, but her story points out many implications for counselors. Ingersoll (1994) delineated seven different dimensions to the integration of spirituality into one's life:

1. One's conception of the divine, absolute, or "force greater than one's self"
2. One's sense of meaning of what is beautiful or worthwhile
3. One's relationship with the divine and other human beings
4. One's tolerance or negative capability for mystery
5. Peak and ordinary experiences that enhance spirituality (which may include rituals or spiritual disciplines)
6. Seeing spirituality as play
7. Viewing spirituality as a systemic force that acts to integrate all the dimensions of one's life (p. 11)

In analyzing my conversations with Mattie, it became readily apparent that her religious and spiritual beliefs gave meaning to her life since early childhood. Mattie's belief in a power higher than herself gave her comfort and security, and brought a centering force to her life. Mattie also saw her God in the natural beauty around her that Ingersoll describes as the ability to "get outside of" oneself and experience the renewal that it brings.

In her conceptions of the divine, Mattie fell primarily within the boundaries of a theistic belief system. Individuals who hold these beliefs relate primarily to a transcendent force or being (Ingersoll, 1994). Mattie definitely believed in one God, but she also saw the beauty of His creation in all things.

In the category of relationships, Mattie saw the divine in all of her interconnectedness with other people, both the good and what she perceived as the "evil" in her life. Mattie resorted to prayer whenever relationships became difficult or when she wanted to offer thanks for the people in her life who cared, helped, encouraged, nurtured, and loved her. She saw her relationship with God as the binding force that enabled her connections with other people. This is especially seen in her concept of forgiveness.

Mattie was an unschooled individual who, because of her inability to read and write, would be labeled illiterate, yet the mystery of divinity didn't faze her. Her unaided intellect led her to the conclusion that there had to be a beginning and this meant that there must be a power higher than herself. She not only accepted this mystery but also gloried in it. Heaven was as real a concept as was earth. She truly believed that God could do all things, even though she may not always understand the "why" of it. This became an immense source of comfort to her.

Mattie's experiences of the divine existed in some peak moments, such as when she finally accepted that she was not at fault in the rape and ensuing pregnancy, but it also existed for her in everyday life as well. She found beauty in the natural world, she hoped for a better existence in an afterlife, she was thankful for family and friends, and she found both strength and solace in her faith. Mattie experienced God on many levels and in many ways.

Ingersoll's (1994) conception of "play" as it relates to spirituality or religion would definitely apply to Mattie. For her, singing hymns of praise and reciting Bible verses appealed to her aesthetic nature as well as her spiritual well-being. This is evident in the joy she experienced even as a young child in the religious services conducted on the plantation as well as in the experiences from her adult life in the "city." She describes them as "freeing her soul" and bringing her closer to her God. Going to church for her was a joy, not just a duty. She found a rhythmic understanding of life in the recitation of her beloved Bible verses and they helped her feel a connectedness to all who believed in Jesus the Christ.

Spirituality and religion were an integrating force in Mattie's life, and any counselor who might have met her as a client would have had to acknowledge that fact before any counseling work could have been effective. Her belief system gave meaning to her life and formed the basis of her value system. To ignore this would have taken away Mattie's chief support system. To deny her an expression of her religious beliefs would have ignored who Mattie really was. This woman, "past 90," illiterate, and infirm, had a rock-solid belief in God and the Bible that transcended everything else in her life. She was truly a self-actualized individual.

Suggested Approaches to Working with the Aging

To intervene effectively with older clients, clinicians must take into consideration many variables, including cultural factors that have influenced the lives of clients in many ways. Clinicians who emphasize independence and individualism only when cultural values encourage self-reliance may have difficulty relating to their aging clients. It is imperative for clinicians to establish a trusting relationship with their client before embarking on a journey toward his or her spiritual awakening in pursuit of peace and ful-fillment—the goal being a state of spiritual well-being.

This state of spiritual well-being parallels Maslow's definition of self-actualization (Ebersole, 1990). If older adults are self-actualized, they are no longer dependent on their social and economic surrounding for life sat-isfaction. They possess the ability to extend the self beyond boundaries of the immediate context and achieve new perspectives and experiences. They realize that even though physical and economic security are society's ac-cepted values of happiness and success, these values do not constitute peace and fulfillment. Clinicians can help their clients become aware that self-actualization can be achieved by identifying behaviors that promote posi-tive thinking and a sense of well-being. Clients are helped to see themselves more clearly as they venture deeper into themselves. They come to realize that their uniqueness that formerly was thought to come from the outside is actually emerging from within their spiritual nature. Clients move away from an external, material, achievement-based definition of self to a more personal, genuine, intimate spiritual definition of self.

The following are examples of suggested clinical activities appropriate for elderly clients adapted from Leetun (1996, pp. 60–70):

- Listen, support, and affirm the clients.
- Obtain the client's personal life history to assist the creative expres-sion of their experiences.
- Review life's accomplishments through reminiscence.
- Practice visual imagery of life's accomplishments, joys, and family events.
- Facilitate dialogue and the sharing of painful events and memories.
- Invite reconciliation with family members and significant others.
- Encourage the discussion of anxieties and uncertainties.
- Suggest journaling as a means of sharing between clinical sessions.
- Discuss the role of religion and spiritual activities in the client's life.
- Discuss time alone and the anxiety that surfaces during these times.
- Explore the client's concerns about the future and encourage living in the moment.

Self-transcending older adults are usually positive, creative, and compas-sionate about humanitarian concerns. Connectedness is demonstrated through behaviors that expand boundaries inwardly through some of the in-trospective activities suggested earlier and outwardly through concerns about the client's welfare. Clinicians can support and intervene to renew con-nectedness through establishing and strengthening self-transcendence when they facilitate the aging client's reminiscences and involvement with others.

The integration of the spiritual dimension is a necessary component of wholeness. Inner healing, if it is to occur, depends on the desire to love and receive love from others and from God or some transcendent power. Belief in a lasting love allows aging clients to experience their own wholeness more fully (McGilone, 1990). From this experience comes new life. Physical frailty in aging clients does not mean they are incapable of making decisions. Accepting the fact that they need help opens them up to the possibility of the many choices available to them to live productive lives. Strength and inner resources are developed through conscious activities of the human spirit, which is ageless. It is essential that older adults be given the help and autonomy to select their own personal way of seeking integration with the self and others, with nature, and with God or their higher power.

To facilitate this growth in the aging client, clinicians must reflect an open sense of hospitality, compassion, and commitment. Hospitality exudes warmth and generosity, creating a free and fearless place for an aging client to become the person he or she wishes to be. This implies that clinicians must be vigilant observers and listeners in order to discover the inner events of the aging client's spirit. Personal reserves of strength, faith, and courage can made real to each aging client as clinicians help them transcend self and understand their joy, pain, and unique situation. Thus, the client is strengthened to proceed on the journey of life.

Effective clinicians are those who avail themselves of the opportunity to discuss spiritual issues rather than referring clients to a priest, rabbi, or minister. This can become a rewarding experience for both the client and the counselor. In the words of two Native American authors, "it is our responsibility to see the world as seen through the eyes of the wisdom figures, to understand their experiences as their hearts feel them so that we may walk alongside them as they seek their true reflection in the water" (Garrett & Garrett, 1998).

A feeling of harmony and relatedness with self is found within and secured through experiences of self-transcendency. Clients can be helped to see that all human beings are called to relate to others, to nature, and to a higher power that transcends them. Through these relationships, all men and women discover meaning in what they do, what they know, and in who they are or become over time. In older adults, these relationships tend to involve moving inward amidst a deep connectedness with others, nature, and with their higher power (Buckhardt, 1994). Essential to these introspective activities is a willingness to interact with and get to know the parts of their lives that are unseen. The capacity to connect with those parts of themselves that remain hidden, namely mystery, love, sorrow, and dreams of wholeness, creates the possibility of rediscovering, recreating, and ultimately transforming the inner life in old age.

Exercises

1. Visit a retirement home in your community and interview one of the residents about the decision they made to move there. Did their personal belief system play any part in their decision?
2. Survey three churches in your community and inquire about programs that are available for persons over 65 years of age.
3. Interview an individual over 65, inquiring about their spiritual journey through life. Write the person's spiritual biography.
4. Role-play a counseling situation where the client expresses concern about his or her inability to attend church regularly because of lack of mobility. This is especially important when the church has always been a major source of comfort and support for the individual.
5. Obtain a listing of TV programs in your viewing area and make a list of programs of a spiritual or religious nature.
6. Visit a church whose membership is primarily of an ethnic group different from your own. Observe the ratio of older to younger members. What roles do the older adults play in the worship service?
7. Visit an older adult and offer to audiotape a message or letter to grandchildren and friends. This will help bring meaning to a person's life.
8. Encourage the possibility of a window box garden being grown by the older adult.
9. Arrange for a visit with a friend from the neighborhood who may be willing to read or pray with the client in order to help him or her get in touch with the beauty of nature.
10. Offer to give the older person a manicure, allowing him or her an opportunity to talk about his or her spiritual journey.
11. Arrange for access to spiritual articles and religious ceremonies that have meaning to the older adult.
12. Investigate the possibility of obtaining some form of therapeutic touch for the older adult to help bring comfort and inner peace.

Case Scenrios

1. Mrs. Brandt is 79 years old and has lived alone since her husband died 10 years ago. She has four daughters and two sons, one of whom lives in close proximity. Recently, Mrs. Brandt fell and broke her hip, which hospitalized her. This was followed by months of intensive therapy. Consequently, she can no longer maintain her home and has become dependent on one of her daughters.

   After consultation with her siblings, the daughter selected one of the best assisted-living residences in the area and Mrs. Brandt took up residence there. Since her arrival, the director of the facility has discussed with the daughter that her mother refuses to take her meals with the other residents, will not avail herself of the many scheduled activities, and has lost weight since becoming a resident. Mrs. Brandt's daughter is worried because her mother was always actively involved in the community and volunteered many hours with her church. Her minister was asked to pay her a visit and he found a drastic change in her.

Questions
- List the various losses that Mrs. Brandt has sustained.
- How would a counselor approach each of these issues from any one of the following theoretical perspectives: person-centered, existential, and reality?
- What spiritual or faith crisis might Mrs. Brandt be experiencing?
- How can a mental health counselor help this client address these issues?

2. Mr. Engles, a retired farmer, has recently moved to a neighboring state to live with his oldest son, Josh. Josh maintains a large farm with many field hands. Since moving in with his son, Mr. Engles has become very opinionated and critical of the way his son is managing the farm. This has caused discord and tension in the family. Since Mr. Engles sold his home, returning is not an option.

   Although not a religious man, Mr. Engles occasionally would attend church services with his wife and children. Josh has invited him to come with the family to their church, but he has refused, saying he doesn't know any of the parishioners.

Questions
- What may be the underlying causes for the apparent negative attitude that Mr. Engles is exhibiting?
- How might a mental health counselor facilitate a counseling session between Mr. Engles and Josh?
- Discuss the pros and cons of Josh's invitation to his father to attend church services with the family.

3. Mrs. Scott, a widow of five years, is seeing a counselor because she says that she has been crying a lot and not feeling herself lately. Her oldest friend died suddenly and she hasn't wanted to do the things she has enjoyed, such as volunteering in the community and belonging to her church group. She was very involved with her grandchildren when they were growing up, but now that they are in college they

seldom come to see her. Her two sons visit with her but not on a regular basis, and she feels isolated and cut off from her family.

Questions
- List the various losses that Mrs. Scott has sustained.
- Identify the feeling that Mrs. Scott is experiencing.
- Describe the approaches that a counselor may use to help Mrs. Scott deal with her feelings.
- How could her pastor become involved?

Assessment Instruments/Inventories
Johnson (1999) has developed a series of exercises for the older client that can serve as their personal workbook: (a) career reorientation, (b) retirement values, (c) personal empowerment, (d) physical wellness, (e) monetary adequacy, (f) quality of life—present, (g) quality of life—future, (h) spirituality/meaning: spiritual life questionnaire, (i) respect for leisure, (j) personal flexibility, (k) spiritual luster, (l) care-giving responsibilities, (m) home life, (n) maturation vitality, and (o) stewardship and service (pp. 136–157).

References

Blazer, D. (1991). Spirituality and aging well. *Generations, 15*, 61–65.

Buckhardt, M. A. (1994). Becoming and connecting: Elements of spirituality for women. *Holistic Nursing Practice, 8*(4), 12–21.

Campbell, A. (1975). *The quality of American life: Perceptions, evaluations, and satisfactions*. New York: Russell Sage Foundation.

Carson, V. B. (1989). *Spiritual dimensions of nursing practice*. Philadelphia: W. B. Saunders.

Coward, D. D. (1995). The lived experience of self-transcendence in women with AIDS. *Journal of Obstetric, Gynecologic and Neonatal Nursing, 24*, 314–318.

Ebersole, P., & Hess, P. (1990). *Toward healthy human aging*. St Louis, MO: Mosby.

Erickson, E. H. (1963). *Childhood and society*. New York: Norton.

Fisher, K. R. (1985). *Winter grace: Spirituality for the later years*. Mahwah, N.J: Paulist Press.

Frankl V. (1963).

Garrett, M. T., & Garrett, J. T. (1998). Therapeutic strategies for the older adult, 3, Lesson 2. Unpublished manuscript.

George, L. K. (1981). Subjective well-being: Conceptual and methodological issues. *Annual Review of Gerontology and Geriatrics, 2*, 345–382.

George, L. K., & Clipp, E. C. (Eds.). (1991). Aging well [Special issue]. *Generations, 15*(1).

Hadaway, C. K., & Roof, W. C. (1978). Religious commitment and the quality of life in American society. *Review of Religious Research, 19*, 295–307.

Heriot, C. S. (1992). Spirituality and aging. *Holistic Nursing Practice, 1*, 22–31.

Idler, E. L. (1987). Religious involvement and the health of the elderly: Some hypotheses and initial test. *Social Forces, 66*, 226–238.

Ingersoll, R. E. (1994). Spirituality, religion, and counseling: Dimensions and relationships. *Counseling and Values, 38*, 98–111.

Johnson, K. M. (1999). *The rising incidence of natural decrease in the United States*. Paper presented to the annual meetings of the Rural Sociological Society, Toronto, Canada. Retrieved February 6, 2000, from http://www.luc.edu/depts.sociology/johnson/p99webnd.html

Johnson, (1999).

Koenig, H. G. (1993). Religion and aging. *Reviews in Clinical Gerontology, 3*(2), 195–203.

Koenig, H. G., George, L. K., & Seigler, I. C. (1988). The use of religion and other emotion-regulating coping strategies among older adults. *The Gerontologist, 28*, 303–310.

Krause, N., & Tran, T. V. (1989). Stress and religious involvement among older blacks. *Journal of Gerontology: Social Sciences, 44*, 4–13.

Larson, R. (1978). Thirty years of research on the subjective well-being of older Americans. *Journal of Gerontology, 33*, 109–325.

Leetun, M. (1996). Wellness spirituality in the older adult. *Nurse Practitioner, 21*(8), 60–70.

Levin, J. S. (1994). Religion and health: Is there an association, is it valid, and is it causal? *Social Science and Medicine, 38*(11), 1475–1482.

Levin, J. S., & Vanderpool, H. Y. (1992). Religious factors in physical health and the prevention of illness. *Prevention Human Services, 9*, 41–64.

McGilone, M. T. (1990). Healing the spirit. *Holistic Nursing Practice, 4*(4), 77–84.

McFadden, S. H. (1995). Religion and aging persons in an aging society. *Journal of Social Issues, 51*, 161–175.

Mehta, K. (1997). Cultural scripts and the social integration of older people. *Ageing and Society, 17*, 253–275.

Pilch, J. J. (1988). Wellness: Wellness spirituality. *Health Values, 12*(3), 29–31.

Reker, G. T., & Wong, P. T. P. (1988). Aging as an individual process: Toward a theory of personal meaning. In J. E. Birren and V. L. Bengtson (Eds.), *Emergent theories of aging* (pp. 214–246). New York: Springer Publishing Co.

Roscow, W. I. (1967). *Social integration of the aged*. New York: Free Press.

Sherman, L. (1991). *Cooperative learning in post-secondary education: Implications from social psychology for active learning experiences*. A presentation to the annual meetings of the American Educational Research Association, Chicago, IL, April 3–7.

CHAPTER 5
Women

Why a chapter on women and spirituality? What can we learn from the inner beliefs and outward practices of women? To study the spirituality of women is to complete the circle. As Carol Ochs (1983) stated, "Since traditional spirituality has been male-centered, it has been regarded as an extension of the male maturational process that emphasizes individuality—coming into selfhood. The new spirituality offered here is an extension of the female maturational process that emphasizes nurturing—coming into relationship" (p. 2). Who would adhere to a spirituality that comes out of partial experience? Who would consider an experience complete that looks at only one sex?

When we move away from a concentration on a male-dominated spiritual reality, we open ourselves up to a more complete look at spirituality that embraces all experiences, including birth. Yet we do not seek a spirituality that is based on experience alone, for to do so would spend too much time concentrating on rapture, ecstasy, out-of-body experiences, and so on. An examination of women's spirituality reveals insights into the joy, despair, loss, trust, and transformation that comprise the whole of human life. It often attempts to find sanctity in the mundane rather than the solitary experiences of many mystics. A woman's role as wife, mother, friend, confidant, and so on places her in a unique position to see God in the face of others, rather than far off on a mountain top.

Does this mean that only women who give birth or who marry can be spiritual? Of course not! It simply means that women who concentrate on their own uniqueness, rather than on trying to be more like men, will discover and rejoice in their own talents and inner being more readily. The

Fourteenth Dalai Lama of Tibet conceived and spoke of spirituality as a concern for the qualities of the human spirit that bring happiness to oneself and to others. The qualities he mentioned are often ascribed to women —love, compassion, patience, tolerance, forgiveness, contentment, and a sense of harmony and responsibility. Some men see these as weaknesses and consider them to be the "soft" virtues. Would any of us, however, want to live in a world without them? Are they not the very entities that provide balance to lives beset with fears of survival, death, war, terrorism, and so on? Would any search for a spiritual sense of the world be complete without them? Although they are certainly not the sole provinces of women, Ochs (1983) contended that a "new spirituality" must arise that includes women's unique contributions. Only then can we formulate a spirituality that is adequate for all of humanities' needs.

It must be noted, however, that the "feminizing of religion" alluded to in this chapter is more a phenomenon of Western religions and faiths than it is of many Eastern religions and belief systems. The "patriarchal" model of church leadership that has left some women in most Western religions suffering from feelings of oppression and disenfranchisement may not resonate in the same way with Eastern women because of cultural differences and traditions. However, what Ochs (1983) said about the uniqueness of contributions that women have to make in the realms of spirituality and religion are universal traits crossing every ocean, every hemisphere, and every continent.

Unique Characteristics

Women face some unique challenges when confronting religion or religious sects. Only in the last 20 years have some churches begun to ordain women for the ministry. Western churches by and large have failed to use women in leadership roles and consequently have underutilized their talents and gifts. Many women feel devalued in today's Western religious sects. Change has come about far too slowly for many women. In many Western congregations, women are allowed to cook, serve, and clean, but not to lead the worship service or participate in the decision-making of the religious hierarchy. Such relegation to subservient roles has caused a groundswell of anger in many women. In an age when women are better educated than ever before and hold many leadership roles in their personal careers, the relegation to second-class citizenship is considered an insult and an injustice.

Winter, Lummis, and Stokes (1994) conducted a survey funded by the Lilly Endowment that elicited women's thoughts on the religious traditions into which they were born. The study focused on a select national sample of women from western cultures who were concerned about religion and spirituality. A total of 3,746 women responded to the survey whose ages ranged from under 30 to over 70, with the majority being between the ages of 35 and 55. The women in the study spoke candidly about religion, how it related to their lives, and about wanting something more in terms of spirituality. They spoke very openly and forcefully about their deep personal pain, their anger, and their frustration about being "discounted," "put down," and even "used" by the churches they attended. Because of the large sample size, the wide geographic distribution, and the percentage of minorities represented in the survey, the findings can be generalized to other populations of women. What many of these women described was a journey into the awareness that they have been present, and sometimes seen, but seldom heard. They spoke about feelings of oppression and marginalization, about the realization of being treated unfairly, and of being ignored in their faith communities.

Yet in spite of these negative feelings of alienation and of being discounted, these women still yearned for a more liberated future where religion is concerned. The majority did not want to leave the religious tradition in which they were raised but definitely wanted change. The women expressed a yearning for a deeper integration between religious expectations and the relationship they are cultivating with the God of their faith experience. Woven through their narratives of disillusionment with religious structures was an amazing resilience of spirit and a tenacious hope that dared to assert a "new age is dawning." The vast majority of the women surveyed were Christian, although Jewish women were represented, as well as some with Eastern religious belief systems.

The following are some thoughts expressed by respondents to the Winters et al. (1994) survey:

> I am constantly saddened by the exclusivity and patriarchal hierarchy of Christian denominations. So many wonderful women are not able to live out their spiritual gifts in this arena. Searching for another place or group in which to live out these gifts is beginning to change how women receive spiritual nourishment and the structures that deliver such services. Telling our stories removes the veil of seclusion and strengthens our connectedness.
>
> —Woman in her thirties, Caucasian, unaffiliated, in the Pacific Northwest

> I look forward to the day when Hispanic women stop being so submissive in ecumenical matters and challenge the system that more often than not doesn't allow them to develop their potential as leaders in the church or any other entity.
>
> —Woman in her fifties, Hispanic, Catholic, in the Northeast

Women's full participation in every aspect of our lives, including organized religion, is vital to the improvement of our world. Religions that limit women's participation shouldn't preach that they believe that God is just and loving, but that their God is prejudiced, biased, and discriminatory.

—Woman in her forties, mixed race, Catholic, in New England

Women must work harder at celebrating each other. There are women in more traditional lifestyles with a profound witness to offer. Let's not forget them. Women have made great strides, but there is a way to go. Let us do more than replace men with women; let's usher in a new way to live in mutual respect.

—Clergywoman in her thirties, African-American,
United Methodist, in the Southeast

Most patterns of western families and education continue to reinforce two roles for women. First, women are socialized to be objects of beauty who must draw acceptance and adulation based on physical appearance, especially from men. Living for "another" or "others" is the second expectation placed on most women; so much so, that few women really are encouraged to develop their own identity. They must wait until they are "found" by a man and then must wait to be "asked" to marry him before they are fully accepted into society. Women are subtlety, or not so subtlety, given the message that it is their duty to submerge themselves into the identity, needs, and interests of another or others. As Schneiders (1986) wrote, "Thus a woman's self-actualizing potential is often anesthetized. She is taught to wait for someone to find her, and then life will take on meaning and purpose" (p. 11). Because true spirituality demands a high level of maturity and independence of thought, a woman's conditioning toward conformity, which leads to passivity, often militates against her questioning the established system. If she does emerge as a "seeker," she often lacks the conditioning self-worth that would allow her to stand up for what she believes in. "Women are led to believe they are virtuous when actually they have not yet taken the necessary possession of their lives to have an authentic 'self' to give in self-donation" (Schneiders, p. 12). Their "holiness" is imposed rather than freely chosen.

Because in many ways this is so diametrically opposed to how women have been taught to operate in the career world, a tremendous paradox exists in the lives of these women. Monday through Friday or Saturday, they are viewed as competent, intelligent, worthy of leadership positions, and valued for their hard work most of the time. Yet when they enter a Western church or synagogue they are expected to regress to an earlier time and culture.

Although progress has definitely been made in the last decade or so, as proven by the increasing numbers of female rabbis and the ordination of women in some Western Christian religions, many Western women still chafe under the male domination that appears to hold them back at every turn. This is particularly so in the realm of spirituality that demands a freedom of thought and self-expression that many middle-aged women are uncomfortable with. This conflict forms the basis of much anger and resentment whether from a social, work, or spiritual context. Younger women who have been socialized in a different manner may not have the same fears. A common approach to spiritual direction maintains that growth in prayer involves the ability to increase the awareness of what one really wants in life and how one really feels in the presence of God or a higher power. These realities may be difficult for women steeped in role conformity, self-doubt, and dependency. Many women are simply too afraid to take a risk, yet western women who have come into their own in the personal and professional realm do not seem to have trouble discerning their own thoughts and beliefs. However, they feel most uncomfortable when they are not viewed as full-fledged members of any congregation.

Western Christianity's teachings and treatment of women have been instrumental in relegating women to a "second-class citizen" role. One of the reasons for this is that for so long virtue was associated with domestic values. Obedience to God was equated with obedience to one's husband or to the needs of children. Humility and selfless devotion were seen and described as "feminine" virtues that made women more desirable and more attractive as wives. Women often found community in religious events. Various church gatherings or societies provided socialization outside the home and were seen as "proper," whereas other social events were seen as "worldly" and "unlady-like." Although these events and activities might appear at first glance to be liberating and a breeding ground for female leadership development, they also encouraged women to fit into limited, clerically defined roles centered on family and subordinated to male authority (Schneiders, 1986). Even today, the refusal to admit women into full participation in some Western churches' leadership continues to restrict women's mature spiritual development.

The very language of worship in Western religions is often male-dominated and excludes and alienates women. When faced with a consistent male-image of God (who in truth is pure spirit), it is easy to understand why women are conditioned to presume that men are more God-like. It prevents a woman from valuing her own female being and affirming herself as an authentic image of God. This can have severe consequences in the development of a healthy self-concept based on a firm feeling of self-worth. This conflict can place a strain on a woman's relationship with her church and even with her God. This often accounts for the number of women who turn away from the Judeo-Christian concept of the God-image in favor of the concept of a higher power that combines both God and Goddess.

Other women have chosen to stay in their respective churches, but they are sure to examine and call attention to how humanly destructive and spiritually traumatic women's exclusion from having a voice and a role in the leadership of the church has been for them. Winters et al. (1994) referred to this as "defecting in place." These women remain within the established churches but *on their own terms*, and in the process they are redefining *church*. As one woman put it, "I believe that women have become church by creating community and serving the needs of each other and those of society." Still another says, "We are learning to find our own way to salvation." A universal theme would appear to be, "Let us create new models of church while being faithful to God." "Women pass on religion through the generations. We are the church." (Winters et al., 1994)

These statements are not made lightly and are the result of much inner conflict and soul-struggle. This is especially difficult for women who were not socialized to function in public or independent roles. Most women were expected to be male-dependent as a wife, daughter, sister, and so on. Even their last names were not truly their own to have or to pass on. It must be emphasized, however, that much of this is changing as younger women choose to keep their birthname or hyphenate their last name to reflect both spouses, but these women are still in the minority. Today vast numbers of women over the age of 40 have not only been prevented from being ordained to ministry but at one time they could not originally set foot in the sanctuary while divine service was taking place. Schneiders (1986) reminded us also that women of that age were not allowed to touch sacred vessels or to read the word of God in public. She stated that in the Catholic Church functions that a 6-year-old boy could perform, such as serving Mass or bearing the processional cross, were forbidden to even the most mature and experienced women.

Eastern Religions and Faith Traditions

Women who are members of Eastern religions or faith traditions may not have felt the "feminizing of religion" to the same extent. Although most Eastern religions of any size—Islam, Hinduism, Buddhism, Taoism, or Shintoism—are thought to be male-dominated, the cultures of the various countries where they are prevalent may not be at the same period of evolution as many western countries. Women in many eastern countries are still struggling for rights that many Western women take for granted, and until their status in terms of civil rights is bettered, it will be hard to accomplish change within the religious structure. Comments in the previous section obviously were taken from a more western perspective because more has been written and published in the western countries about these issues. However, the Internet has sites that attest to the fact that women in some Eastern religions want more of a voice in their respective religions or faith traditions. For instance, Web sites have been dedicated to "Women in Buddhism" and "Women in Hinduism." As women are allowed to take their place as equal partners in human affairs, church, synagogue, or temple hierarchies will feel the result of this. As women in many eastern countries become better educated, they will have a better comprehension of what women in other countries have achieved, and many may want to do the same. History definitely shows that this has been the logical progression in the western world.

Suzie's Story

Suzie is a middle-aged woman who grew up in the Midwest in a town of 40,000 people. Her parents were professionals, a pharmacist father and a nurse mother. She has two younger sisters and one brother. She describes the family life of her youth as being rather typical of the times, with an adherence to routine and a focus on church and school—boring, but stable. Suzie describes herself as being a leader from an early age and popular with her peers during her school years. Her reflections about her home life revealed that, as the oldest child, she enjoyed a very close relationship with her mother. Although she admired her father greatly, she felt that he was a rather distant and reserved figure.

Her earliest memories of religion were of being brought to church on Sundays, first in the church nursery and then in a type of Sunday school. Suzie thinks she was in first grade when she began to attend the regular church service. She still speaks vividly about the remembered smells of incense, beeswax, and the beautiful flowers in the sanctuary. Her parents were regular churchgoers, although they rarely spoke of religion outside of church in any public way. She does remember having conversations with her mother, however, about God, heaven, and hell. These memories are also very vivid and in some way comforting, but Suzie is not sure if it was because of their content or because it was the one-on-one time with her mother that she enjoyed. Looking back, she muses it was probably a combination of both. Although things like sin, the devil, hell, and punishment frightened her greatly, she also took comfort in the image of God as a merciful father.

As an Episcopalian, she was very caught up in the beauty of her church's liturgy throughout her school years. She loved the pageantry and history that guided the worship services. Music has always been a special love of hers and she sang in the church choir. She credits this for her love of classical music and her knowledge of many forms of music. Singing has always constituted a special form of worship for her and she favors it over other types of community prayer.

Although her association with the her parents' church brought Suzie feelings of security and belonging, she also feels that it engendered feelings of unworthiness and fear in her, especially around the issue of sin. She remembers trying very hard to be good but always feeling that she did not measure up to her parents or her church's expectations. In retrospect, she feels that too much emphasis was placed on punishment and not enough on love and forgiveness. She feels that the Episcopalian priests with whom she came in contact, as well as an order of Anglican nuns, did not really understand or appreciate human nature, regardless of how well educated they were.

These feelings of guilt became more acute as she approached adolescence and began experiencing the first stirrings of sexuality and the physical changes that puberty brings. This was a troubling time for her because everywhere she turned people warned of sin, but no one acknowledged that the changes she was going through were natural and normal. They made her feel ugly and unworthy in God's eyes. Shame entered into her consciousness, although she couldn't quite explain it because she really wasn't doing anything terribly wrong. She just knew that she had somehow left the happy, carefree days of childhood behind and entered a moodier, more troubled time in life.

Even though most of the Episcopal priests she knew were married, she didn't feel comfortable talking to them about these things anymore than she would have with her father. The few Anglican nuns she knew seemed too far removed from such "unclean thoughts." Religion was far from a comfort in this stage of her development.

Today Suzie ardently wishes that someone had had the foresight to think of talking about the changes she was experiencing as beautiful and part of God's plan, rather than always warning about sin, temptation, and "going too far" with boys. She also wonders if her younger sisters went through the same feelings when they became adolescents. The three of them never talked about these specific things, although they had snickered often about how reluctant their parents had been to talk about sex, even though their mother was a nurse.

It was not until many years later, in her late thirties, when Suzie joined a women's group and took part in services based on the Goddess theory, that she truly began to see and feel the beauty of her woman's body with its power to conceive and give birth. Although she definitely sees these services as a turning point in her life, she does recall feeling very comfortable about her body during her two pregnancies. In spite of some physical discomfort, Suzie had really enjoyed being pregnant and feeling a human life growing within her. To her, this was mystical and spiritual, and she felt connected to God and His creation.

Suzie's adolescent feelings, while she acknowledges that they were probably somewhat typical, were definitely related to her own perceptions of sin and punishment. Unfortunately, they also carried over into much of her adult life. Growing up seeing God as a father image, she naturally projected feelings and trepidations about her own father onto Him. It was only when Suzie joined with other women in worship that she felt the feminine side of her was validated.

Suzie attended college in the East and while there her church attendance and religious observances were sporadic. She attended religious services with some of her friends and sampled everything from a Roman Catholic Mass to a Southern Baptist revival. She enjoyed going to these various events and they made her weigh her commitment to her own Episcopal background. Suzie also took a course in world religions and began to read about various Eastern religions and belief systems. These appealed to her greatly because they seemed so peaceful and less judgmental than her own faith. In the end, however, she migrated back to her religion of birth.

She wonders today how much guilt and parental expectation may have played a part in her return to Episcopalianism. She is glad, however, that she opened herself up to these new experiences, and she speaks of this time in her life with great enthusiasm. She definitely feels it was a liberating experience and something that she needed to undertake on her spiritual journey.

Young adulthood was also fraught with ambiguity about matters of sex and relationships. Her upbringing did not allow her to see sex outside of marriage as a proper thing to do, and she battled her sexual frustrations in silence, wondering how many young women were going through the same thing. Her friends talked about sex often but were hesitant to get too personal about their private lives. When a young woman that Suzie played cards with became pregnant without the benefit of marriage, Suzie was genuinely surprised. Comparing herself in her twenties to the world of the twenty-first century, when television has made talk of sex and even the act itself such an open thing, Suzie sees her younger self as very naive. She envies young people's ease with the subject of sex and the fact that many of them live quite openly with a significant other before marriage. She does wonder, however, if in spite of their openness with sexual matters, they do not have some of the same insecurities she labored under. She really doesn't see the younger generation as being happier despite their openness.

Suzie married in her mid-twenties, and both of her children were born by the time she was 30. Those years were filled with babies, housework, and family. Even though Suzie and her husband attended church services, she does not remember feeling particularly spiritual or religious except during her pregnancies. She describes this time as one of running to God when something awful happened or when she really wanted a favor, but she did not feel particularly close to Him at other times. She does remember feeling a greater obligation to attend church, though, because she wanted to serve as an example to her children, but she often felt hollow in doing so.

As Suzie approached her mid-thirties, she began to realize her marriage was unraveling. She suspected her husband of cheating on her and she didn't know what to do. The panic she often felt increased her church attendance, and she prayed privately much more often. Although Suzie felt that again she was turning to religion only in times of trouble, God seemed to be the one constant in a world that was changing rapidly. A priest at her church suggested counseling to help her deal with the decisions that lay before her, and Suzie was lucky to be directed to a an slightly older woman therapist who happened to be divorced.

In the counseling sessions, Suzie was able to release a lot of the anger she had been harboring for a long time. Her husband's unfaithfulness and her recurring feelings of unworthiness were difficult to cope with. She prayed, but more to comfort herself than to give worship. An all-male clergy seemed odious to her and even the fact that God was pictured as a man unsettled her.

It was at this point that Suzie joined the women's group and began to revel in her own femaleness. The group was definitely spiritual in nature and helped to calm Suzie as well as give her new confidence. Strangely, the more Suzie confronted her problems in her marriage and went through the grieving process, the more at ease she began to feel with men in general. Was this actually a maturing process in some way?

Eventually, Suzie was able to face the fact that the marriage was not viable and divorce was inevitable. The battle for the primary custody of her sons was the most difficult part and she found herself edging into bitterness. She spent time both in and out of the therapy sessions, ruminating about all that had happened to her in the last few years. She attended church, but her thoughts were more on her own problems than on the religious service. She wanted to believe in God, but everything seemed so empty. She cried out for help but often felt very alone.

Someone finally suggested a group devoted to divorced people, or in the process of obtaining a divorce, sponsored by a local church. With her therapist's encouragement, Suzie began attending the group's sessions and found others who were in the same stages of grief from a broken marriage. Listening to their stories and finding the courage to tell her own seemed much like a spiritual experience to her. She felt the clouds of gloom and failure gradually fading from black to gray. She attended this group for almost 18 months and kept in touch with some of the members she had become close to in the process of facing her own fears.

As her forties loomed before her, Suzie found herself single, the mother of adolescent boys, and totally on her own for the first time in more than 15 years. Although she had moments of trepidation and anxiety, she actually felt calmer than she had in a long time. Her individual therapy had allowed her to see herself in a different and more realistic light, and she felt stronger as a result. The group for divorcees that she joined had been a powerful support system during a very difficult time in her life. There was still an occasional crying spell and almost daily moments of some anxiety, but overall Suzie knew that she was freer than she had ever been in her life and more confident in almost all aspects of her life.

Now in her mid-forties, Suzie looks back reflectively on her journey. Spiritually, she has grown a lot, almost in tandem with her maturing in other areas of her life. She is still an Episcopalian, even though she believes that no organized religion could ever truly meet her needs. She wants to believe in God and the age-old prayers and ceremonies, familiar since her childhood, that give her comfort and a sense of belonging. She is drawn to communal worship and her church provides an outlet for this. Looking back, Suzie wishes that more female spiritual leaders or guides had been available to her in her formative years. She feels that a woman might have understood better than a man her adolescent turmoil, her spiritual awakening during pregnancy, and the doubts and fears she felt throughout much of her life. She expresses sorrow over the fact that this was not available to her through her religion of choice.

Suzie is also a staunch advocate for the ordination of women, even though she has had no desire for this herself. She has long felt that the domination of men in the hierarchy of the church is a paternalistic dimension that has to be resolved. Although still in the minority, women are being heard in ways never possible before.

Most of all, Suzie has begun to understand how powerful an inner spiritual life really is. Her counseling sessions helped her to see that nothing outside of herself is ever truly going to meet all her needs, yet at the same time counseling helped her get in touch with the true values in her life. Even though she has fought against it at times, religion is an important element in her world. At different times in her life she has sought out various ways of expressing this need, but she is continually drawn back to the religion of her birth. This definitely fulfills a special dimension of her life, and she feels less than a whole person without it. She still questions many things and has moments of doubt, but therapy has helped her gain the inner strength and confidence to deal with them. Therapy also has helped her to see that her religious faith, regardless of how she expresses it, is a support system for her and a constant that she has come to value even more than before. Suzie feels that it is only one dimension of her life, but an important one to her.

In spite of this newfound confidence, Suzie still finds herself searching for answers, just as all human beings do. All of her doubts and questions are by no means resolved, and she has come to realize that much of the anger she felt at times was not really towards God, but the people who represent Him. She works hard to resolve this but has no quick answers or solutions. She no longer feels guilty about occasionally missing services on Sundays, as she once did, but instead sees it as a matter of personal choice. Spirituality for her is accepting life, one day at a time. She rarely prays any more to change something, but rather to have the courage to face it. Some days are filled with the radiant feelings of God's love and on other days His face is hidden from her, yet she struggles forward, attempting to nourish the spiritual life within her. At times she struggles with the very notion of a God, but intellectually she feels that she cannot deny the existence of a Supreme Being who was the Beginning. In spite of all of this, she feels more inner contentment in some ways than ever before. Prayer to her is both a comfort and a way of resolving some of her doubts. She no longer pictures herself as a child with a parent all the time, but rather as an adult in the presence of someone of greater authority. The one thing Suzie expresses with absolute surety is the fact that some of these doubts and frustrations will be present all of her life, and she tries to accept this with some equanimity.

Implications for Counselors

As already covered in the previous two chapters, Ingersoll (1994) delineated seven different facets to the integration of spirituality into one's life:

1. One's conception of the divine, absolute, or "force greater than one's self"
2. One's sense of meaning of what is beautiful or worthwhile
3. One's relationship with the divine and others
4. One's tolerance or capability for mystery
5. Peak and ordinary experiences that enhance spirituality (which may include rituals or spiritual disciplines)
6. Seeing spirituality as play
7. Viewing spirituality as a systemic force that acts to integrate all the dimensions of one's life (p. 11)

In analyzing conversations with Suzie, it became readily apparent that her religious and spiritual beliefs have given meaning to her life since early childhood. Suzie's conception of a power higher than herself has provided her with comfort, security, and a centering force to her life. Suzie's earliest memories of church, spirituality, and religion are positive ones and seem appropriate for a child. Church membership made her feel part of a community that in some ways mirrored her family life.

In her conceptions of the divine, Suzie had a tendency to project the image of her father onto this being, someone caring but rather distant. Her search for a different type of spirituality during her college days was probably an effort to find a more "personal" type of connection to the divine. Freeing herself to search and to question was a healthy and maturing force in Suzie's life. The lack of a feminine force in her religious background, however, appeared to have created a void for Suzie. Although she saw her early experiences within her church as beautiful and meaningful, part of her, her feminine side, felt alienated.

In the category of relationships, Suzie tried to make the connection with others through attending churches and worship services, obviously searching for a group to belong to. Some individuals are not attracted to the "organization" of religion and prefer to worship on their own through prayer and meditation, whereas others like Suzie prefer to be a member of a community. Suzie was interested in developing a rich inner life, however, and she seemed to have acquired some balance between her inner and outer self. Many individuals turn to their image of God only when in need, but Suzie had matured to the point that she wanted a relationship with a Supreme Being as a "guide" rather than a "rescuer." Spiritually, this marks an elevated level of maturation for an individual.

Growing up in the Episcopal Church, Suzie demonstrated a definite capacity for "mystery" and the ability to develop faith in an entity that could not be perceived through the senses. She valued and respected the liturgy and ritual that gave substance to the sacraments. Suzie could speak coherently and intelligently about her beliefs and her reasoning behind them. Her intellect demanded that she continue this search for meaning throughout the many phases of her life.

Suzie has gone through many transformative phases in the growth of her inner or spiritual self. She regrets that her earlier faith experiences did not support her in embracing her sexuality more, but she has been able to realize that part of this was because of not only the church that she belonged to but the time period in which she grew up. Suzie has also accepted in an adult manner that we can do nothing to change the past, but we must go forward. Suzie has returned to her faith of origin as an adult and embraced it as an act of will, not of convenience or habit. She sees worship as joyful and fulfilling and not merely as a duty. She appears to have come almost full circle.

No doubt exists that as a result of the searching and pain in her life that Suzie has grown as a human being. She has survived divorce, restlessness, and doubt in her life and emerged as a healthy, intact human being. Her spiritual life has sustained her through all of this, and she has integrated her belief system into the rhythm of her life. What she possesses in the church of her choice is right for her, not necessarily for everyone, and she is comfortable with it. Suzie knows that life holds many unknowns, but she feels she has found a way to center herself for whatever the future might hold.

Suggested Approaches

Counselors need to help clients investigate and question their concepts of authority, power, and domination. Many of these concepts, and our reactions to them, come out of the religious traditions we were exposed to in our childhood. The lack of female clergy and other feminine role models in positions of religious or spiritual leadership have deeply affected the way in which women have viewed themselves in relation to a God-figure. Gloria Steinem maintains that a relationship exists between images of God and images of oneself. What does this do for a woman when all images of God and the hierarchy of the church are male? What does it do for men when they can never rejoice in the feminine side of their nature?

Counselors should be able to understand how this problem has created a feeling of sacral unworthiness in women. To this day in the Catholic Church and in some Protestant sects, only men may be ordained as deacons, let alone priests. Women are almost exclusively bound to men for their sacramental needs. Schneiders (1986) made the point that "We have perhaps not even begun to fathom the extent to which *a priori* exclusion of women, solely because they are women, from ordained ministry has limited, distorted, and subverted the Christian identity of women" (p. 34). Women in Eastern religions may not feel this to the same extent because men are still dominant in the home as well as in the temple or mosque, but even in these religions some women are asking for more autonomy in their personal spiritual development and more equality in their religious life.

Exercises

1. Imagine you are counseling a woman who has recently become ordained as pastor of a local Protestant church. What issues might she need to address? What concerns might she have? What obstacles might she need your help in overcoming?
2. Design a group that invites women of all faiths to come together and discuss their ideas for change in their churches. What can women of different faiths learn from each other about the struggles they all face in being marginalized in the church? What are some common themes in their spiritual beliefs that they can share with each other?

Carolyn's Case

Carolyn is the provost at a public institution and is applying for the presidency of a moderate-sized private institution owned by the Lutheran Congregation. Carolyn is a nonpracticing Protestant but was ordained as a Protestant minister. She hasn't practiced her ministry in about 15 years. Carolyn sees this employment as an opportunity to return to her ministry and to continue her work in higher education. When questioned regarding the mission of the institution, Carolyn expressed her desire to reenter her ministry. She isn't knowledgeable of the Lutheran religion and questions whether or not she is matched for the position. She is in the final round and is considering withdrawing her name because of what she perceives as a possible conflict between her religious practices and that of the institution to which she is applying. She seeks counseling from a licensed professional counselor to explore her options and to express her concerns.

Case Discussion

- What resources would a counselor need to help Carolyn explore her conflicts?
- What information would a counselor need from the client in order to accurately address her concerns?
- If the counselor were not of the same religious persuasion, what would he or she need to know in order to effectively counsel Carolyn in her decision-making process?
- How could the values of the counselor impact his or her ability to be of assistance?

References

Ochs, C. (1983). *Women and spirituality.* Totowa, NJ: Rowman & Allanheld.
Schneiders, S. M. (1986). The effects of women's experience on their spirituality. In J. W. Conn (Ed.), *Women's spirituality: Resources for Christian development.* Mahwah, NJ: Paulist Press.
Winter, M. T., Lummis, A., & Stokes, A. (1994). *Defecting in place: Women claiming responsibility for their own spiritual lives.* New York Crossroad Publishing Company.
www.lifepositive.com/mind/philosophy/feminism/women-spiritual.asp#top

CHAPTER 6

Gay and Lesbian Populations

BOB BARRET

Gay and Lesbian Spiritual Issues: A Personal Reflection

An unusual intersection occurs between religion and sexuality. Throughout history, religious institutions have consistently taken positions on the appropriate expressions of sexuality. Over generations, many of those stances have been retracted as religious leaders developed new understandings about scripture and human behavior. However, today one of the most entrenched issues continues to be the morality of homosexuality. Each year Christian denominations deliberate the complex issues inherent in coming to understand gay and lesbian sexuality more fully. Although the pace of change seems terribly slow to most gay and lesbian persons, the fact of the debate indicates that it is simply a matter of time until gay men and lesbians find themselves welcomed fully into religious practice. In the interim, the domains of religion and spirituality continue to be sources of emotional distress for many sexual minorities. The purpose of this chapter is to take a look at some of the issues that gay men and lesbians ordinarily face as they embrace or reject religious institutions.

This is also my story. It is a story of struggle, rejection, abandonment, spiritual recovery, and transformation. And it is written with the understanding that these themes, like those of others, are not linear but more circular, evolving through crisis toward an emergence into new levels of spiritual awareness (Tessier, 1997). Over time I have made peace with the fact that the answers to the spiritual and religious mysteries are rarely as definite as I might wish. I have shifted my focus away from seeking answers as I have realized that, over time, my questions change, reflecting an internalization of insights I have gained along the way. I hope that in this brief writing I can convey some of the anger, joy, and wonder I have found as I explore my questions.

As complex as writing this will be, it is a story that will illuminate many of the spiritual issues faced by gay men and lesbians, and I hope this approach will bring the reader closer to the intense internal experience that being gay and being spiritual demand. Of course, as an academic, I understand that professional writing usually does not involve data derived from only one subject, and it is even more rare that the data come from the writer's own experience. At the same time, I have come to believe that summary data often loses the depth and impact that can be gained from a more personal exploration. Heuristic research typically involves "reaching into deeper and deeper regions of a human problem or experience and coming to know and understand its underlying dynamics and constituents more and more fully" (Moustakas, 1990, p. 13). The emphasis in this kind of research is direct experience, responsive awareness, and conscious perception (Douglas & Moustakas, 1985). In telling my story, I will be open to those dimensions while I keep in mind some of the findings on gay and lesbian spirituality from more traditional research.

From my previous writing on gay and lesbian spirituality (Barret, 1988; Barret & Barzan 1996, 1998; Barret & Logan, 2002; Barret & Robinson, 2000), I have come to a reasonably full understanding of these issues as gay men and lesbians attempt to step over the many barriers that exist between organized religion and sexual orientation. As I have learned about various strategies and issues useful for reconciling with religion, I have come to understand my own experience more fully. I also make my bow to traditional *academe* by including a section at the end of the chapter that provides references to current research findings.

In writing my own story, I do not presume to speak for all sexual minorities. Without intending offense and for the sake of easy reading, I will use the word *gay* to refer to both gay men and lesbians unless greater specificity is appropriate. Also, I will not address the unique experience of bisexuals and transsexuals in this writing. This chapter will instead reflect in some depth on one gay man's experience. I have organized my story chronologically and will begin with some background on my family and some of the themes that surround my own spiritual development.

Background and Themes

Growing up in the South in the 1940s and '50s, especially in a "Christian" family that espoused "traditional values," was an experience I pretty much took for granted. My parents, my two older brothers, and I lived what seemed to be a fairly typical life similar to my peers. My mother's parents lived in a town some 70 miles away, and I had cousins and friends who seemed very much like me. The Presbyterian faith had been a bedrock of family tradition through many generations, and I internalized it fully. My great-great grandfather was one of the founding members of the Presbyterian Church in my hometown, and the church building was decorated with marble plaques honoring my ancestors. I spent a lot of time in that small town and, partly as a result of the lack of connection within my own family, I needed to be connected to something larger than my small world. I felt a relationship to all of these ancestors, and part of being present with them involved belonging to their church and living a life founded on moral principles and behaviors that would meet their approval. It never really occurred to me to question the teachings.

I grew up in a large southern city, I was a good student and a student leader, and I was active in my church youth group. I even ended up attending a small Presbyterian liberal arts college that reinforced the values I had previously been taught. Did I question the existence of God? Did I wonder about the "truth" of Jesus? Did I struggle with accepting creeds and even the words of hymns and prayers? I am sure I did, but whatever doubts I had never seemed significant.

All of this began to change one Sunday when the church leaders called police to arrest a group of black persons who wanted to worship with us. Although these leaders pointed to scripture to justify their action, I knew what they were doing was wrong and that I would no longer worship there. Of course, in 1960 in the South, not many alternatives were available for most congregations who believed as the Presbyterians did. I drifted into the Episcopal Church where I found immediate comfort in the liturgy and with the more liberal perspectives. My own sense of a personal search for truth had been discovered, and I began to feel a tug toward a more active role in religious life. I began to give serious thought to going to seminary, an inclination I feared and resisted. Nevertheless, this idea did not go away.

Death had been a constant in my life from a young age. My grandparents "lost" three of their four children before I was 5 years old. Going to visit them always involved a visit to the cemetery, and there was an almost palpable sense of grief in their home. After the deaths of my great-grandmother and grandfather, I confronted some questions about life after death but held on to the belief that they had found the afterlife promised by God. When my grandmother died, I was comforted by the image of her reunion with my grandfather.

Following graduation from college, I got married, took a job in business, and became a father. When I learned that my best friend in college had died in an automobile accident, I sat up all night, stupefied that he (who had so much to give to others) was dead, and I was alive. My last visit with him had been intense, and we had argued over his assessment of my life as self-centered and void of any expression of spiritual belief. In my heart I knew he was speaking a truth, but I had defended myself and accused him of being out of touch after spending three years in Africa. When he died, I began to realize that the time had come for me to live with a greater sense of integrity. I knew I wanted a career that centered on service, but I had no clue how to go forward. I also found myself plummeted into an intense religious crisis. I asked myself, "What do I really believe about religion? What am I going to do about these sexual urges that were becoming increasingly burdensome? What do I do with all of these confusing feelings?" I turned to the priest at my church for help, and fortunately he encouraged me to seek counseling. Thus began a period of intense self-exploration and understanding.

The counselor helped me break through my religious denial and begin to see myself more realistically. I realized that from a young age I had worried about religion and the church. I also felt significant estrangement when it came to religious teachings and Sunday school attendance. I was not exactly a loner, but I certainly was teased in school, at home, and at church. Although not your typical "sissy boy," I had no interest in sports and avoided any activity that was "rough." I was sort of a social misfit, even though I always had one or more friends (usually other boys). I have never been the quiet, shy boy that many might label as queer, but I was called queer and sissy often. The distress this caused was intense, and I felt so ashamed and fearful about it. I also had no one to talk to about these things so I just shut down. I built a wall of denial that was virtually impenetrable.

Reflections on Emerging Sexuality

Becoming aware of one's own sexuality is usually an isolated and individual experience. As I grew up, I did not think about the ways my interests might reflect my sexuality. About the only sexual message I internalized from my parents, teachers, and religious teachers was the importance of not having sex. I had crushes on girls and developed the typical kinds of hopes and dreams about the future like most boys and girls. I would get married, be a father, and live a life like those I saw all around me.

Once I became a teenager, however, I began to fear that I was, in fact, very different from my peers. I'm not sure exactly when I became aware that I had sexual feelings for boys. Those feelings were conflicted by my feelings about my own body, fear of my family's reactions, and my hope that if I could place this enormous suffering before God in the right form, He would take it away. My greatest fear was that I would be abandoned by all who knew me and that no one would want to associate with me. Struggling with these intense feelings alone was overwhelming. I was frequently depressed and too afraid to tell anyone what was going on. With great desperation I began the process of denial that only partly covered the intense internal torment, a torment that God seemed indifferent to regardless of the fervor of my prayers or the degree of my bargaining.

Back in the 1950s and 1960s, homosexuality was only talked about in negative terms, and the popular belief was that homosexuals needed to be locked up—either in prison or in a mental hospital. I knew I was not a criminal and did not think I was mentally ill. And I combined those two beliefs to convince myself that I must not be homosexual. Since I was not having sex with anyone, the logic sustained itself, and I felt generally at peace in my family, social, and religious lives.

This began to change once I got married and became a father. My awareness of my sexual attraction to men would result in intense, unexpected feelings of guilt, and I found myself ashamed that I had married and fathered children. I became a monster to myself for placing these people I loved so much in such a shameful situation. Once again, I would turn to my prayer life and the church, hoping for some kind of relief. I desperately wanted to be like my peers, to be relaxed about being a husband and a father, and to feel confident about my future. Even today it seems odd that I had so much awareness about myself even though I had had no sexual experience with men. At my core, I knew who I was.

The problem was that I could not imagine that others, including God, would ever accept me. I realized that I had made many bargains with God. If he would take these sexual feelings away, I would do *anything* for Him. I had convinced myself that both of us were living up to the bargain even as my defenses were crumbling. Following my friend Dan's death, I forged one more agreement with God: I would go to seminary and he would take my attraction to men away. I took the steps toward becoming a minister, but the feelings persisted. It did not take me long to realize that being a minister or priest was not a solution.

Let me be clear about a couple of things. My high school and college years were good years for me. I had great friends, did lots of fun things, explored the world, and began to become the adult I am today. There were easily more laughs than tears. My strong denial kept me in place, and the days I thought about my sexual orientation were certainly few. Denial can be such a strong force in one's life. My need to connect, to be included, to belong has been great most of my life. Simultaneously, my fear of disconnectedness, separation, and marginalization has been an underlying driving force. That I did not come to understand this until later in life is a disappointment but also represents reality. The interplay of the connect/

disconnect themes often drove me into situations that might have turned out differently with more insight, but, like most of us, I was doing the best I could with the knowledge I had at that time. And while I was doing this, I was loving being a father and creating a wonderful life with a woman I loved very much.

My career emerged as I became a teacher, then a school counselor, and later a psychologist. My family life continued to be stable and rich. I drifted away from the church, exploring Eastern religion and other expressions of spirituality. Although my denial had broken down, my commitment to my family remained intact. I would not be gay, but I could not face God with this denial, so I just stayed away. Fear and anger rose up every time I even went into a church. I could not resolve the issue of living with integrity with the reality of hurting so many people I loved so much. Somehow approaching God brought these issues to the forefront, so I just avoided thinking about Him.

Death = Life

Shortly after I began my work at the university as a counselor educator, I began to volunteer as a cancer counselor. My mother-in-law had died of ovarian cancer, and I knew the isolation and fear all of us experienced as we watched her die. I wanted to use my skills with those facing similar losses. The men and women I worked with during those years nudged me closer and closer to claiming my own integrity. At times their courage made my own life seem empty. This work brought so many of the spiritual themes mentioned earlier into full focus, and my questions became more urgent. What happens when one dies? Why does so much suffering have to be experienced? Where is God in these situations? What does my life mean, and what am I doing that *really* matters? The relationships were intense but so very rich. They challenged me on virtually every level of my life to take some steps I doubt I would ever have taken without them.

As the HIV crisis began to emerge, I had a strong urge to get involved. In the early 1980s, people with HIV were routinely subjected to very inhumane treatment. Many hospital workers refused to bring food into their rooms, employers and landlords rejected them, no real treatment was provided, religious groups refused to offer comfort, and death was prominent. Initiating a counseling program for people with HIV gave me the opportunity to use the skills I had learned from the cancer work; it also introduced me to gay men who challenged the negative stereotype I had introjected.

Watching these men die was probably the most powerful moment in my life. They lived with more integrity than I could muster. They died and called me to live more fully. As I sought to make sense of their suffering, they brought me back to religious life. Their suffering and love showed me that my own personal spiritual experience had just as much validity as the religious experience espoused by churches. I began attending church again, and I had many important theological conversations with religious teachers. I was buoyed by a new kind of love I felt in the small but growing community of religious persons responding to people with AIDS (Barret, 1989). I also found enormous comfort in my return to the church. Trying to get religious organizations involved with AIDS victims brought me face to face with men and women of various faiths who did not seem concerned about judging gay people. As I realized the kind of compassion and love they were offering, I began to reconnect with religious life.

Coming Out

At this stage in my life, I was approaching coming out in the context of a new relationship with the church. I felt God's presence in my life, and I knew that I was headed toward a more honest life. This awareness both terrified and reassured me. I did not know what I was going to do; I felt the pull towards change, and I prayed. For the first time I did not seek the personal relief of my confusion or for God to take away my attraction to men. I just asked to express more fully the love I felt inside, and I began to more intensely feel a sense of wonder and acceptance of the unique person I am. Realizing that God wants all of us to simply be who we are gave me the courage to begin to tell those I loved that I could no longer be who they wanted me to be. I *had* to be who I am, and I wanted to be that with as much integrity as I could muster. Both spiritual and religious energy were pulling me forward, and even though I was hurting people I loved, I knew I had no choice. Coming out was *the* moment when I would be standing before God with maximum integrity. I would not hide from that moment again.

There is no need to recount the tumult of those years. Even though my daughters were grown, leaving the family was the most painful moment I had ever faced. As I was going through that time, I was also liberating myself from the authority of a church that wanted to impose rules on me that did not support my own experience of God. I suppose I began to be more spiritual and less religious, even though I continued to attend church each week. I found great comfort in the readings and sermons. I felt connected there throughout the period of disconnection from my wife and daughters.

Being Gay and Christian

It would be nice to say that affirming myself as gay before God solved all of my problems and that I lived blissfully in a new and whole relationship with Him. I rejoiced at participation in the liturgy. I love church music and the sacraments; to be able to participate in these moments as an openly gay man seemed like a miracle. I would walk the labyrinth in Grace Cathedral whenever I went to San Francisco. I participated in church retreats by leading workshops on gay and lesbian experience. I was in church virtually every Sunday. I liked the community of the church and felt personally more focused from my worship experiences.

Of course, spiritual life is rarely serene. Maybe it is just the searcher in me who continues to pull up questions. Most mainstream Protestant churches, some Catholic churches, and some Jewish groups struggle intensely over the "homosexual question." Do we allow *them* to worship with us? Do we allow *them* to serve in leadership roles? Do we allow *them* to become ministers, priests, or rabbis? And do we allow *them* to participate fully in all religious ceremonies?

These questions brought me into a new conflict with my church. As my gay identity matured and I began to understand the politics of oppression more fully, I found myself uneasy in many of my worship experiences. Gay men and lesbians who accommodate the church's homophobia have constant reminders of their second-class status. Baptisms, ordinations, and weddings are sacred and wonderful moments in a religious group's life. Participating in them as an outsider became a distressing experience for me. Although I believe that God would not act in such a manner, I felt offended that humans who guide the church would be so blind to the harm they were causing. Once again I found myself on the margin, and that was no longer acceptable. When I went to my priest and told him about my feelings and my decision to leave the church, he told me to be patient, that change would come. He seemed indifferent to my reaction to the oppressive nature of having to sit in the back of the bus.

The Metropolitan Community Church (MCC) was founded to respond to the spiritual needs of sexual minorities and has congregations in most major cities in the United States and other countries. It is truly a gay celebratory church, and it is filled with persons who have found a safe place to bring themselves before God. But it just did not work for me. Once again I found myself in a kind of self-imposed exile. When I spoke with a priest who knew me well, he pointed out that I would probably never find peace in a Christian church that placed an emphasis on sin, asking for forgiveness, and redemption because those were not my issues. He encouraged me to understand myself as an Old Testament person, a man, like the Jewish people, who seeks a home, thinks he has found it, but is cast off and must begin his search once more.

Understanding this wandering as a way of spiritual evolution has enabled me to keep my focus on the many challenges of living a spiritual life more fully. Today I seek to respond to each person with an attitude that expresses my awareness of the sacred within each of us. I want to be gentle and loving with everyone I meet. Far too often I do not live up to this challenge, but I continue to try and that is what is important for now. I try to bring the sacred into each moment of my life, a spiritual life that seems to have the most integrity for me. There is both joy in this kind of living and a kind of sadness borne from doing this without the support of a larger spiritual community. I am mostly at peace with this expression at this time in my life. Will I ever return to formal organized religion? I don't know the answer to that right now, but history suggests that such a movement will undoubtedly occur, that my present understandings are likely to be tested, and that my restlessness will once again lead me into the uncomfortable but stimulating search for a greater awareness of God's mystery. When the student is ready, the teacher will appear. I expect that is the way my spiritual life will continue to unfold.

Gay and Lesbian Spirituality in the Literature

Gay men and lesbians face an enormous challenge as they attempt to participate in traditional religious life. Most religious organizations see the lives of gays and lesbians as sinful and do not welcome them as fellow believers. Some groups go so far as to create conversion or "reparative" therapy experiences that purport to change people's sexual orientation from gay to straight (Barret & Logan, 2002). In order to participate, many gays and lesbians choose to go back into the closet or subject themselves to harmful reparative approaches to be found acceptable. Both of these coping strategies (going back into the closet and using reparative strategies) merely push them back into inner lives of shame, fear, and self-condemnation.

Gay men and lesbians who refuse to accept self-denial as a means of accommodating a religious organization may elect to participate as openly gay men and lesbians and let whatever happens, happen. Others frequently seek out alternative spiritual paths. Native American spiritual rituals have become a source of meaning for some sexual minorities (Brown, 1997). Some seek out eastern forms of meditation or even explore paganism as a resource for spiritual practice and understanding. Some find solace in separating spiritual and religious experiences, giving validity and authority to both as a means of accessing metaphysical life. It is clear that many gay men and lesbians engage in their religious and spiritual lives with an intense desire to live out an inner truth.

In the past, it was rare to hear gay men and lesbians mention spiritual and religious questions. Today in the gay community a growing awareness of various paths toward spiritual understanding is emerging (O'Neil & Ritter, 1992).

Lee & Busto (1991) collated the results of a survey printed in a national magazine read largely by gay men and lesbians. From the 648 responses,

83% reported being raised in the Christian tradition, 11% identified as Jewish, and the remaining 6% had no particular religious instruction during their childhood. By 1990, most respondents reported not participating in their family's religious organizations. Forty-six of these subjects continued to maintain an affiliation (Protestant 22%, Jewish 6%, gay Christian 2%, Eastern faiths 4%) with the largest group (28%) naming their religious affiliation as a 12-step recovery program. Over one third of the participants in this survey reported they did not belong to any religious or spiritual community, and over 84% stated that their spirituality was very or somewhat important to them. Only 52% saw religion as similarly important. These results parallel those reported by a 1988 Gallup Poll and a similar survey conducted by the *San Francisco Chronicle* (Ritter & Ternrup, 2002). Although these data may be out of date now, they do reflect a level of disaffiliation with religious life within the gay community.

The reasons that some gay men and lesbians give for abandoning all spiritual activity are varied. Many report that during their adolescence and young adulthood they were very active in religious life. They talk about how devout they tried to be and the alienation and sense of loneliness that evolved as they realized that their spiritual figure was not going to take away their homosexuality. Because of the intensity of their suffering and the acute judgment they receive from most mainstream religious organizations, they conclude that trusting any spiritual or religious teaching will just lead to more suffering.

Challenges in Claiming Spiritual Life

The primary challenge that gay men and lesbians face in embracing their spirituality is giving up the worry of condemnation that comes so loudly from the religious organizations that do not accept them. Counselors may find themselves taking on the task of consciousness-raising by participating in traditional religious organizations. For example, as gay men and lesbians seek accommodation in traditional religious organizations, they are likely to receive a mixed welcome. Some embrace them warmly, whereas others tolerate them but encourage them to be quiet about their sexuality. Few religious organizations seem to genuinely understand the oppressive experience of gays and lesbians who participate in religious activities that continue to marginalize them. The frequency of baptisms, bar/bat mitzvahs, and even weddings reminds gay and lesbian members of their differences. Few moments honor, much less acknowledge, their relationships. Some religious groups even bless their members' pets and homes but still refuse to provide community support for gay and lesbian relationships. Many religious groups hide behind the fact that they cannot bless these relationships because they are illegal. Although coming out of a loving tradition, most of these organizations fail to recognize an opportunity to creatively bless nontraditional relationships. By not addressing this issue, gay men and lesbians must find a faith that recognizes the failure of the organization to properly reflect the teachings on which it is based (McNeil, 1995).

Some gay and lesbian clients will undoubtedly project onto their religious organizations their own internal shame. Helping them see that the real problem lies within is a step toward opening more fully to the idea of a religious or spiritual practice. Some totally reject the religious life and hold on to a bitterness and cynicism that will arise in counseling sessions. Others chose nontraditional beliefs and practices such as Wicca and other nature-based connections to the spiritual world. A growing number continue to participate in organizations that outwardly reject them but appear to be tolerant and "welcoming."

The Emergence of Literature on Gay and Lesbian Spirituality

A growing body of literature is devoted to the discussion of gay and lesbian spirituality. This literature unfortunately does not come from well-designed research studies. As is true with homosexuality in general, research into the spiritual lives of gay men and lesbians is scarce. However, various authors are beginning to provide books that allow readers to understand the complex issues surrounding this topic. Although I will not present an exhaustive list, mentioning a few of them will provide a sense of the topics being discussed.

As early as 1984, Catholic theologian Matthew Fox outlined a four-step process for the spiritual development of gay men and lesbians: (a) creation, in which the gay self is truly embraced; (b) letting go, in which the pain of rejection is acknowledged and released; (c) creativity, which leads to the rebirth of the soul; and (d) transformation, in which the individual extends compassion and a sense of celebration to others. These steps mirror the coming-out process but employ a different language. Gay men and lesbians who participate in religious communities display similar needs to their nongay peers: a sense of something greater than self, a sense of community, answers to universal questions, and moral guidance (Perlstein, 1996).

In his book *Gay Soul*, Michael Thompson (1994) recounted interviews with 16 gay men, including writers and thinkers like James Broughton, Clyde Hall, Ram Dass, Malcolm Boyd, and Robert Hopcke, all of whom have contributed to the understanding of gay spirituality. The interviews focused on one specific question: What is gay soul and how might it be expressed? Later in his career, Thompson (1997) described the development of gay identity through spiritual reflection.

In other works, Peter Gomes (1996), former minister at Harvard Memorial Church in Boston, outlined a way to read the Bible that shows the way understanding scripture has changed over the years with a particular emphasis on the issue of homosexuality. Mel White (1995), a former colleague of Jerry Falwell and Pat Roberson, told his coming-out story against the backdrop of the fundamental Christian movement. Chris Glaser (1998) encouraged gay men and lesbians to affirm the deeply spiritual experience of gaining integrity and wholeness through coming out. Along those same lines, McNeil (1995) urged gay men and lesbians to celebrate their sexuality as a gift from God. M. C. Wann (1999) detailed various ways congregations can affirm their gay and lesbian members. Also, Scanzoni & Millenkott (1994) raised the issue of the appropriate Christian response to gay and lesbian neighbors.

Books like these serve as beacons to gay and lesbian people who seek a greater spiritual life. They also help inform the debate between religious organizations and homosexuality. It is clear that gay men and lesbians are forging change within religious and spiritual communities.

Suggested Approaches

Counselors can assist gay men and lesbians explore their spirituality in many different ways. *Keeping an open mind or opening a closed one* is an essential task as counselors explore the religious and spiritual lives of their gay and lesbian clients. As in all aspects of exploring religious beliefs within counseling, it is important to suspend personal religious beliefs about homosexuality to give the client a nonjudgmental and safe environment for this important work.

Understand the wounds that may be left from previous religious rejection and condemnation. Many gay men and lesbians have suffered at the hands of a judgmental and restrictive religious organization, and they may be resistant to opening themselves to new spiritual and religious experiences. Institutionalized religion has been a source of oppression for gay men and lesbians for centuries (Davidson, 2000). It may be appropriate to simply explore these harmful events without suggesting the presence of safer options that exist today.

Be aware of the connection between spirituality and eroticism. Many people find that a highly erotic experience in the context of committed relationships has a deep spiritual component (Connor, 1993). It may be that some find their way back to spiritual life by exploring these moments of contact.

Learn about local resources. Knowing of community-based religious groups that accept gays and lesbians will enable you to make sound recommendations to those who are troubled spiritually. However, encouraging a client to speak with a religious leader without prior knowledge of that leader's views on homosexuality can be very dangerous. Too many times clients turn to religion for help and experience rejection anew. Of course, having a counselor simply recognize that spiritual and religious participation may be an important element in the lives of gay men and lesbians will create an openness to exploring this important aspect of their lives.

Discussion

1. What are your personal religious understandings about homosexuality? If a conflict exists between your views and your client's sexual orientation, what would you do?

2. Consider the person presented in this chapter. If he were your client, and he told you about his sexual orientation immediately prior to his marriage, how would you encourage him to explore his decision further? If he came to you after his marriage for continued assistance, what feelings might you have about him? How would you resolve or express these feelings?

3. The last part of the chapter identifies some of the issues that gay men and lesbians face as they attempt to reconcile their religious and spiritual lives with their sexual orientation. Using this discussion as a basis, examine the case in this chapter and point out where these issues are apparent.

4. How might you become more of an activist in your community for an increased understanding about gay men and lesbians as religious people?

5. All of us learn prejudices as we mature. What prejudices do you have about gay men and lesbians? How might these attitudes affect your work with gay and lesbian clients?

6. What community resources or church organizations would you recommend to your gay men and lesbian clients?

7. What are your thoughts regarding gay and lesbian clergy and religious leaders?

References

Barret, B., & Barzan, B. (1996). Spiritual experiences of gay men and lesbians. *Counseling and Values, 40*(1), 4–15.

Barret, B., & Barzan, B. (1998). Gay and lesbian spirituality: A response to Donaldson. *Counseling and Values, 42*(3), 222–225.

Barret, B., & Logan, C. (2002). *Counseling gay men and lesbians: A practice primer.* Belmont, CA: Brooks/Cole.

Barret, R. L. (1988). The spiritual journey: Explorations and implications for counselors. *Journal of Humanistic Education and Development, 26*(4), 154–162.

Barret, R. L. (1989). Counseling gay men with AIDS: Human dimensions. *Journal of Counseling and Development, 67*(10), 573–575.

Barret, R. L., & Robinson, B. E. (2000). *Gay fathers.* San Francisco: Jossey Bass.

Brown, L. B. (1997). *Two spirit people: American Indian lesbian women and gay men.* Binghamton, NY: Herrington Park Press.

Connor, R. P. (1993). *Blossom of bone: Reclaiming the connection between homoeroticism and the sacred.* San Francisco: Harper.

Davidson, M. G. (2000). Religion and spirituality. In R. M. Perex & K. DuBord (Eds.), *Handbook of counseling and psychotherapy with lesbian, gay, and bisexual clients* (409–433). Washington, D.C.: American Psychological Association.

Douglas, B., & Moustakas, C. (1985). Heuristic inquiry: The internal search to know. *Journal of Humanistic Psychology, 25*(3), 39–55.

Glaser, C. (1994). *The word is out: The Bible reclaimed for lesbians and gay men.* San Francisco: Harper.

Glaser, C. (1998). *Coming out as a sacrament.* New York: Geneva Press.

Gomes, P. (1996). *The good book: Reading the Bible with mind and heart.* New York: Avon Books.

Lee, K., & Busto, G. (1991). When spirit moves us. *Outlook, 14,* 83–85.

McNeil, J. (1995). *Freedom, glorious freedom. The spiritual journey to the fullness of life for gays, lesbians, and everybody else.* Boston: Beacon Press.

Moustakas, C. (1990). *Heuristic research: Design, methodology and applications.* Newbury Park, NJ: Sage Publications.

O'Neil, C., & Ritter, K. (1992). *Coming out within. Stages for spiritual awakening for lesbians and gay men.* San Francisco: Harper.

Perlstein, M. (1996). Integrating a gay, lesbian, or bisexual person's religious and spiritual needs and choices into psychotherapy. In C. Alexander (Ed.), *Gay and lesbian mental health: A sourcebook for practitioners.* Binghamton NY: Herrington Park Press.

Ritter, K., & Ternrup, A. (2002). *Foundations of affirmative psychotherapy for lesbians and gay men. A mirroring experience.* New York: Guilford Press.

Scanzoni, M., & Mollenkott, V. (1994). *Is the homosexual my neighbor? A positive Christian response.* San Francisco: Harper.

Tessier, L. J. (1997). *Dancing after the whirlwind: Feminist reflections on sex, denial, and spiritual transformation.* Boston: Beacon Press.

Thompson, M. (1994). *Gay soul: Finding the heart of gay spirit and nature.* San Francisco: Harper.

Thompson, M. (1997). *Gay body: A journey through shadow to self.* New York: St. Martin's Press.

Wann, M. C. (1999). *More than welcome: Learning to embrace gay, lesbian, bisexual, and transgendered persons in the church.* St. Louis: Chalice Press.

White, M. (1995). *Stranger at the gate: To be gay and Christian in America.* New York: Simon & Schuster.

CHAPTER 7

Persons with Disabilities

SUSAN NIEMANN

Spiritual beliefs and practices play an important role in the lives of millions of people worldwide, yet spirituality has been largely overlooked in the field of counseling for disabled individuals. Historically, disabled people have been seen as damaged or flawed, often unable to make choices or decisions for themselves. Modern counseling approaches to the disabled often focus on helping individuals overcome the challenges associated with functional limitations without addressing the mental, physical, and spiritual dimensions of counseling. However, spirituality has been a constant source of meaning for individuals and families facing the challenges associated with physical, cognitive, and psychiatric disabilities. Addressing spirituality as a core theme is essential to providing holistic mental health services to this diverse population.

The Experience of Disability
A disability is best understood in the context of how it is perceived by society, the meaning of the disability being a social construct. Additionally, understanding the experiences of disabled people requires understanding how society views those individuals. Historically, three major social constructions of disabilities have been present: the moral model, the medical model, and the diversity model.

The Moral Model
The oldest social construction of disabilities is the moral model. This model is based on religious traditions that often describe disabilities, such

as blindness or physical challenges, as the representation of sin, a failure of faith, a moral lapse, or evil. Whether congenital or acquired, many theologies have historically constructed disabilities to be a curse, one often associated with the attribution of shame onto an individual or family.

The moral model also includes the view that disabilities are tests of faith or strength, whereby only the truly holy or righteous can bear such a burden. From this perspective, individuals and families are specially selected by God to receive a disability and are given the opportunity to redeem themselves through their endurance, resilience, and piety. Psychologist and disability rights proponent Rhonda Olkin (1999) and others asserted that the moral model has served to disempower and marginalize individuals with disabilities, because a fundamental assumption of this model is that any disabling condition is inherently tragic and burdensome.

In more recent times, the moral model has been reframed to include the positive attributions associated with disabilities, yet this controversial view that persons with disabilities are "special" or "chosen" is often debated within the disabled community. Olkin (1999) asserted that the moral model provides the underpinnings for the concept of a disability as a metaphysical blessing. In this view, individuals are chosen to receive disabilities in order to reach a greater level of consciousness. Those who espouse this philosophy may believe that as a disability impairs one sense, it heightens another, often bestowing previously untapped gifts to the individual. In this way, individuals are selected by God or a higher power to receive a disability not as a curse or punishment but to demonstrate a special purpose or calling. Vash (2001), speaking of her own experiences as a rehabilitation counseling professional with a disability, believed that a disability can be a metaphysical gift, providing the impetus for personal growth and spiritual transcendence. Some mental health professionals describe this view as an unhealthy coping mechanism or a reflection of a societal need to impose order and purposefulness on random events (Olkin, 1999).

The Medical Model

The medical model of disabilities gained momentum in the mid-nineteenth century with the advent of increasingly enlightened and humanistic medicine. In this view, the cause of the disability is rooted not in sin or mysticism but in science. Disabilities are viewed as mental or physical defects, the unfortunate byproducts of illnesses, accidents, or genetic mistakes. The goals of working with disabled people include curing or correcting defects as much as possible and helping these individuals adapt to a nondisabled society given their limitations.

The medical model has been hailed as a revolution by many members of the disabled community, spurring medical and technological advances that have improved the lives of disabled people. This model's approach of addressing functional limitations has served as the historical foundation of the rehabilitation counseling profession. With the advent of the medical model, societal attitudes toward disabled individuals as evil and cursed have been abated and continue to be eroded. However, the medical model posits that the challenges associated with disabilities reside in the individual, and solutions are primarily limited to medical interventions, aid in adjusting to disabilities, and modifications to the person's lifestyle. Little or no consideration is given to the negative societal attitudes that create and maintain barriers to a full range of beneficial opportunities (Olkin, 1999). In addition, the medical model does not routinely address the spiritual concerns of disabled individuals and their families, such as a need for meaning, connectedness, and faith.

The Diversity Model

During the last few decades, the civil rights movement has raised awareness of how societal attitudes have created barriers for groups of historically marginalized people. The diversity model (also called the minority model) posits that, as with negative projections upon persons of color, negative perceptions of disabilities have been socially constructed, based on a desire to keep power in the hands of the dominant, privileged group. Aside from reframing disabilities as positive from the moral model perspective, both the moral and medical models often carry the implicit assumption that disabilities themselves are inherently negative, and that persons with disabilities are sick, impaired, or flawed. In general, these models frame the disabling condition as separate from an individual's identity, assuming that the primary goal of each person with a disability is to be disability-free and therefore problem-free.

The diversity model, however, asserts that the most profound problems faced by individuals with disabilities lie not within the disability per se but in the society that fails to accommodate them and that maintains a pervasive negative attitude toward them. The diversity model emphasizes that it is not the functional limitations of the disability itself that create barriers to meaningful living, but the societal attitudes and policies that prevent persons with disabilities from fully integrating into society. This model emphasizes the need for the acceptance and appreciation of disabled people as unique and integral to a diverse community, rather than flawed and in need of repair. Embedded in this model is an implicit spirituality coupled with the notion that as a society we must work in cooperation to find meaningful roles for all individuals, with or without disabilities.

Prejudice, Stereotyping, and Discrimination

According to the diversity model, the major challenges associated with disabilities for most individuals are rooted in discrimination and prejudice. Fine & Asch (1988) listed five assumptions rooted in the medical model often applied by researchers and practitioners to persons with disabilities in the United States. First, it is generally assumed that a disability is rooted in a biological dysfunction and that this dysfunction or pathology is the driving force in the lives of individuals with disabilities. The use of terms such as "confined" to a wheelchair or a "victim" of polio reinforce the notion that having a disability is a horrible fate. Second, a disability is considered to be the cause of all the problems or crises an individual may face, without consideration of ecological factors. Third, persons with disabilities are conceptualized as victims in need of sympathy, because their situation is sad and tragic. Fourth, a disability is considered central to an individual's self-concept, and that all problems or challenges faced by that individual are related to the disability. Fifth, regardless of the disability type, the individuals are seen as inherently helpless; they are thought to be too childlike and simple to make decisions or advocate for themselves.

Perpetuating Stereotypes of Persons with Disabilities

Outside the realm of rehabilitation counseling, the counseling profession has perpetuated many negative attitudes toward people with disabilities. Several negative views attributed to mental health professionals have been described, including the apparent invisibility of the disabled, the fear of the disabled, the belief that people with certain disabilities are also limited in other ways, and attitudes of paternalism and pity (Wenig, 1994). In viewing individuals with disabilities as invisible or without hopes and dreams of their own, mental health professionals often focus on how a family copes with the needs of a family member with a disability. In this model of family therapy, the disabled person is viewed as separate from the rest of the family and as an abnormal event requiring the rest of the family to adjust. For example, the following passage from a recent (1999) marriage and family therapy article on the family life cycle includes the assumption that a child with a disability will cause stress in a "normal" family:

> We need to plan therapeutically for the lifelong implications that a handicapped child has for all family members, especially for the adjustment and caretaking responsibilities of the siblings. . . . Normal siblings become especially stressed when parents expect them to treat

a disabled sibling as normal or when parents expect them to be pre-occupied with the needs of the disabled sibling. (McGoldrick, Watson, & Benton, 1999, p. 157)

Mental health research prior to the 1980s generally assumed that family dysfunction and pathological reactions were an inevitable result of having a disabled child (Stainton & Besser, 1998). The "burden literature," which emphasized negative impacts on families and assumed "grieving" would be pervasive and lifelong, discounted positive outcomes and family growth attributed to spirituality as denial or attempts by parents to alleviate their guilt.

The Need for Connectedness

For individuals with disabilities, feeling connected to supportive people can provide a tremendous source of strength. Being able to find and maintain satisfying intimate relationships, to achieve career goals that show one's worth in relation to others, and to contribute to family and society all serve to enhance self-esteem and self-efficacy, especially for women (Nosek & Hughes, 2001). However, for persons with disabilities, the risk of social isolation is high, perhaps resulting from parental overprotection, inaccessible environments, a lack of assistive devices for mobility, barriers to employment, and a lack of opportunities to develop social interaction skills. Expectations communicated by family early in life and efforts to integrate school and recreational activities play an important role in setting the stage for a life of participation versus a life of isolation. Meaningful participation in faith communities throughout the family life cycle is one way to address the need for spiritual connections for persons with disabilities.

Challenges Associated with Specific Disability Types

Although persons with disabilities share commonalities, they are a diverse group. Understanding the experience of having a disability involves understanding how different types of disabilities may present unique challenges. For some, these challenges are associated with spiritual questions and crises of faith.

Persons with Mobility Impairments

Individuals with a mobility disability are those whose physical differences compel them to conduct physical activities in a variety of alternate ways. Mobility impairments include congenital conditions, such as cerebral palsy and spina bifida, and conditions acquired later in life, such as a spinal cord injury and multiple sclerosis.

Whether a mobility-related disability is acquired before birth, at birth, or later in life, persons with mobility disabilities experience prejudice, stereotyping, and discrimination. In a culture that defines beauty in a narrow and restricted sense, persons with mobility impairments are often viewed as unattractive and asexual. Hahn (1988) asserted that due to the cultural inculcation of certain mores from Judeo-Christian heritage, American society has developed an "existential anxiety" toward persons with obvious physical disabilities and differences. This anxiety manifests itself in avoiding the physically disabled as a result of their own fears about potential disabilities, illnesses, and, eventually, death.

A major challenge for persons with mobility impairments is gaining access to public and private facilities. Even with the advent of the Americans with Disabilities Act of 1990, wheelchair riders are often denied access to places of commerce, certain types of housing, parks and recreation areas, private and public transportation, and places of worship (Mackelprang & Salsgiver, 1999).

According to Zink (1992), accepting and adapting to an acquired mobility-related disability may be easier for younger rather than older individuals. As their self-concepts are still developing, young persons are generally able to successfully integrate a disability into their self-concepts. Also, more years with a disability increase the opportunities to be exposed to role models, leaders, and cultural and political movements centered on the strength, power, and beauty of disabilities and differences.

A study of the physical disabled, including those with mobility impairments, identified five factors that facilitate coping and positive adaptation. The combined elements of spiritual transformation, hope, personal control, positive social supports, and meaningful engagement in life enable individuals to empower themselves and come to terms with their respective conditions (DoRozario, 1997). Inherent in these findings is the role spirituality plays in the lives of persons with physical disabilities.

Deaf and Hearing-Impaired People

About 21 million deaf or hearing-impaired people live in the United States, constituting over 8% of the population. When discussing deafness, an important distinction must be made between "nonlingual" and "lingual" as applied to persons with hearing impairments. Nonlingual deafness occurs when a deaf child does not acquire language at a normal developmental age. Lingual deafness occurs when a person develops either spoken or manual language at a normal developmental age (Zak, 1996). Thinking and learning patterns can be markedly different for nonlingual individuals, and they may struggle with communicating in a hearing world.

Since the late 1960s, Deaf people have presented themselves as sharing unique social and cultural characteristics, using an uppercase *D* to characterize their common identity as the Deaf culture. Lowercase *deaf* refers to noncultural elements of deafness, such as medical conditions. Although definitions of who is included in Deaf culture vary, the broadest definition includes all those who embrace American Sign Language (ASL) and other characteristics of Deaf culture, including hearing children of Deaf parents.

Stokoe (1989) noted that mainstream American culture has marginalized members of Deaf culture, expecting them to act as if they hear, and that Deaf Americans have a way of life that is different but not inferior to mainstream Americans. Many Deaf Americans prefer to socialize and worship together in an environment where ASL is the preferred mode of communication. Although Deaf Americans are likely to be affected by societal actions and policies that define them as disabled, they generally reject the disability label (Mackelprang & Salsgiver, 1999). Members of the Deaf culture assert that if everyone knew ASL, no one would consider deafness to be a disability. A current trend in counseling the deaf is to assist them in developing a bicultural identity so that these individuals feel comfortable working and socializing in the hearing world without losing their sense of community and uniqueness as a part of Deaf culture.

A great deal of diversity exists among deaf and hearing-impaired people. Some feel strongly aligned with Deaf culture and frame deafness as a source of pride and identity, whereas others see their deafness as a "hearing disability" that requires accommodation in a hearing world. People who develop deafness later in life, referred to as the "postlingual" deaf, may need time and resources to adjust to their loss. Their emphasis in coping may be geared primarily to adapting to a hearing world through compensation strategies, technology, and legal protections.

Persons with Visual Disabilities and Blindness

The medical profession defines a legally blind person as having 20/200 vision or worse when corrected. Persons with blindness are particularly vulnerable to the moral model's assertion that this disability is synonymous with evil and immorality. Many negative images of blindness are related to Judeo-Christian heritage, where blindness is often associated with death, a lack of enlightenment, or punishment for sins. Overall, most blind or visually impaired people view themselves as having a difference rather than a dysfunction, despite persistent stereotypes of them as helpless and dependent. For many, the real problem is not the loss of eyesight, but the misunderstanding the general public has about blind people's abilities (Mackelprang & Salsgiver, 1999).

One of the greatest challenges for persons with visual disabilities is in finding meaningful employment. The unemployment rate for this population is approximately 70% for persons aged 16 to 64 (Mackelprang & Salsgiver, 1999). Many who do have jobs are underemployed or working in positions that do not suit their talents or interests because of persistent societal attitudes and a lack of accommodations. Professional identity issues often center around feelings of worthlessness and a lack of meaning in life, including a sense of having a spiritual void.

Persons with Developmental Disabilities

Developmental disabilities are acquired during childhood and persist throughout one's life. The term has been generally applied to individuals who require ongoing support in more than one major life activity in order to fully participate in an integrated community. For persons with developmental disabilities, support may be required for mobility, communication, self-care, and learning as necessary for independent living, employment, and self-sufficiency (Brown, 1991).

Developmental disabilities are often associated with intellectual disabilities, a more current and appropriate term than "mental retardation." Most people with intellectual disabilities and their families are offended by the mental retardation label, because of the stigma associated with "retard." Persons with intellectual disabilities generally learn at a slower rate (particularly with complex tasks), are slower to generalize information, and may not learn from past situations. Processing social information can be particularly challenging, and they may respond to social situations differently than most people (Winnick, 1995).

Autism is a developmental disability that impacts an individual's ability to communicate with others, understand language, and relate to others. Persons with autism often have inconsistent patterns of sensory responses and vary widely in their abilities as a group and as individuals. Although many autistic individuals are unable to develop meaningful verbal language, other notable individuals with a mild form of autism called Asperger's disorder have become professors, scientists, and authors. For most, however, the disability is pervasive and lifelong, and development can be inconsistent and idiosyncratic. A child with autism, for example, may be able to name all of the world's countries and their capitols while being unable to recall and follow basic classroom instructions.

Societal strategies for addressing the needs of people with developmental disabilities and their families have changed drastically over the past three generations. Two generations ago, children labeled as "mental defectives" were institutionalized as "patients" and were provided with no education or meaningful life skills. A generation ago, while private and governmental institutionalization was still common, increasing numbers of families opted to keep children with developmental disabilities in the family home. Without services or attitudes that promoted independence, these individuals often became "perpetual children," remaining dependent and sheltered throughout their lives. Today's young adults with developmental disabilities represent the first generation of individuals who have been provided with education and community services designed to promote independent living. A medical model approach has often neglected the rights of individuals with developmental disabilities to make decisions for themselves. This model persists today, with both disabled persons and their parents being fearful of taking steps towards self-determination.

The stigma associated with developmental disabilities in general and intellectual disabilities in particular reflects the pervasive attitudes about the values placed on intelligence and independence in society. Mental health literature abounds with examples of how parents must "grieve" for a child with a developmental disability, and this tragedy may create "chronic sorrow" in the lives of families. However, a diversity model approach would suggest that parents grieve more for the lack of opportunities and resources afforded their child. Parents who perpetuate grief for the "normal" child they expected are actually grieving the birth of a child that society has taught them is not as valuable as children without disabilities (Niemann, 2000a). Conversely, parents who maintain a sense of spirituality report placing greater value on their child and their child's progress and abilities (Niemann, 2000b).

Persons with Psychiatric Disabilities

The needs of persons with severe and persistent psychiatric disabilities, such as schizophrenia, major depression, and bipolar disorder, are increasingly being included in the movement for improved awareness, rights, and resources for those with disabilities (Wedenoja, 1999). Perhaps no other group has encountered more negative attributes than those diagnosed with mental illness. Psychiatric disabilities have often been associated with violent and/or evil behavior, despite no evidence that suggests persons with psychiatric diagnoses are responsible for any more violent acts or crimes than those without diagnoses. Historically, such individuals have been characterized as being "possessed by Satan" in Judeo-Christian traditions. The mental health community has also contributed to the stigma associated with psychiatric disabilities, often blaming parents, especially mothers, or blaming the weak moral character of the individual.

Recent medical research regarding brain dynamics and chemistry has been helpful, however, in increasing the social awareness of psychiatric disabilities. In popular culture, the critical and commercial success of the movie *A Beautiful Mind* (2001) has increased public awareness of schizophrenia from a disability perspective. However, media images still abound with images of "psycho killers" and "lunatics" who are evil and subhuman.

Psychiatric disabilities encompass a wide variety of conditions with a complex range of variable effects. Adding to the uncertainty and stress for persons experiencing psychiatric disabilities and their families is the inability to predict the course or severity of symptoms (Roland, 1994). At the time of onset, which may be gradual or sudden, few reliable predictors occur that would foretell whether the person will face a future of episodic effects, persistent and/or severe impairments, or no further impairments at all. Shock and disbelief are common reactions when the diagnosis of a psychiatric disability is made because of the severe social stigma, a lack of apparent cause or warning, and the significant behavioral and personality changes that may occur. Acceptance of the diagnosis, along with accepting responsibility for disability management, is considered central to adapting to life with a psychiatric disability.

Perhaps no other disability population is as severely stigmatized as a family with a psychiatrically disabled child. Because the family has historically been blamed for the occurrence of psychiatric disability, remnants of this belief system are still found in the mental health delivery system and in society. Families are often left out of decision-making, denied information, and given inadequate resources for overall family health. An increasingly family-oriented focus, however, has been emerging with an emphasis on family empowerment, family education, and the building of collaborative relationships (Lefley & Wasow, 1994).

Persons with mild cognitive disabilities

In the past two to three decades, increasing attention has been devoted to the needs of individuals with less severe cognitive disabilities, such as learning disabilities and attention deficit hyperactivity disorder (ADHD). Mild cognitive disabilities may also result from a traumatic head injury (TMI). Sometimes termed "hidden disabilities," mild cognitive disabilities affect not only academic learning but important social skills. To varying degrees, these individuals struggle with intuiting and applying complex rules governing social behavior, and they may be rejected or misunderstood by their peer group.

Individuals with mild cognitive disabilities often fall between the cracks regarding special education and rehabilitative services. Children with mild cognitive limitations (MCLs) are often expected to become independent adults with little or no access to specialized supports beyond special education services received during the school day, if they qualify. Adults with MCLs face challenges in every aspect of life, including income security, employment, housing, health, and spiritual well-being. Termed the "forgotten generation," these adults represent the first generation of people with MCLs who have been diagnosed with learning challenges and educated in the same schools as their peers without disabilities, but who have not been provided with the resources to live fully integrated lives in adulthood (Tymchuk, Lakin, & Luckasson, 2001).

A great deal of controversy surrounds the diagnosis and treatment of mild cognitive disabilities. Some argue that disabilities such as ADHD are largely overdiagnosed and that a disability label stigmatizes a child and steers his or her family toward a simplistic pharmacological solution to behavior problems embedded in family dynamics. Others feel that being able to employ a common language in describing the learning/social/behavioral challenges makes them more understandable and manageable.

Common Spiritual/Religious Themes

"Why did God do this to me? What have I done to deserve this? Why is God punishing me this way?"

According to Helen Betenbaugh (2000), an Episcopal priest with a mobility disability, these are the near-universal questions asked by those newly experiencing a permanent disability. Although clergy from nearly every faith would assure any disabled person that their disabilities had nothing at all to do with God's wrath or God's need for vengeance, these questions persist as individuals struggle to find the meaning of their condition.

Whether a disability is congenital or acquired, individuals and families will face feelings of fear, loss, and anger. Many encounter crises of faith, yet most individuals with disabilities report that having strong spiritual convictions prior to encountering the disability led to positive coping and even spiritual growth. Increasingly, spirituality is being recognized as a tremendous source of comfort, support, and meaning for those with disabilities and their families.

Adaptation to Acquired Disabilities

Adults who were already incorporating spirituality into their lives as a core dimension of their identity before acquiring a disability tend to use those preexisting spiritual resources when adapting to their situations. On the other hand, those without strong spiritual beliefs prior to acquiring a disability are less likely to incorporate spirituality into their adaptation (Houston, 2000). Although participating in religious activities is cited as important to a positive adaptation, it may not be as significant as individuals' personal relationship with a perceived higher power. For many, cherished spiritual beliefs cannot be separated from the experience of acquiring a disability through illness or accident. For individuals embedded in faith traditions that include participation in religious communities, encountering challenges or difficulties in adapting to acquired disabilities often contributes to eventual spiritual growth. Ultimately, preexisting spiritual beliefs have been found to provide meaning, assistance with coping, and other intrapersonal, interpersonal, and societal benefits (Treloar, 1999).

Spiritual Meaning Through a Disability

For many individuals, particularly those with mobility or sensory disabilities, finding meaning in their experience means seeing their disabled bodies as valuable and crucial to their holistic identities. They view their existence as having spiritual gifts bestowed rather than as having afflictions, and they are more concerned with removing societal barriers than with changing themselves, especially when such "cures" are unlikely. For some, a disability is a blessing rather than a curse, and brings rewards to those whose lives are affected.

Are we going to engineer disabling illness out of existence? I don't think so; I think I chose my disability before I came into this life for distinct learning purposes. Since it has taught me to develop trust, patience, tolerance for dependency and frustration, laser-like attention, and clear, sharp, memory images, I have to wonder if such characteristics were among my soul's intentions. If vulnerability to poliovirus had been engineered out of existence, I have to wonder if I would have experienced a spinal cord injury—yielding paralysis plus disrupted sensory and autonomic functioning—to accomplish them? (Vash, 2001, p. 34)

Creating Family Meaning

Increasing attention has been given to the positive ways families derive meaning from having a disabled child (Stainton & Besser, 1998). Spirituality, often expressed as transformative growth and change, has emerged as an integral component of a family's search for meaning.

Mothers raising children with chronic physical disabilities such as spina bifida or cerebral palsy report for themselves lower levels of disability-related stress when they maintain a higher intrinsic (as opposed to extrinsic) religious orientation. This suggests that an internal sense of spirituality helps these mothers cope with the challenges associated with a disability (Horton, 1999).

Stainton & Besser's (1998) qualitative study examined the effects of spirituality on the families of children with an intellectual disability. It concluded that spirituality served as a source of joy and happiness; it increased one's sense of purpose and priorities; it expanded personal and social networks, as well as community involvement; and it led to family unity. It also increased tolerance and understanding, personal growth and strength, and positive impacts on the community. Furthermore, parents' statements about a child's disability provide an insight into how families incorporate spirituality into their lives, such as "Whatever God gives you, He has prepared you for, and He won't give you any more than you can handle" (Weisner, Beizer, & Stolze, 1991, p. 659).

Reflecting on raising a child with a disability, many parents report positive spiritual experiences. Parents often find meaning in their parenting roles and feel that their special children are blessings from God. Parents make comments such as "It's God's plan . . . he was the child that was meant for us" (Haworth et al., 1996, p. 277), reflecting a view that parents are specially chosen by a higher power to receive a child with special needs. In this way, parents view their child as an opportunity for a greater connection with God rather than as a burden to be shouldered.

Moreover, Fewel (1996), in her work with mothers of children with developmental disabilities, suggested that belonging to a religious organization provides families with a variety of support for assisting with the daily living realities of raising the child. A church, temple, or other house of worship may provide disabled children and their families with structural support, including the opportunity to participate in religious ceremonies such as baptism and marriage. From activities such as these, families may obtain a sense of welcomeness and belonging. Faith communities often offer a number of ministry projects that may be meaningful for disabled members. Reporting the comments of a mother of a child with a developmental disability, Weisner et al. (1991) noted the importance of religious participation: "It's a nice experience for the entire family. Jason (a child with developmental disability) loves Sunday school" (p. 655).

Sense of Self and Self-Efficacy

Research has suggested that having a positive sense of self is more significant than the severity of the disability in predicting how well all persons adapt to the disability itself (Nosek & Hughes, 2001). In a philosophical framework, a sense of self can be interpreted as a construct with strongly spiritual dimensions, and the strength that comes from it can be interpreted as having divine origins. A sense of self includes three aspects: self-esteem, the self in connection to others, and self-efficacy. All of these have been shown to be enhanced through a meaningful and positive relationship with a higher power.

As applied to individuals with disabilities, self-efficacy is the power to manage the practical challenges of a disability, to accept limitations while engaging in behaviors to promote wellness, and to counter the barriers and discrimination in society while not resigning oneself to a life of resentment and frustration. Individuals with high self-efficacy often draw upon a spiritual power that is inherent to their sense of self. Although this spirituality is often identified with a higher power, it may also be defined as a personal belief system that allows one to overcome and even thrive in the face of obstacles and challenges.

Finding a Community of Worship

For many individuals with disabilities, finding a community of worship that meets their spiritual needs is an essential component of their faith. Membership in a church, temple, or other house of worship satisfies the need for a connection to a higher power as well as the need to be part of a community of like-minded worshipers. Belonging to a faith community provides support and opportunities for interaction with others though common acts of good will and service to a higher power.

For some with disabilities, the need for structure, order, and sensate experiences is essential to experiencing spiritual connectedness. Kathy Lisner Grant, an adult with autism, articulates the importance of finding a spiritual home in the Orthodox Christian Church:

> . . . as a person with autism, the liturgy appealed to all my senses. For my eyes, there were icons of saints, the Theotokos, and Jesus. For my nose, there was the incense that the priest used. For my ears, there was the music, because the entire service is sung. And for my mind, there was the theology, history, and lives of saints, the Theotokos, the apostles, Jesus, and the Bible. I also like the vestment the priest wears. (Grant, 2000, p. 245)

Margaret Nosek, a rehabilitation counselor and researcher who describes herself as having a severe physical disability, details a spiritual journey that lead to her finding a home in the Quaker faith while retaining her Eastern spirituality:

> . . . I finally understood that the value of suffering is your ability to transcend it as Christ and Shri Ramakrishna both did. My disability is almost irrelevant in this context. The meeting had taken extraordi-

nary efforts to make their facilities accessible, and offers of help when needed flow freely. . . . My involvement with the Quakers has opened a new channel in my identity that has burst through the feelings of disconnection and isolation that I have struggled with all my life as a single, career oriented, disabled woman. I can now add (an additional) characteristic—I am part of a community of worshipers. (Nosek & Hughes, 2001, p. 26)

Spiritual Needs of Caregivers

Much attention has been given to the "caregiver burden" caused by caring for a person with a disability. Although families are frequently stressed when it comes to finding time and resources for those with special needs, much of this stress could be alleviated with increased community resources. Finding opportunities for the disabled individual to be more independent and involved in the community is another solution as well. The caregiver/care receiver relationship is recursive, and concordance between the care receiver and the caregiver's emotional distress may be high, meaning that caregivers and care receivers frequently contribute to the emotional well-being of one another (Rabkin, Wagner, & Del-Bene, 2000). Caregivers of persons with Alzheimer's disease experience less of a burden when they report a higher level of spirituality or a more satisfying relationship with God in their lives (Mullins-Rivera, 1998). Also, caregivers of persons with intellectual disabilities in residential facilities experience fewer burnout symptoms when they report satisfying religious affiliations and practices (Shaddock, Hill, & van Limbeck, 1998).

An Overlooked Dimension of Counseling

Although it is important to recognize that spirituality has been neglected in the field of rehabilitation counseling, it is also crucial to examine the reasons for this problem. These include counseling's emulation of empirical science, an overgeneralized separation of Church and State, and the counseling profession's immersion in technocratic society (McCarthy, 1995).

As previously discussed, concepts such as the medical model and the evolving genetic model of disabilities have shaped the way disabilities are socially constructed and consequently the way disabled people are treated. The constructions of disabilities also operate to define and confine the spiritual journey of disabled people (Fitzgerald, 1997). Specifically, spiritual needs have been identified as a neglected element in community-integration programs for persons with brain injuries (Minnes, Buell, Lou-Nolte, McColl, Carlson, & Johnston, 2001).

Challenges in Accessing Client Spirituality

Despite the importance of spirituality in the lives of many disabled individuals, several barriers and challenges persist in helping clients access their spirituality as a source of comfort, support, and meaning. Counselors need to be aware of the potential obstacles to spirituality in the lives of clients with disabilities.

Overcoming Negative Attributions Rooted in Traditional Theologies

Rose (1997) examined the treatment and attitudes of religious institutions toward persons with physical or mental disabilities, theorizing that they stem from ancient beliefs about the nature of disabilities and their relationship to God. It has been hypothesized that several potentially disempowering themes have been implicit or explicit in Jewish and Christian religious teachings. As previously mentioned, these include seeing a disability as a sign of punishment or an evil incarnation, as a challenge to divine perfection, as a reason for pity and charity, and as incompetence and exemption in religious practice. In a study of children with developmental disabilities, one parent commented, "I just went through a phase of blaming myself . . . that Amy was the way she was because of my past sins" (Haworth, Hill, & Masters, 1996, p. 274). Perhaps these Judeo-Christian constructions of disabilities, rooted in ancient times and rejected by a majority of Jews and Christians today, arose from a primitive human fear of difference (from the "norm"). This fear has provided the impetus for labeling certain groups as "others" and excluding them from moral communities and worship traditions (Fitzgerald, 1997).

Miles (1995) suggested that disabilities have been constructed within Eastern cultures in terms that are similar to the Judeo-Christian constructions of disability:

> . . . [at] the "surface level" of history, these religions [Islam, Buddhism, and Hinduism] have produced little different from the bag of ideas that Christianity held . . . Disability did not figure in creeds or articles of belief. Insofar as disabilities were found meaningful it was as misfortunes, sent by deity, fate, karma; often associated with parental or personal sin. (Miles, 1995, p.52)

Many religious traditions are rooted in a construction of disabilities as punishments for sins of the family, as great blessings (the "holy innocent"), or as vehicles through which others can gain spiritual status (the object of pit and service). The common thread in all these constructions is that people with disabilities remain outside the norm, unaccepted for what and who they are as individuals (Fitzgerald, 1997). A higher power is often credited with healing powers that may cure disabilities or heal afflictions. However, individuals with disabilities feel most empowered and supported by a spiritual approach that takes a broader view of the concept of healing.

Many persons with permanent disabilities fall away, discouraged and disgusted by the church's inability to separate healing and cure, as well as their failure to recognize that a person can be healed, whole, and still live in a visibly broken, "malfunctioning" body. The church, by its teachings both explicit and implicit, says that we are the visible objectification of sin, that we are victims needing the patronization, the pity, and "charity" of the church, rather than a source of wisdom, of an experience of God and the Holy Spirit that may be far deeper, far richer, and far fuller than that of a "normal" person (Betenbaugh, p. 207).

Gaining Access to Faith Communities

Accessibility in general is frequently cited as a problem for individuals with disabilities. At times, religious communities can apply overly rigid standards for participation in rites or services, or they lack the motivation to provide meaningful accommodations. Individuals with disabilities may not feel welcome or be able to fully participate in faith communities that do not actively address their needs. "Our minister is not flexible. He thinks either you're there on time or you don't need to bother coming," commented a parent of a child with a developmental disability, reflecting the unhelpful attitudes found in some faith organizations (Haworth et al., 1996, p. 274.)

Jill Peyton, a marriage and family counselor with a strong Christian identity, frequently encounters barriers in advocating for her adult daughter's full participation in their family's church activities and ministries. Although Kristen, a young woman with a developmental disability including autistic traits, was initially welcomed into the church choir, she was asked to withdraw when it was determined that her tendency to sing along with the soloist would be distracting and confusing to the other parishioners (personal communication, 2002). People suffering from various forms of dementia, especially Alzheimer's disease, may be unable to gain access to houses of worship or find spiritual meaning by attending traditional religious services. In theory, faith communities and churches as organizations can assist these people in a variety of ways. Rehabilitation counselors can take a role in assisting religious communities by helping congregations in minimizing communication difficulties during one-to-one pastoral visits, simplifying religious services for nursing home residents, and providing guidance when a practicing church minister develops symptoms (Elliot, 1997).

Addressing Anger Toward a Higher Power

Anger is a component of loss, and most individuals and families experience loss when encountering a disability. Expressions of anger toward a higher power are often developmental and expected in the face of losses associated with a disability. Although for most this can lead to a deeper understanding of the role of spirituality in their lives, some become mired in anger and find themselves unable to establish meaningful dialogues with a higher power or to participate in faith communities.

Both the disability and the associated existential questions of "why" can initiate a crisis of faith for some individuals. Some parents have spoken of the anger they feel towards God because of their children's disabilities (Haworth et al., 1996; Weisner et al., 1991):

> When Michelle was born—there was no God. I was angry, I was extremely angry. There just couldn't have been a God at that point, nobody could have brought that on. There was just no reason for it. And I do have trouble resolving that, to accept that God gave me a child that's handicapped is not my picture of the way things are supposed to go. In spite of other people having it, it wasn't supposed to happen to *me*, and that's not resolved with me, yet. But I do believe in God, but this is a conflict I have. And to say that God created Michelle this way—I don't like that idea at all. This is something that happened beyond control, and I don't have it fully reckoned with myself.
>
> . . . And I said to my husband, before we got the results, I said, "If they turn up something wrong with Sean, I'll never set foot inside a church again, because I kind of feel like, why should I go there and sing these songs of praise to God, when this has happened to me? I think I need to talk to the minister about it, and maybe he could explain to me why this has happened." (Weiser et al., 1991, p. 649)

Lane (1995) examined why anger is necessary and how it empowers people with disabilities to seek justice and equality in their efforts to live a full and active life. Anger is a component in the grief cycle and is experienced when loss occurs, as in the losses associated with a disability. Individuals with disabilities feel anger due to the actual and societal impositions of their limitations, lack of power, fear of desires and needs, and feeling unimportant. Anger can become destructive when the losses and needs of people with disabilities are repeatedly ignored. Expressing anger against God and forgiving God are important aspects of the faith journey. The ability to question God is in direct relationship to one's relationship with God. Part of the faith journey of many people with disabilities lies in their ability to question God.

For those with disabilities associated with chronic pain, loss of mobility or senses, or degenerative illness, suffering is an undeniable component of a disability:

> Suffering is a radical challenge to the meaning of human existence. The problem of suffering raises the questions about good and evil, and the source of evil. Much of our anger at God may come in the form of asking hard questions, for which there may be no answers. Most of the questions have to be asked in order for us to struggle toward the answer — which will be different for each of us. We find God in our questioning, not in ready-made answers from those who know nothing of suffering. We discover God in seeking to question the meaning of life, the meaning of suffering, and the meaning of evil. Questioning is costly: it can be as painful as the suffering itself. (Lane, 1995, p. 105)

Forgiveness is an important element in every healthy and deepening relationship. If managed well, anger can play a positive and creative role in the lives of persons with disabilities.

Suggested Approaches and Interventions

Although mental health literature has often either omitted the needs of clients with disabilities or relied on a primarily medical model for providing services, the rehabilitation counseling profession has increasingly called for more reliance on the diversity model in order to craft counseling interventions for disabled persons. Mental health counselors are also being challenged to actively incorporate spirituality as a component of wellness in counseling individuals and families facing the challenges associated with disabilities.

Assessment of Spirituality

Dunbar (2002) described spiritual energy as an innate presence that takes the form of a passionate, driving, focused, and resilient energy. A pastoral counselor, Dunbar developed a clinical instrument to measure the spiritual strengths of those facing long-term disability rehabilitation, such as that stemming from a stroke or accident. The Pastoral Assessment of Spirituality Scores (PASS) incorporates the three constructs of holistic spirituality, (a) spiritual energy; (b) faith, including formal or informal theological or credo elements and specific beliefs, and (c) faith acting, including faith behaviors such as active participation in faith community worship, practices, and service. PASS helps counselors determine the client's level of spirituality and develop interventions for incorporating spirituality as a resource in order to achieve rehabilitation goals and spiritual growth. Specific factors of the PASS include:

- Degree of relationship with God or higher power
- Sense of meaning and purpose in life
- Hope for present or future
- Positive attitude toward cooperating with others in achieving goals
- Passion and energy to devote to progress in achieving goals
- Passion and energy to devote to adapting to disability-related lifestyle changes

Spirituality Incorporation

In incorporating spirituality as a part of individual, family, and group counseling, counselors need to consider the following suggestions:

Check Attitudinal Biases Towards Disability

The attitudes of those who are able-bodied towards disabilities and those with disabilities are a significant factor in the lives of disabled persons (Olkin, 1999). Although counselors may feel that they are less judgmental and more rooted in unconditional, positive regard than the public in general, counselors are human and may hold attitudes based on fear, lack of information, or discomfort. It is important that counselors examine how their own faith traditions regard disabilities and that they be mindful of imposing a disempowering construction on their clients. Well-meaning comments or interventions can be unhelpful at best and harmful at worst. Some examples of counselor statements that reflect an attitudinal bias toward disability include the following:

- Parents should "grieve the loss of the normal child."
- The client's disability is "God's will."
- The client must be very special to have encountered the disability.
- Clients should establish career goals for helping others "like them."

Addressing attitudinal biases towards disabilities is similar to addressing biases against members of ethnic or cultural minority groups. It makes counselors uncomfortable to consider that all human beings hold some prejudices, regardless of their good intentions. It is also understandable when individuals living with a disability hold on to disempowering views of themselves and their worth.

Incorporate Spirituality into a Diversity Model Approach

Helping clients view their disability as an element of diversity is an important approach in working with individuals and families. Although spirituality may be seen as implied in the diversity model, this model does not directly address the spiritual needs of disabled individuals or the importance of spirituality as a source of strength. Many disability rights advocates point to religious traditions as historically marginalizing and stigmatizing those with disabilities. A direct discussion of individual and family spirituality for disabled clients is often omitted. Counselors are challenged to view disabilities from the perspective of the diversity model while incorporating client spirituality as a positive force for growth and change.

Evaluate Client's Level of Identification with Disability

How clients view their disabilities varies widely. Some disabilities, such as mild mobility disabilities or cognitive disabilities, may not even be seen as disabilities at all. For these individuals, a disability label may be a relatively unimportant part of a client's identity and have little impact on their relationship with God or a higher power. For those with pervasive or degenerative disabilities, disability is likely a key component of their identity and is instrumental in a client's construction of spirituality.

Determining a client's level of identification with his or her disability must be carefully assessed. Although it may seem intuitive that severe disabilities are associated with an increased identification of being disabled, this is generally not the case. Determining the meaning of the disability over the course of one's life is client-specific and is based more upon individual introjects along with family and societal messages than on the level of functional impairment.

Another factor within the formation of a disability identity involves recognizing the different stages at which a client or family adopts the disability as a component of their identity. Based on the diversity model and Helms's (1995) racial identity development model, the family disability identity development model posits that families go through stages when adapting to a disability, much as persons of color encounter stages in developing positive ethnic identities (Niemann, 2000b):

- Stage I: Conformity—Despite living with a disability, the family conforms to societal norms, devaluing the disability and strongly identifying with able-bodied or nondisabled persons as ideal or preferable. This stage may be associated with a desire to disguise the disability, keep it from public view, deny its reality, or deny that it represents a need to alter family structures. Families in this stage may incorporate spirituality by praying for a cure or for strength through trying times.
- Stage II: Dissonance—Often triggered by events that feel marginalizing, such as exclusion from social activities or an inability to obtain

services, this stage is characterized by ambivalence and confusion regarding the disability status. No longer able to pretend that the disability does not exist or that society does not in fact view the person as "just like everyone else," families may incorporate spirituality by questioning God, becoming angry at God, or looking to a higher power or faith traditions to find meaning or support.

- Stage III: Immersion/Emersion—During this stage, families of a disabled individual may isolate themselves from other families without a disability factor and strongly identify with others facing similar challenges. Observers (for example, counselors, spiritual leaders, friends, and so on) may define such a family as "obsessed" or "overinvolved" in their quest to join with a disability community in order to learn more and obtain needed services and social connections. Spirituality may be incorporated through a continued reliance on a higher power for strength and meaning, including finding a positive meaning in the disability. Some families may search for faith communities with proactive policies toward individuals with disabilities.

- Stage IV: Internalization—This stage occurs when families continue their identification with others facing similar challenges, but they work toward a positive commitment to the emotional health of all family members. During this period, the disability is incorporated as a component of family identity but does not generally overshadow other family characteristics. Families in this stage of development are characterized by logical problem-solving approaches to disability-related challenges, often mobilizing support from the disability community and culture.

  This is a less crisis-oriented stage for families and is often a period of reentry into worship activities and faith communities. As families begin to incorporate the disability into their identity, they become increasingly tolerant of their differences and increasingly mindful of the challenges posed by the outside world. For many, spirituality is a key component of the journey toward addressing such challenges with a clear sense of purpose.

- Stage V: Integrative Awareness—At this stage, families begin to see themselves not only as part of the disability community or culture but as part of the community at large. Families at this stage often describe a transformative process whereby they can now empathize and collaborate with members of other marginalized groups. Families at this stage may still see themselves as crusaders, but they can process information about the disability with increasing flexibility and complexity. Family decisions may be guided by a sense of social justice based on deep spiritual convictions.

Spirituality is a powerful force in the lives of families who have reached the stage of integrative awareness. These families become committed to the rights of others who face discrimination as they continue to strive for the rights of their disabled family member. Regardless of faith traditions or the degree of religiosity, these are families who operate at a high level of moral reasoning. Having a member with a disability has brought the best out in them collectively and individually, and they have found meaning in growing through their experience, however difficult the challenges associated with the disability may be.

It is important to assess where family members are with respect to disability identity development before implementing counseling interventions. Clients at earlier stages may not benefit from counseling strategies emphasizing empowerment. Recall that all change involves grieving, and periods of grieving may be longer for families who embrace religious traditions or ideologies that view a disability as tragic. Often, these families need time and nonjudgmental support while they grapple with their fear, sadness, and anger. It is not possible to propel families to different stages if they are not ready or willing; families must find their own way to make meaning out of their losses and may do so in ways that do not fit a stage model.

Family members also may not encounter stages at the same times. Anecdotally, it is noted that mothers of disabled children often react with strong emotions, followed by an intense desire for information and action, quickly entering stages I, II, and III. Fathers may lag behind, sometimes worrying more about pragmatic matters such as finances and in-home care without addressing family identity issues until later. Furthermore, families may revisit early stages during times of stress or developmental milestones. For example, the parents of an adolescent with a developmental disability may experience dissonance followed by immersion when they realize that their child may not be able to drive, date, or achieve a diploma in the same manner as his or her peers.

Call upon Existing Spiritual Resources of the Client

Counselors need to be aware of the existing spiritual resources of their client. These include not only faith traditions but the client's sense of hope, passion, meaning, and relationship with a higher power. For clients who struggle to find a meaningful sense of spirituality or relationship with a higher power, a powerful intervention is to construct a "spirituality story," or a history of one's spirituality. This may take the form of a written journal, a series of taped prayers or conversations with God or a higher power, or a collection of pictures or visual representations. Regardless of the disability, clients can use this to identify when and how spirituality was present in their lives in the past, and how they might invite spirituality to become a part of their lives in the present. For some clients, it may be helpful to encourage them to identify a spiritual mentor, perhaps a clergy member or spiritual leader in the community, who will guide them toward a greater sense of connectedness or direction on the spiritual path of their choosing.

Prayer and meditation have been noted as helpful for individuals facing specific challenges associated with a disability. For example, prayer has been effectively used as a coping skill in managing pain with adults (Rapp, Rejeski, & Miller, 2000).

Consider Client Gender and Culture

Other important factors in counseling persons with disability-related challenges include gender and culture. Women with disabilities may benefit from narrative approaches by learning to understand and tell their stories as part of a spiritual journey. Spirituality teaches them to consciously rather than passively live their stories, to find empowerment and freedom in order to transcend disability, and to recreate a positive self-image (Lane, 1992). Women with disabilities are also more inclined to need interconnectedness as a component of their spirituality and often seek a community of worship. Studies conducted by the Center for Research on Women with Disabilities suggest that women's journeys to find a sense of self in connection to others is a fundamental determinant of self-esteem. Self-efficacy, when perceived as power drawn from a divine source, is an important mechanism used to transcend the challenges that often accompany a disability (Nosek & Hughes, 2001).

It is also important to note how culture may affect the role of the church in the lives of families facing a disability. For example, Latino families with cognitively disabled children have been described as largely affiliated with formal religions. These families describe their faith as a very important component of finding meaning in a child's disability (Skinner, Correa, & Skinner, 2001). In urban African-American families with a disabled child, research has suggested that religious practices in both the home and in the community are associated with positive outcomes (Rogers-Dulan, 1998).

Conclusion

Millions of individuals and families encounter disabilities at various times in their lives. Understanding how people address and create meaning in the face of disability-related challenges involves understanding how society has historically marginalized disabled individuals. Regardless of the disability type or its severity, persons with disabilities have faced prejudice, stereotyping, and discrimination. It is important for counselors to incorporate a diversity approach into their disability-related interventions. Incorporating spirituality into counseling includes gaining an understanding of the unique disability-related challenges faced by the individual as well as his or her own spiritual coping resources. Each disability group is associated with an array of challenges, some based on functional limitations, others on societal and attitudinal barriers. Historically, some theologies have described various disabilities as a symbol of shame or a curse on the family. Some disability categories, such as developmental and psychiatric disabilities, are associated with a particular stigma, evil, or sin. A major challenge for many in finding a "spiritual home" is addressing and overcoming the negative attributions rooted in traditional theologies and replacing these with more empowering and accepting notions of God or a higher power.

In accessing spirituality, persons with disabilities may grow angry at God, but often they will come to find spiritual meaning through living with their disability. For many, it is important to find a community of worship that supports and accepts them for who they are, with or without a disability. Without such acceptance, individuals and families may not connect with others as a component of their spiritual journeys and may find themselves isolated and lonely.

Using a diversity-based approach also means assessing the level of identity development in families and individuals. The degree to which people with disabilities address and incorporate ideas such as disability culture and advocacy influences their response to various therapeutic interventions and strategies. It is also essential that counselors recognize and respect the existing spiritual framework of each client, along with gender and other cultural factors. Maintaining an interpersonal stance that incorporates spirituality as a primary component of strength and growth provides the foundation for counseling.

Case of Bernard and Shari

Bernard and Shari have been referred to couples counseling. They have been married for 15 years. Bernard is an attorney and Shari is freelance writer. They have three children; Brandon, 12; Brenda, 9; and Brianna, 5. Brianna was born very prematurely and as a result has developmental disabilities and health impairments. Her health impairments have improved, but she remains visually and mobility impaired. Her cognitive impairment seems permanent, she requires a number of special interventions, and she has been placed in a special education kindergarten class.

Shari feels that Bernard has abandoned her and the family. He works long hours and is rarely home before their youngest child is in bed. She is also harboring pain over a comment he made several years ago that he wished the doctors had "just let her go to God" instead of saving Brianna to face a life without meaning. Bernard claims he is doing all he can to provide for his family, especially his daughter's future needs. He also feels abandoned because Shari's life seems to revolve around Brianna, and she has little time for him or anything else. Increasingly, Barnard is using alcohol as a means to unwind when he returns home from work.

Shari and Barnard used to attend church in the Baptist faith and belonged to the same church when they first started dating. Since their daughter's birth, they have not found the time to go as a family, although Shari still attends with her mother and sister each Sunday. Shari expresses strong faith in God and credits Him with saving her daughter's life and giving Shari the strength to help her daughter. She is worried, though, that church members will pity Brianna because of her impairments. Barnard is not sure of what he believes anymore and questions a God that would allow Brianna to suffer.

Case of Mark

Mark, a 32-year-old man with multiple sclerosis (MS), moved in with his parents following a difficult transition from using a cane to using a wheelchair. Mark is a copy editor and works full time, though he tires easily and is having increasing difficulty with his eyesight. His parents George and Louise, determined to take care of Mark, are having trouble letting him do anything for himself. Louise in particular treats Mark as if he were helpless and often bursts into tears when she sees her son struggle with various tasks. "I feel like they think I've come home to die," he laments, hoping he can find a way to retain his adult status while living with his parents so he can save money for his own apartment. Mark fears that, although he is likely to live many more years, his quality of life will continue to decline until he has nothing to look forward to. Although he has had several meaningful relationships with women, he has avoided dating since his diagnosis five years ago, thinking few women would be interested in him as a person with MS.

Raised as a Catholic, Mark turned away from his parents' church in his late teens. Since that time, he has considered himself agnostic. However, Mark has begun reading about Buddhism and is becoming increasingly interested in spiritual matters. George and Louise remain devout Catholics.

Case Discussion

For each of the two cases, explore the following questions:

- How would you assess the spirituality of the family members? In what ways would you address spirituality as part of your counseling intervention? How would you use the diversity model to help clients generate alternatives? How would you assess the family identity developmental level regarding the disabilities? How would you use the existing spiritual resources as building blocks for increased spiritual growth?

- If you belong and participate in a faith community, consider the following. How accessible is your temple or church to individuals with mobility impairments? To your knowledge, how many individuals with disabilities are active members? How might your faith community respond to individuals with cognitive disabilities who behave in nontypical ways during worship services? How open would your faith community be to embracing individuals with mobility disabilities, visual disabilities, deafness, developmental disabilities, psychiatric disabilities, and mild cognitive disabilities? Which type do you think your faith community would find hardest to accept and why?

- Consider the following statement regarding the differences in disability types and spirituality. From your own spiritual and therapeutic point of view, how would you respond? "Although the diversity model is fine for purely physical disabilities, it doesn't really apply to individuals with illness, mental disorders, or severe cognitive impairments. These people suffer all their lives, and you can't tell them they are just 'different' or 'special.' Regarding spirituality, these people are hoping and praying for a cure for themselves or their loved ones. Changing society, attitudes, or access doesn't lift the very real burdens of genetic abnormalities and deformities."

- One paradox regarding the parents of those with disabilities is that although "chronic grief" models of how parents react to a child's disability are considered disempowering and outmoded, many parents still express feelings of grief following a diagnosis of disability. How does the family disability development model address this apparent contradiction? What is the role of spirituality in this model?

- Describe ways in which a disability has touched your life. What was your first encounter with a disability? How have your encounters with disabilities affected your spiritual journey? In what ways do you feel you still need to grow regarding disabilities?

References

Betenbaugh, H. R. (2000). Disability: A lived theology. *Theology Today, 57,* 203–210.

Brown, L. (1991). Who are they and what do they want: An essay on TASH. In L. H. Meyer, C. A. Peck, & L. Brown (Eds.), *Critical issues in the lives of people with severe disabilities* (pp. xxv–xxvii). Baltimore, MD: Paul H. Brookes.

Byrd, E. K. (1997). Concepts related to inclusion of the spiritual component in services to persons with disability and chronic illness. *Journal of Applied Rehabilitation Counseling, 24*(4), 26–29.

DoRozario, L. (1997). Spirituality in the lives of people with disability and chronic illness: A creative paradigm of wholeness and reconstruction. *Disability and Rehabilitation: An International Multidisciplinary Journal, 19,* 427–434.

Dunbar, W. C. (2002). *Pastoral assessment of spirituality scores (PASS).* Unpublished manuscript.

Elliot, H. (1997). Religion, spirituality, and dementia: Pastoring to sufferers of Alzheimer's disease and other forms of dementia. *Disability and Rehabilitation: An International Multidisciplinary Journal, 19,* 435–441.

Fine, M., & Asch, A. (1988). Disability beyond stigma: Social interaction, discrimination, and activism. *Journal of Social Issues, 44*(1), 3–21.

Fitzgerald, J. (1997). Reclaiming the whole: Spirit, self, and society. *Disability and Rehabilitation: An International Multidisciplinary Journal, 19,* 407–413.

Grant, K. L. (2000). My Story. *Focus on Autism and Other Developmental Disabilities, 15,* 243–245.

Hahn, H. (1988). The politics of physical differences: Disability and discrimination. *Journal of Social Issues, 44*(1), 3–21.

Haworth, A. M., Hill, A. E., & Glidden, L. M. (1996). Measuring religiousness of parents of children with developmental disabilities. *Mental Retardation, 34,* 271–279.

Helms, J. E. (1995). An update of Helm's white and people of color racial identity development model. In J. Ponterotto, J. Casas, L. Suzuki, & C. Alexander (Eds.), *Handbook of multicultural counseling.* Thousand Oaks, CA: Sage.

Horton, T. V. (1999). The role of religion in the adjustment of mothers of children with chronic physical conditions. *Dissertation Abstracts International, 60 (3B),* 1302.

Houston, E. M. (2000). What are the roles of spiritual and religious practices, attitudes, and beliefs in the lives of people with acquired disabilities? *Dissertation Abstracts International, 61 (2B),* 1065.

Howard, R. (Producer/Director), & Grazer, B. (Producer). (2001). *A beautiful mind* [Motion picture]. United States: Universal Pictures.

Lane, N. J. (1992). A spirituality of well-being: Women with disabilities. *Journal of Applied Rehabilitation Counseling, 23*(4), 52–58.

Lane, N. J. (1995). A theology of anger when living with disability. *Rehabilitation Education, 9,* 97–111.

Lefley, H. P., & Wasow, M. (1994). *Helping families cope with mental illness.* Newark, NJ: Gordon Breach Publishing Group.

Mackelprang, R. W., & Salsgiver, R. O. (1999). *Disability: A diversity model approach in human service practice.* Pacific Grove, CA: Brooks/Cole.

McCarthy, H. (1995). Understanding and reversing rehabilitation counseling's neglect of spirituality. *Rehabilitation Education, 9,* 187–199.

McGoldrick, M., Watson, M., & Benton, W. (1999). Siblings through the life cycle. In B. Carter and M. McGoldrick (Eds.), *The expanded family life cycle: Individual, family, and social perspectives* (3rd ed.) (pp. 153–167). Boston: Allyn and Bacon.

Merrick, J., Morad, M., & Levy, U. (2001). Spiritual health in residential centers for persons with intellectual disability in Israel. A national survey. *International Journal of Adolescent Medicine and Health, 13,* 245–251.

Miles, M. (1995). Disability in an Eastern religious context: Historical perspectives. *Disability and Society, 10,* 52.

Minnes, P., Buell, K., Lou-Nolte, M., McColl, M., Carlson, P., & Johnston, J. (2001). Defining community integration of persons with brain injuries as acculturation: A Canadian perspective. *NeuroRehabilitation, 16,* 3–10.

Mullins-Rivera, E. E. (1998). Predicting burden in caregivers of persons with Alzheimer's disease. *Dissertation Abstracts International, 58 (12B),* 6490.

Niemann, S. H. (2000, February 18). Coping with child's special needs. *The New Orleans Times-Picayune,* p. B-7.

Niemann, S. H. (2000, October). *Reframing disability in family theory and practice.* Paper presented at the annual national conference of American Association of Marriage and Family Therapy, Denver, CO.

Nosek, M. A., & Hughes, R. B. (2001). Psychospiritual aspect of sense of self in women with physical disabilities. *The Journal of Rehabilitation, 67,* 20–31.

Olkin, R. (1999). *What psychotherapists should know about disability.* New York: Guilford Press.

Rabkin, J. G., Wagner, G. J., & Del-Bene, M. (2000). Resilience and distress among amyotrophic lateral sclerosis patients and caregivers. *Psychosomatic Medicine, 62,* 271–129.

Rapp, S. R., Rejeski, W. J., & Miller, M. E. (2000). Physical function among older adults with knee pain: The role of pain coping skills. *Arthritis Care and Research, 13,* 270–279.

Rogers-Dulan, J. (1998). Religious connectedness among urban African-American families who have a child with disabilities. *Mental Retardation, 36,* 91–103.

Rose, A. (1997). "Who causes the blind to see:" Disability and quality of religious life. *Disability and Society, 12,* 395–405.

Shaddock, A. J., Hill, M., & van Limbeck, C. A. H. (1998). Factors associated with burnout in workers in residential facilities for people with an intellectual disability. *Journal of Intellectual and Developmental Disability, 23,* 309–318.

Skinner, D. G., Correa, V., & Skinner, M. (2001). Role of religion in the lives of Latino families of young children with developmental delays. *American Journal of Mental Retardation, 106,* 297–313.

Stainton, T., & Besser, H. (1998). The positive impact of children with and intellectual disability on the family. *Journal of Intellectual and Developmental Disability, 23,* 57–70.

Stokoe, W. (1989). Dimensions of difference: ASL and English-based cultures. In S. Wilcox (Ed.), *American deaf culture: An anthology* (pp. 49–59). Burtonsville, MD: Linstock.

Treloar, L. L. (1999). Perceptions of spiritual beliefs, response to disability, and the church. *Dissertation Abstracts International, 60*(2A), 562.

Tymchuk, A. J., Lakin, K. C., & Luckasson, R. (2001). *The forgotten generation: The status and challenge of adults with mild cognitive limitations.* Brookes Publishing Co.: Baltimore, MD.

Vash, C. L. (2001). Disability, spirituality, and the mapping of the human genome. *The Journal of Rehabilitation, 67,* 33–41.

Wedenoja, M. (1999). Persons with psychiatric disabilities. In R. W. Mackelprang & R. O. Salsgiver (Eds.), *Disability: A diversity model approach in human service practice* (pp. 167–190). Pacific Grove, CA: Brooks/Cole.

Weisner, T. S., Beizer, L., & Stolze, L. (1991). Religion and families of children with developmental delays. *American Journal on Mental Retardation, 95,* 647–662.

Wenig, M. M. (1994). Women with disabilities: A challenge to feminist theology. *Journal of Feminist Studies in Religion, 10,* 129–134.

Winnick, J. P. (1995). *Adapted physical education and sport* (2nd ed.). Champaign, IL: Human Kinetics.

Zak, O. (1996). *Zak's politically incorrect glossary.* Retrieved July 13, 1996, from http://www.weizmann.ac.il/deaf-info/zpig.html

Zink, J. (1992). Adjusting to early- and late-onset disability: A personal perspective. *Generations, 16*(1), 59–61.

CHAPTER 8
Spirituality and Grief

SUSAN FURR, PhD

"I questioned God today." These poignant words were spoken by a grand-mother after learning of a highway accident that led to the deaths of her daughter, son-in-law, and three grandchildren. Just when she most needed the strength of her spiritual beliefs, she was left with questions rather than answers. Often a source of great comfort in times of loss, our spiritual and religious beliefs also can trigger a time of questioning and examination.

In times of loss, spiritual beliefs can provide solace but also can be a source of confusion when life events contradict these beliefs. The relation-ship between spirituality and grief is complicated and often is approached with trepidation by counselors. Although a majority of people in the United States profess some form of religious belief (Kelly, 1995), counselors have been reluctant to explore spiritual issues in counseling. Yet spiritual issues are intricately woven into the loss experience.

A traumatic loss challenges the way in which a person views the world. When spiritual beliefs provide a source of support and an understanding of how loss fits into the larger scheme of life, these beliefs can facilitate coping with the loss. However, the magnitude of the loss may exceed the explana-tory capacity of the beliefs. In either situation, the counselor needs to be comfortable exploring the meaning that the client gives to the beliefs.

Ivey, Ivey, & Simek-Morgan (1997) emphasized the importance of coun-selors addressing spiritual beliefs with clients, because these beliefs influence both the way in which clients construct the meanings of life events and the coping strategies they use to confront challenges. However, counselors may avoid exploring spiritual issues for many reasons. First, many major counseling theories have not incorporated spirituality in their views of human development. In addition, counselors may not believe they are trained to deal with a client's spiritual identity, so they may fail to take into consideration how spirituality influences the way in which a client constructs meaning in his or her life. Finally, counselors may not be knowledgeable about the different beliefs held by clients from diverse cultural backgrounds (Shimabukuro & D'Andrea, 1999). Given these reasons, counselors may not recognize the importance of spiritual issues in addressing loss.

Spirituality and grief are connected in three ways. Two of these connections can be addressed by the question of whether spiritual beliefs are a help or a hindrance to grieving. The resolution of this question leads to the third connection, the role of grief in facilitating spiritual growth. Each of these three areas will be addressed separately as a prelude to examining the ways to utilize spiritual beliefs in grief counseling.

Spiritual Beliefs as a Source of Comfort

For many individuals, spiritual beliefs are expressed through an organized religious community. Kallenburg (2000) examined research on physical health to find that "a religious attitude to life makes traumatic events easier to bear" (p. 123). He stated that religion is an asset in that it provides a social network for support, supplies a system to make meaning of life, and gives hope to the individual. He concluded that an intrinsic religious attitude facilitates good mental health.

In many instances, spiritual beliefs and practices are linked with psychological adjustment after a loss. Spiritual beliefs and practices, the importance of religion, comfort from religion, and optimism emerge as important predictors of psychological well-being among bereaved spouses (Frye, 2001). An indirect link between well-being and religious participation has been found among parents who lost a child in that religious participation is related to perceived social support, which in turn is related to higher levels of well-being (McIntosh, Silver, & Wortman, 1993). In addition, the importance of religion is related to greater cognitive processing of the loss and finding meaning in the loss. Those parents who are more able to find meaning experience less distress.

Bereaved partners of men who died of AIDS respond to the grief of their loss differently according to their spiritual beliefs. Those partners who expressed spiritual beliefs are found to use more positive coping reappraisals, planned problem-solving, and confronting coping methods than those who did not express spiritual beliefs (Richards & Folkman, 1997). In a study examining the factors associated with adapting to the death of a significant person, intrinsic spirituality was found to be one of four factors associated with bereavement adaptation (Gamino, Sewell, & Easterling, 2000). The other factors were seeing some good resulting from the death, having a chance to say goodbye, and spontaneous positive memories of the deceased.

The previously mentioned studies illustrate the positive, measurable effects of spiritual and/or religious beliefs on adapting to a significant loss through death. Traumatic events challenge the individual's cognitive organization of the world. Spiritual beliefs can be a buffer to that challenge in that these beliefs may provide meaning to the loss. Often the first question asked after a loss is "Why did this happen?" This is soon followed by "What does this mean to my life?" In order to help the client discover his or her own answers to these questions, the counselor must first be willing to examine the spiritual and religious framework within which the client functions. When the framework is well developed, the client may find comfort in the tenets of his or her beliefs about how death or loss is viewed or the support provided by the beliefs. Golsworthy and Coyle (1999) found a high value placed on the support provided by an individual's spiritual beliefs. The permanence of this support appeared to be important to the bereaved, and a connection between spiritual and personal support was recognized.

The existing framework of meaning may help contain the impact of the loss, because this belief system influences how loss, particularly death, is viewed (Braun & Berg, 1994). Death may be viewed in terms of an afterlife or a transformation of life's meaning (Marrone, 1999). Individuals with these views seem to have an easier time assimilating the meaning of the loss into their existing belief systems.

Rituals are another important component of many spiritual belief systems and can provide an important strategy for addressing existential challenges. By engaging in rituals, the individual can integrate the meaning of the loss into his or her personal narrative. Rituals offer reassurance and guidance in a structured way that provides support and encourages positive coping (Pargament, 1996). Because many rituals are a part of a shared, communal experience, the individual experiences a connection with others of similar beliefs, both past and present.

Spiritual Beliefs as a Source of Discomfort

In the wake of some traumatic events, answers to the question "why" are not easily found. Doubts and questions may arise about previous beliefs, and the grief experienced may be difficult to reconcile with one's faith (Gamino, Sewell, & Easterling, 2000). Anger toward God is one possible result when the loss is incongruent with one's spiritual beliefs (Batten & Oltjenbruns, 1999). Anguish over being fundamentally mistaken may be expressed unless the belief system is reexamined and expanded to accommodate the loss experience.

Most people want to see the world as a fair and just place where chance plays a limited role. When random events lead to a traumatic loss, this view of the world is upset, and a crisis in faith may result (Marrone, 1999). This crisis may send some on a quest to find new ways of making meaning of the loss, whereas others may reject spiritual beliefs altogether and become bitter over the loss. Such a rejection of beliefs without a reconstruction of new beliefs may lead a person to become "stuck" in his or her grief.

In some cases, an individual may have experienced rejection from the very institutions that had been a source of spiritual meaning. For example, the mother of a child born outside of marriage or the gay teenager who begins to express his sexuality openly may move away from spiritual beliefs after being abandoned by the religious organization. Consequently, prior negative experiences with religion may interfere with the pursuit of spiritual exploration, even though those who are not religiously affiliated have been found to be comforted by spiritual beliefs at the time of loss (Richards & Folkman, 1997).

Although intrinsic (or internal) religiosity has been associated with psychological well-being after a loss, extrinsic (or outward) religiosity may lead to guilt and self-blame. The person experiencing the loss may feel shame due to the belief of letting God down and may question his or her faith in not accepting God's purpose in the loss. If beliefs are built around the concept of divine punishment for sinful acts, then the loss may be conceptualized as the consequence for some lapse in personal behavior and therefore be deserved. The ensuing self-blame and guilt only serve to disrupt the process of grieving.

Spirituality as Both a Source of Comfort and Discomfort

A common experience for those experiencing a loss is to find at times that spirituality is a source of support, but at other times it leads to questioning and doubting one's beliefs. This oscillation between the meaning given to the loss by the spiritual belief system and the uncertainty created by the limits of the beliefs can be an additional source of anxiety to the mourner. Vacillating between these two views may lead the grieving person to feel that grief comes in waves. While hopeful one moment that the loss can be survived, the next moment only brings doubt and misgivings about the future.

Many spiritual individuals are shocked when their beliefs do not protect them from the pain of grieving. A person may believe that a strong faith will buffer him or her from feelings of loss and grief, yet these feelings will inevitably arrive and may leave the mourner overwhelmed with their intensity. Rather than view spiritual beliefs as a protection against grief, it may be more helpful to see spirituality and loss as two separate processes

(Golsworthy & Coyle, 1999). Feelings of loss and the ensuing grief are inevitable but are unrelated to the strength of spiritual beliefs. However, these same spiritual beliefs are a source of support in living with the grief, even if the beliefs do not serve to reduce the grief.

Spiritual Growth Through Grief

Bereavement is a life crisis that can be an impetus for spiritual growth. Adolescents who lost a sibling have reported developing a new perspective of a higher power (Batten & Oltjenbruns, 1999), and college students who lost a family member have expressed positive changes in their life goals (Edmunds & Hooker, 1992). Other mourners describe themselves as becoming more caring toward others, reevaluating what was meaningful in life, and reordering life priorities (Hogan, Morse, & Tason, 1996).

Balk (1999) identified three conditions that are necessary for a life crisis to produce spiritual change. First, the event must create a psychological imbalance that is not easily stabilized. Bereavement, characterized by the disruption of cognitive functioning and emotional upheaval, creates such an imbalance. As mentioned previously, current belief structures may not be adequate to accommodate the loss. Second, there must be time for reflection. The process of working through grief takes time and cannot be rushed. This time allows for reflection and an examination of long-held values and beliefs that can lead to new spiritual insights. Third, the person's life must be forever changed by the crisis. Grief involves a permanently changed reality in that the loss transforms the person's life forever (Hogan & DeSantis, 1992). A significant grief experience provides all of the conditions necessary for spiritual growth to emerge from the loss. But this growth will occur only if the counselor is willing to venture into the client's spiritual world and help the client construct meaning from the loss. We will now examine two approaches that may help facilitate this growth in clients.

Suggested Approaches

Constructivist Approach in Counseling

To understand a client's view of a grief event, the counselor must first recognize that each person is the constructor of his or her phenomenological world (Neimeyer, 1999). Rather than looking for the same grief reaction to the same sort of loss, it is important to begin counseling from a position of "not knowing." Included in the client's perspective is the client's view of spirituality. This view is highly personal and carries strong cultural connotations. Constructivist approaches are particularly helpful when working with culturally diverse clients who maintain a variety of spiritual perspectives (Shimbukuro & D'Andrea, 1999). Spiritual beliefs and traditions have been recognized as important components in Native American psychology (Garrett & Garrett, 1994), in the mental health of the African-American community (Richardson & June, 1997), and in the healing practices favored by Asian immigrants (Chung, Bemak, & Okazaki, 1997). Unless the counselor explores the meaning of spirituality from the viewpoint of the client, the counselor will be unable to assist the client in utilizing the strengths that the spiritual beliefs provide to the client.

To assess the meaning of spirituality for the client, the following questions may be asked. Because spirituality often is not discussed in counseling, it may be necessary to preface the questions with remarks such as, "In times of loss, people often have emotional and spiritual issues they would like to discuss but may not know how to bring them to the attention of the counselor. I would like to ask you some questions that will provide you with the opportunity to explore these issues, if they are important to you."

1. What role, if any, have religion and spirituality played in your life?
2. What religious/spiritual traditions have been important to you (and your family)?
3. How have these traditions influenced the way you have responded to your loss?
4. Often religious rituals are important at a time of loss. What rituals have assisted you in dealing with your grief? What rituals have created difficulties for you in facing your grief?
5. Do you hold any belief in a higher power? If so, what are your perceptions of your higher power during this time of grief?
6. How do people who share your spiritual beliefs or culture normally respond to loss? How does your experience compare to their responses?

These questions are just suggestions for the counselor to use in examining the client's perspective. An atmosphere of total acceptance for the client's worldview must be established. It is important that the counselor develop an understanding of how the construction of the spiritual beliefs is connected to the way the client is responding to the loss. The client needs to tell his or her story as a way of making sense of the loss experience. It is also crucial that the counselor understand the cultural and spiritual context of the client's grief; otherwise, the counselor may misinterpret the client's responses and assess pathology where none exists. The client's spiritual beliefs will influence his or her thoughts about the afterlife, mourning practices, and the relationship between the deceased and the living.

Cognitive Strategies in Grief Counseling

To make sense of a loss, the loss experience must be assimilated into an already existing belief system. These cognitive schemas incorporate any spiritual beliefs valued by the individual. Holding on to cognitive rules that help make sense out of life is important in developing coping strategies. In response to a loss involving death, a belief in an afterlife is one of the most common religious-based assimilation strategies employed by the bereaved (Marrone, 1999). Other spiritual coping strategies include the concept of eventual reunion with the deceased and the belief that the loss served some spiritual purpose, such as inspiring people to do good works or to form closer relationships.

When a loss cannot be assimilated into the existing belief system, a dramatic upheaval in beliefs may occur. For example, an unexplained illness after a lifetime of practicing good health habits may not fit into a client's conceptualization that one will be rewarded for taking care of oneself. An incongruency between what one expects to happen based on his or her beliefs and the actual outcome may render a person's spiritual belief system ineffectual in providing comfort. Thus, the client's spiritual schema may have to expand in order to accommodate the idea that not all events are under the client's control or that God allows bad things to happen to those with strong spiritual beliefs. Often this cognitive perspective is challenged in a search for meaning by reflecting on personal values and learning to appreciate the important things in life.

Counselors can facilitate this process by helping the client identify spiritual beliefs and the impact of these beliefs on grieving. Although the beliefs might provide comfort, the beliefs also create spiritual questions. To be effective, the counselor must be open to the client suspending or even rejecting spiritual tenets and beliefs. During this time of turning away from past beliefs, the client may need additional emotional support until a new set of beliefs is developed that can accommodate the loss.

Before the cognitive aspects of grief can be addressed directly, the counselor needs to be willing to listen to the client's stories. Clients who are grieving can be described as being held captive by their memories, so a need exists to process these memories that hold powerful emotional content (Harvey, Barnes, Carlson, & Haig, 1995). As the counselor listens to these stories, it is important to determine the spiritual beliefs that help sustain the client as well as those beliefs that have been challenged by the loss. Some questions to consider using with the client are listed here:

1. You have mentioned that you just don't know what to believe about God anymore. What were your beliefs prior to this loss?
2. Which of these beliefs has comforted you?

3. Which beliefs have you questioned since your loss?
4. How have your spiritual beliefs been challenged by your loss?
5. Based on what you have learned from your loss, what other beliefs have helped you cope?

Clients need to be able to identify their spiritual beliefs and to question those that are not sufficient in helping with the reconciliation of grief. The client may need permission to see that some long-held beliefs are not rational given the nature of the loss. Instead of feeling guilty over the questioning of beliefs, the client will benefit from a supportive atmosphere where reconstruction of meaning is encouraged. For many adults, spiritual beliefs are not questioned until a significant life event occurs. Consequently, the exploration of beliefs may be viewed as part of a life development process in which the client develops a more adaptive approach to finding meaning in life.

Spirituality and Grief Among the Dying

Our discussion thus far has focused on spirituality and grief among the survivors of loss. However, spiritual issues are prominent among those who are aware they are dying. The dying person experiences repeated losses of control that may overwhelm his or her coping ability (Marrone, 1999). Often, a search for meaning and spiritual purpose is undertaken. Three principle spiritual tasks have been identified for those who are dying (Doka, 1993). First is the need to find meaning in or the significance of life. This meaning may come from a belief system that provides a sense of purpose to life. Second, the person needs to approach death from a framework that is congruent with personal values and lifestyle. Making decisions about the way in which the person will die, such as dying at home, is part of this framework. Finally, the individual has a need to transcend death, meaning that he or she is searching to identify the ways in which his or her life will have meaning after death. For some, this transcendence may take the form of an afterlife, whereas others may take comfort in knowing that their deeds and memory live on in the lives of their loved ones.

To assist the client who is facing death, the counselor must first serve as a companion on this journey. Just being present with the client in a supportive, nonjudgmental way is of immense importance as long as the counselor is comfortable with grief, loss, and death issues. The counselor can use many approaches but may find that creative approaches that help the client open up and expand his or her thinking are more facilitative than traditional ones (Smith, 1993). The use of metaphor and imagery may help the client visualize the meaning he or she seeks from death (i.e., help the client reflect on a life well lived or seek forgiveness for transgressions). Creating rituals may also assist the client in establishing a strong relationship with his or her higher power. In addition, keeping a spiritual journal can foster an ongoing examination of the journey to the end of life.

Exercises

1. If you were counseling a client who recently lost her husband and children in a car accident, what rituals might you and the client think of to help her work through her grief? What spiritual strengths might you explore? What spiritual difficulties might she face?
2. Create a list of questions that a counselor who has not worked with grieving clients might need to address and research prior to the counseling session.
3. As a counselor, how have you dealt with grief and loss in your own life? What helped you through the process? What could have helped you at the time that you didn't know about? Write a brief story about this experience and how you felt about it.

Thomas's Case

Thomas, a 13-year-old boy, was referred to grief counseling following the death of his older brother. The boys were close and were united in trying to be successful while growing up in a high crime neighborhood. They were both bright and inquisitive, with the older brother taking the role of the leader. Thomas adored his older brother and depended on him for emotional support and physical protection. After his brother was accidentally caught in neighborhood gunfire, Thomas experienced a dramatic shift in behavior. He no longer cared about school and began acting out in a rebellious manner. When he was initially referred to counseling, he was sullen and refused to interact with the counselor on more than a superficial level. However, he continued to attend the counseling appointments. The counselor gently persuaded him to talk about his relationship with his brother, and this opened the door for Thomas to eventually talk about his feelings of loss. The counselor then asked what Thomas believed his brother would want for him in the aftermath of his grief. This exploration evolved into an existential examination of how Thomas could best honor his brother's memory. Thomas was able to recapture the meaning school success had given to both his brother's life and his own. For Thomas, this search for meaning came not from a higher power but from recognizing a power greater than himself in the form of his deceased brother.

Case Discussion

- Grief issues frequently are intertwined with spiritual beliefs. How could counselors approach spirituality as an issue of diversity because each individual constructs spiritual meaning from a highly personal perspective?
- How would being open to the importance of spiritual issues as an absolute necessity for clients who have experienced loss foster effectiveness?
- Explain how the following could enhance a counselor's effectiveness with issues of grief and loss:
  a. Striving for personal awareness concerning spirituality.
  b. Openness to the multiplicity of spiritual views that could provide a foundation for an effective exploration of the client's grief.
  c. Awareness of clients' spiritual views in order to enable them to draw strength from integral beliefs and address the core conflicts preventing a reconciliation of grief.

References

Balk, D. E. (1999). Bereavement and spiritual change. *Death Studies, 23*, 486–493.

Batten, M., & Oltjenbruns, K. A. (1999). Adolescent sibling bereavement as a catalyst for spiritual development. *Death Studies, 23*, 529–546.

Braun, M. J., & Berg, D. H. (1994). Meaning reconstruction in the experience of parental bereavement. *Death Studies, 18*, 105–129.

Chung, R. C., Bemak, F., & Okazaki, S. (1997). Counseling Americans of southeast Asian descent: The impact of the refugee experience. In C. C. Lee (Ed.), *Multicultural issues in counseling: New approaches to diversity* (pp. 207–232). Alexandria, VA: American Counseling Association.

Doka, K. J. (1993). *Living with life-threatening illness.* New York: Lexington.

Edmunds, S., & Hooker, K. (1992). Perceived changes in life meaning following bereavement. *Omega, 25*, 307–318.

Frye, P. S. (2001). The unique contribution of key existential factors to the prediction of psychological well-being of older adults following spousal loss. *The Gerontologist, 41*, 69–81.

Gamino, L. A., Sewell, K. W., & Easterling, L. W. (2000). Scott and White study phase 2: Toward an adaptive model of grief. *Death Studies, 24*, 633–660.

Garrett, M. T., & Garrett, J. T. (1994). The path of good medicine: Understanding and counseling Native Americans. *Journal of Multicultural Counseling and Development, 22*, 134–144.

Golsworthy, R., & Coyle, A. (1999). Spiritual beliefs and the search for meaning among older adults. *Mortality, 4*, 21–40.

Harvey, J., Barnes, M., Carlson, H., & Haig, J. (1995). Held captive by their memories: Managing grief in relationships. In S. Duck & J. Wood (Eds.), *Confronting relationship challenges: Understanding relationship processes series, Vol. 5* (pp. 211–233). Thousand Oaks, CA: Sage Publications, Inc.

Hogan, N. S., & DeSantis, L. (1992). Adolescent sibling bereavement: An ongoing attachment. *Qualitative Health Research, 2*, 159–177.

Hogan, N. S., Morse, J. M., & Tason, M. C. (1996). Toward an experiential theory of bereavement. *Omega, 33*, 43–65.

Kallenberg, K. (2000). Spiritual and existential issues in palliative care. *Illness, Crisis, and Loss, 8*, 120–130.

Kelly, E. W. (1995). *Spirituality and religion in counseling and psychotherapy: Diversity in theory and practice.* Alexandria, VA: American Counseling Association.

Ivey, A. E., Ivey, M. B., & Simek-Morgan, L. (1997). *Counseling and psychotherapy: A multicultural perspective* (4th ed.). Boston: Allyn and Bacon.

Marrone, R. (1999). Dying, mourning, and spirituality: A psychological perspective. *Death Studies, 23*, 495–519.

McIntosh, D. N., Silver, R. C., & Wortman, C. B. (1993). Religion's role in adjustment to a negative life event: Coping with the loss of a child. *Journal of Personality and Social Psychology, 65*, 812–821.

Neimeyer, R. A. (1999). Narrative strategies in grief therapy. *Journal of Constructivist Psychology, 12*, 65–85.

Pargament, K. I. (1996). Religious methods of coping: Resources for the conservation and transformation of significance. In E. P. Shafranske (Ed.), *Religion and the clinical practice of psychology* (pp. 215–240). Washington, D.C.: American Psychological Association.

Richards, T. A., & Folkman, S. (1997). Spiritual aspects of loss at the time of a partner's death from AIDS. *Death Studies, 21*, 527–552.

Richardson, B. L., & June, L. N. (1997). Utilizing and maximizing the resources of the African-American church: Strategies and tools for counseling professionals. In C. C. Lee (Ed.), *Multicultural issues in counseling: New approaches to diversity* (pp. 155–170). Alexandria, VA: American Counseling Association.

Shimabukuro, K. P., & D'Andrea, J. D. (1999). Addressing spiritual issues from a multicultural perspective: The case of the grieving Filipino boy. *Journal of Multicultural Counseling and Development, 27*, 221–239.

Smith, D. C. (1993). Exploring the religious-spiritual needs of the dying. *Counseling and Values, 37*, 71–77.

SECTION II

CHAPTER 9
African-Americans

Recent demographic reports indicate that approximately 35.4 million African-Americans are living in the United States. This represents almost 13% of the total U.S. population (Russell, 1998). This 35.4 million represents an 11% increase over the 30.8 million African-Americans who lived in the United States in 1991 (Locke, 1992) and a 33% increase over the 26.4 million African-Americans who resided in this country in 1980 (U.S. Bureau of the Census, 1986). Given the multifaceted problems many African-Americans encounter as a result of being subjected to racism, poverty, and other forms of social and political disadvantages, it is incumbent on mental health professionals to seek ways of helping to promote the well-being of persons in this cultural/racial group (Parham, White, & Ajamu, 1999).

Spirituality and religion have been essential components in the cultural heritage of African-Americans and served as major sources of strength and survival. However, few attempts have been made to discuss the central role these issues can play in the clinical work of mental health professionals for this population (Boyd-Franklin, 1989; Stevenson, 1990).

Although spirituality and religion are often connected, they hold very different meanings in the lives of African-Americans. Many within this ethnic population have an internalized sense of the spirit but are often not affiliated with an organized religion or church (Boyd-Franklin, 1989). African-American men see spirituality and religion as two distinct entities (Watts, 1993). Spirituality refers to an outlook on life and a personal relationship with God, whereas religion refers to church doctrine. Brisbane and

149

Wamble (1985/1986) stress that African-American spiritual power and a belief in something higher than themselves provide a reinforcing function of conviction and fulfillment.

Research within the last 10 years has reported that the majority of African-Americans are affiliated with a religious denomination (Taylor, Chatters, Jayakody, & Levin, 1996). Fifty-two percent of African-Americans report their religious denomination as Baptist, almost 12% identify themselves as Methodist, and 6% identify themselves as Catholic (Taylor & Chatters, 1991). Additionally, an estimated 30% of American Muslims are African-American (Hoge, 1996). Affiliation with a particular ideology is viewed as an important component of the psychological health of many African-Americans (Ellison, 1993; Moore, 1991), and nonaffiliation with a specific religion may also represent a form of spiritual expression (Taylor, 1988).

The church to which African-Americans belong often presents a means of coping with adversity, preserving family life, and encouraging involvement in current social issues (Moore, 1991). Although some mental health workers may view the African-American Church as one that tends to be narrow in its perspective on values or morals, it is important to remember that African-Americans often combine theology and psychology. This blend influences their mental health issues (Millet, Richardson, & June, 1977; Sullivan, Schwebel, & Myers, 1996). Furthermore, McCullough's (1999) study indicated that people's religious involvement was positively associated with good mental health, including lower degrees of depression and suicidal behavior.

It is important to note that not all counselors can work effectively with clients who have certain spiritual or religious beliefs. These include counselors who rigidly adhere to their own personal beliefs, overidentify with their clients' beliefs, or fail to see their clients' pathological use of spirituality or religion (Mendes, 1982). Such practices may have important implications for a counselor effectively working with many clients, especially African-Americans because of their high emphasis on religion and spirituality. Despite this, it would be a serious mistake to put all African-Americans into the same mold, because this culture is so diverse and much variability will be manifested among its members.

Spiritual and Religious Issues Generally Ascribed to This Group
Regardless of their spiritual beliefs, most African-Americans are cognizant of the role of the church in responding to their needs. Both the inner spirit of the individual and the collective spirit of the church are important resources for mental health providers working with African-American clients. Above all, African-American spirituality is communal. Traditional

religions exist foremost for the community rather than for the individual (Nobles, 1980). The individual is a reflection of the community and the community is a reflection of the individual. African-Americans share each other's sufferings and joys and recognize the dead as spirits that are active in their lives (Mbiti, 1991).

Therefore, spirituality plays an essential role in the African-American community. Spirituality is considered to be the "whole of life" (Frame & Williams, 1996). Many African-Americans consider themselves to be spiritual beings who live in a spiritual universe. According to Blaine and Crocker (1995), spirituality, as recognized by the African-American Church experience, is a coping mechanism as much as a unifying social entity. "As an established social institution, the church engenders perceptions of belonging and connectedness among its adherents and members" (p. 1033).

Jackson (A Conversation)

Jackson Smith is an African-American male in his late forties. He lives in a midwestern town where he has worked for the local utility company for the last 20 years. Jackson has been successful in his work and was recently promoted to foreman of his crew. The author met him in a hospital waiting room where both were waiting for news of loved ones who were ill and in surgery. Jackson was a wonderful conversationalist and spoke readily about himself and his family.

Jackson was born in the South and grew up on a farm/plantation. He was raised by his mother and grandmother, and knew very little about his father. His mother was the cook for the family who owned the tobacco plantation, as her mother before her had done. Both women had known little else in their lives and had always lived there. Jackson's earliest memories were of playing with the other African-American children who lived on the place. He described his childhood as very happy because of the type of existence that it provided. As he said to the author, "I just didn't know any better at the time."

Jackson, his mother, and grandmother lived in a house on the plantation that was loaned to them by the owner. It was located in a group of similar dwellings inhabited by other plantation workers and their families. These were rather crude houses of three or four rooms, but most had running water and even indoor plumbing in some of them. Because his mother was the main cook, their house was probably a little nicer than some of the others. Jackson loved the camaraderie of the other children and the fact that they lived in such close proximity. Almost all the families also attended the same church, a Baptist church located in the nearest town. Jackson related that a large church bus would come every Sunday morning and Wednesday night to take them to services. As a child, Jackson found the services long and rather tedious, but he knew that any attempt to get out of going would not be met with success. What gave him some measure of comfort was knowing that when the service was over a large communal meal would take place on the church grounds. Each family brought a dish that was put on a long table to be shared with the other families. These Sunday church meals were a highlight of the week for him. They provided an extended family that nourished more than just his body.

I asked Jackson how he felt about his family being absent. He thought for awhile and then responded slowly and deliberately. "I remember lying awake at night and wondering what it would be like to have a father who would take me hunting and fishing, a father who would tell me what it is like to be a man. Yes, I missed having a father sorely, down to the depth of my soul." However, he went on to explain, this was only one facet of my childhood. Other aspects were not so bad. "I had a house which was a home, and my mother had a steady job. She didn't make much cash, but we had plenty to eat, and I had plenty of room to run, and to play, and to be a boy. My grandmother and my mother made most of our clothes, and I had plenty of hand-me-downs from the son of the plantation owner who was a couple of years older than I was," Jackson said. It's strange. Talking about it now, I feel some anger about the situation, but honestly, at the time, I just accepted it as the way things were."

The area that caused Jackson the most resentment was education. When he was growing up, schools still operated under the premise of "separate but equal." According to Jackson, they were certainly separate, but they surely were not equal. He graduated from eighth grade with second-grade reading skills. Classrooms were overcrowded, and teachers had little more education than the students. There were never enough textbooks to go around and consequently they were never taken home at night to study from. His mother and grandmother were both illiterate and therefore could not help him much. The school buildings were old and in desperate need of repair. Most teachers were kind, but they did not really encourage their young charges to aspire to greater things. Jackson started high school but dropped out in the tenth grade, once he was 16. He later received his GED when he was in the army. He felt very grateful for what the armed services had provided for him.

Jackson's teenage years were turbulent ones for the county and for the South. The demise of segregation was at the forefront of everyone's attention. The black churches played a pivotal role in this endeavor and Jackson was active in the movement. He recalled several marches that he participated in and the beatings he endured at the hands of the policemen who sought to stop such activity. It was an exhilarating time and a time when he felt very closely connected to his family, his church, and his African-

American heritage. He felt that the young people of today, including his own children, do not really appreciate the struggles and sacrifices the preceding generations went through to give them the freedoms they have today. They took too much for granted according to Jackson.

In our discussion, he remembered the days of segregated movie theaters and doctors' offices. He remembered riding on the back of the bus when he visited large southern cities and being allowed to only go into certain restaurants and stores. It was definitely second-class citizenship at best. It engendered anger in him even today. Jackson admitted that he probably should seek professional help to deal with some of this residual anger.

Jackson talked a lot about the role of the church in his adult life. During his days in the army, belonging to a particular religion gave him a place to go, particularly on Sundays. It also provided companionship for him, but most importantly, from his perspective, it gave him the opportunity for a personal relationship with Jesus Christ. This relationship with his God gave Jackson much joy and also carried him through some tough times.

After the war, Jackson moved to the Midwest hoping to find a better life for himself. When asked if this actually happened, Jackson smiled sadly and said, "Places may change, but human nature doesn't. Prejudice looks and feels the same whether it is in Alabama or in Kansas. You can run away, but you can't hide." When he settled in a midwestern town, Jackson joined a black Baptist church. Once again he felt at home with the prayers, the preaching and singing, and the socializing. He felt "at home." He met his future wife at a church social and they were married in the church to which they both belonged.

Jackson wanted several children because he had been an only child and he had missed having siblings. Although his wife had come from a family of five, she also wanted more than one child. Four children were born in rather rapid succession, yet on the birth of the fourth child the doctors knew immediately that something was wrong. The child was born with multiple birth defects, and the prognosis for his survival was not good. Jackson and his wife were devastated. They had three daughters and this was their first boy, a longed-for son. For five weeks, the couple practically lived in the hospital and rarely left the baby's crib. The doctors did everything that they could, but to no avail. The baby died, and Jackson and his wife experienced a grief that was almost unbearable.

The only way they survived this blow was through the kindness and generosity of family, friends, and particularly the support of their church. Their pastor came every day and prayed with them both during the time they spent in the hospital and at first when they returned home. Although the death of this child was hard to reconcile with the image of a merciful God, prayer helped them find some solace and to accept what had occurred, even though they may not have understood it. Fortunately, Jackson and his wife were able to have two other healthy children—both boys.

Jackson also spoke of other times when he sorely needed the comfort of his religious faith and his church. Both Jackson and his wife experienced the death of their parent figures. There were times when finances were troublesome, and times when teenagers upset the peacefulness of their lives. Through all of this, their church served as a meeting place and as a source of comfort and support. Jackson and his wife felt that this was a place where they really belonged and were accepted.

When asked if their church membership had any negative aspects, Jackson spoke of a few times when the administration of the church had disappointed them. One pastor had had illicit affairs with female members of the church, one of the elders of the church had embezzled money, and a youth director had been accused of having an affair with a minor. Each of these incidents had shocked and dismayed Jackson and his wife and had even caused them to actually change churches once. Looking back, Jackson became rather philosophical about these times. "In many ways," he said, "these incidents made my faith stronger. I came to realize that religion is not about men or women, but about God. People are human, and with all the best intentions, some are going to hurt and disappoint us. We have to accept that and not base our faith on an individual but remember that it is because of God that we are a member of any church or faith group."

There was a time, however, when Jackson even stopped going to church. "I just wasn't getting anything out of it," he explained. "Nothing moved me any more. I felt empty and bored, and I wanted to be any place but there." When asked what had led him back to church, Jackson replied, "After being away for a year or so, I missed it. I missed it like a child misses his Mama. I felt lost and without something to anchor me. I also realized that during my absence from church I was drinking more and frequenting gambling halls more. I guess I was hiding from the Lord, wanting to do my own thing. I didn't enjoy it nearly as much as I wanted to and I missed my church. So I asked for forgiveness and went back. It was where I belonged."

Implications for Counselors

Jackson was an acquaintance of the author, but his story points out many implications for counselors. As stated in previous chapters, Ingersoll (1994) delineated seven different dimensions to the integration of spirituality into one's life:

1. One's conception of the divine, absolute, or "force greater than one's self"
2. One's sense of meaning of what is beautiful or worthwhile

3. One's relationship with divinity and others
4. One's tolerance or capability for mystery
5. Peak and ordinary experiences that enhance spirituality (which may include rituals or spiritual disciplines)
6. Seeing spirituality as play
7. Viewing spirituality as a systemic force that acts to integrate all the dimensions of one's life (p. 11)

According to Ingersoll's *Spirituality Integration* model, Jackson definitely had a conception of the divine as a "force greater than one's self." Jackson's faith beliefs gave meaning to what is beautiful and worthwhile. It allowed him to survive a "separate and totally unequal society" and to rebound after the death of his infant son. Jackson spoke often about the relationships in his life and their importance, but most of all he valued his personal relationship with his God. There were many things in life that Jackson admitted not understanding, but he came to accept them as "mysteries" that would only be explained in the afterlife. Jackson's church membership provided peak and ordinary experiences and the familiarity of ritual and communal prayer. The camaraderie of his fellow church members allowed Jackson to see worship as play, rather than just a duty. Religion and spirituality were at the center of Jackson's life so that when he left his church, he felt lost and missed it, "like a child misses his Mama."

Unique Needs of African-Americans

It is important to recognize that for African-Americans the psychic and the spirit are often seen as one (Knox, 1985). Psychological pain is frequently expressed in spiritual terms as "God will solve my problems" and "God never gives you more than you can carry" (Knox, 1985, p. 32). Spirituality often refers to a belief in a "higher power" or God. References to prayer and God are ingrained within African-American culture; even individuals who do not consider themselves to be religious incorporate these references into their everyday lives (Levin, 1984). Often rebellious young people forsake religion and spirituality, and as a result engender very strong conflicts with their families. Yet these same individuals are very likely to draw on the strong beliefs given to them in childhood when they are in a crisis. Often these same, once rebellious young men and women return to their spiritual roots when they have children of their own (Boyd-Franklin & Lockwood, 1999).

In addition to the African-American population, over 250,000 Black Africans are currently residing in the United States (U.S. Immigration, 1990). The idea of Western therapy is very alien to the African. Because of the relational culture of Africans, they are more likely to respond to a therapist who is more active and personal (i.e., someone who gives clients something "to do" rather than just to think about), and who shows dignity and respect to the institutional family and its structure, roles, and boundaries (Nwadiora, 1996).

The primary ethnicity of an African-American can be used as a therapeutic resource to help discover practices that enhance continuity and belonging, thereby propelling life forward while affirming past ties. For example, African families, as other immigrant families, experience acculturative stresses as they attempt to integrate into the American mainstream. Faced with the experience of being Black and African and residing in a predominately white culture, African families undergo a unique psycho-cultural encounter.

In order to gain an understanding of African-Americans' worldview, knowledge of the history of African spirituality and of African-American churches is necessary for the mental health professional. Because of the oral tradition and the ancestral importance of African culture, the past is part of the present for many African-Americans. Churches have played a key role in retaining as much of the African spirituality as possible, despite the dehumanizing conditions of slavery and the domination of institutionalized racism. Perhaps the combination of African spiritual roots and the remarkable survival of an oppressed people contribute to the African-American's strong belief in a real and loving God (Mitchell & Mitchell, 1989).

Some psychological and cognitive reframing interventions, such as empathic understanding, are congruent with what African-Americans frequently receive from their pastors when they go for counseling. However, some aspects of traditional therapy are incongruent with African-American traditions. For example, it is typical for therapists to begin counseling by completing an intake questionnaire. Often this is perceived as rude and intrusive if it is done without first having established a trusting relationship. For many African-American clients, history taking must be coupled with genuine caring and mutual sharing. Then the storytelling can take place in a nonthreatening environment.

Mainstream religious practices are very important sources of comfort, solace, and support for African-Americans when they are combined with practices indigenous to their culture. The cultural practices can help the clinician integrate the best of the past with modern clinical practices and open the doors to healing and hope for the client. Perhaps Aponte (1994) says it best:

> When it comes to our work, however, spirituality is an arena where we need our clients. It will require that we see ourselves not as proprietary experts on the subject but as companions on a journey. We do not own the expertise about the spirit. As therapists, we are not

the new priesthood. We all have our own personal, philosophical, social, and spiritual perspectives. We have varying degrees of commitment to our values. We have, in effect, our respective "religions." However, the poor come to us sometimes clothed only with their ethnicity, culture, and spirituality. It is not for us to dress them in our apparel. (p. 246)

Likewise, referrals for medical evaluations and psychological testing must be negotiated carefully because African-Americans have been used as involuntary subjects for clinical treatment trials and have also been mislabeled as a result of biases in testing (Helms & Cook, 1999). African-Americans are more likely than whites to drop out of therapy. According to one report, 52.1% of blacks dropped out, compared with 29.8% of whites (Sue, 1977). One issue that causes clashes between black clients and their white middle-class therapists is the interpretation of time. Wilkinson and Spurlock (1986) found that black clients at a mental health clinic were consistently 15 to 30 minutes late despite clinician's efforts to interpret the resistance and get clients to change their behavior.

Resistance from Within

Many mental health professionals fail to take into consideration the importance of spirituality and religion in the lives of their African-American clients. This has led the client to view the clinician as "antispiritual." Ignoring the key components in their congregants' core belief systems has led ministers to view the mental health professional as narrowly secular, and they have been reluctant to refer their troubled congregants to such a professional (Boyd-Franklin, 1989). This issue is very significant when considered within the broader context of the African-American community. The legacy of racism and discrimination has compelled many African-Americans to view clinics, hospitals, schools, and other social institutions with a healthy cultural suspicion, leading to a reluctance to discuss "family business" in public (Boyd-Franklin, 1989).

Given this view of therapy, it is incumbent upon the mental health professional to establish a comfortable, trusting relationship with the African-American client. Clinicians who fail to incorporate spirituality and religion into the counseling process may be missing a major therapeutic tool in working with their clients.

Mental health providers also need to be aware of the influences of the church on the African-American client. Although perceptions of counseling and psychotherapy vary across denominations, African-American churches have in the past been suspicious of counseling and therapy for reasons other than those previously discussed. The position of the churches was that all the members needed was Jesus. However, in recent years, churches have become more accepting of counseling as the pastors have become more educated in regards to mental health practices. Their pastors tend to be more accepting of counseling if the pastors are confident that the mental health providers are open to the racial and cultural lives of the African-Americans. Mainline Protestant and Catholic denominations tend to be more open to counseling, but mainline Pentecostal and Holiness churches tend to be more conservative and not so open to counseling (Cook & Wiley, 2000).

Black churches have long served a multitude of needs for the African-American communities. During the tumultuous years of desegregation, they provided an opportunity for African-Americans to feel respected for their abilities. Therefore, it is important for the clinician to beware of the concepts "church home" and "church family" (Smith, 1985). The "church home" is the one the family attends, often for generations. Families who move to a new community often travel a long distance to attend this church, and they continue to support this church even though they may be unable to attend regularly. "Church family" is a concept that illustrates the fundamental role of a Black church as a support network. This network provides a place where people share meals and fellowship before and after services. "Church families" often are considered extended families where the minister's spouse, deacons, deaconesses, prayer partners, and "sisters and brothers" in the church provide support in times of need and can be a highly cohesive network (Boyd-Franklin, 1989).

Mental health professionals would benefit greatly from meeting with ministers of African-American churches because of the powerful leadership positions these ministers hold. Nye (1993) found that the role of the Black church had played a salient role in the life of the elderly African-American women he interviewed in southwestern Virginia. He expanded the work of E. Franklin Frazier (1963) in identifying six sub-themes of the function of the African-American church:

- An expressive function as an outlet for one's deepest emotions couched in religious terms
- A recognition of the uniqueness of the person that is denied by American society
- A meaning for their lives
- A haven in a hostile society
- A release of pent-up emotions and frustrations felt by an oppressed minority

- An otherworldly orientation that helps them see that they will find eventual fulfillment in life after death

Boyd-Franklin and Lockwood (1999) added two additional valuable functions to Nye's list, namely

- A social function as the opportunity to meet, socialize, and share fellowship with persons of similar interests and backgrounds
- A child-rearing and support function, especially for young, single parents

Relationships with Clients

Many African-American clients may seem to be more trusting with African-American therapists; however, Cook and Wiley (2000) felt that a similarity in spiritual traditions is as important or even more important than race to the success of therapy. The importance of validating the spiritual identity of the clients and openly addressing their issues can be a powerful tool in developing a trusting relationship. Clients for whom spirituality is important may be more receptive to therapy when the therapist initiates the discussion of spirituality early in the therapeutic process. Furthermore, by acknowledging their own spiritual traditions, therapists can build a deeper trust in the relationship if they assure clients that they are equally accepting of the client's spiritual traditions. This does not suggest that therapists know all about the client's traditions, but rather that they are open to learning and that they feel free to ask the client questions when they need further clarification. An open discussion of attitudes about counseling and therapy may also be helpful. If the client has received messages that oppose therapy, it may be helpful to identify biblical scriptures that advocate seeking help or counsel from others.

Mental health professionals can help African-American clients claim their spiritual legacy and capitalize on the strong influence of spirituality and religion in their lives. Thus, the richness of the African-American culture and the importance of spirituality can be combined into the therapeutic process from intake to termination. By so doing, the therapists can work towards a successful intervention with the client.

Suggested Approaches for Working with African-Americans

The following are guidelines adopted from Boyd-Franklin and Lockwood (1999) for incorporating spirituality or religion in clinical work with African-American clients:

- The decision to integrate spirituality into therapy should be contingent upon a careful assessment and diagnosis of a client's spiritual or religious worldview and the role or impact it has had on the client's life (Boyd-Franklin, 1989).
- Clinicians should be aware of the risk of an African-American client leaving therapy prematurely because the clinician failed to address the client's spirituality or belief system. It is important that the clinician be able to initiate this type of dialogue and empower clients to discuss their spirituality or belief system as they would any other area of relevance to them. Otherwise, the client may become confused and doubt that the therapeutic relationship is the appropriate arena for spiritual concerns.
- Clinicians must be aware that being in therapy may generate conflicts for African-American clients. Clients may feel that being in counseling goes against their religion, particularly when ministers have communicated derogatory views of therapy. In addition, individual clients may be suspicious of therapy, viewing it as antispiritual or antireligious. In the event that psychological scarring resulted from shame or guilt originating in religion, therapists' sensitivity to these issues can help clients experience a release from that pain.
- Clinicians should be aware that the church can be utilized in times of crisis and offer aid to an African-American in need. The client may be more receptive to help from a church that is familiar than from an outside agency or person. In addition, a church can help clients who are socially isolated and emotionally cutoff from their extended families to reconnect with their "home church" or help find a new church that will provide the same support.
- When doing genograms (family trees) or ecomaps (drawings of other social systems involved in the client's life), the clinician should be careful to assess the role of the "church family" in the lives of African-Americans who report church affiliations (Boyd-Franklin, 1989).
- Differences in spiritual or religious beliefs may trigger intergenerational disagreements in African-American families. In such cases, the clinician needs to bring together key family members to discuss issues in ways that foster mutual understanding and tolerance for different beliefs and practices.
- Clinicians need to be aware that psychological symptoms such as depression, anxiety, psychosomatic illness, and acting-out or conduct-disordered behaviors may mask issues of unresolved guilt or loss. Often these issues involve spiritual pain. For a person who has a strong spiritual or religious orientation, the incorporation of these issues into therapy can expedite the healing process.

- Clinicians working in Black communities should make a special effort to interact with the ministers and other church leaders. This personal contact with revered individuals builds trust and credibility for the clinicians who work with African-American clients.

Although the mental health profession has become aware that in order to be effective with African-American clients nontraditional methods of service delivery are essential, these approaches have rarely addressed the spiritual dimension of the client's life (Lee, 1990). This is contrary to the belief that God is found in all of God's creation (Mitchell & Mitchell, 1989). The concept of spirituality as inseparable from all other aspects of human experience undergirds the African-American culture. The spiritual and physical are undistinguishable (Mbiti, 1991). Spirituality is woven into everything one experiences (Boyd-Franklin, 1989). It is especially important to note that a significant mode of spiritual expression is music and dance (James, 1993), thus providing a historically acceptable way to connect body, mind and spirit.

According to Ivey (1995), one of the most important contributions of multicultural counseling theory and research to the mental health field has been the move from a narrow focus on the individual to the broader view of the person within a cultural context. This shift has prompted the recognition of spiritual and healing systems indigenous to ethnic American cultures. The standards for multicultural counseling competencies include the requirement that counselors refer to religious and spiritual healers and leaders when working with African-Americans or other ethnic clients (Sue, Arredondo, & McDavis, 1992). It is imperative that clients' needs and dilemmas concerning religion and spiritual beliefs be given the same importance as issues of gender, race, and ethnicity (Richards & Bergin, 1997).

Religion and spirituality are a vital part of most cultures. When these issues are ignored, one of the most powerful facets of human experience is neglected. These entities can offer hope and solace to those who are suffering. The following strategies can help address these concerns.

Strategies for Addressing Spiritual Issues of African American Clients

Although basic counseling skills are necessary for any client, certain strategies are often more effective when working with those from different cultures. The following strategies have been adapted from Frame and Williams (1996):

Use of Metaphor: The African tradition of storytelling uses metaphor extensively (Wimberly, 1993–1994). By combining the metaphor with narrative therapy, the clinician can help the client weave a new story about him- or herself, thus introducing new metaphors of transformation. By generating these new metaphors of transformation, the clinician can generate hope and thus enable the client to rewrite a life story that exhibits success, courage, and empowerment.

Social Change: The civil rights movement and other human rights struggles have been powerful instruments of social and psychological change for African-Americans. These movements presented a clear vision of dignity and humanity for untold numbers of people within this culture. Spiritual and religious symbolism, in addition to music and songs containing powerful lyrics that speak of liberation, raised the hopes of a downtrodden people. Thus, the unity of personal transformation and social action can be used as a tremendous resource for counseling African-Americans. The appeal of the music of spirituals and rap should be explored. What do the lyrics say to the client? What is it about the words and music that appeal to the client? The powerful liberating and transforming function of music in the African-American tradition can be utilized with the client to help him or her develop a sense of hope and positive self-esteem.

Communalism: The therapist should consult with the client about how and to what extent family and friends are involved in his or her life. If there is a family bond, as there is for many African-American families (McDavis, Parker, & Parker, 1995; Nobles, 1980; White, 1984), the therapist might suggest a family meeting that includes nuclear and extended family, friends, pastor, teachers, and other significant persons in the client's life. At this meeting, held in a safe and nurturing place, the participants would be asked to encircle the client and present him or her with "gifts" in the form of messages and affirmations of worth and meaning to the client. The clients' disillusionment could be reframed in terms of personal power and a journey toward spiritual wholeness.

Use of Proverbs: The proverb is a means by which African wisdom is passed down through generations as a means of communicating interdependence and reliance on family members. One such proverb was translated by McCrary (1990): "The small hand of the child cannot reach the high shelf. The large hand of the adult cannot enter the narrow neck of the gourd" (p. 119). The client might be asked to collect African proverbs and discuss their meaning in his or her life. This process helps the client reconnect with family traditions and reclaim the spiritual support that is life giving for generations of African-Americans.

Giordano and Giordano (1995) suggested nine guidelines to use when responding to cultural diversity:

- Assess the importance of ethnicity to clients and families.
- Validate and strengthen the ethnic identity of the clients. Be prepared in case clients may have low self-esteem.
- Be aware of and use the client's natural support systems. The extended family is an extremely valuable resource.
- Serve as a "culture broker" when addressing value conflicts. Emphasize positive aspects of all value systems.
- Be aware of "cultural camouflage" as a defense against change. An example would be "I'm late because I'm in Black time."
- Know that being of the same ethnic group as the client has advantages and disadvantages (e.g., unresolved issues about one's own ethnicity).
- Do not feel that you have to know everything about all cultures. Know as much as possible about the client's culture and enter the relationship as a learner.
- To avoid polarization, always try to think in categories that allow for three possibilities.
- To be effective with African-American clients, counselors need to be aware of the history and culture of this population. They also need to be sensitive to the role religion has played in their lives for generations. Having hands-on experience in the black community will provide opportunities for counselors to learn first-hand what role spirituality plays in the lives of their clients.

Exercises

1. Visit an African-American family and discuss the role church has in their lives.
2. Interview an older African-American person regarding the role that spirituality and/or religion played in the lives of African-Americans prior to integration.
3. Interview an African-American who has reconnected with his or her African roots. Have the person identify the spiritual implications of this experience.
4. Organize a panel of Black ministers from the local community to discuss intergenerational influences on religious and/or spiritual practices.
5. Attend services at a church whose membership is predominantly African-American.

Ethel's Case

Ethel is a 41-year-old African-American woman who is currently married with six children, two of which are from a previous marriage. She was pregnant with her second child when her husband was killed in the line of duty as a policeman.

Ethel is a Southern Baptist and has been a member of her grandmother's church since childhood. She is still very close to her grandmother, and her first husband also belonged to this church. Ethel's present husband belongs to another Baptist church where he was a member before meeting and marrying Ethel. Ethel thought that after her children were born he would join her church so that they could attend as a family, but he has refused to leave his church.

Ethel is also a member of the choir and has befriended a fellow choir member who lost his wife to cancer. Ethel has not told her husband that she sees this man after choir practice, and she has begun lying when he asks why practice is so late. Because her husband does not attend her church, she is not afraid that he will learn about her relationship. She has talked to her pastor because she feels guilty about lying to her husband and is afraid of the consequences of her actions. She doesn't want to hurt her husband, but she is getting deeper into this relationship.

Ethel's pastor referred Ethel to a mental health professional who serves on a civic board with him. Ethel has begun seeing the counselor on a regular basis. The counselor suggested that Ethel's husband attend the sessions with her because she stated that she has been having marital problems

Case Discussion

- What assumptions will assist the counselor as he begins to work with Ethel and how will these assumption be addressed?
- If the male counselor is of another ethic, cultural, and religious background, how could this assist or impede the process?
- What would be a good starting point for this clinician?
- How could he or she effectively incorporate Ethel's religious affiliation in counseling?
- How important would it be for the clinician to have an understanding of the importance of the "home church" to this African-American client?
- What insights would the clinician obtain by having both spouses talk about the influence of their "home church?"
- How can Ethel's family support system, particularly her grandmother, help Ethel in this dilemma?
- How will the clinician address issues of trust with this couple?

- How will the clinician help this woman explore what the needs are that this new relationship is fulfilling in her life?

Assessment Strategies
- Intergenerational Ecomap to assess the impact of other systems such as the church in the lives of African-American clients.
- Genogram to assess multigenerational influences.
- Tennessee Self-concept scale to assess the degree of satisfaction of religion.
- A spiritual autobiography highlighting persons and events that had an impact on their spiritual and religious development.
- A journal of how their spiritual and/or religious practices impact their daily lives.

Questions for Further Discussion
1. What is the role, if any, of religion and spirituality in the client's life?
2. Does the client still identify with his or her own traditional religious practices?
3. To what extent is the African culture clashing with the American culture?
4. How would the problem be solved at home without therapeutic intervention?

References

Aponte, H. J. (1994). *Bread and spirit: Therapy with the new poor.* New York: Norton.

Blaine, B., & Crocker, J. (1995). Religiousness, race and psychological well-being: Exploring social psychological mediators. *Personality and Social Psychology Bulletin, 21,* 1031–1041.

Boyd-Franklin, N. (1989). *Black families in therapy: A multisystems approach.* New York: Guilford Press.

Boyd-Franklin, N., & Lockwood. (1999). Spirituality and religion: Implications for psychotherapy with African-American families. In F. Walsh (Ed.), *Spiritual resources in family therapy.* New York: Guilford Press.

Brisbane, F. L., & Wamble, M. (1985/1986). Treatment of black alcoholics. *Alcoholism Treatment Quarterly, 2*(3/4), 28–30.

Ellison, C. S. (1993). Religious involvement and self-perception among Black Americans. *Social Forces, 71,* 1027–1055.

Frame, M. W., & Williams, C. B. (1996). Counseling African-Americans: Integrating spirituality in therapy. *Counseling and Values, 41,* 16–28.

Hoge, D. R. (1996). Religion in America: The demographics of belief and affiliation. In E. P. Shafranske (Ed.), *Religion and the clinical practice of psychology* (pp. 21–41). Washington, D.C.: American Psychological Association.

Ivey, A. E. (1995). Psychotherapy as liberation: Toward specific skills and strategies in multicultural counseling and therapy. In J. G. Ponterotto, J. M. Casas, L. A. Suzuki, & C. M. Alexander (Eds.), *Handbook of multicultural counseling* (pp. 53–72). Thousand Oaks, CA: Sage Publications.

Lee, C. C. (1990). Black male development: Counseling the "native son." In D. Moore & F. Leafgren (Eds.), *Problem solving strategies for men in conflict.* Alexandria, VA: American Association for Counseling and Development.

Locke, D. C. (1992). *Increasing multicultural understanding: A comprehensive model.* Newbury Park, CA: Sage Publications.

Mbiti, J. S. (1991). *Introduction to African religions* (2nd ed.). Oxford, England: Heinemann Educational Publishers.

McCrary, C. (1990). Interdependence as a normative value in pastoral counseling with African-Americans. *Journal of Interdenominational Theological Center, 18,* 119–147.

McDavis, R. J., Parker, W. M., & Parker, W. J. (1995). Counseling African-Americans. In N. A. Vacc, S. D. DeVaney, and J. Whittmer (Eds.), *Experiencing and counseling multicultural diverse populations* (3rd ed., pp. 217–250). Bristol, PA: Accelerated Development.

McCullough, M. E. (1999). Research on religion-accommodative counseling: Review and meta-analysis. *Journal of Counseling Psychology, 46,* 92–98.

Mendes, H. A. (1982). The role of religion in psychotherapy of Afro Americans. In B. A. Bass, G. E. Wyatt, & G. J. Powell (Eds.), *The Afro-American family: assessment, treatment, and research issues* (pp. 203–210). New York: Grune and Stratton.

Millet, P. E., Sullivan, B. F., Schwebel, A. I., & Myers, L. J. (1996). Black Americans' and white Americans' views of the etiology and treatment of mental health problems. *Community Mental Health Journal, 32,* 235–242.

Mitchell, R. P., & Mitchell, H. H. (1989). Black spirituality: The values in that of time religion. *Journal of the Interdenominational Theological Center, 17*(1/2), 98–109.

Moore, T. (1991). The African-American church: A source of empowerment, mutual help, and social change. *Prevention in Human Services, 10,* 147–167.

Nobles, W. W. (1972). The psychology of Black Americans: An historical perspective. In R. L. Jones (Ed.), *Black psychology* (2nd ed.). New York: Harper & Row.

Parham, T. A., White, J. L., & Ajamu, A. (1999). *The psychology of Blacks: An African centered perspective* (3rd ed.). Upper Saddle River, NJ: Merrill/Prentice Hall.

Richardson, B. L., & June, L. N. (1997). Utilizing and maximizing the resource of the African-American church: Strategies and tools for counseling professionals. In C. C. Lee (Ed.), *Multicultural issues in counseling: New approaches to diversity* (pp. 155–170). Alexandria, VA: American Counseling Association.

Russell, C. (1998). *Racial and ethnic diversity* (2nd ed.). Ithaca, NY: Strategist Publications.

Stevenson, H. (1990). The role of the African-American church in education about teenage pregnancy. *Counseling and Values, 34*, 131–133.

Sue, D. W., Arredondo, P., & McDavis, R. J. (1992). Multicultural counseling competencies and standards: A call to the profession. *Journal of Counseling and Development, 70*, 477–486.

Taylor, R. J. (1988). Correlates of religious non-involvement of Black Americans. *Review of Religious Research, 29*, 126–139.

Taylor, R. J., & Chatters, L. M. (1991). Religious life. In J. S. Jackson (Ed.), *Life in Black America* (pp. 105–123). Newbury Park, CA: Sage.

Taylor, R. J., Chatters, L. M., Jayakody, R., & Levin, J. S. (1996). Black and White differences in religious participation: A multi-sample comparison. *Journal for Scientific Study of Religion, 35*, 403–410.

U. S. Bureau of the Census. (1986). *Population Profiles of the United States*. Washington, D.C.: Government Printing Office.

Watts, R. (1993). Community action through manhood development. *American Journal of Community Psychology, 2*(3), 333–359.

White, J. L. (1984). *The psychology of Blacks*. Englewood Cliffs, NJ: Prentice Hall.

Wimberly, E. P. (1993/1994). Pastoral counseling with African-American males. *Journal of the Interdenominational Theological Center, 21*(1/2), 127–144.

CHAPTER 10
Asian Americans

Recent demographic reports indicate that of all the Asian American people living in the United States, 63% are foreign born. Immigration trends show that 34% of all persons who immigrated to the United States in 1996 came from Asian countries (U.S. Bureau of Census, 1997). Although many Asian Americans have achieved considerable academic and financial success, many more have experienced heightened levels of stress and failure in different areas of their lives. As Baruth and Manning (1999) noted, language problems, dismal employment opportunities, and conflicting familial roles and expectations represent serious risk factors that compromise the mental health and well-being of many Asian immigrants who live in the United States.

The traditional Asian American family structure provides stability, interpersonal intimacy, and social support for its members (Hsu, 1972). However, the process of immigration and cultural transition to Western culture puts a great stress on families. The limited interpersonal interaction outside the family forces greater demands and more intense interaction within the nuclear family. This can cause many unresolved conflicts and require different levels of mental health services. According to Ho (1987), generally the mental health professional sees three types of Asian American families:

- Recently arrived immigrant families—These families tend to require information, referral, and advocacy services such as English language instruction, legal aid, and child care. These families seldom seek personal or psychological help.

- Immigrant Asian American families—These families consist of foreign-born parents and American-born children; therefore, a great degree of cultural conflict exists in the home. These issues require help in resolving communication problems and clarification and negotiation of their place in the family.
- Immigrant descendent families—These families are usually second- or third-generation American-born parents and their children who speak English at home and are acculturated to Western culture. Generally, these families seek help from many of the same agencies from whom the primary culture gets its services.

Unique Needs of Asian Americans

Asian immigrants bring to their new land their cultural heritage, a major part of which is spiritual in nature. This spiritual influence serves as a major support for maintaining their identity. These immigrants come from diverse ethnic groups, including Chinese, Japanese, Korean, Filipino, Asian Indian, Southeast Asian, and Pacific Islander. This diversity represents more than 50 groups speaking more than 30 different languages (Sue, Nakamura, Chung, & Yee-Bradbury, 1994). Although they are anxious to adapt to their new environment, they cling to their cultural traditions, which serve as a spiritual support and a way of maintaining their identity. Initially, Asian immigrants may experience strong feelings of alienation. They fear discrimination because they have come to the most advanced country in the world. They cannot disguise their origins because their physical appearance is different. Some may also feel that others regard their countries and cultures as inferior. These factors can lead to anxiety and/or feelings of inferiority. These feelings often cause younger Asians to develop a more Western manner merely to cover up what they think is inferior within their own culture.

To truly appreciate Asian Americans, it is important to understand the cultural diversity and sociopolitical history of this group, which is a major task. The Indian subcontinent alone includes Pakistan to the west; India in the center; Nepal, Tibet, and Kashmir to the north; and Burma to the east. Several languages are spoken in each nation, and each region has its own cultural traditions, beliefs, and values, with the religions ranging from Hinduism to Islam.

Clear demarcation lines define the male and female gender roles, which originate from ancient Confucian doctrines. In this belief system, a woman has only three pathways; first, she must be subject to her father, then to her husband, and then to her son (Ibrahim, 1992, 1994). Islam, a recent religion in the Indian subcontinent, gives a woman several rights that are hardly ever practiced; these include the right to divorce without providing a reason and the right to remarry as often as she becomes single (Ibrahim et al., 1997). Some authors contend that if women are limited to certain roles, that would also limit the flexibility that men can enjoy. Others state that respect given to women is based on their maternal status. Once motherhood is achieved, women are held in high esteem and are more highly revered if they have male children (Woollett, Marshall, Nicolson, & Dosanjh, 1994).

Men traditionally have managed the domain outside the home and women manage the home, however, this is changing. Gender identity varies with generational and educational levels, social class, and economic stability. The family would insist that the men are in control of the family in order to give this impression to dominant culture groups. In reality, the power and control is held by the oldest member of the family, even if that person, regardless of gender, is thousands of miles away (Ibrahim et al., 1997).

The goal of many Asians is to reach the highest form of self, the true self that dominates the culture. This process is seen as the consummation of all human efforts and confers the charisma of the holy man onto the person (Bharatic, 1985). This higher-order status of psychological development progresses from material to nonmaterial, from materially needy to the highest order of purity (Bharatic). In the Islamic tradition, the highest order of the self purports a denial of material needs to achieve a oneness with the purest or God. Asian Americans holding these values and beliefs often find themselves in conflict with the values of their new homeland, which defines success primarily in economic and social status standards.

Some knowledge of Asian immigration to the United States may be helpful to the mental health professional. According to Ibrahim et al. (1997), Asian immigrants have not been welcome in the United States. European Americans have been accepted as conquerors, African-Americans are accepted as people who were severely wronged, Native Americans are accepted as the original people of the land, and most Latino Americans are accepted as colonized people. Asian Americans have not been accepted because of cultural and certain racial differences. The earliest arrivals from Asia came as laborers (Takaki, 1989) in hopes of earning enough to return to their homeland. A major uproar occurred in California, where it was made quite clear that Asians were not welcome. The Asian Exclusionary Act of 1924 prohibited Asians from immigrating to the United States. This continued until 1946 when the right of naturalization was attained (Chandrasekhar, 1982). The exclusionary tactics directed at Asian Americans tended to be more severe than those directed at other ethnic groups. Some authors believe that these injustices may live in the psyche of South Asian Americans and influence their trust of mainstream American society (Ibrahim et al., 1997). Counselors and mental health professionals must have some knowledge of the history of this cultural group in order to be able to walk with their clients on the journey toward wholeness.

Cultural Identity and Worldview of the Client

The cultural identity and worldview of the client are variables that will influence how the counselor should approach the client. The following six basic beliefs and values are generally held by most Asian Americans. The strength of these values depends on the length of time the immigrant has spent in the United States. These are adapted from Ibrahim et al. (1997):

- *Self-respect, dignity, and self-control:* From early childhood, the importance of these three variables is emphasized in Asian cultures. Each person is empowered to achieve them, while all excesses are abhorred. The person is seen as an individual in a familial context, and this individuality is encouraged within the boundaries and limits of the family. The highest ideal is to achieve a self-identity free of material needs.
- *Respect for the family/filial piety:* Parents are to be honored and revered. The family extends horizontally and laterally. These various relationships are valued, and appropriate respect is given to each family member.
- *Respect for age:* It is assumed that the older a person gets, the more maturity and knowledge he or she has. Older persons are respected for these attributes, and families go to elders to resolve familial conflicts. They also turn to older family members for advice and support when they are in a crisis or when relationships are disrupted in social or work relationships.
- *Awareness and respect for community:* This idea derives from the earliest values where the community is seen as an extended family and one has responsibilities to the community. This value decides how self-respect, dignity, and self-control are mediated for each person.
- *Fatalism:* A belief that no matter what one does or does not do, certain challenges are preordained and must be handled appropriately.
- *Humility:* It is extremely important not to make oneself the center of attention or to discuss one's accomplishments. It is expected that the more people achieve, the more humble they will be. Others in the group and the community are expected to extol the virtues and accomplishments of group members. It is also important not to

draw attention to yourself by posing as someone who is superior to others. Humility is misunderstood in the United States and those who practice it are seen as having low self-esteem or as not being very accomplished. This value can also backfire in the competitive employment world. A South Asian American may share his or her knowledge, talent, and skill but never receive the due credit for his or her ideas because he or she shuns the recognition based on the importance of humility.

In addition to the cultural identity and worldview of Asian Americans, special attention must be given to those who view their spiritual needs as of primary importance and their material gains as secondary. For such people, the hereafter, or long-term well-being of the soul, is valued over immediate gains or gratification. If, however, material success and an active, positive spiritual dimension are achieved, both are reflected in the lines of the Asian American. In working with Asian American clients, a counselor must keep this viewpoint uppermost in his or her mind. Spiritualism is not only an integral part of the client's life; it is the most important and unifying aspect. The highest form of personal achievement is to renounce all material gains and become a holy person in the quest for purity of soul that would allow oneness with God or the cosmos based on religious beliefs (Ibrahim, 1993). Neglecting to acknowledge this dimension of the client's life would be a major deficiency.

Li Anh's Story

Li Anh is a middle-aged Chinese woman who has lived in the United States for the last 30 years. She is married and the mother of four children, two boys and two girls. She has recently experienced the death of her mother and is seeking help in dealing with this loss. Her husband has prevailed upon her to come for counseling. Li Anh is slight of stature and rather bowed, which makes her look somewhat older than she really is. Deep sorrow is etched in her face and tears are in her eyes as she speaks.

She related how she immigrated to this country as a rather young bride and how she and her husband saved for years in order to bring her mother to this country. She described the loneliness she went through when she first arrived in America and how much she had missed her family. Li Anh's mother was always supportive, and Li Anh felt that her mother loved her unconditionally. Her father died shortly after she left China, which is when she began to make plans for her mother to join her. With her mother's arrival, Li Anh felt a peace that she had not felt since coming to America. Her mother represented wisdom, safety, and security to her. Having her mother in her home also allowed Li Anh to feel that she was honoring her elders and paying her mother her due respect. It was a mutually beneficial and happy arrangement for both.

Li Anh spoke at length about the void that her mother's death had left in her life. She missed the companionship that her mother's presence in her home had afforded, because her prosperous husband worked very long hours. She appreciated the wisdom and experience her mother shared about raising children and about life in general, and Li Anh didn't know who to turn to now for the same sort of support. Li Anh enjoyed doing things for her mother and even buying things for her. Because her mother was a widow, Li Anh had felt responsible for her welfare, and her husband had agreed to the arrangement and had been supportive of both of them. Li Anh felt lost and lonely without her.

It was obvious that if Li Anh was to emerge from her period of mourning healthy and intact she had to connect with every support system at her disposal. Her relationship with her husband seemed to be strong and supportive, and her relationships with her children seemed to afford her a source of satisfaction and pride. Li Anh did not, however, have very many close personal friends. She felt it was her duty to stay close to home and care for her husband and children, which left her little time to socialize with other women or to form close bonds with them. Her mother's presence in her home had provided companionship for many years, and her lack of friends was not a problem.

Li Anh and her family were Buddhists and attended a local temple. She and her mother had created several small shrines in her home where they worshiped daily. The town where she lived was mainly Christian in orientation, and she often missed the larger Buddhist population of China, even though she had known Christians even in her country of origin. We began to explore how her religious and spiritual beliefs might be a comfort to her at this time. Li Anh was willing to explore this with me and was also willing to teach me about some of her beliefs. As the counselor, I began to read everything I could about the Buddhist faith.

Li Anh had practiced meditation for most of her life and reported that it was a source of comfort and enlightenment for her. She reported feeling very close to her mother while meditating, as though the two were communicating. Sometimes her meditation was accompanied by chanting, something she had learned as a child and that brought her peace and helped her focus. She told me about the use of chanting in the Buddhist faith and the occasions when various chants are used. This was an area that Li Anh wanted to explore further because of the peace and calmness that resulted from this practice.

The Buddhist faith states that "all life entails suffering," and even though one part of Li Anh saw death as a normal and natural life passage, on a more personal and human level her grief at the loss of her mother was enormous. We both agreed that the practice of meditation could help to center her and help her work through some of her grief. Li Anh reported that her meditation time was also a time when she could give vent to her feelings at their deepest levels. She reported that as she meditated the tears often flowed. This was not typical of Buddhists, but because Li Anh was rather stoic in most areas of her life, she welcomed this time and emotional release it provided.

Li Anh also felt that her religious beliefs prompted her to reach out to others who were suffering as well. She knew of other women who had lost a husband, a parent, a child, or other loved one. She resolved to reach out to these individuals, even though her shy nature made it hard to do so. We talked about ways she could make contact with such people. Through her temple and the social gatherings that her local Chinese community provided, Li Anh gradually began to make friends with women who had experienced a loss similar to hers. Several of them agreed to meet once a week at each other's homes just to talk. Although not a therapy group with a trained leader, this group of women provided a source of comfort and support that Li Anh sorely needed. None of these things happened overnight; in fact, they took quite a while, but Li Anh worked at it with courage and determination.

It took quite a bit of persuading on my part to make Li Anh realize how valuable her bilingual abilities could be. The city in which she lived had a rather large Chinese population, and I suggested that she might want to volunteer as an interpreter at a hospital or other community agency. This would be a wonderful way in which to help people who were suffering or in need of help. Venturing out of her home to perform these deeds was also a big step for Li Anh. She started in a small way, a couple of hours a day or one day a week. It was a tremendous effort for her, but it was also a great source of healing for others.

Li Anh believed in reincarnation and we discussed what this meant in terms of her mother. Li Anh believed that people who lived a good life were entitled to return to life in a more enlightened form, and she definitely felt that her mother fell into this category. This led to discussions about the Buddhist terms *karma* and *nirvana* and what this meant to Li Anh. She explained that in order to reach the higher states of Buddhism one had to live a good, moral life. She felt that her mother had exemplified many of the highly regarded qualities and this was a comfort to Li Anh. She described her mother as a woman who truly cared about others. In the Chinese community, her mother was regarded with respect and even veneration. Many people would come to visit her mother and seek her advice. Li Anh missed this flurry of activity in her home. We talked about the need to keep in touch with these friends and about the opportunity it could provide to talk about her mother. Li Anh acknowledged that this would be a source of comfort for her.

We explored the whole concept of suffering within the context of the Buddhist tradition. Linked with this was also the concept of denial. Li Anh explained that Buddhists expected life to contain trials and tribulations, and that in denying oneself certain earthly pleasures and avoiding things deemed to be immoral, one was strengthened to accept the hardships of life, such as death. Li Anh knew that she was struggling with her acceptance of these hardships. She needed to be able to accept that her mother's death was final—that she was not ever coming back. The mere thought of this was painful to her.

Li Anh truly wanted to work through her grief. She attempted to accomplish the things we discussed, and she turned more and more to her Buddhist belief system for calmness and serenity in this difficult time. She felt that her mother had "passed through" to a better life and that one day she would also. By remaining in contact with her mother's friends, she in turn felt connected to her mother. Li Anh accepted that she had to assume responsibility for her own healing. She did, however, acknowledge that a higher power governed the universe and directed all things. She needed to find her place within this universe now that her daily female companion was no longer with her. Her faith was an important key to this acceptance. It preached orderliness to the rhythm of life. There was a time to be born and a time to die. One generation succeeded another and the karma of each lifetime determined the level of satisfaction of the next. Li Anh clung to these beliefs as she sought solace in her grief.

Li Anh also realized that her closeness to her mother could have intruded somewhat on her relationship with her husband. In her need to honor her mother, she may have shut him out of many things in her daily life. She realized that at times she confided more in her mother than her husband. Li Anh resolved to work harder at reestablishing her husband as the primary relationship in her life. She often felt torn in dealing with her ethnic group, the traditions of her faith and nationality, and her present-day American existence. American women seemed to navigate these things with much more ease, or at least that's what Li Anh believed.

Implications for Counselors

In looking at Ingersoll's (1994) seven different dimensions to the integration of spirituality into one's life, one can analyze Li Anh's use of her religious beliefs to work through grief:

1. One's conception of the divine, absolute, or "force greater than oneself"
2. One's sense of meaning of what is beautiful or worthwhile
3. One's relationship with divinity and others
4. One's tolerance or capability for mystery
5. Peak ordinary experiences that enhance spirituality (which may include rituals or spiritual disciplines)
6. Seeing spirituality as play
7. Viewing spirituality as a systemic force that acts to integrate all the dimensions of one's life (p. 11)

Li Anh was not just from a religion different from the counselor's; she was from a whole different cultural background and ethnic group. This can stretch even the most astute professional's abilities, but it can also be an opportunity for immense personal and professional growth. This is truly a time to let the client lead the counselor. Li Anh was an open individual, albeit a shy one. She was willing to discuss her feelings and emotions in the context of the grief she was experiencing. She was searching for something to hold on to in these difficult days and for something that made sense or gave meaning to her suffering. In turning to the tenets of her Buddhist faith, she was able to bring balance to her life.

As a Buddhist, Li Anh's conception of the divine was different from that of a Protestant, Catholic, or Jew. Her beliefs were Eastern in origin while she was living in a very western civilization. Spirituality took on a very different meaning for her from Western religious thought, but the centering force that it held in her world was much the same. The application of the word karma, for instance, applied to the many worlds that have passed away and also to the many worlds that are to come. Articulating this gave Li Anh reason for hope. This is different from the afterlife espoused by most Western religious thought.

As a Buddhist, Li Anh was very much in touch with the meaning of life and saw beauty in the entire natural world. No plant or animal was too small to be of consideration to her. Her reverence for life also gave nobility to death. She missed her mother in a very human way but firmly believed that she was in a "better" or "higher" place because of the good life she had led.

Li Anh's religious beliefs also prompted her to reach out to others and realize that other people had suffering to bear also. She found it difficult to relinquish her grief long enough to leave her home and seek companionship, but with effort she did accomplish this. Her religious traditions became a common bond between her and others who had befriended both her and her mother in the past. Her skills as a translator were put to good use, and this was something she could give to those in need. She saw all of this as a source of growth in a spiritual dimension.

Belief in things or spirits she could not sense in a physical way did not constitute a problem for Li Anh. Her Eastern background made her very sensitive to the mystery of a life or lives that existed in another realm. Meditation and chanting were the means she used for peak experiences and to find comfort and peace.

The quality of sacrifice and self-denial that her religion preached made it easier for her to understand and tolerate the sorrows of this life. Li Anh had grown up believing in a strict moral code and this was a comfort to her as it preached a right order to life that helped her achieve balance. Basically, she had been taught to think positively about life, and in spite of her grief she was intent on doing this.

The absence of her mother forced Li Anh to establish and strengthen other relationships, and this was an area of personal growth and connectedness for her. She and her mother had always worshipped together, and now she had to seek this out on her own or with her husband. Li Anh believed in the order of life—we are born and we die, but it had never been so close to home for her before.

Part of her healing was to reach out beyond herself and be open to new experiences. Her meditation and chanting took on new meaning as she worked through her grief. It was not just a ritual that she performed but also an act of healing and emotional awareness. Her mother's friends became her friends in a new way and provided comfort for her. She also made new friends who held the same religious beliefs and were also suffering, and they formed a support group for each other.

Li Anh worked hard to achieve a peaceful state of mind, and she used all the means at her disposal. Her religion served as a source of solace and gave meaning to her suffering. She worked to integrate the various components we discussed into her daily existence. Most of all, she prayed for acceptance of her mother's passing. She went through all the typical stages of grief— denial, hoping for a miracle, anger, and sorrow—and she often felt exhausted from the effort. In spite of this, Li Anh's core belief in the sanctity of life and the solemnity of death gave her strength for this journey.

Suggested Approaches to Working with Asian Clients

The concepts of mental health and illness are ultimately derived from a worldview that prevails in society. Eastern immigrants (Muslims, Chinese, Koreans, etc.), despite modernization, scientific revolution, and modern technology, remain conditioned by a respect for elders, a respect for beliefs, and a tendency to appreciate group activities and norms rather than individualistic ideas. Das (1987) suggested that religious traditions define the lives of Asians if they want to attain a good life. Psychological stress and disorders are explained within a religious framework in terms of either spiritual possession or a violation of religious values as moral principles. Healing may take the form of invoking supernatural powers or restoring the sufferer to a state of well-being by prescribing right conduct and beliefs.

Overall, Asian immigrants, a diverse group with many nationalities and cultural traditions, present special challenges for mental health professionals who would integrate spirituality into counseling. Many Asian immigrants are bicultural, working to hold Asian and Western values together, as well as Christian and traditional beliefs (Chao, 1992; 1983; Tan, 1991). The values of honoring the family and community groups, of duty and obligation, of hierarchy and status, and of deference and self-control also influence the ways Asian immigrants embody their religious and spiritual beliefs (Tan & Dang, 2000). The fact is, among many Asian immigrants, a stigma is attached to psychological distress. Many perceive it as punishment from the spirits, a sign of weakness, or a negative reflection on one's family (Lee, 1996; Moy, 1992). These and other considerations are critical for the mental health professional to take into consideration when entering a therapeutic relationship with Asian immigrants.

Professionals need to avoid falling prey to the "model minority" stereotype that many people have adopted about Asian immigrants (Baruth & Manning, 1999). It is important that counselors gain a knowledge and appreciation of the rich cultural diversity that characterizes persons from different Asian backgrounds. For example, one must realize that the values, language, and traditions of a Japanese man or woman will not be useful when working with a Filipino client whose life is strongly influenced by his or her own values and traditions.

In order to narrow the gap between immigrant clients and mental health professionals, therapists must understand and respect the client's spiritual beliefs. If clients perceive that therapists respect their worldview, religion and spirituality provide a real source of strength to the client. Any effort made by a clinician to learn the spiritual traditions of the immigrant will result in a better understanding of their client and a more effective and rewarding experience for the Asian individual who seeks his or her services.

As a means of avoiding some of these pitfalls, the following are some specific guidelines that may prove helpful:

- Determine the client's level of cultural adjustment to the United States.

- Take time to explain the counseling process and discuss counseling expectations.
- Realize that immigrants may have a different time perspective based on the present, because the future may be seen as not being under their control.
- Be aware that it is important for therapists to spend a considerable amount of time, more than generally required, building rapport.
- Consider using active problem-solving techniques rather than depending primarily on reflective approaches.
- Be aware that some guidance or direction may be expected during the counseling process.
- Use knowledge about religious and/or spiritual systems to contribute to meaningful interventions.
- Be aware that some immigrants are likely to maintain their language, cultural values, and unique group characteristics.
- Discuss the possible participation of family in therapy.
- Enlist the help of clergy or spiritual leaders when appropriate.

Realize that, when working with Asian American immigrants, therapists must be able to embrace a view of diversity that recognizes the immigrant's differences as a necessary and beautiful part of creation that is all too often silenced and underrepresented.

To successfully assist Asian Americans, mental health professionals need to understand how this population views counseling services. Asian Americans often feel stigma and shame in talking about their personal problems. They prefer to attribute their problems to external forces such as the death of a loved one, the loss of a job, or a physical illness. The suffering may also be attributed to a person's violation of some duty such as filial piety. In this case, family members or community elders would exhort the individual to change his or her behavior and improve (Ho, 1992).

It is also essential for the clinician to encourage the client and family members to openly discuss their culture and religious viewpoints as to the cause of the problem, their past coping styles, and their treatment expectations. Questions to ask might include the following (Lee 1990):

- What are the symptoms and problems as perceived by family members?
- What would be the diagnostic label given in the client's home country?
- What are the family's cultural explanations of the causes of the problem?
- What kind of treatment would the family receive if they were back in their home country?

- Where did the family go for help before they came to see the clinician?
- What is the family's experience with herbal medicine, indigenous medicine, and Asian exercises such as tai chi and chi gang?
- What were the family's previous experiences with health and mental health care systems?
- What is the family's exposure to mental health professionals?
- What are the family's treatment expectations?

It is obvious from these questions that the family is central to the whole process of working with the Asian American client. Effective clinical strategies need to incorporate unique cultural values and family.

Because Asian Americans are usually unfamiliar with family therapy, the following suggestions may be effective in addressing the cultural and family issues (Lee, 1996):

- In view of the traditional family power structure, the initial appointment should be made with the "decision maker" of the family, mostly the father. Requesting the English-speaking children to inform the parents of an appointment may reinforce the role reversal in the family. If necessary, ask the interpreter to make the arrangements. Be sure to set an appointment time that is convenient to the working parents because they value work more than therapy. Detailed explanations of the reasons for such an appointment and the location of your agency may be necessary.
- Many immigrants do not understand the role of the mental health professional and may confuse him or her with a physician. A brief explanation of the therapist's role and training background may be helpful.
- During the first session, the clinician should address the family in a polite and formal manner. In addition, he or she needs to pay attention to "interpersonal grace" and show warm expressions of acceptance both verbally and nonverbally. Greeting the family with a smile, offering a cup of tea, and providing comfortable chairs to the older family members are examples of pragmatic expressions for conveying genuine concern and can add greatly to the beginning of a positive relationship (Ho, 1987).
- Many Asians are used to receiving help from their friends or village elders for advice. They may ask the clinician many personal questions, such as his or her country of origin, marital status, number of children, and so on. The clinician needs to feel comfortable in answering such questions. Appropriate self-disclosure may facilitate positive cultural alliance and a level of trust and confidence.

- Forming a social and cultural connection with the family during the first session is very important. For the clinician who has lived in the same Asian country or has extensive experiences in working with Asians, it will be beneficial to disclose your familiarity with that culture to make the "cultural connection." For the clinician who is not very familiar with the client's culture, it is important to show his or her interest and appreciation of the client's cultural background. Pictures of Asian countries and culture on the office wall can also convey the clinician's interest.
- Because many Asian family members are not used to the type of required verbal communication in therapy, asking nonthreatening personal questions can put the family at ease. Engaging the clients in small talk may also help to allay fears. It is important to avoid direct confrontation, a demand of greater emotional disclosure, or a discussion of culturally taboo subjects such as sex or death before an adequate rapport has been established.
- For many Asians, a public admission of mental health problems can bring intense shame and humiliation. The clinician may counter those emotions by empathizing with his or her Asian clients and encouraging them to verbalize their feelings. It is important to assure Asian family members about confidentiality and anonymity. One helpful technique is to reframe their courage in seeking help as love and concern over family members. If appropriate, the mobilization of the family's sense of obligation to receive help to achieve family harmony or for the sake of the children can be very effective.
- Many Asian clients come to their first session believing that the clinician is an authority who can tell them what is wrong and how to solve their problems. It is helpful for the clinician to establish credibility right away in order to ensure that the client will return. Confidence, empathic understanding, maturity, and professionalism are all important ingredients. Other ways to establish credibility and authority include: (a) using professional titles when making introductions; (b) displaying diplomas, awards, and licenses in the office; (c) obtaining sufficient information about the client and his or her family before seeing them for the first time; (d) offering some possible explanations for the cause of the problem; (e) showing familiarity with the family's cultural background; (f) providing a set of cues that help the family judge the clinician's expertise (i.e., "According to my experience working with Asian families during the past 20 years . . . "); and (g) utilizing the crisis intervention approach to offer some immediate solutions to the problems. It is important for the family to

feel that they are in good hands leave the first session with a sense of hope.

- Many Asian Americans do not comprehend the significance and sometimes lengthy procedures of evaluation. They are either not used to detailed history taking, or they do not understand the relationship between the questions and the problems. Some may even suspect such information will be put to political use, thus jeopardizing their immigration status. The clinician needs to help the client understand the reasons behind such questions.
- Most of the families come to the first interview during a family crisis. The clinician should plan to allow more time than a usual 1-hour session, especially when an interpreter is used.

Although it is desirable to have family members come to therapy, the Asian American family may not be willing to cooperate. A flexible subfamily system approach may be helpful at the beginning so that a comfort level can be established for all. For example, have the parents come first, then the identified client on his or her own, and finally the siblings. Each would have an opportunity to discuss their concerns or express emotions freely. When all parties feel "safe," they may be more willing to talk openly with the family group.

Asian American families often come to counseling with specific behavioral or physical problems, and they expect the clinician to fix them immediately; therefore, it is essential that the clinician adopt a problem-focused, goal-oriented, and symptom-relieving approach at the beginning of therapy. Many clients find loosely targeted and emotionally oriented goals incomprehensible, unreachable, and impracticable (Ho, 1987). Once success has been achieved with short-term goals, the clinician can then introduce more long-term or insight-oriented ones or renegotiate plans with the family.

To establish this working relationship with the client and his or her family, the clinician needs to engage all involved in an active exchange in which they perceive giving and receiving on the part of both those seeking help and the counselor. Most clients are familiar with the physician/patient relationship, which entails a brief encounter, a series of questions from the doctor, concrete answers from the patient, and subsequently some sort of payment by the patient followed by symptom relief. Minority clients often generalize from this relationship to that of the mental health worker. When these expectations are not met, the client becomes disillusioned with the process. However, a reciprocal exchange with the physician enables that patient to experience tangible gains as a result of participating in the process.

The necessary factors on the client's side include a willingness to meet with the helper, self-disclosure and receptivity, and some form of payment for the service, be it a nominal fee or third-party payment. The therapist agrees to meet with and listen to the client, shares personal credentials or qualifications, empathizes with the client's frustration and emotional pain, and acknowledges the client's explanation for the issues presented.

Construing the working relationship as an active exchange serves to counter the image of the client as debtor. Inherent in most Asian cultures is an unwillingness to incur obligation. The fear of being indebted to someone often forces the Asian client to discontinue therapy. An active exchange promotes a sense of partnership in the helping process and transforms the client from a passive recipient to an active participant attempting to gain control over his or her life (Huang, 1998).

Effective communication skills are the most important prerequisite for functioning anywhere. English proficiency opens an opportunity for employment and success, as unemployment is a major problem for some Asian immigrants. Even those with professional training in their own countries sometimes find it difficult to find employment in the United States because they may possess poor communication skills.

Other important factors in assimilation and acculturation for Asian immigrants include their places of settlement, their opportunity for direct interaction with Americans, and their rejection of cultural biases. Living in minority-concentrated areas adds to the isolation of Asians. Any immigrant's interaction with citizens of the host country not only reduces probable segregation but also helps them adapt to American society (Wenhao, Salomon, & Chay, 1993).

A therapist who has practical experience with Asian clients or the Asian community will know what will facilitate the counseling process. As stated earlier, it is an invaluable asset to be familiar with the particular cultural groups being served.

Exercises

1. Visit an area with a large Vietnamese population or attend a Vietnamese worship service. Observe the family interactions during this visit.
2. Interview an Asian American student and ask about his or her experiences concerning the observance of one of the national holidays.
3. Compare the cultural practices of at least two different Asian groups.
4. What questions regarding religious observances would you ask in order to better understand Asian American religious practices?
5. Talk to an Asian American student about his or her grandparents.

6. Interview an Asian American who belongs to an Eastern religious sect about the tenets of his or her faith.

Case of an Indonesian Family

A family from Indonesia recently moved to your area, and the teenage children have enrolled at a local school. As one of the school counselors, you have been asked by the principal to facilitate the acculturation of these students. You have had an initial session with both students and you've planned to meet with them on a weekly basis for the next three weeks. In the meantime, the principal has informed you that the parents called and indicated that they would prefer that their children have no further private sessions with you until the father has spoken with you.

Case Discussion

- What information will the counselor need prior to meeting with the father?
- What information would have been helpful prior to seeing the teenagers?

  How can the counselor continue to assist the students in their orientation and what suggestion would you make for facilitating this process?
- To what extent is the Asian culture clashing with the new American culture?
- To what extent are gender roles the major source of stress for the Asian students?
- How could the teenagers' religious belief system help or hinder their assimilation process and what would the counselor need to know regarding their religious practice?
- Are the students temporary residents, permanent residents, or citizens?

References

Baruth, L. G., & Manning, M. H. (1999). *Multicultural counseling and psychotherapy: A life span perspective* (2nd ed.). Englewood Cliffs, NJ: Merrill/Prentice Hall.

Chandrasekhar, S. (Ed.). (1982). *From India to America: A brief history of immigration, problems of discrimination, admission and assimilation*. La Jolla, CA: Population Review Book.

Chao, C. (1992). The inner heart: Therapy with Southwest Asian families. In L. Vargas & J. D. Koss-Chioino (Eds.), *Working with culture: Psychotherapeutic interventions with ethnic minority children and adolescents* (pp. 157–181). San Francisco: Jossey-Bass.

Das, A. K. (1987). Indigenous models of therapy in traditional Asian societies. *Journal of Multicultural Counseling and Development, 14,* 25–36.

Gibbs, J. T., & Huang, L. N. (1998). *Children of color: Psychological interventions with culturally diverse youth*. San Francisco: Jossey-Bass.

Ho, M. K. (1987). *Family therapy with ethnic minorities*. Newbury Park, CA: Sage Publications.

Ho, M. K. (1992). *Minority children and adolescents in therapy*. Newbury Park: Sage Publications.

Hsu, F. L. K. (Ed.). (1972). *Psychological anthropology*. Cambridge, England: Schenkman Publishing Company, Inc.

Huang, L. N. (1997). Asian American adolescents. In E. Lee (Ed.), *Working with Asian Americans: A guide for clinicians* (pp. 175–195). New York: Guilford.

Ibrahim, F. A. (1992, April). *A curriculum to enhance the cultural and gender identity of youth*. Symposium on cultural and gender identity development at the annual meeting of the American Counseling Association, Atlanta, GA.

Ibrahim, F. A. (1993). Existential worldview theory: Transcultural applications. In J. McFadden (Ed.), *Transcultural counseling: Bilateral and international perspectives* (pp. 23–58). Alexandria, VA: American Counseling Association Press.

Ibrahim, F. A. (1994). Developmental guidance from a culture and gender perspective. Dialog, Fall.

Ibrahim, F. A., Ohnishi, H., & Sandhu. (1997). Asian-American identity development: South Asian Americans. *Journal of Multicultural Counseling and Development, 25,* 34–50.

Ingersoll, R. E. (1994). Spirituality, religion, and counseling: Dimensions and relationships. *Counseling and Values, 38,* 98–111.

Lee, E. (1990). Family therapy with Southeast Asian families. In M. P. Mirkin (Ed.), *The social and political contexts of family therapy,* (pp. 331–354). Needham Heights, MA: Allyn and Bacon.

Lee, E. (1996). Chinese families. In M. McGoldrick, J. Girodano, & J. Pearce (Eds.), *Ethnicity and family therapy* (2nd ed.). New York: Guilford Press.

Moy, S. (1992). A culturally sensitive, psychoeducational model for understanding and treating Asian-American clients. *Journal of Psychology and Christianity, 11,* 358–367.

Sue, S., Nakamura, C. Y., Chung, R. C., & Yee-Bradbury, C. (1994). Mental health research on Asian Americans. *Journal of Community Psychology, 22*(2), 61–68.

Takaki, R. (1989). *Strangers from a different shore*. Boston: Little, Brown and Company.

Tan, S. Y. (1991). Counseling Asians. *Urban Mission, 9,* 42–50.

Tan, S. Y., & Dang, N. J. (2000). Psychotherapy with members of Asian American churches and spiritual traditions. In P. S. Richards & A. E. Bergin (Eds.), *Handbook of psychotherapy and religious diversity* (pp. 421–444). Washington, D.C.: American Psychological Association.

U. S. Bureau of Census. (1986, 1989, 1995, 1997, 1998). *Population profiles of the United States*. Washington, D.C.: Government Printing Office.

Wenhao, J., Salomon, H. B., & Chay, D. M. (1993). Transcultural counseling and people of Asian origin: A developmental and therapeutic perspective. In J. McFadden (Ed.), *Transcultural counseling: Bilateral and international perspectives* (pp. 239–250). Alexandria, VA: American Association for Counseling and Development.

Woollett, A., Marshall, H., Nicolson, P., & Dosanjh, N. (1994). Asian women's ethnic identity: The impact of gender and context in the accounts of women bringing up children in East London. *Feminism and Psychology, 4,* 101–114.

CHAPTER 11
Latino Population

A journey of migration to a new land, language, and culture involves many losses and the challenge not merely to adapt but to reinvent a life. The process of acculturation challenges the immigrant to develop this new life by assimilating new elements without forfeiting old ones. During cultural, developmental, and other life cycle transitions, many immigrant Latino families turn to the comfort and continuity of past traditions such as prayer and folk medicines. The human tendency to find comfort and stability in the midst of change by revisiting cultural beliefs and rituals has been called *ideological ethnicity* (Harwood, 1981).

The 1990 Census counted 22.3 million Latinos in the United States. This represents 46% of the international population of the United States and about 9% of the total population. Of these, 61.2% are Mexicans and 7% Puerto Ricans and Cubans. By the year 2010, it is estimated that Latinos will become the largest minority group in the United States. By 2050, it is projected that Latinos will comprise one fourth of the entire U.S. population. Demographic studies indicate that overall the Hispanic population is younger, less educated, poorer, and more likely to live in inner-city neighborhoods than the general population. These factors, coupled with their linguistic minority status, make Hispanics particularly vulnerable to psychological problems requiring mental health services (Aponte & Wohl, 2000).

Hispanic or *Latino* are terms used to describe people who come from different countries with different cultures. Once they arrive in the United States, they are officially categorized as "Hispanics" by the U.S. Census

Bureau. This is seen as a politically conservative term and a source of conflict. The terms Latinas/Latinos are seen as more progressive (Gonzalez, 1992). For the purpose of clarity, the term Latinos will be used.

Even though it is important to differentiate the ethnic identities of Latinos, certain commonalities are helpful for therapists to acknowledge. Spanish is a common language, except for Brazilians who speak Portuguese, and most Latinos belong to the Roman Catholic Church. In the Latino culture, an emphasis is placed on spiritual values and a commitment to the inner qualities of personhood as opposed to the individualism and material achievement valued so highly in American culture. Perhaps the most significant value Latinos share is the importance of family unity, welfare, and honor. Validating these and other values in their culture is essential to help Latinos maintain dignity as a people and foster a sense of community (Boyd-Franklin & Garcia-Preto, 1994).

Most of the literature portrays Latinos as maintaining a dual system of beliefs and practices: of beliefs in traditional or natural folk approaches on one hand, and beliefs in the supernatural, magic, or witchcraft on the other. Shorris (1992) discussed how spiritual beliefs influence the worldview of many Latino clients. The most common folk illnesses are fear, indigestion, nerves, and nervous attacks (Harwood, 1981). Underlying folk illnesses are beliefs in the power of strong emotions, one's own or another's, that influence bodily health (Falicov, 1999).

Because of the predominance of Catholicism in Latin America and on Latinos in the United States, Roman Catholic beliefs have influenced this culture's attitudes regarding mental and physical health. Basic beliefs include belief in a Supreme Being, life after death, the existence of one's soul, a hell, a heaven, sin, guilt, free will, and many of the beliefs attributed to the Christian faith. Devotional prayers and pilgrimages play an important role as well, especially devotion to the Virgin of Guadalupe who has had a profound influence on Latinos since 1531. This devotion began when a poor priest, Juan Diego, reported that he saw the Mother of God appear miraculously to him as a brown-skinned indigenous Aztec. Her portrait hangs in almost every Latino home and is venerated by the people because they attribute having enormous psychological protection from her, and she unifies them in their religious devotions (Falicov, 1999). Being knowledgeable about the importance of this devotion in Latino lives can help build the counselor/client relationship.

When working with clients whose dominant language is not the same as their own, mental health professionals must identify if their client's bilingualism is affecting their perceptions of the client. Research has shown that clinicians can misinterpret the disrupted speech and reduced affect of their clients as psychological problems, rather than merely a difficulty with the language. Translators may be necessary in cases such as this, but care must be taken that the translators have a knowledge of both the verbal and nonverbal nuances within the language in addition to the mental health background.

Diversity is the hallmark of Latino Americans. The richness of their cultural and religious backgrounds greatly influences their heterogeneity. Racially, Latino Americans are composed of indigenous American, African, European, and Asian ancestry and all possible combinations (Zea, Mason, & Marguia, 2000). Into this kaleidoscope of peoples comes a variety of religious and spiritual influences: Roman Catholicism from Spain and Portugal; indigenous traditions based on Aztec, Mayan, and Andean worldviews (Ramirez, 1983); and African practices that survived slavery (Zea, Quezada, & Belgrave, 1997).

Despite the widespread importance of religion and spirituality for Latinos, very little has been written about the interaction of religion and psychotherapy. Churches and church life provide support and a sense of community. Church functions not only as a place of worship but as a social setting where both adults and children can socialize.

Adherence to church doctrine varies with different Latino groups. For Mexicans, especially the older population, the church provides spiritual support in the form of hope. For Puerto Ricans, the church is a place for weddings and funerals. It is not considered necessary to reach God or the supernatural. Puerto Ricans have a special relationship with the saints whom they believe can be personal emissaries to God (Garcia-Preto, 1998). They emphasize values that relate to the spirit as distinguished from physical nature and are willing to sacrifice material wealth for spiritual goals; therefore, being is more important than having or doing (Papajohn & Spiegel, 1975). Many Puerto Ricans believe in Spiritism, an invisible world inhabited by good and evil spirits who influence behavior (Delgado, 1978). Cubans share Catholic values and rituals but without much vigor. Exposure to other religions has led to the incorporation of other beliefs and rituals for many Cubans.

Great diversity exists within the Latino culture, as each culture and racial group has its own religious and spiritual traditions. Because they represent so many cultures, their needs are very challenging for therapists.

Unique Needs of the Latino Population

Some Latino groups have no experience in seeking help from therapists. They are more likely to seek help from a priest, a physician, or a family member. Those who believe in an indigenous worldview will seek help from a *curandero,* who combines clinical skills, traditional remedies, and spiritual considerations. When these authority figures suggest an action, few Latinos would ever dare to not follow the suggestions. However, the therapist's authority is not seen in the same light. Merely listening, reflecting, and using the interventions of the mental health profession are often not seen as sufficient by the Latino client (Zea, Mason & Marguia, 2000). Their natural inclination is to be more active.

To get Latinos to discuss their spiritual beliefs requires great skill on the part of the therapist. In order for the therapy to be effective, therapists must have a deep understanding and respect for the Latino's religious and spiritual beliefs. Many Latinos, especially those with an indigenous worldview, will fear that the therapist will label them as abnormal just because of their spiritual perspectives. Zea et al. (2000) maintained that a great deal of prejudice is held by Latino and non-Latino therapists alike against clients who proffer from indigenous spiritual beliefs. Consequently, this prejudice hinders the ability of the therapist to suspend judgment and listen to the client.

It is important to emphasize the major significance of the therapeutic relationship. It takes a long time for persons of this culture to develop trust in the therapist, but once this trust relationship is established, clients will treat the therapist almost as a family member or a close friend. Once the cultural barriers are broken, therapists are viewed in almost the same manner as priests, who are considered to be in a sacred position in the lives of Latinos.

Psychological interventions that emphasize individualistic approaches are less congruent with a Latino worldview than those that emphasize collective approaches. Because of the collective nature of the Latino culture, the degree of closeness among family members can sometimes be interpreted by outsiders as being pathological. For Latinos, however, the opposite is considered to be pathological. Not to care for a family member in need or not to support a relative is pathological.

Carmela (Case Notes from a Client)
Carmela (her real name and identifying information has been changed) came to counseling because a recent breakup with her boyfriend/fiancé had left her depressed, tearful, and with very poor self-esteem. Carmela was a young woman in her mid-twenties of Latin American descent. Both of her parents had been born in Central America and had come to the United States as adults. Carmela's older siblings had also been born in Central America, but Carmela, as the youngest of the family, and her next-oldest brother had been born in America. Carmela lived in a major eastern city on the Atlantic seacoast. She still lived at home with her parents, as did two of her unmarried siblings. The other siblings were married and had homes of their own, but they lived in close proximity to their parents' house.

Carmela and all the members of her family were Roman Catholics. A mixture of Spanish and English was spoken in the home, but because Carmela had always gone to school in America, her English was flawless, although spoken with a slight Spanish accent. Carmela's family had lived in the same neighborhood since her birth and had attended the same Catholic Church where she had been baptized, made her first communion, and been confirmed. She also attended the parochial grammar school attached to the church parish.

Carmela's family was a blue-collar family, and none of her siblings had attended a four-year college or received a college degree, but all had graduated from high school. Carmela was presently enrolled in a junior college and was in her third semester there. She had been recommended to the therapist by one of her teachers.

It was obvious that Carmela was very nervous when she first came to the therapist's office. She failed to make eye contact readily and she twisted a handkerchief in her hands almost the entire time. Carmela spoke in a low voice that was hard to hear at times, and she seemed on the verge of tears throughout the initial interview session. She was a small, young woman slightly less than 5 feet tall. Although small boned, she had a very feminine and well-developed figure. She was olive skinned with enormous brown eyes and long, lustrous black hair. All in all, she was a very attractive young woman, although a sad one. The therapist sensed that establishing trust with Carmela would not be easy and have to develop over time. In spite of this, or because of it, Carmela exuded a sweet vulnerability that was endearing, but almost childlike in essence. She appeared sad, frightened, and rather overwhelmed at times.

In response to the counselor's questions regarding why she had come to counseling, Carmela stated that she felt that every relationship in her life was unsatisfactory. She didn't know where to turn for comfort. The breakup with her boyfriend had left her shaken and feeling overwhelmed with grief. She thought that everything in their relationship was going very well, although they did have heated arguments at times, until she found out from a friend that he had been cheating on her with someone she thought was a friend. This left her shaken and feeling totally adrift. She couldn't concentrate on her studies, and she was nervous about telling the whole story to her parents, although they certainly knew something was wrong. She had gone into one of her teacher's offices to try to explain why she did not have the research paper that was due and all she could do was cry. This teacher gave her the name of the therapist.

In the second session, Carmela began to talk about her family and how close they all were. All the children were expected to live at home until they married, and those who were married with families were expected to come for Sunday dinner or at least to visit once a week if not more. As the baby, Carmela had been dominated by her mother and her older sisters. Her brothers were overprotective of her and had threatened other boyfriends she had in the past. They had never liked the most recent man in her life, because he was 10 years older than she was and he lived alone in an apartment, among other things. Although his mother was Latino, his father wasn't, and family didn't seem to mean as much to him.

As therapy progressed, the counselor was able to discern some of the real causes of Carmela's distress. Carmela confided that her faith had always been a source of comfort and even joy for her. She believed in God with all of her mind and heart, and the rituals and ceremonies of her church were beautiful and even magical to her. St. Paul's Catholic Church had been a home away from home for her. School and church had always been intertwined and in that mix was her family. The therapist noted, however, that whenever Carmela spoke of these things she seemed far from happy, but rather on the verge of tears.

In about the fourth session, Carmela burst into tears shortly after starting the session, and between sobs the real issues began to surface. Carmela felt guilt more than any other emotion. Underneath her sadness was an enormous amount of anger. She was angry because of being forced to live at home. She wanted to be free to move into an apartment like many of her friends had done, but she was afraid of hurting and angering her parents. Carmela had always been the "baby," the good little girl. How could she disappoint them now?

Carmela loved the religion of her birth in many ways, but also resented its strictness. She felt that many of the church's regulations were out of date, yet disobeying them made her feel guilty. In the course of discussing this, Carmela burst into tears once again. She revealed she was currently taking birth control pills because she and her former boyfriend were having sex during their relationship. She felt that, as an adult, she should have the right to make these decisions for herself, yet she could not seem to lose the enormous burden of guilt that she carried. It was guilt where God was concerned, but it was also guilt where her parents, her ethnic heritage, and the community of Latinos were concerned. At times this was almost more than she could bear. The breakup with the man in life only intensified these feelings. She felt like God was punishing her for breaking His laws.

Carmela wanted to return to the carefree, happy days of her youth where innocence and a love of God and her family prevailed and were unsullied. The counselor recognized a young woman in extreme pain and conflict. Therapy began with attempts to help Carmela realize she was an adult, and that as such, she had to assume responsibility for her actions and decisions. She had to step out of the role of the "baby" who obeyed to please everyone and become the young adult who had the responsibility and privilege of defining her own life.

Carmela resisted this, claiming it would cause her parents too much pain. The counselor guided Carmela to recognize that to stay in her current situation was only causing her parents more distress because she was angry and resentful most of the time and they did not really understand why. Carmela decided to try to tackle these problems one by one. The first question she tried to resolve was where she would reside. She began to read the newspaper want ads and figure out what moving into an apartment would cost her. She felt that having a roommate would be an easier first step for her and, and even though it may have appeared cowardly, it would also be easier for her parents to bear. The therapist commented that Carmela had to do whatever it was she could bear in the present moment. Transitioning in small steps was nothing to be ashamed of, and she had the right to do whatever felt comfortable for her. They practiced confronting her parents with the news that she wanted to move out on her own. Although very fearful, Carmela realized this was a necessary step for her in establishing her independence.

On the question of birth control and sex outside of marriage, these were questions of such a personal nature that the counselor was careful to act as a sounding board but not to interject her own opinion on these subjects in any way. Carmela came to realize that these were not "yes" or "no" subjects. Why was she consenting to having sex in the first place? Was she doing this only to please someone else? Was she trying to hold on to someone possibly for all the wrong reasons? Was it truly her decision? As Carmela attempted to explore these issues, she began to fully realize how complicated, yet how essential, they all were. In no way did she resolve all of these immediately in therapy, but she was able to make the decision not to get into another sexual relationship until she had been able to discern her true feelings around these issues. As attractive as she was, it would have been easy to simply find another partner to help ease the hurt and reassure herself of her attractiveness, but she recognized the folly of this and how much more her self-esteem would suffer in the end.

Carmela grew emotionally as a result of wrestling with these issues and reclaimed her identity from such decisions. It also helped her to look at her previous relationship in a new way. This helped to ease the hurt and allowed her to view her ex-boyfriend in a more objective light. She began to see how immature he really was and how the breakup was really in her best interest, but this took some time and did not happen overnight.

Carmela felt that her relationship with her religion was at the core of many of her difficulties. She came to see that her religion in many ways was a metaphor for her family—an entity that afforded her much joy and a definite sense of belonging, but that at times seemed to suffocate her and hold her back from independence. Once Carmela could really see this, she determined to treat her church in the same way she sought to maintain membership in her family. She had absolutely no intention of rejecting her family and refusing to associate with them even as difficult as it might have been to be a part of a unit that in some ways was so unrelenting. She felt the same way about her church membership.

She did change Catholic parishes and began to attend Mass at the Catholic chapel that was a part of a local university campus. Here she found priests who were more attuned to the problems of young adults and who were more open to discussing these things without the need to enforce guilt and shame. She also joined a young Catholic singles group that frequently held group discussions about many issues and also offered study groups focusing on spirituality and personal growth from a scriptural context. Carmela really felt like she had come home. She knew she would wrestle with some of these issues all of her life, but she felt more at peace, and the amount of guilt she had carried was greatly lightened. She definitely felt more in control of her life and her decisions.

Implications for Counselors

As stated in previous chapters, Ingersoll (1994) delineated seven different dimensions to the integration of spirituality into one's life:

1. One's conception of the divine, absolute, or "force greater than one's self"
2. One's sense of meaning of what is beautiful or worthwhile
3. One's relationship with divinity and others
4. One's tolerance or capability for mystery
5. Peak and ordinary experiences that enhance spirituality (which may include rituals or spiritual disciplines)
6. Seeing spirituality as play
7. Viewing spirituality as a systemic force that acts to integrate all the dimensions of one's life (p. 11)

Carmela was imbued with a sense of the divine almost from birth. The ethnic group she belongs to has a long history of religious fervor. She definitely believed in a power higher than herself and saw this as the source of what was beautiful and worthwhile. Even in her struggles with some of the tenets of her faith, Carmela still received joy from the rituals and ceremonies of her church. Her relationship with the divine was a personal one and had been fostered from birth. Even when angry at the church for what she perceived to be overly strict regulations and beliefs, Carmela had no desire to leave her religious faith. She had the ability to believe in and appreciate mystery, and religion was not just a duty but had also been a source of joy at different times in her life. Her religious faith was a source of consolation for her once she could reconcile her own needs and her right to explore her own conscience. Spirituality was at the center of her life, or it would not have had the power to cause such pain. Through therapy Carmela matured as an individual and as a member of her church.

Suggested Approaches for Working with the Latino Client

Mental health researchers and anthropologists are beginning to realize that Latino spirituality is not a solitary individualistic path (Goodman, 1988; Koss-Chioino, 1999). Therefore, the first step for the therapist is to determine how important these complex traditions are in the lives of their clients. To what extent is the tradition central to the person's sense of self? What role does it play psychologically, socially, and spiritually? How does the tradition explain the client's current circumstances (Comas-Diaz, 1981)?

Most Latinos share a core belief that is very important for the therapist to understand: When illness or troubles come, the cause is often attributed to forces outside of themselves. Many Latinos will add "God willing" when speaking of their future plans, thus conveying the idea and belief that their lives are governed by a higher power. On the other hand, Cisneros (1997) saw the relatively infrequent use of this linguistic expression among other Anglo-Americans as evidence that they must feel in control of their own destiny.

The notion that little in life is under one's direct control is a worldview ascribed to minority groups, but it is important to distinguish various meanings that are attributed to external forces when working with clients of diverse cultures. Sue and Sue (1999) suggested that "high externality may be due to (a) chance luck, (b) cultural dictates viewed as benevolent, and (c) political force (racism and discrimination) that represents malevolent but realistic obstacles" (p. 143).

Fatalism, a cognitive orientation or belief system, may resemble some of these aspects of externality (Comas-Diaz, 1989). It is thought to be more prevalent among poor people because they learn through a lifetime of experiences that powerful people and unpredictable forces control their lives. Limited opportunities to get ahead only fuel these feelings of helplessness and increase psychological distress (Ross, Mirowsky, & Cockerham, 1983). It is important for clinicians to distinguish between this type of fatalism and more cultural inclinations that are evident in Latinos who see problems as a result of God's will. Sometimes mental illness is perceived as God's test; at other times it is seen as God's will.

Another form of coping related to the locus of control lies in somatization, those medically unexplained physical symptoms that commonly denote emotional distress. Depression is correlated with somatization, according to Barsky and Klerman (1983). Among the poor and refugees, somatization is found more often because health care is more readily available for medical than for psychological complaints.

Therapists' views of Latino clients differ depending on their training and experience with Latino clients. Given the complexity of Latino culture, many non-Latino therapists consider themselves unqualified to work with Latinos. Many barriers to treatment stem from non-Latino therapists' lack of knowledge of Latino culture and their unwillingness to be in an apprentice role in the therapeutic session (Tyler, Brome, & Williams, 1991). Despite this, because of the increase in the numbers of Latino immigrants, Anglo therapists have no choice but to work with Latino clients.

As a result of being inadequately trained in working with Latinos, therapists often neglect to address the client's spiritual identity as an integral part of the counseling process. A lack of knowledge of the different spiritual beliefs and religious traditions is a barrier in the client/therapist relationship (Ivey et al., 1997; Richardson & June, 1997).

Acculturation Process of Latinos

Cultural groups interpret and act on the acculturation process differently. Smart and Smart (1995) suggested that six unique characteristics of the Latino immigration experience tend to foster and sustain acculturative stress and impede movement through the stages of adjustment. Counselors must incorporate knowledge of and responsiveness to the following needs if they are to be successful with Latino clients:

1. Discrimination on the basis of skin color
   Because of the unfortunate problem of racial discrimination in American culture, it is important for counselors to realize that acceptance into American society may be easier for someone who is light-skinned than for someone who is dark. For example, Mexican Americans may be of mixed Spanish and Native American descent. When a Mexican American has similar physical characteristics to a Native American, he or she may experience prejudice and discrimination similar to Native Americans and African-Americans (Avila & Avila, 1995). Wide variations in skin color are the norm in Latin countries, and Latinos are accustomed to accepting people of color. It is necessary for the counselor to take into consideration not only the ethnicity of the client but also the race with which the client most closely associates.
2. Unique emphasis on social and family ties

Because Latino cultures stress affiliation and cooperation, competition and confrontation are particularly difficult for them (Lum, 1986). They view American society as more impersonal and cold. On the other hand, the Latino open-door hospitality, which invites unusually large numbers of extended family members to live under one roof, causes problems for landlords and housing authorities. Establishing parenthood or guardianship for Latino children is often a complicated problem for public school authorities.

3. Illegal immigration

Many Latinos, especially Mexican Americans, enter the United States by crossing the border illegally. These undocumented immigrants live in constant fear of deportation. They are vulnerable to exploitation by unscrupulous employers who often expect them to work for wages that are below market value. According to Espi (1987), the psychological impact of the immigration experience on women may be more traumatic because of repeated rape or other forms of sexual abuse and harassment they may have experienced.

4. Geographic proximity

The geographic proximity of Latin American countries allow for constant travel to and from the United States. This migration pattern militates against acculturation because of a constant flow of new arrivals who are not pressured into learning the English language or changing from their Latino culture. These people take much longer than other immigrants to be acculturated.

5. The legacy of armed conflict

It is important to remember that many Latino cultures did not originally become part of the United States voluntarily. Many, like the Mexican Americans, were conquered by armed conflict (McLemore & Ramo, 1985). American foreign policy toward Cuba and Nicaragua are also examples of such conflict. Counselors who are unaware of these armed conflicts may unintentionally insult clients by their lack of sensitivity to history and natural loyalties.

6. Latino reliance on physical labor

In the past, the United States needed large numbers of physical laborers. Today the United States is affected by the global economy, which depends on information technologies and fewer physical laborers. As a result, it is more difficult for Latino Americans who are less educated and socialized to obtain satisfying work that rewards them for their efforts and dedication. Although little information is available concerning the education of immigrants, what is available suggests that education is one of the main factors influencing the rate of assimilation of immigrant children into American society.

The counseling literature has emphasized critical differences among ethnic groups and has stressed the need for culture-specific techniques to address these differences. Sue and Sue (1999) listed the following characteristics as typical. Latino clients prefer to: (a) be active during counseling because they are action-oriented; (b) receive some guidance, direction, and advice from the counselor; (c) focus on the present because the future is not seen as being under their control; (d) look for immediate short-range goals, immediate cause and effect, and little delay in gratification; and (e) have a concrete, structured approach to counseling.

Given these groups' characteristics, Cruz and Littrel (1998) suggested that brief counseling would be a good fit for this cultural group. They conducted a study with a group of Latino American college students and found that brief counseling was most effective in dealing with (a) academic concerns such as grade improvements, study skills, and time management; (b) career concerns such as preparation for a job interview; and (c) personal social issues such as family relationships, friendships, or separation problems. However, they cautioned that very brief counseling has some limitations. It is not suitable for problems such as potential suicide, sexual abuse, eating disorders, crisis intervention, and other severe situations because this form of counseling incorporates a solution-focused approach within a limited time frame.

Exercises

1. Visit an area with a large Latino population and attend a worship service. Observe the family interactions during this visit. What spiritual strengths do you notice that you can relate to that will help you in working with Latino clients? What do you need to learn? Write this in your journal.
2. Talk to a Latino American student about his or her grandparents. What spiritual strengths have they learned from their elders? What do they want to pass on to their own children? What questions regarding their spirituality are they working through?

Martina's Case

Martina is a first-generation Latino teen struggling with the values of her parents and rebelling against their rules. She says that they are keeping her from fitting in with the crowd, and she frequently violates curfew. She has joined a group of girls who call themselves the Latino Sisterhood, who are known for their body piercing and cult practices. Martina's father has been verbally abusive and has threatened to send her to his mother who lives in Argentina. Martina said she would run away before she would go to

Argentina. Martina's mother is a devout Catholic and believes that Martina is involved in devil worship. She has spoken to her pastor who is willing to talk with Martina; however, she refuses to see him. Martina's family is close-knit, and her aunts and uncles have been trying to use their influence to no avail.

Case Discussion

- What are your impressions of this family system?
- How could Martina's religious upbringing be useful in helping her to look at her behaviors?
- Who could be a possible influence to intervene in this case?
- Where is Martina developmentally?

References

Aponte, J. F., & Wohl, J. (Eds.). (2000). *Psychological intervention and cultural diversity.* Boston: Allyn and Bacon.

Avila, D. L., & Avila, A. L. (1995). Mexican Americans. In N. A. Vacc, S. B. DeVaney, and J. Wittmer (Eds.), *Experiencing and counseling multicultural and diverse populations* (3rd ed., pp. 119–146). Bristol, PA: Accelerated Development.

Barsky, A. J., & Klerman, G. I. (1983). Hypochondriasis, bodily complaints, and somatic styles. *American Journal of Psychiatry, 140*(3), 273–283

Boyd-Franklin, N., & Garcia-Preto, N. (1994). Family therapy: The cases of African-American and Hispanic women. In L. Comas-Díaz & B. Greene (Eds.), *Women of color: Integrating ethnic and gender identities in psychotherapy* (pp. 239–264). New York: Guilford Press.

Cisneros, S. (1997, Fall/Winter). In two humors. *Si Magazine, I,* 68–70.

Comas-Diaz, L. (1981). Puerto Rican espiritismo and psychotherapy. *American Journal of Orthopsychiatry, 51,* 636–645.

Comas-Diaz, L. (1989). Culturally relevant issues and treatment implications for Hispanics. In D. Koslow & E. Salett (Eds.), *Crossing cultures in mental health* (pp. 31–48). Washington, D.C.: SIETAR International.

Cruz, J., & Littrell, J. M. (1998). Brief counseling with Hispanic-American college students. *Journal of Multicultural Counseling and Development, 26*(4), 227–239.

Delgado, M. (1978). Folk medicine in Puerto Rican culture. *International Social Work, 2*(2), 46–54.

Espi, O. M. (1987). Psychological impact of migration on Latino women. *Psychology of Women Quarterly, 11,* 489–503.

Falicov, C. J. (1999). *Latino families in therapy: A guide to multicultural practice.* New York: Guilford Press.

Garcia-Preto, N. (1996). Latino families: An overview. In M. McGoldrick, J. Giordano, & J. K. Pearce (Eds.), *Ethnicity and family therapy* (pp. 141–154). New York: Guilford Press.

Garcia-Preto, N. (1998). Puerto Rican families. In C. J. Falicov (Ed.), *Latino families in therapy: A guide to multicultural practice.* New York: Guilford Press.

Gonzalez, F. (1992, February). Schools can involve Hispanic parents. *IDRA Newsletter, 19*(2), 2–4.

Goodman, F. (1988). *How about demons: Possession and exorcism in the modern world.* Bloomington, IN: Indiana University Press.

Harwood, A. (1981). *Ethnicity and medical care.* Cambridge, MA: University Press.

Ivey, A. E. (1995). Psychotherapy as liberation: Toward specific skills and strategies in multicultural counseling and therapy. In J. G. Ponterotto, J. M. Casas, L. Suzuki, & C. Alexander (Eds.), *Handbook of multicultural counseling* (pp. 53–72). Thousand Oaks, CA: Sage Publications, Inc.

Ivey, A. E., Ivey, M. B., & Simek-Morgan, L. (1997). *Counseling and psychotherapy: A multicultural perspective* (4th ed). Boston: Allyn and Bacon.

Koss-Chioino, J. D. (1999). *Working with Latino youth: Culture, development, and context.* San Francisco, CA: Jossey-Bass.

Lee, E. (1996). Chinese families. In M. McGoldrick, J. Giordano, and J. Pearce (Eds.), *Ethnicity and family therapy* (2nd ed.) New York: Guildford Press.

Lum, D. (1986). *Social work practice and people of color: A process, stage approach.* Monterey, CA; Brooks/Cole.

McLemore, S. D., & Ramo, R. (1985). The origins and development of the Mexican people. In R. de La Garza, F. D. Beans, C. M. Bonyean, R. Ramo, & R. Alvare (Eds.), *The Mexican American experience: An interdisciplinary anthology* (pp. 3–32). Austin, TX: University of Texas Press.

Moy, S. (1992). A culturally sensitive, psychoeducational model for understanding and treating Asian-American clients. *Journal of Psychology and Christianity, 11,* 358–367.

Papajohn, J., & Spiegal, J. (1975). *Transactions in families.* San Francisco, CA: Jossey-Bass.

Ramirez, M. (1983). *Psychology of Americans: Western perspectives on personality and mental health.* New York: Pergamon Press.

Richardson, B. L., & June, L. N. (1997). Utilizing and maximizing the resource of the African-American church: Strategies and tools for counseling professionals. In C. C. Lee (Ed.), *Multicultural issues in counseling: New approaches to diversity* (pp. 155–170). Alexandria, VA: American Counseling Association.

Ross, C. E., Mirowsky, J., & Cockerham, W. C. (1983). Social class, Mexican culture, and fatalism: Their effects on psychological distress. *American Journal of Community Psychology, 11,* 383–399.

Shorris, E. (1992). *Latinos: A history of the people.* New York: W. W. Norton.

Smart, F., & Smart, D. W. (1995). Acculturation stress of Hispanics: Loss and challenge. *Journal of Counseling and Development, 73,* 390–397.

Sue, D. W., & Sue, D. (1999). *Counseling the culturally different: Theory and practice* (3rd ed.). New York: Wiley.

Tyler, F., Brome, D. R., & Williams, J. E. (1991). *Ethnic validity, ecology, and psychotherapy—A psychosocial competence model.* New York: Plenum Press.

Zea, M. C., Mason, M. A., & Marguia. (2000). Psychotherapy with members of Latino-Latina religious and spiritual traditions. In P. S. Richards & A. E. Bergin (Eds.), *Handbook of psychotherapy and religious diversity.* Washington, D. C.: American Psychological Association.

Zea, M. C., Quezada, T., & Belgrave, F. S. (1997). Limitations of an acultural health psychology for Latinos: Restructuring the African influence on Latino culture and health-related behaviors. In J. G. Garcia & M. C. Zea (Eds.), *Psychological intervention and research with Latino populations* (pp. 255–266). Boston: Allyn and Bacon.

CHAPTER 12
Native Americans

The Native American population in 1998 numbered 2.3 million in the United States (Russell, 1998). An analysis of this group shows that they are culturally heterogeneous, geographically dispersed, and remarkably young. Thirty-nine percent of these people are under 29 years of age as compared to 29% of the total U.S. population (LaFromboise, 1993). Fewer Native Americans are high school graduates relative to the general population, and the annual income level is 62% of the U.S. average (Sue & Sue, 1999; U.S. Bureau of the Census, 1995).

A quote from *Native American Religions* by Hirschfelder and Molin (1992) is instructive:

> ... the North American public remains ignorant about Native American religions. And this, despite the fact that hundreds of books and articles have been published by anthropologists, religionists and others about native beliefs. . . . Little of this scholarly literature has found its way into popular books about Native American religion. . . .

Yet Natives American culture and religion should be valued, if for no other reason than the many contributions they have made to North American society.

Many followers of Native American spirituality do not regard their spiritual beliefs and practices as a "religion" the same way many Christians do. Their beliefs and practices form a integral and seamless part of their very being. Because of the wide range of habitats in North America, different native religions evolved to match the needs and lifestyles of the individual tribe. Religious traditions of aboriginal peoples around the world also tend to be heavily influenced by their methods of acquiring food, whether by hunting wild animals or by agriculture. Native American spirituality is no exception. Their rituals and beliefs show an interest in promoting and preserving their hunting and horticulture.

Native Americans today follow many spiritual traditions, and many families have been devout Christians for generations. Other tribes, particularly in the Southwest, have kept their aboriginal traditions more or less intact. Most Native Americans follow a personal faith that combines traditional and Christian elements. Pan-Indianism is a recent and growing movement that encourages a return to traditional beliefs and seeks to create a common native religion.

The Native American Church is a continuation of the ancient Peyote religion that has existed for about 10,000 years. Incorporated in 1918, the church's original aim was to promote Christian beliefs and values, and to use the Peyote sacrament. Although the use of peyote is restricted to religious rituals (which are protected by the U.S. Constitution), is not harmful or habit forming, and has a multimillennia tradition, considerable opposition has come from Christian groups, from governments, and from within some tribes (Web site: Native American Spirituality).

No study of Native Americans would be complete without first acknowledging the need on the part of non-native people to recognize the intrinsic worth of native spiritual beliefs and practices. In fact, such beliefs and practices are a part of long-held Native traditions that have struggled to sustain their authenticity in the face of a dominant culture denial. Any introduction to these traditions requires respect, patience, and a commitment to understanding even the most elementary aspects of Native American life and culture. The disturbing history of religious persecution and the denial of native religious rights, coupled with an often irresponsible public exposure of beliefs and practices, have led to a sheltering of native spirituality from the public eye. The consequence of this irresponsible behavior on the part of non-natives has created a climate of caution or mistrust that only additional generations of reciprocal care, listening, and responsiveness can fully heal (Irwin, 1996).

One must understand that spirituality as practiced by Native Americans has a deep connection to their core values and beliefs. Spirituality is a pervasive quality of life that develops out of an authentic participation in values and real-life experiences meant to connect members of a community with the deepest foundations of personal affirmation and ideality. Essentially, spirituality is inseparable from any sphere of activity as long as it connects with affirmative values and sources of authentic commitment and genuine concern. This spirituality is remarkably diverse and embedded in unique ethnic histories. The changes in contemporary American society and the numerous political, economic, and social upheavals that constantly batter Native American communities create a very complex problem.

Irwin (1996) painted this complexity in graphic and colorful language:

> When I think of the image of the Native person in the context of popular culture, it seems more like a Thanksgiving Day parade balloon-figure, blown up out of proportion and painted with artificial colors and cartoon designs. The non-native people holding the ropes are marching in a display of cultural images far more reflective of themselves than of the peoples such images claim to represent. From "noble savages" to "shaman healers" and from "blood-thirsty warriors" to "political radicals," these images seem to speak of something other than real people whose complexity and concerns cannot be reduced to such inadequate images. Furthermore, such images deny the actual, deeply held communal aspects that inform the lives of many Native peoples, the kinship connections and the sense of obligations that unite the community in its struggles against internal and external tensions. The isolated, inflated, and artificial images created by non-natives seeking a simpler, inauthentic overview need to be thoroughly collapsed and deflated. A more complex, nuanced view of Native diversity and difference can be created out of a context of meaningful communal dialogues. The value of diversity and identity within a specific community is that they foster a better understanding of the rich inheritance of the past and present (p. 328).

Unique Needs of This Group

Complex and richly diverse, Native American family life is difficult to describe because the roles of specific family members and the structure of extended families vary across tribes and among families within tribes. Yet obvious contrasts emerge when Native American families are compared with Anglo families.

Traditionally, Native American people live in relational networks that serve to support and nurture strong bonds of mutual assistance and affection. Many tribes still engage in a traditional system of collective interdependence with family members responsible not only to one another but also to the clan and tribe to which they belong. When problems arise among Native American youth, for example, these problems become problems of the community as well. The family, relatives, and friends join together to observe the youth's behavior, draw him or her out of isolation, and integrate the youth back into the group. Extended family members, such as uncles, aunts, and grandparents, function as important teachers.

They share wisdom, influence values, serve as role models, and reinforce tribal traditions, especially spiritual values. The early introduction of children to the spiritual life of the tribe fosters a loving respect for nature, as well as independence and self-discipline. Traditionally, tribal spirituality is the same as tribal life. The two are not deliberately separated (Hungary Wolf & Hungary Wolf, 1987).

Also, no particular tribal spirituality remains paramount among Native American people. Families encourage and expect all members, including children and adolescents, to participate in various ceremonies. Unfortunately, this participation in ceremonies sometimes militates against the attendance policies of dominant Anglo culture and therefore causes problems with negative consequences for the Native Americans.

Even though Native people suffer from many of the same problems that lead others to counseling, traditional counseling interventions have not been effective. Duran and Duran (1995) suggested four reasons why:

- Mental health professionals lack an understanding of Native people's traditions, values, and worldviews.
- Mental health professionals fail to include spirituality in the therapeutic process.
- Not enough outreach is extended to Native people at high risk for psychological problems but who lack the resources (e.g., money and transportation) to access a mental health care system.
- Counselors are unwilling to address contextual factors (e.g., cultural oppression and racism) that compromise the mental health of many Native people.

Regardless of the immense diversity and varying demographics, common threads are woven throughout this population. For example, a prevailing sense of "Indianess" based on a common worldview appears to bind the Native Americans together as a "people of many peoples" (Garrett & Garrett, 1994).

The challenge of counseling Native Americans is to create a dialogue of growth with individual clients and their communities across the cultures. Embedded in this goal is a respect for indigenous cultural values. The counselor must keep an open mind when assessing the client's worldview (Ibrahim, 1991; Pedersen, Firkuyana, & Health, 1984). This worldview serves as a background for the collage of identity one develops that is grounded in the individual, group, and universal levels of human behavior (Sanford & Donovan, 1984).

Native Americans are affected by several cultures (Peregay, 1991), and several studies have indicated that such clients are looking for someone who understands the practical aspects of tribal culture, can give sound advice about their lives, and is culturally sensitive to their needs (Dauphinais, Dauphinais, & Rowe, 1981). One way of demonstrating respect for the traditional way of healing is to encourage family members and friends to participate in the therapy, which is closer to the natural process of conducting events in Native American culture (Garrett & Garrett, 1994). According to Herring (1999), family therapy with Native Americans will have more positive results than individual sessions because it reflects not only cooperation but also the high motive of talking together as a group.

Suggested Approaches for Working with Native American Clients

Arredondo (1986) proposed a systematic model for working with refugees (or those whose culture is different from the dominant culture that is applicable to working with Native American clients. This model is holistic and encompasses six dimensions of the client's life, including: (a) the historical era, (b) sociopolitical factors, (c) sociocultural factors, (d) individual workables, (e) developmental tasks, and (f) esteem and identity themes. The initial interview is key to developing the therapeutic alliance and establishing a rapport with Native American clients. Showing respect and concern for the client could mean being open to, or suggesting, the possibility of consultation with a traditional healer. Perhaps joint services could be provided by traditional healers in conjunction with the traditional therapy. An assessment of cultural commitment and tribal structure, as well as customs and beliefs, will provide useful information on how to proceed (Garrett & Garrett, 1994).

The more traditional the clients, the more they view the counselor as an elder, expecting the therapist to speak more than they do. It is of the utmost importance that the therapist discuss the counseling process and the importance of confidentiality before beginning the session. By doing this, the therapist provides the client with an understanding of the counseling process and enhances the client's trust in a relationship that may not be familiar to him or her. By using this framework, the therapist may be able to help the client feel more comfortable and more open to the process (LaFromboise & Bigfoot, 1988).

Time spent helping the client feel comfortable should also be used to formulate the issue from the client's point of view. Therefore, the therapist needs to assess the client's level of acculturation, which will provide a better understanding of the issues the client may be facing (LaFromboise, Tremble, & Mohatt, 1990; Peregay & Chapman, 1989). The therapist must be aware of influences the dominant culture may be having on the client's self-depreci-ating beliefs. Beliefs that are irrational by standards of the dominant culture may be perfectly legitimate given the course of Indian-White relations (LaFromboise et al., 1990). The counseling goal may be to help the client see the patterns of irrational thought, behavior, or negative self-assessments, thus facilitating growth in the client toward a more self-satisfying and posi-tive self-image (Arredondo, 1986). According to Garrett & Garrett (1994), the chasm between mainstream expectations and the cultural values of the Native American people can be referred to as "cultural discontinuity." This conflict leaves many clients not "knowing what to do" (p. 136).

McFadden (1999) suggested that the counseling goal may then be facil-itated by cognitive therapies such as self-monitoring, behavior change, and social validation. He also suggested the use of guided imagery as a means of helping the client see how perceptions of self may be changed using a cul-turally sensitive intervention for enhancing the Native person's coping skills.

From aboriginal times, religion and spirituality have played an impor-tant role in the life and survival of the Native American people. Yet it was not until 1978 that the American Religious Freedom Act made it legal to practice native religions. The religion and spirituality of the Native Ameri-can had undergone a history of persecution through legislation that lasted from the late 1800s to 1978. Despite this persecution, religion and spiritu-ality have remained viable and provide meaning to the lives of Native American people. Religion and spirituality serve as the focal point for their view of life. Respect is given to those who protect the sacred knowledge, ways, and practices by which religion and spirituality continue in the lives of Native Americans (Beck & Walters, 1977).

Even though the various tribes maintain their respective traditional val-ues, beliefs, and practices about religion and spirituality, the following are a number of shared views that most tribes have in common (Beck & Walters, 1977):

- A belief or knowledge exists about the unseen powers, and reference is to deities, mystery, and great powers.
- They share the knowledge that all things in the universe are depend-ent on each other, and reference is to the notion of balance and harmony.
- Personal worship creates the bond among the individual tribal mem-bers and the great powers; worship is a personal commitment to the source of life.
- The responsibility of those knowledgeable in the sacred is to teach and guide the Native American way of life.

- For most tribes, a shaman is responsible for specialized, even secret, sacred knowledge; an oral tradition is used by the shaman to pass sacred knowledge and practices from generation to generation.
- A belief exists that to be human is a necessary part of the sacred and an acknowledgement that human beings make mistakes.

For Native Americans, the consideration of religion and spirituality in the treatment process is essential because both are an integral part of their lives. To address these issues effectively, the therapist must possess cultural competence, exemplified with respect and an awareness of the sacred boundaries (or boundaries between the supernatural and the natural, and the transpersonal and the personal). To the Native American, the mental health professionals who demonstrate a sincere interest in being culturally aware, sensitive, competent, personally and professionally responsible, and able to recognize their own limits have a good chance of being successful with their clients (Trujillo, 2000).

Integrating religion and spirituality into the counseling process with a Native American client is a venture into the life experience of the person because these people have a serious regard for assuring that the sacred will be addressed properly. It is crucial to acknowledge that the integrity of their religion and spirituality will remain intact in a respectful and effective way (Trujillo, 2000).

The importance of the person-to-person relationship with the client cannot be overstressed. It is the trust that comes from this relationship, coupled with cultural competence, that opens the door for a successful clinical treatment to occur. Native American culture exists in the context of the sacred. Religion and spirituality guide the Native American through the developmental life span to pursue the source of life. They are the fundamental cornerstones to a way of life that has existed since aboriginal times and that has been the source of life for the Native American to live and survive (Trujillo, 2000).

Roy Lightfoot (An Interview Conducted by One of the Authors)

Roy Lightfoot is a Native American residing in one of the southern states. He is a Wise Man in his tribe and has made quite a study of Native American cultures. He consented to be interviewed in order to allow the author more insight into the beliefs of his people and their unique type of spirituality. Roy explained that over 1,000 different tribal peoples were indigenous to the North American continent. Each tribe had its own set of festivals, rituals, and spiritual beliefs; however, common beliefs were apparent across all tribes.

Spirituality has played a central role in the lives of many of these people. Roy explained that the powers of nature, the personal quest of the soul, the acts of daily life, and the solidarity of the tribe were all considered to be religious, and they were celebrated in dance and ritual. Above all, their spirituality was a land-based spirituality, where the land and the people were mystically interdependent. Different tribes worshiped different aspects of nature. The Great Plains Indians worshiped the Sun God and the Great Sky. Those who were more agriculturally oriented worshiped the Corn God, and others worshiped the buffalo or the bear. As Roy went on to relate, the Indian thought of the earth as his mother. Earth was *home* and therefore not a "dumping ground" or something to be used carelessly and thoughtlessly.

Common to virtually all Native American tribes is a belief in an all-knowing, all-powerful deity known as the Creator or Master Spirit. This being made the universe and may be represented by the sun, and according to Roy Lightfoot, is referred to as the Father. The Goddess is sometimes referred to as Mother Earth and represents the divine feminine. There are also the gods of the elements, namely the Rain God, the Thunder God, and the God of the Wind.

Roy spoke of a spiritual culture made up of three layers. The first of these is the underworld, often considered to be a dangerous and mysterious place. The middle world is where humans dwell with nature, and the third layer is represented by the heavens and is inhabited by powerful spirits. Roy learned these things from his grandmother when he was a young boy. Out of all the members of his family, she was the one who held on to her ancient beliefs the most. She explained to Roy that the three layers were represented by a tree that had its roots in the underworld, its trunk passed through the middle world or earth, and its top was in the sky. She went on to explain that a serpent lived in the trunk of the tree and when the serpent moved, it caused the tree (or the earth) to shake. To her, this explained why earthquakes happened. Roy went on to say that not all Native Americans believed in this three-layered world but that virtually all believed that these three things were united in some way.

I asked Roy about the various ceremonies that Native Americans might have taken part in as a sign of their religious or spiritual beliefs. Giving thanks to their various gods and to the earth was vastly important in Roy's culture. This gratitude was often expressed through elaborate dancing ceremonies and tribal reunions. In Roy's lifetime, a conscious effort was being made to retain the Indian culture in all of its aspects, whereas in his father's generation, much had been neglected or lost.

The focus of many religious ceremonies was "renewal" in its various forms. Roy explained the act of giving thanks as a form of renewal of the bond with the Creator or Master Spirit. The elaborate dances, complete with costumes, often represented the renewal with the Mother Earth. These ceremonies were also a time of renewing bonds of love with family and friends. In other parts of the country, dance rhythms were played on eagle bone whistles as dancers gave thanks to this majestic, sacred bird for giving life to the tribe. Dancers from another region wore hides of buffalo as thanks was given to the powerful animal whose meat and skin were so vital to the survival of the tribe.

I queried Roy about the idea of an afterlife within Native American spirituality and he answered with the assertion that belief in an afterlife is shared by almost all Native American cultures, but that exactly the nature of this afterlife might vary greatly. Some tribes believed in the reincarnation of the person as another human being or even as an animal. Some tribal beliefs incorporated the presence of ghosts, whereas others believed that the soul of the dead person dwelt in another world. In general, Roy stated that most Indian cultures he had studies believed that the spirits of Native Americans live on and that they were able to inspire the next generation with values such as taking care of the earth, working for the common good, and remaining true to oneself. Ancestor worship, according to Roy, is common among the tribes. The dead are respected, as evidenced by the sacredness of burial grounds in the tribal cultures.

According to Roy, everything in the natural world to a Native American is imbued with spirit. He was also taught to believe that constant dialogue existed between all manifestations of creation. In order to survive well in Native American culture, human beings must avoid insulting the spirits of the wind, rain, earth, and so on. Rather than being given domination over all creatures, man is supposed to regard animals, plants, and minerals as companions to learn from and live with. Mutual respectfulness is required of all.

Roy went on to say that this "spirit" that resides in all things is reflected in Native American languages where most nouns are animate. He also said that although all things are thought to be imbued with spirit, certain places are considered to be more sacred than others. Certain landscapes, mountains, land formations, or locations are thought to be very powerful and very holy. Native American literature is full of references to these sacred sites, and they are often used in key rituals and rites of passage. Therefore, when a sacred place is desecrated, one can expect that there will be consequences.

Roy further noted that shapes have a definite meaning in Native American spirituality, as do colors. A circular shape is considered to be a sign of the sacred or divine because the sun, earth, and moon are all round. The circle of life is sometimes represented by the Medicine Wheel. This wheel is forever evolving, bringing new truths and lessons to mankind. Native Americans call life the "Earth Walk" and that in traveling this sacred walk each human being steps on the spokes of the Medicine Wheel many times. Because it is a circle, every direction is honored. The Medicine Wheel teaches that all lessons taught are equal, and all individual talents and abilities are equal. This Magic Wheel is a Native American pathway to truth, peace, and harmony. The circle is never-ending and also represents eternity.

In Native American spirituality, the colors the dancers wear often represent virtues or feelings, just as the colors of the vestments worn in Roman Catholic or Episcopal churches represent certain seasons or events. For instance, red symbolizes success, victory, or power; blue represents defeat or trouble; black is a sign of death; and white signifies peace and happiness.

Two numbers also had sacred meanings to one Native American tribe, the Cherokees. Four (4) represented the primary directions of North, South, East, and West, and seven (7) represented the seven ancient ceremonies that formed the religious cycle of the Cherokee year. In some cultures, there were seven sacred directions, because *above*, *below*, and *middle* or *center* were added to the four points of direction previously cited. The center of a circle was the place of the "sacred fire."

Roy also spoke of how the arts were related to Native American spirituality. Art, music, and dance were at the soul of every celebration. Religious festivals were a time for rejoicing and were looked forward to with joyful anticipation. Native Americans celebrated the earth, its bounty, its seasons, and each other. They did not use the earth in their religious worship—it *was* their religion.

Rather than having a book of scriptures, such as the Bible or the Koran, most Native American religious beliefs were passed on by word of mouth. Oral communication became the standard method for passing on stories, customs, and rituals. Special ceremonies were held to pass on this wisdom to the younger members of the tribe. Because Native American tribes existed all over North America and Canada, religious beliefs varied somewhat and no source of unification existed. In the twentieth century, a Native American church was institutionalized as the Peyote Religion, but by that time many Native Americans had joined more mainstream religions depending on where they were located. Their choice of religion was also dictated in part by the religious groups that sought to colonize and sometimes educate the Native Americans.

Implications for the Counselor

Looking at Ingersoll's (1994) seven different dimensions to the integration of spirituality into one's life, one can analyze and apply the Native American traditions:

1. One's conception of the divine, absolute, or "force greater than one's self"
2. One's sense of meaning of what is beautiful or worthwhile
3. One's relationship with divinity and others
4. One's tolerance or capability for mystery
5. Peak and ordinary experiences that enhance spirituality (which may include rituals or spiritual disciplines)
6. Seeing spirituality as play
7. Viewing spirituality as a systemic force that acts to integrate all the dimensions of one's life (p. 11)

To the Native American, the conception of the divine is embodied in the deity known as the Creator or the Great Spirit. Although one cannot generalize over all tribes and all locations, it is safe to say that an image of the divine as a spirit to be revered and worshipped is rather universal. There is also a reference to the Divine Goddess in the form of Mother Earth.

The natural world is seen as beautiful and a bounty from the Great Spirit. Therefore, water, earth, fire, rain, and so on are to be revered and respected. A connection to the earth is an essential aspect of Native American spirituality. The belief that everything in nature has a soul also echoes the beliefs of certain Eastern religions. This connection with nature is also seen in the depiction of the universe in the form of a tree or a multilayered entity.

Native American spirituality stresses both a personal and a communal relationship with the Creator. Individual prayers and sacrifices are required, but community worship is integral to the Native American sense of religion. Many religious ceremonies focus on both spiritual and temporal renewal, with family life, tribal life, or friendship being exalted in the tribal celebration.

Mystery is an integral part of the Native American psyche, and the spirit world is as real as the temporal one. Therefore, belief in a higher power that can neither be seen nor accessed with the senses is not difficult for Native Americans. Mystery is a part of tribal lore and manifests itself in many forms, including dance. Ingersoll (1994) spoke of the capacity to endure "negative capabilities," and the Native American is more suited to this because of tribal tradition and culture than almost any other group of people.

Joy is an earmark of religious observance among the various tribes of North America. Elaborate and colorful dancing accompanied by singing and the beating of drums mark religious observances. Native American tradition says that there is a time to work and a time to worship. One does not interfere with the other but rather completes it. Gratitude is a defining characteristic of Native American culture and the act of giving thanks to a higher power marks the seasons of the year and the bounty of the earth.

Symbolism and ritual are also earmarks of Native American spirituality and religion. Geometric shapes, colors, numbers, and natural elements are all seen as sacred and representing the divine. Traditions handed down from generation to generation have been preserved in spite of monumental and cruel efforts to eradicate them. A proud people has managed to preserve a history and a set of traditions that date back almost to the beginning of time.

The integration of spirit and temporal worlds gives a sense of meaning to individual experiences for the Native American. Nature and its manifestations form the core or center of their worship. They view life as a vibrant experience that unites them with the entire natural world. Peak experiences are achieved through movement, song, and color. Ordinary life, planting, harvest, and banquets are celebrated and become the focus of religious observances and festivals. Life and religion are seen as one entity.

Spirituality for the Native American is a systemic force that acts to unite and integrate all the separate dimensions of life for an individual or the tribe. Spirituality is to be lived, not just revered. It takes the common elements of everyday life—dirt, water, corn, grass, fire—and sanctifies them. It offers back to nature what nature has chosen to bestow in a sanctified form and in the name of the Great Spirit or Creator. Religion is not a part of life but is life itself.

The history of this proud people is contained in story, myth, and song rather than in a Bible or Sacred Scrolls. The stories of the gods in their various forms explain creation and the works of nature. The destruction of nature is a sad and cruel act of desecration to the Native American people. The earth is their cathedral and its gifts form the core of their ritual and ceremonies. One must understand this, along with the indignities and sufferings these people have endured, in order to understand the core of their existence and their spirituality.

Approaches to Therapy

The Native American idea of therapy consists of families working together to solve problems. Culturally sensitive and nondirective approaches work well with this population. Strategic interventions and brief therapy models are least effective because of the value of "presence" and heartfelt listening. As stated earlier, Native Americans come to therapy hoping that the therapist is an expert who can give them practical and concrete advice about their problems (LaFromboise, Tremble, & Mohatt, 1990). In the past, missionaries, teachers, and social workers have tried to "help" by imposing values and alienating the Native person from the strength and support of families and traditions (LaFromboise et al., 1990). Historically, the Native Americans have been frightened by these well-meaning professionals; thus, the most important credentials for the counselor to possess are authenticity and genuine concern for the client. The therapist who is willing to listen carefully will gradually learn more about the family structure and dynamics, because the individual tribe determines roles and family obligations for the tribal members. Self-disclosure by the therapist can be a way of modeling the counseling process and serve as a nonthreatening way for the counselor to help develop a rapport with the client.

The therapist may treat silence and indirectness by the client as signals of resistance, when actually they represent respect, thoughtful reflection, or other forms of nonverbal communication. How one enters a room, greets another, and reacts to silence are all forms of communication the therapist needs to be aware of when working with Native American clients. Because a therapist cannot be familiar with all the subtle nuances of Native American culture, he or she needs to ask questions when on unfamiliar ground and find out which particular values the client cherishes and wants to maintain. These include family customs, spirituality, language, or other parts of their culture. The therapist may want to explore with the client the available support systems, including involvement with Native American organizations or centers, participation in local ceremonies at a powwow, or the support available through family ties. For some clients, the feelings of grief for a lost culture or a culture he or she did not experience may be something the client has never acknowledged to anyone (Sutton & Broken Nose, 1996).

Garrett and Garrett (1994) offered some basic recommendations for counseling with Native Americans:

- Ask permission whenever possible and always give thanks.
- Never interrupt—allow sufficient time for responding.
- Be patient.
- Use silence whenever possible.
- Use descriptive statements rather than questions.
- Model self-disclosure through anecdotes or stories.
- Make use of metaphors and imagery when appropriate.
- Try not to separate the person from the spirituality or from an affiliation with the tribal group. Honor those sacred relationships.
- Recognize the relative nature of value judgments such as "right and wrong" and "good and bad" (p. 143).

The importance of Native American cultural practices cannot be over-stated when addressing the mental health needs of this population. Some authors (Attneave, 1982; LaFromboise & Low, 1998) suggested that social cognitive interventions, systems therapy, and traditional Native American interventions are most effective because they incorporate the environment and social context into treatment and therefore better accommodate the Native American cultural practices.

In contrast to the disease model psychopathology, the theory behind cognitive therapies holds that most psychological problems are learned within the social milieu and maintained through cognitive reinforcement (Michenbaum, 1977). A therapist working with Native American clients must be highly sensitive to the possibility that self-deprecating beliefs may be a reflection of the internalization of the dominant culture's attitudes toward ethnic minorities. For example, a Native American youth who has broken a cultural taboo may experience anxiety that a therapist in the dom-inant culture may label as catastrophic. Yet given the Native American youth's beliefs, the fear of spiritual consequences may be well founded. The rationality of the beliefs within the cultural context must be assessed by the therapist and, once identified as dysfunctional, treatment should be focused on the present as opposed to the past (LaFramboise & Low, 1998).

Native Americans may expect immediate results and may not appreciate the length of time it takes to establish rapport and trust in therapy. Asking clients to keep behavior logs or solicit help from the extended family may actively involve the clients in therapy and help them gain some insight into the nature of the problem in a more timely manner.

Ivey, Ivey, & Simek-Morgan (1997) suggested that systems therapy inte-grates the inherent strengths of the extended family. These authors argued that the most helpful therapeutic interventions are those that enhance an individual's interaction with others or with the environment, therefore en-suring lasting change outside the context of the therapeutic relationship. Extended family, as opposed to the immediate family or the conventional service delivery (one-on-one counseling) agency, needs to be involved in order to ensure success. A therapist who limits his or her work to the client's nuclear family may miss the significant contributions that can be made by the more extended family members.

Identifying the extended family may be difficult but can be made a less daunting task by having the client (a) draw a genogram, (b) draw a portrait of the family, or (c) tell a story involving all the extended family members. Engaging the family in therapy may require the support of the tribe or the Native American community, in addition to numerous requests by the therapist or referring agency as well as visits to the home to establish a rapport before beginning therapy. To establish this rapport, the following techniques are suggested:

1. Use self-disclosure.
2. Exercise patience.
3. Build relationships using humor and small talk.
4. Listen attentively.
5. Establish credibility through genuine care and concern.
6. Solicit the support of family members by asking them to accompany the client(s) to therapy.

Once the key family members begin to attend the sessions, they should be asked to define the family structure, including such issues as hierarchy, triangulation, and alliances. Care must be taken not to view the family as "enmeshed" because of its interdependence on one another, as opposed to the independence of the American family (Shangreaux, Pleskac, & Freeman, 1987).

In addition to the systems therapy, the use of traditional Native American interventions may be particularly effective for those clients who have been raised in traditional ways. A collaboration by the therapist with a traditional healer usually follows a client assessment that determines if such ceremonies are desired. Manson, Walker, and Kivlahan (1987) suggested the following three Native American strategies be used: (a) sweat lodge ceremonies, (b) four circles, and (c) the talking circles.

The sweat lodge ceremonies are often conducted for purification and prevention purposes. The ceremonies consist of preparatory fasting, prayer, and offerings using several purification sessions called "rounds." The ceremony lasts several hours while participants make offerings for health and a balance of life.

The four circles consist of the symbolic organization of life's important relationships. Of the four circles, the centermost circle represents the Creator, the second represents the relationship with one's spouse or partner, the third represents the immediate and extended family, and the fourth represents the tribal members. The circles are used as a symbolic search for a balance in relationships and are used to clarify or assign importance to allegiances and social responsibilities.

The talking circle is similar to group therapy where participants sit in a circle and remain there until the ceremony is complete. Sweet grass is burned to produce purifying smoke and give direction to the group conversation. The leader begins and each person is free to speak when moved to do so. No one is permitted to interrupt and the ceremony ends with the joining of hands in prayer.

The combination of traditional Native American healing practices and contemporary therapy can be very effective in garnering community support for the client, for the therapist's work with the client, and for legitimizing the natural skills of Native American helpers and community advisors (LaFramboise & Low, 1998). Working in collaboration with the Native American community is a primary goal for the therapist who wants to be successful with this population. In the words of Garrett and Garrett (1994), "If counselors and educators first come to meet with Native American clients as learners, and second, as professionals, they might be surprised at how much growth would take place by members of both worlds" (p. 143).

Exercises:

1. Spend a weekend visiting a Native American reservation. Observe their way of life. How does their spiritual view of life differ from yours? What can you learn from them that will help you in counseling Native Americans?
2. Native Americans have traditionally been marginalized. Design a support group to address how their faith has helped bind them together through years of oppression. How have their spiritual beliefs contributed to their ability to cope?

John's Case

John's family has lived on the Swanee Indian Reservation all of John's life and have been devoted to the practice of their Native American spirituality. John has had little to no contact with peers his own age, other than those residing on the reservation. A high school teacher encouraged John to pursue medical studies because his interest and aptitude indicated a strong potential in this area. John applied and was accepted at a prestigious Ivy League institution. Because he received a full scholarship, his parents decided to allow him to enroll. However, John was not prepared for the bigotry and prejudice he faced when first arriving at this institution. The representative for Indian Affairs has been in contact with John and recommended that he seek his family's counsel as to how to deal with this. John's mother suggested that he return home and attend the state university. John has been unwilling to accept this option and has been directed to the university counseling center.

Case Discussion
- What resources would John's counselor need in order to help John cope with the bigotry and prejudice he faces?
- How could John's practice of spirituality be of help to him as he learns to cope?
- What person-of-the-counselor issues, if any, would you have in working with John?

References

Arredondo, P. M. (1986). Immigration as a historical moment leading to an identity crisis. *Journal of Counseling and Human Service Professionals, 1*(1) 79–87.

Attneave, C. (1982). American Indians and Alaska native families: Emigrants in their own homeland. In M. McGoldrick, J. K. Pearce, & J. Giordano (Eds.), *Ethnicity and family therapy.* New York: The Guilford Press.

Beck, V., & Walters, A. L. (1977). *The sacred ways of knowledge: Sources of life.* Tsaile (Navajo Nation), AZ: Navajo Community College Press.

Dauphinais, P., Dauphinais, L., & Rowe, W. (1981). Effects of race and communication styles on Indian perceptions of counselor effectiveness. *Counselor Education and Supervision, 20,* 37–46.

Duran, E., & Duran, B. (1995). *Native American post-colonial psychology.* Albany, NY: State University of New York Press.

Garrett, J. T., & Garrett, M. T. (1994). The path of good medicine: Understanding and counseling Native Americans. *Journal of Multicultural Counseling and Development, 22,* 134–144.

Herring, R. D. (1999). *Counseling Native American/Alaskan native populations.* Thousand Oaks, CA: Sage Publications.

Hungary Wolf, A., and Hungary Wolf, B. (1987). *Children of the sun.* New York: Morrow.

Irwin, L. (1996). Themes of North America: Spirituality. *American Indian Quarterly, 20,* 309–332.

Ivey, A. E., Ivey, M. B., & Simek-Morgan, L. (1997). *Counseling and psychotherapy: A multicultural perspective* (4th ed.). Boston: Allyn and Bacon.

LaFromboise, T. D. (1988). American Indian mental health policy. *American Psychologist, 43*(5), 388–397.

LaFromboise, T. D., & Bigfoot, D. S. (1988). Cultural and cognitive considerations in the prevention of American Indian adolescent suicide. *Journal of Adolescence, 11,* 139–153.

LaFromboise, T. D., Trimble, J. E., & Mohatt, G. V. (1990). Counseling intervention and American Indian tradition: An integrative approach. *The Counseling Psychologist, 18*(4), 628–654.

LaFromboise, T., & Low, G. K. (1998). American Indian children and adolescents. In J. Gibbs, & L. Huang (Eds.), *Children of color: Psychological interventions with culturally diverse youth.* San Francisco, CA: Jossey Bass.

Manson, S. M., Walker, R. D., & Kivlahan, D. R. (1987). Psychiatric assessment and treatment of American Indians and Alaska natives. *Hospital Community Psychiatry, 38*(2), 165–173.

Russell, C. (1998). *Racial and ethnic diversity* (2nd ed.). Ithaca, NY: Strategist Publications.

Sanford, L. T., & Donovan, M. E. (1984). *Women and self-esteem: Understanding and improving the way we think and feel about ourselves.* Harrisonburg, VA: R. R. Donnelley Sons.

Shangreaux, Pleskac, & Freeman. (1987).

Sue, D. W., & Sue, D. (1999). *Counseling the culturally different: Theory and practice* (3rd ed.). New York: Wiley.

Sutton, C. T., & Broken Nose, M. A. (1996). American Indian family: An overview. In M. McGoldrich (Ed.), *Ethnicity and family therapy* (2nd ed.). New York: Guilford Press.

Trujillo, A. (2000). Psychotherapy with Native Americans: A view into the role of religion and spirituality. In P. S. Richards & A. E. Bergin (Eds.), *Handbook of psychotherapy and religious diversity* (pp. 445–466). Washington, D.C.: American Psychological Association.

U. S. Bureau of Census. (1995). *Population Profiles of the United States.* Washington, D.C.: Government Printing Office.

www.religioustolerance.org/nataspir.htm This Native American section of the Ontario Consultants on Religious Tolerance homepage is a good starting point of reference. In a short space the page defines key concepts and explains general trends.

CHAPTER **13**

Judaic Population

Judaism Defined

Today a Jew is someone who is a member of a Jewish religious or cultural group or who practices the religion of Judaism. The origins of Judaism began in Israel approximately 2000 BCE (Before the Common Era) (Fishbane, 1993). According to Morrison and Brown (1991), the word *Jew* is derived from the term Judah, the southern kingdom of Israel that existed from 922 to 586 BCE. The Latin name for Judaism is *Judaeus*, meaning "a resident of Judea." The name was later shortened to *Jew*. According to Langer (2003), at its most fundamental level, the definition of "Jew" is neither religious nor theological, but ethnic.

So what is Judaism? Is it a religion, a theology, and an ethic reality? Gelernter (2002) stated that Judaism is one continuous sacred text, founded on the written Torah (or Bible) and the spoken Torah (or Talmud). In Jewish law, a Jew is someone whose mother is Jewish or who has converted to Judaism (Morrison & Brown, 1991).

Gelernter (2002) has written that there are 13.2 million Jews in the world today. The Jewish nation has had a significant impact on Western civilization, yet Judaism itself is all but unknown. It is difficult if not impossible to grasp or discover Judaism's view of a particular topic. Educated and sophisticated people (including Jews) believe that if you want to know what a Jew believes, you look it up in the Hebrew Bible. Nothing could be farther from the truth. To use the simile used by Gelernter, to attempt to discover Judaic impressions or views on controversial topics is like identifying the Atlantic Ocean with the basin that contains it while forgetting about the

221

water. The Bible is the ocean bed of Judaism. The Talmud and more than two centuries' worth of rabbinic literature are the substance of Judaism.

Judaism has no official creed. Various belief statements have been formulated over the centuries, the best known of which is the *Thirteen Principles of Faith* crafted by Moses Maimonides in the twelfth century. Although it is found in declaratory form ("I believe with perfect faith in . . .") and in poetic renditions, it is not among the obligatory prayers required of those practicing the Jewish faith (Langer, 2003, pp. 255–278).

Basic Tenets of the Judaic Tradition

To know Judaism, you must first become acquainted with its fundamental beliefs. The most basic tenet of Judaism is monotheism: the belief that there is one God (Yahweh) who created the universe and governs it (Sarason, 1993–1996). Judaism is specifically the religion of one people, Israel (Langer, 2003). Another tenet is that Jews believe that they were chosen and blessed by God, who will reward them if they keep His commandments. If they fail to do this, He will punish them. The Jewish people await the coming of the Messiah who will restore them to sovereignty in their land (Sarason, 1993-1996).

In addition to knowing the basic tenets of Judaism, it is also important for the therapist to recognize the role that dietary laws have in Jewish life. "Keeping kosher" is the observance of the dietary laws and includes not eating certain fish and animals that are considered unclean.

The Sabbath (or the seventh day of the week), the five major festivals, and the two minor ones are the significant times of the Jewish calendar but are often overlooked in a pluralistic society. Yom Kippur, or Day of Atonement is the holiest of the Jewish holidays and is spent in fasting, prayer, and repentance. Strict adherence to these practices depends on which of the three major forms of Judaism one belongs to: Orthodox, Conservative, or Reform. These terms are modern designations, arising only in the mid-nineteenth century. For purposes of clarity and lay understanding, Langer (2003) offered this distinction:

> It is generally more useful to designate the ends of the spectrum of contemporary Judaism as "traditional," referring to those groups who see themselves in total continuity with 2000 years of rabbinic Judaism, and "liberal," referring to those groups who do not accept the authority of this system in part or in full. Reform and Reconstructionist Judaism, as well as parts of the conservative world, can be considered "liberal" (and new groups such as Renewal, New Age, Humanistic Judaism) while the rest from the more conservative end of the Conservative Movement through the Ultra-Orthodox may be termed "traditional" (pp. 255–287).

Most American Jews are descendents from European Jews who immigrated in the mid-nineteenth century or from those who were survivors of the Holocaust. All three major forms of Judaism can be found in America today. Orthodox Jews are traditionalists committed to maintaining their practices amid the demands of modern life. They believe that the Torah is the ultimate religious authority and reject modern interpretations of it as mythical (Morrison & Brown, 1991). They adhere to the strict laws of their religion and dutifully observe the Sabbath through rest and worship. Conservative Jews respect traditional Jewish law and practice, yet they are more flexible, less mechanical, and attempt to update the Law in response to contemporary life. Reform Judaism emphasizes reason and tends to be liberal and nonauthoritarian (Sarason, 1993–1996). Innovative changes have taken place in Reform Judaism, such as allowing families to be seated together instead of segregating males and females. Sermons are preached in English rather than Hebrew, and women are permitted to become rabbis (Morrison & Brown, 1991).

Classical Judaism, like other world religions, is traditionally patriarchal, and modern feminists and liberal Jews have worked to change this. Within contemporary feminist orthodox and liberal circles, women are attaining higher levels of learning and spiritual leadership. Scholars view this tension between classical and modern sensibilities as a source of comfort and creative integration (Fishbane, 1993).

Judaism is a religion of memory and narrative. The Torah, the foundation text of Judaism, explains the formation of the ancient Israelite nation and its relationship with God. It is the core of a rich and varied tradition that extends from ancient times to the present. Interpretation and study are the key spiritual activities in Judaic practice. Almost nothing is more valued than sacred learning. Through prayer, learning, and rituals, the past is constantly reinforced.

Spirituality and study in the Jewish tradition are not separate tasks. Judaism is not a religion that encourages isolated spiritual quests. Rather, the journey takes place in the context of a fellowship of seekers, worshippers, or students. Study is a collaborative and relational process. Judaism evolves and responds to the demands of the present historical period. Continuity is ensured in Judaism by parents teaching their children, and the parent's obligation to teach the child is mirrored by the child's obligation to honor the parent. This tradition connects honoring parent with honoring God. The Jewish tradition is adamant about requiring children to honor their parents, which includes giving parents everything they need until the end of their lives.

However, these traditions are no longer widely accepted by non-Orthodox Jews. In liberal Jewish American circles, creativity and personal authenticity tend to be more highly valued than strict adherence to religious law. The traditional Jewish view of the person is very relational; one is tied to family, community, and Yahweh. By contrast, popular psychology in the United States has made relationships with parents optional; growing away from or beyond parents is an acceptable development of this culture. In this view, the person is accountable primarily to self, and the good of the individual is paramount (Bellah, Madsen, Sullivan, Swidler, & Tipton, 1985). Modern American Jews, raised on the Freudian and American narratives, are caught between two opposing worldviews. The clash of values is especially poignant around the issues of intermarriage. Finding a balance between family religious practice and personal autonomy is a challenge, especially for the modern American Jew.

The Role of Gender and Family

The great themes of Jewish history are exodus and liberation, chosen and revelation, exile and redemption, community and peoplehood (Gelernter, 2002). An effective counseling program for a Jewish individual or family must consider the context of family within the Judaic tradition, especially its emphasis on maleness and femaleness. It would be difficult to understand Judaism unless we had a heightened awareness and sensitivity to the male and female aspects of everything in the universe. Gelernter remarked that Jewish thought is steeped not in sex but in sexuality: in maleness and femaleness, and the power between them. The whole makeup of the biblical family, as of all western families until modern times, put the wife as the possession of the husband—in order words, in his power. He acquired her, received a dowry from her father, and brought her home. "Every man who has no wife," says the Talmud, "lives without joy, without blessing, without goodness"(Gelernter, pp. 31–41).

At the very core of Judaism is the ritual of the Sabbath. On the Sabbath, the married couple is exalted as God's culminating masterpiece. Remember on the sixth day of Creation that God created male and female? Whether or not a child is born of this union, the sexual union of husband and wife is inherently blessed. It has given the Jewish family a unique centrality and stability. The Sabbath is female, and Judaism embodies its femaleness by having women create and embody it (Gelernter, 2002).

Understanding the role of gender in Judaism helps to shed light on how coupleness is perceived. The ideal male is a courageous aggressor. Judaism has two versions of the ideal woman. She is heroically brisk, efficient, and brilliant. She also reaches out to the poor and extends her hands to the needy (Gelernter, 2002). Ordinarily, Judaism puts males in charge of the public, outer world and females in charge of the private inner sanctum. Women can take on as much as they want and can get involved in the outer world—as long as it is the secular world. The religious world remains partitioned, like the synagogue itself. Men are in charge of public religion; in private, at-home religion, women take precedence. And of these two, the inner, private domain is more important.

In the 1970s, a Jewish women's reform movement similar to that of the feminist movement emerged. This was a movement away from the traditional practices of Judaism, yet elements of the traditional practices were incorporated. Jewish women, committed to transforming Judaism into a more woman-friendly religion, gathered regularly to create Jewish feminist liturgies and rituals. In this way, they were able to fashion a new vision and concept of Judaism that responded to a more feminine perspective. Over time, reformed or liberal congregations responded, and women began to assume a place within the Jewish congregation. Many became rabbis.

Because Judaism is not the dominant religion in the United States, and because Jews have been oppressed, disenfranchised, and marginalized, many Jews are able to identify with the plight of women. According to Eller (1993), many Jewish women stayed connected to their traditional practices despite the obvious patriarchal worldview because "it is an identity not easily cast aside" (p. 224).

Feminist spirituality is largely a separatist movement. Although some women remain connected to traditional religions such as Christianity, Islam, and Judaism and adhere to the basic principles of feminist spirituality, they are in the minority.

In a Jewish household, the conversion of a child to Judaism is not binding, nor are they considered to have reached religious maturity until the age of 13 for the boy and age 12 for the girl, at which time they celebrate bat mitzvah or bar mitzvah. This rite of passage gives evidence of positive identification with the Jewish community. It also serves as a ratification of the parent's decision.

Unique Needs of This Population

To be accepted in Western society, the Jewish people have been asked to assimilate with Christians and to lose their cultural distinctiveness (Langer, 2003). The challenge for the American Jew is to have a voice and still stay connected to the values of the Jewish tradition, which demands honoring one's father and mother (Carter, 1999; McGoldrick, 1995). Holding one's own heritage, balancing autonomy and loyalty, and having respect for parents are complex relational skills. It requires learning to make a relational claim that honors both self and others. Parents are often able to respond with reciprocal respect when approached in this matter. As this process unfolds, respect tends to beget respect, generating a relational rather than an adversarial cycle between generations. If the parent is not able to respond positively, the adult child has at least acted in accord with the Torah and has not responded to the parent with rage or humiliation. When an individual finds a way to be constructively loyal to his or her parents and is not stuck in blame or resentment, that person may be freer to live his or her life without carrying burdens of resentment into other relationships (Boszormenyi-Nagy & Spark, 1973).

Aaron (A Teenage Male Client)

Aaron was a 13-year-old boy who had been referred to counseling because he had been in a fight at school and been suspended. Counseling was one of the stipulations for having him reinstated. His parents had been noticing that he had been very quiet lately and his grades had been slipping. Aaron appeared for his first session dressed in blue jeans, a very large T-shirt, and a pair of designer tennis shoes that from the scuff marks and the holes in them evidenced a lot of wear and tear. His hair was somewhat long and shaggy, and he suffered from a mild case of acne. He appeared sullen and would not make direct eye contact at first.

Although he was halting in his answers and appeared bored and annoyed throughout the interview, Aaron did begin to loosen up a bit. Whenever the counselor touched on subjects concerning his parents, Aaron appeared more agitated than usual. Questions about school evoked an "I don't care" response. However, as time progressed and the conversation became easier, it was obvious from his body language that Aaron was feeling more comfortable just being in the counselor's office.

In subsequent sessions, the counselor began to probe further into Aaron's difficulties with his parents. At first, Aaron offered a lot of resistance, but gradually he became more talkative. One day he blurted out, "My parents are so old-fashioned that they just make me sick!" His eyes were filled with tears. The counselor waited for some of the emotion to subside and then asked Aaron to give some examples.

"You know," he said, "they aren't at all modern. They act and dress like people who lived a long time ago. I hate to bring my friends home from school because I don't want them to see my house and the way that I live. I have refused to wear a yarmulke at school, and my parents are really angry with this. I refuse to cut my hair and wear forelocks, and they think that I am a horrible creature. It's just too hard and everyone makes fun of me! I want to be just like everyone else!"

Aaron also was angry because his parents preferred for him to associate only with other Jewish boys from his synagogue, even though Aaron attended a public school and had made friends with kids of all nationalities. He went on to express his pain and discomfort over his upcoming bar mitzvah. He felt that his parents were asking him to come of age in a religion he was not sure he wanted to practice. He certainly could not deny his Judaism, but he would prefer to belong to a more liberal sect, whereas his parents staunchly upheld the more traditional or conservative aspects of the Jewish faith. Aaron was torn between his love for his parents and his own perceived need to express his individuality. Being a minor, his options were somewhat limited.

Once this floodgate had been opened, it was easier to see the whole picture of Aaron's distress. His slipping grades were a result of being teased at school. His schoolmates perceived him as "different," because he adhered to at least some of the tenets of traditional Judaism as espoused by his parents. Of course, "different" is not what the typical American teenager wants to be. Aaron felt alienated both from his parents, because of his anger and resentment over their practices, and from his classmates, because he felt guilty if he did not acknowledge his religion of birth. In the midst of all of this, Aaron was trying to figure out who he was as an individual. It was enough to make anyone stressful and angry.

The counselor recognized how much Aaron profited from being able to vent his feelings and thought how wise it was of Aaron's parents to put him in counseling. This must have been a big step for them, considering their conservative beliefs, but it was evident that they truly loved their son and wanted the best for him. The counselor and Aaron explored the particular instances when Aaron felt most vulnerable. He talked about expected modes of dress (which he completely ignored except for synagogue), the inability to play soccer because most games were held on Saturday mornings, and the dietary laws that made it uncomfortable for him to be in the homes of his friends, especially overnight. These things were hard for an adolescent to contend with.

At the same time, the counselor encouraged Aaron to explore the things he liked about being Jewish. The counselor was quite impressed with Aaron's rather in-depth knowledge of historical Judaism. At the core of his being, Aaron was proud to be Jewish and proud of his personal family history. Aaron's grandparents had been survivors of the atrocities of World War II. His grandfather had been a Holocaust victim interred in a concentration camp during the last two years of the war. His grandmother had escaped the concentration camps because her parents left Europe at the outbreak of the war, but they had to move to several different places and leave behind all that was familiar and beautiful. Aaron had heard these stories many times, and they never failed to evoke in him a mixture of fear and pride. He couldn't imagine himself enduring such hardships.

Gradually, Aaron began to see one of the possible reasons why his parents and grandparents had clung so tenaciously to the more conservative or traditional practices of Judaism. It might not have been entirely because of tradition but because these practices had been denied them during the horrible sufferings of World War II. They must have wondered if they would ever be able to practice them again without fear of reprisal. Aaron was encouraged to talk with his grandparents in an effort to better understand his parents. The counselor seriously doubted that the grandparents would consent to join in family therapy, but he intended to recommend it anyway. Family counseling was definitely an option that should have been considered, but Aaron's parents were not ready. Although disappointing, it was a situation that could not be forced.

Aaron spoke at length about the study of the Torah he had begun at a very early age. Aaron definitely believed in the existence of one true God and thought that the various prayers and ceremonies were very beautiful, even if he felt that they were somewhat outdated in his adolescent opinion. He expressed a true reverence for the major holy days of the Jewish calendar and related in loving detail the observance of Yom Kippur. He talked about the long hours spent in synagogue and then the celebratory meal that followed when the fast was broken. He recounted Seder suppers, the rituals that accompanied them, and how close he felt to his family on these occasions. His pride in his heritage was very evident.

Aaron eventually began to realize how much he really identified with being Jewish. He also came to the realization that the teasing he suffered from his classmates was more from ignorance than true animosity. Aaron was very intelligent and his insights into things constantly impressed the counselor. This was a young man who, underneath a sullen exterior, had a very warm heart, an exceptionally keen mind, and a great sincerity. Aaron hated disappointing his parents and other family members, but his intellectual honesty compelled him to constantly search for the truth and for his own identity.

Aaron and the counselor explored ways he could broach some of his reservations and confusion regarding his parents. They role-played various scenarios until Aaron felt comfortable going to them and being open about his true feelings. The counselor felt that none of this was going to be a great shock to them, although it might cause them some distress.

On the question of his bar mitzvah, Aaron decided this was a rite of passage and that by participating in it he was linking himself with a long, unbroken line of other faithful Jews. What it symbolized was actually very important to him. When he could see it in this light, he was able to accept and even embrace it. He no longer regarded it as controlling his future, and therefore it was not something to be feared. This decision and the insights it provided brought Aaron considerable relief.

As he explored his historical past and his future in the context of counseling, Aaron began to realize that shutting his classmates out of his home life and his religious traditions only increased their speculations and teasing. He resolved to take more visible pride in his heritage and attempt to educate his friends rather than hiding his true self from them. Although his parents might never be totally comfortable with his non-Jewish relationships, he wanted to invite his friends for the Friday night Shabbat service and other Jewish observances. He realized his friends would mirror his pride, just as they had quickly picked up his discomfort. He was firmly convinced that his parents loved him enough to welcome his Gentile friends into their home, and the counselor tended to agree. This was true progress on Aaron's part.

As the counselor and Aaron explored the differences between the traditional and liberal branches of the Jewish faith, Aaron accepted the fact, if somewhat reluctantly, that decisions about the course of his religious life might have to wait until he was older. In the meantime, he planned to attend other, more liberal synagogues from time to time to see how services and rituals might differ. He planned to be open about this with his parents, even though he suspected they might not fully approve. He also planned to continue to study the history of the Jewish faith and increase his knowledge of the Torah.

Because Aaron could gradually let go of his anger and focus more clearly on the real issues, he was able to make plans for the future and strategize carrying them out. He was truly remarkable for a young man of 13. He emerged as a thoughtful, sensitive person who was very different from the disheveled, sullen teenager who first came into the counselor's office.

Implications for Counselors
Ingersoll (1994) delineated seven different dimensions to the integration of spirituality into one's life:

1. One's conception of the divine, absolute, or "force greater than one's self"
2. One's sense of meaning of what is beautiful or worthwhile
3. One's relationship with the divinity and others
4. One's tolerance or capability for mystery
5. Peak and ordinary experiences that enhance spirituality (which may include rituals or spiritual disciplines)
6. Seeing spirituality as play
7. Viewing spirituality as a systemic force that acts to integrate all the dimensions of one's life (p. 11)

Aaron was enthralled by the divine, especially as it related to the story of his people and their struggles. He currently railed against a sect that he saw as outmoded and not in touch with modern times. This in no way, however, caused him to lose belief in a power greater than himself or in the mystery that surrounded his God and His teachings. Aaron had a distinct tolerance for mystery and his very brilliant mind sought answers that less intelligent people might not have wrestled with. When he was angry and embarrassed by his religious traditions, he sought to abandon them, but as he came to value and respect them his joy in their existence greatly increased. Aaron wanted desperately for a personal spirituality to be a systemic force that would bring together all the different facets of his life. He just wasn't sure it should take the same form as the religious observances of his parents. Aaron was searching for meaning, not for an escape from the traditional.

Anti-Semitism

Anti-Semitism probably reached its peak in history during World War II with the ethnic cleansing by the Third Reich and the atrocities of the concentration camps. Holocaust survivors are living proof of the depth and extent to which humankind can inflict its most deplorable acts. Anti-Semitic acts, though probably at their lowest ebb, continue to be a defining issue for the Jewish community. Groups such as the Jewish Advocacy Organizations (JAOs) have been created, and their mission is to collect and disseminate information on anti-Semitic incidents and shape the dialogue for the greater Jewish community. However, the proliferation of such organizations has been a cause of tension within the Jewish communities because few rabbis are members of the JAOs. Even so, the JAOs are frequently viewed as the first line of defense.

Prejudice against Jews has waned in the twentieth century, making experience with anti-Semitism far less likely to be commonplace in the United States (Djupe & Sokhey, 2003). However, evidence still persists, especially among adolescents, that anti-Semitic acts can inflict deep wounds and damage trust. Mental health practitioners, particularly those practicing in school settings, must be vigilant and ready to intervene when these acts occur. Such prejudice can precipitate hate crimes and destroy communities. Traditional youth, in order to remain faithful to their beliefs, are required to take part in Jewish rituals.

Suggested Approaches to Working with a Jewish Client

As covered previously, much of the current struggle within Judaism is between those rooted in Jewish traditional customs and those open to change, or essentially between the Orthodox and liberal Jews. The approach to working with Jewish clients revolves around helping them establish a delicate balance between integrating a commitment to egalitarian principles on one hand and a deep respect for the spiritual richness of the Jewish religious tradition on the other. Failure to do so for a Jewish client would assure spiritual suffocation (Fishman, 1993).

Also, understanding the role gender plays is critical if the counselor is to intervene effectively. The Jewish woman is honored in her home and blessed by her husband and her children. The purpose of life is to marry and rear children. Her family is her life. According to Gelernter (2002), the modern world's view that career and not family is the point of life is un-Jewish. Because man cannot exist except where male and female are one, the Jewish self is a strange, unfamiliar self, made of two separate beings. And a self that includes another person is a hint of a self that includes God or Yahweh.

Joshua's Case

Joshua is a lawyer who declared himself to be of the liberal Jewish faith. He and his wife Pamela have been married for 10 years. She is an Episcopalian and their two boys, ages 6 and 8, are being raised in both traditions. Josh's parents are both living and practice Jewish Orthodox customs. Josh's parents have refused to accept that Josh was marrying outside of his tradition, and they have disowned and written Josh out of their will. They refused to attend the wedding, even though Josh invited his rabbi to be a part of the ceremony. They have refused to see their son and have never seen their grandchildren.

Josh feels as though his boys are missing an important part of their Jewish heritage by not having a relationship with their grandparents. To complicate matters, Josh's younger brother, Samuel, has three children, two boys and a girl, and the two families have remained close. Sam's children have a close relationship with their paternal grandparents, and Josh's oldest son, who is close to his cousins, cannot understand why he is not permitted to visit his paternal grandparents and why they have not asked to see him. Pamela cannot fathom why Josh's parents have shut them out of their lives; her parents have accepted Josh and are warm and supportive. This has placed a strain on the marriage and both have agreed to see a counselor.

Josh and Pamela's counselor is not familiar with the Jewish tradition. Although he considers himself to be a spiritual person, he is not affiliated with any organized religion. He has asked Josh if he would like to invite a close friend of Josh's parents, Rabbi Ruben, to some of the sessions in order to help facilitate this difficult situation, and Josh has reluctantly agreed.

Discussion

- Explore with Josh the depth of loss he has experienced in being disowned by his parents.

- Have a family session and ask the children to describe their feelings about not having contact with their paternal grandparents.
- Explore with Josh how his Jewish upbringing has influenced his need to reconnect with his parents.
- Identify someone who practices traditional Judaism and discuss the customs and beliefs that are important to them.

Exercises

1. Research the role of the family, particularly the obligations of children to parents in the traditional Orthodox Jewish tradition.
2. Have a discussion about the meaning of the commandment "Honor thy father and thy mother."
3. Compare and contrast the interpretation of this commandment for Orthodox Jews, liberal/reformed Jews, and other major faith traditions.
4. Investigate the role of grandparents in the lives of their grandchildren.
5. Discuss how faith traditions are passed on through generations.
6. Discuss any anti-Semitic experiences of which you are aware. How would you intervene?

References

Bellah, R. N., Madsen, R., Sullivan, W. M., Swidler, A., & Tipton, S. M. (1985). *Habits of the heart: Individualism and commitment in American life.* Berkeley, CA: University of California Press.

Boszormenyi-Nagy, I., & Spark, G. (1973). *Invisible loyalties: Reciprocity in intergenerational family therapy.* Hagerstown, MD: Harper & Row.

Carter, R. B. (1999). Counseling Muslim students in school settings. *Professional School Counseling, 2*(3), 183–189.

Djupe, P., & Sokhey, A. (2003). The mobilization of elite opinion: Rabbi perceptions of and responses to anti-Semitism. *Journal for the Scientific Study of Religion, 42*(3), 443–444.

Eller, C. (1993). *Living in the lap of the goddess: The feminist spirituality movement in America.* New York: Crossroad.

Frame, M. W. (2003). *Integrating religion and spirituality into counseling.* Pacific Grove, CA: Thomson-Brooks/Cole.

Fishbane, M. (1993). Judaism: Revelation and traditions. In H. G. Earhart (Ed.), *Religious traditions of the world.* San Francisco: HarperSanFrancisco.

Fishman, S. B. (1993). *A breath of life: Feminism in the Jewish American community.* New York: Freepress/Macmillan.

Gelernter, D. (2002). Judaism beyond words. *Commentary, 113*(5), 31.

Langer, R. (2003). Jewish understanding of the religious other. *Theological Studies, 64*(2) 255.

McGoldrick, M. (1995). *You can go home again: Reconnecting with your family.* New York: Norton.

Morrison, M., & Brown, S. F. (1991). *Judaism.* New York: Oxford.

Sarason, R. S. (1993–1996). Judaism. *Encarta 97 Encyclopedia.* Redmond, WA: Microsoft Corporation.

The largest religious tradition in the world is Christianity, which includes approximately 2 billion members. Islam is the second largest religion with approximately one and a half billion members. Judaism contains approximately 13.2 million members, and Hinduism has approximately 750 million members with about 1,250,000 followers currently living in the United States. Finally, approximately 353 million Buddhists exist in the world, with 2 million in North America. All statistics have been rounded upward for brevity (Barrett & Johnson, 1998).

Although Christianity has the largest numbers, not all Christians have similar beliefs. For purposes of clarity, this chapter will divide Christianity into Catholics and Protestants, the two major groups, with Mormons, Jehovah's Witnesses, Pentecostals, Seventh-Day Adventists, and Christian Scientists comprising the remaining smaller groups. Each group has its own unique tenets, which clinicians should be familiar with when assisting Christian clients in living fuller and more satisfying lives.

Basic Tenets

Christianity began in the first century and is founded on the life and teachings of Jesus Christ, who is considered to be the promised Messiah. Christians believe (a) that Jesus Christ is both human and divine, (b) that He is the Son of God, (c) that He suffered and died on a cross for the sins of the world, (d) and that He arose again on the third day and ascended into heaven 40 days later (Frankiel, 1993). Christians also believe that there are three persons in one God—the Father, the Son, and the Holy Spirit—and that the Christian community is the church consisting of all the believing members. For Christians, the Bible is the Word of God and consists of the Old and New Testaments to which they give the same level of credence. Most Christian churches have at least two sacraments, baptism and Holy Communion, which are signs of the grace of God given to believers.

Divisions Within Christianity

The largest major division within the Christian Church is Roman Catholicism, which has seven sacraments and acknowledges the supreme authority of the Pope, the bishop of Rome. The church is a hierarchical structure consisting of clergy: cardinals, bishops, priests (who are celibate), and the laity, or members of the church. The church emphasizes its continuous unbroken succession to St. Peter, the first bishop of Rome. Roman Catholics believe in the real presence of Jesus in the Eucharist or Holy Communion, which takes place during the liturgy of the Mass.

Roman Catholics believe in the Trinity—Father, Son, and Holy Spirit—in one God Almighty, the incorporated spirit. They also believe that Jesus Christ is God's only incarnation, the Son of God and God. Some Catholics believe in a literal translation of the Bible, especially the book of Genesis, but the church holds that God gave mankind both a supernatural revelation in the Bible and a natural revelation through the rational human mind. Catholics have also disagreed on issues such as evolution. Some hold to a strict interpretation of creation, but all believe that God created the universe from nothing. Thus, if the "Big Bang" theory were true, then God created this event. If evolution did occur, it only occurred under the choice and control of God, and only with the understanding that God breathed the first soul into the first man; all souls are immediately created by God.

Catholics believe that after death God immediately judges who goes to heaven or hell, and some Catholics still believe in purgatory, a place of punishment and purification before one is ready for heaven. Reward and punishment are considered to be relative to one's deeds on earth. Hell is traditionally considered a literal place of eternal torture, but the Pope has also described hell as the condition of pain that results from alienation from God, a thing of one's own doing, not an actual place. It is also believed that God will return to judge all for eternity in heaven, on Earth, or in hell.

Evil was first experienced on Earth with Adam and Eve, according to church doctrine. Their sin was transferred to all mankind through original sin. All are sinners and prone to the influence of Satan unless they find salvation in God and the church. All are believed to be saved through Christ's death and resurrection, and all are still being saved through the church and will be in the future (the second coming of Christ). Salvation, according to the Roman Catholic Church, demands faith in and prayer to God and Jesus Christ, good works, and reception of the sacraments, including infant baptism. Mortal sin separates man from God, and this union can only be restored by the sacraments of repentance and confession.

Roman Catholics believe that suffering is allowed by God to test, teach, or strengthen belief in Him. The greater the suffering of innocent believers, the greater will be their reward in heaven.

In addition, Roman Catholics believe that abortion is considered to be a form of murder. The church also does not accept homosexuality. Women are afforded the highest regard as wives and mothers, but are not allowed to be ordained as priests. Marriage is a sacrament and is believed to be permanent. Divorce is allowed, but remarriage is not acceptable without an annulment of the first marriage. Remarriage without an annulment results in the inability to receive the sacraments.

Roman Catholics revere the Virgin Mary as the Mother of God and accord her a place of prominence, but they do not worship her. The Pope is considered to be the teaching authority of the church and is considered to be infallible in matters of faith and morals. Saints are revered because of their holy lives and are asked to intercede on behalf of sinners.

Along with the multitude of issues that cause a client to see a counselor, counselors must be aware of certain topics that relate specifically to Roman Catholics. These include divorce, remarriage after divorce, abortion, birth control, and disagreement with church laws. Counselors need to know the general church laws and related issues but must be fully attentive to the client whose personal interpretation of the laws may be entirely different.

The Eastern Orthodox Church has many beliefs in common with the Roman Catholic Church but does not subscribe to the supreme authority of the Pope of Rome (Esposito, Fasching, & Lewis, 2002). Its members are led by patriarchs and bishops in Eastern Europe. The patriarch is chief among equals who cannot interfere with any of the workings of the national Orthodox Churches. It is important for counselors not to confuse these two Christian groups, because the differences, though few, are very significant.

The Eastern Orthodox Christians believe in the Trinity, three Gods in one (the Father, the Son, and the Holy Spirit), and that God judges individuals immediately after they die. Those who keep faith in God and the church, who do not sin after baptism or repent before death, and who do good works will find happiness after death. Those who do not keep faith in Christ and fail to do good works will be dealt with accordingly. Eastern Orthodox Christians believe that Christ will return to resurrect and judge everyone for all eternity. Salvation is attained through Christ's death and resurrection, but it also requires faith and good works. Required sacraments include one baptism at infancy and the Holy Eucharist with confession and repentance. Adherence to the church's moral laws is essential.

Eastern Orthodox members believe that some suffering is an inheritance from Adam and Eve and their sin. This also includes a vulnerability to illness and disease. Abortion is considered a sin and homosexuality is not an accepted practice. Marriage is a sacrament, but divorce and remarriage are not condemned if reconciliation attempts are pursued in earnest.

Protestants

Protestantism began in the 16th century in a protest to reform Roman Catholicism led by Martin Luther in Germany (Pollock, 2002). This Christian group now consists of a number of mainline Protestant denominations, including Episcopalians, Lutherans, Presbyterians, Methodists, and Baptists. Although these groups have developed over the past 400 years and have many differences among them, all hold to the authority of the Bible and the importance of individual faith.

These mainline Protestant churches tend to be liberal and open to scientific discovery. They question the Bible and church traditions, and minimize the distinctiveness of the denominations (McCullough, Weaver, Larson, & Aay, 2000). An appreciation of these similarities by the counselor is helpful in working with mainline Protestants. Yet enough differences exist that counselors need to have the client describe his or her perception of the particular situation as it relates to that person's denomination. Consulting with a minister in any given denomination in order to become more knowledgeable of that faith is always desirable.

The smaller subdivisions of Protestantism tend to be classified as Evangelical Christians and Fundamentalist Protestants (Frame, 2003). As the names imply, these groups tend to be conservative in their approach to social issues, including opposition to abortion, divorce, homosexuality, and sex outside marriage (Thurston, 2000). Some see women as subservient to men and oppose wives working outside the home. Both Evangelicals and Fundamentalist Christians put a great emphasis on converting nonbelievers to their faith. These groups make up a significant number, 77 million of American Christians, and this number continues to grow yearly (Thurston, 2000). Counselors need to be familiar with all these groups because, although similarities exist among them, the differences can be challenging and confusing unless counselors know the various nuances. Counselors should also strive to recognize the unspoken feelings that clients have deep in their hearts.

Common Features in Protestant Christianity

Tenets of Protestant Christianity as listed here will help to frame commonly held beliefs:

- Christians believe that "God was in Christ reconciling the world to Himself."
- God created mankind in His image and desires that everyone live in a relation of love and fellowship with Him.
- Every person has "sinned" against God and become less than what God intended.
- Sin breaks fellowship with God and leads to a guilty conscience.
- The penalty for sin is death and eternal separation from God's fellowship.
- God sent His Son, Jesus of Nazareth, to demonstrate His love for mankind and to take the penalty for sin upon Himself.
- Jesus of Nazareth, Christ the Messiah, died for the sins of all mankind.
- God raised Jesus from the dead.
- Those who trust Jesus as Lord and Savior are saved (restored to an eternal relationship of love and fellowship with God).
- Faithful disciples of Jesus live in a relation of love and fellowship with God and others.

Protestant Faiths

The following sections will attempt to briefly describe some of the major Protestant church groups. This list is not all inclusive. It focuses on the groups with the largest membership and those most commonly found in the United States. The sections are meant to provide major characteristics that counselors may find interesting and helpful in their practices. This is only a place to start, but it may inspire counselors to seek more information in books, monographs, pamphlets, and on the Internet.

Episcopalians

The Anglican Church, or the Church of England, broke with the Roman Catholic Church (1534) during the reign of the English King, Henry VIII. The Episcopal Church, the American offshoot of the Church of England, does not recognize the role of the papacy, or in other words does not recognize the Pope of the Roman Catholic Church or the authority of the Vatican in matters of faith and morals. The mainstream Episcopal Church, however, has retained many of the ceremonies and rituals of the Roman Catholic Church. The basic tenets of the Episcopal Church can be found in documents published by the bishops of the church. Three documents in particular contain the basic beliefs of the church: The Thirty-nine Articles of Religion (a modified American version based on the original document written for the Church of England in 1563) adopted in 1801, the Book of Common Prayer, and the Catechism of the Episcopal Church. For someone seeking to better understand the religious beliefs of an Episcopalian, any or all of these documents would prove very helpful.

Episcopalians believe that all people are part of God's creation, made in the very image of God. They believe that human beings are free to make choices, to love, to create, to reason, and to live in harmony with their fellow man and with God. Man does not always live in harmony with God because humans sometimes make poor choices and misuse their freedom. However, God is viewed as a merciful God and He is there to help us in spite of our occasional abandonment of Him.

God revealed himself and His will to man through nature and history, through many seers and saints, and especially through the prophets of Israel. From these sources we learn there is only one God, but He exists in Trinity with Jesus Christ and the Holy Spirit. The Father is God, the Son is God, and the Holy Spirit is God. This is not easily understood from a human prospective but is regarded as a major matter of Episcopalian faith. These beliefs are contained in a document named the Athanasian Creed (Quicunque Vult).

Episcopalians believe that God has made two covenants with His people. The Old Covenant was the one God made with the Hebrew people and its provisions are found in the books of the Old Testament. These books also contain the Ten Commandments that Episcopalians believe are still binding and contain God's will for humankind. They define mankind's relationship with God and humans.

Episcopalians believe in the concept of sin and infant baptism. Sin is viewed as the seeking of one's own will instead of the will of God. Man was freed from sin by the coming of the Messiah, in the person of Jesus of Nazareth, the Christ, the only Son of God. Jesus received His human nature from the Virgin Mary, his mother, and He did this so that through Him human beings might be adopted as children of God, and be made heirs of God's kingdom. Through Jesus Christ we are freed from the power of sin and reconciled to God. The New Covenant is the renewed relationship with God given by Jesus Christ, the Messiah, to the apostles, and through them, to all who believe in Him.

The Episcopal Church makes reference to the Summary of the Law and the New Commandment. The first is the commandment to love God with all one's heart, soul, and mind. This is referred to as the first and the great commandment. The New Commandment is to love one's neighbor as one's self. These tenets are found in virtually all Christian religions, although the interpretations may differ somewhat.

What Episcopalians believe is summarized in two creeds: the Apostles' Creed and the Nicene Creed. The Apostles' Creed is the ancient creed of Baptism and is used in the Episcopal Church's daily worship to recall the baptismal covenant. The Nicene Creed is the creed of the universal church and is used at the Eucharist. We have already alluded to the Athanasian Creed, an ancient document proclaiming the nature of the incarnation and of God as Trinity.

Episcopalians also refer to the two great sacraments given by Jesus Christ to His church: Holy Baptism and the Holy Eucharist. These two sacraments are seen as essential for all people. Episcopal Church members also believe that other sacramental rites evolved in the church under the guidance of the Holy Spirit and these include confirmation, ordination, holy matrimony, reconciliation of a penitent, and unction (anointing the sick). They are viewed as means of grace, but they are not necessary for all persons in the same way that baptism and the Eucharist are.

The Catechism of the Episcopal Church also refers to the "Christian hope," which is defined as the ability to live with confidence in newness and fullness of life, and to await the coming of Christ in glory for the completion of God's purpose in the world. Episcopalians, like most Christians, believe in heaven and hell. By heaven, they refer to eternal life in our enjoyment of God, and hell is defined as eternal death in our rejection of God. The Episcopal Church also adheres to the belief in an afterlife or "everlasting life," which will be a new existence in which the faithful will be united with all the people of God in the joy of fully knowing and loving God and each other. The church speaks of the "assurance" as Christians: "nothing, not even death, shall separate us from the love of God which is in Christ Jesus our Lord" (The Catechism of the Episcopal Church, Book of Common Prayer).

Lutherans

A Lutheran is a person who believes, teaches, and confesses the truths of God's Word as they are summarized and confessed in the Book of Concord, which contains the Lutheran confessions of faith. When a pastor is ordained, he promises that he will perform the duties of his office in accord with the Lutheran Confessions. When people are confirmed in the Lutheran Church, they are asked if they confess the doctrine of the Evangelical Lutheran Church.

These solemn promises indicate to all just how important the Lutheran Confessions are for the church. This section will explain the various items contained in the Book of Concord and why the Lutheran Confessions are so important for Lutheranism.

The three ecumenical creeds in the Book of Concord are the Apostles' Creed, the Nicene Creed, and the Athanasian Creed. They are described as "ecumenical" (or universal) because they are accepted by Christians world-wide as correct expressions of what God's Word teaches.

In the year 1530, the Lutherans were required to present their confession of faith before the emperor in Augsburg, Germany. Philip Melanchton wrote the Augsburg Confession, which was read before the imperial court on June 30, 1530. One year later, the Lutherans presented their arguments in defense of the Augsburg Confession, which is what "apology" means here, and it was written by Melanchton as well. The largest document in the Book of Concord, its longest chapter, is devoted to the most important truth of the Christian faith: the doctrine of justification by grace alone, through faith alone, in Christ Jesus.

Martin Luther realized early on how desperately ignorant the laity and clergy of his day were when it came to even the most basic truths of the Christian faith. Around 1530, he produced two small handbooks to help pastors and the heads of families teach the faith. The Small Catechism and the Large Catechism are organized around six topics: the Ten Commandments, the Apostles' Creed, the Lord's Prayer, Holy Baptism, Confession, and the Sacrament of the Altar. So universally accepted were these magnificent doctrinal summaries by Luther that they were included as part of the Book of Concord.

In 1537, Martin Luther was asked to prepare a statement of Lutheran belief for use at a church council, as it was called. Luther's bold and vigorous confession of faith was also incorporated into the Book of Concord. It was presented to a group of Lutheran rulers meeting in the town of Smalcald. Philip Melanchton was asked to expand on the subject of the Roman Pope and did so in his treatise, which was included in the Book of Concord as well.

After Luther's death in 1546, significant controversies broke out in the Lutheran Church. After much debate and struggle, the Formula of Concord in 1567 put an end to these doctrinal controversies, and the Lutheran Church was able to move ahead united in what it believed, taught, and confessed. In 1580, all the confessional writings mentioned here were gathered into a single volume, the Book of Concord, with Concord meaning "harmony." The Formula of Concord was summarized in a version known as the "Epitome" of the Formula of Concord. This document is also included in the Book of Concord.

Lutherans confess that "The Word of God is and should remain the sole rule and norm of all doctrine" (FC SD, Rule and Norm, 9). What the Bible asserts, God asserts. What the Bible commands, God commands. The authority of the Scriptures is complete, certain, and final. The Scriptures are accepted by the Lutheran Confessions as the actual Word of God. The

Lutheran Confessions urge the faithful to believe the Scriptures for "they will not lie to you" (Lutheran Catechism, V, 76) and cannot be "false and deceitful" (FC SD, VII, 96). The Bible is God's "pure, infallible, and unalterable Word" (Preface to the Book of Concord).

The Lutheran Confessions are the "basis, rule, and norm indicating how all doctrines should be judged in conformity with the Word of God" (FC SD RN). Because the Confessions are in complete doctrinal agreement with the written Word of God, they serve as the standard in the Lutheran Church to determine what is faithful, biblical teaching, insofar as that teaching is addressed in the Confessions.

The Lutheran Reformation, according to the Lutheran Church, was not a "revolt," but it rather began as a sincere expression of concern with the false and misleading teachings, which, unfortunately, even to this very day, obscure the glory and merit of Jesus Christ. What motivated Luther was a zealous concern about the Gospel of Jesus Christ.

> Human beings have not kept the law of God but have transgressed it. Their corrupted human nature, thoughts, words, and deeds battle against the law. For this reason they are subject to God's wrath, to death and all temporal afflictions, and to the punishment of the fires of hell. As a result, the Gospel, in its strict sense, teaches what people should believe, namely, that they receive from God the forgiveness of sins; that is, that the Son of God, our Lord Christ, has taken upon Himself the curse of the law and borne it, atoned and paid for all our sins; that through Him alone we are restored to God's grace, obtain the forgiveness of sins through faith and are delivered from death and all the punishments of our sins and are saved eternally. . . . It is good news, joyous news, that God does not want to punish sin but to forgive it for Christ's sake.

The word "confession" is used in a variety of ways, but when one speaks of a "confessional" Lutheran, what is meant is a Lutheran who declares to the world his or her faith and most deeply held belief and conviction, in harmony with documents contained in the Book of Concord:

> Therefore, it is our intent to give witness before God and all Christendom, among those who are alive today and those who will come after us, that the explanation here set forth regarding all the controversial articles of faith which we have addressed and explained—and no other explanation—is our teaching, faith, and confession. In it we shall appear before the judgment throne of Jesus Christ, by God's grace, with fearless hearts and thus give account of our faith, and we will neither secretly nor publicly speak or write

anything contrary to it. Instead, on the strength of God's grace, we
intend to abide by this confession. (FC SD, XII, 4)

Confessional Lutheran pastors are required to "subscript" unconditionally to the Lutheran Confessions, because they are believed to be a pure expression of the Word of God. This is the way pastors, and every layman who confesses his or her belief, are able to say what it is that he or she believes to be the truth of God's Word.

Dr. C. F. W. Walther, the Missouri Synod's first president, explained the meaning of an unconditional confessional subscription in words as clear and poignant today as they were during the time of Martin Luther:

An unconditional subscription is the solemn declaration which the individual who wants to serve the church makes under oath that he accepts the doctrinal content of our Lutheran Confessions, because he recognizes the fact that they are in full agreement with Scripture and do not militate against Scripture in any point, whether the point be of major or minor importance; and that he therefore heartily believes in this divine truth and is determined to preach this doctrine.

A Lutheran is a person who believes the truths of God's Word, the Holy Bible, as they are correctly explained and taught in the Book of Concord. To do so, according to Lutherans, is to confess the Gospel of Jesus Christ. Genuine Lutherans, confessional Lutherans, dare to insist that all doctrines should conform to the standards contained in the Lutheran Confessions. They believe that whatever is contrary to these standards should be rejected and condemned as opposed to the Lutheran faith.

Such a statement may strike some as boastful, but to Lutherans it is not. Rather, it is an expression of the spirit-led confidence that moves them to speak of their faith before the world.

To be a confessional Lutheran is to be one who honors the Word of God. That word, according to the Lutheran Church, makes it clear that it is God's desire for His church to be in agreement about doctrine, and to be of one mind, living at peace with one another. It is for this reason that Lutherans so treasure the precious confession of Christian truth found in the Book of Concord. For confessional Lutherans, no other collection of documents, statements, or books so clearly, accurately, and comfortingly presents the teachings of God's Word and reveals the Biblical Gospel as does the Book of Concord.

Hand in hand with the commitment to teaching and the confession of the faith, Lutherans are supposed to have an equally strong commitment to reaching out boldly with the Gospel and speaking God's truth to the world.

This is what the "confession" of the faith is all about according to the Lutheran faith in the final analysis. This is what it means to be a Lutheran (www.lcms.org).

The United Methodist Church

On April 23, 1968, the United Methodist Church was created when Bishop Reuben H. Mueller, representing the Evangelical United Brethren Church, and Bishop Lloyd C. Wicke, of the Methodist Church, joined hands at the constituting General Conference in Dallas, Texas. With the words, "Lord of the Church, we are united in Thee, in Thy Church, and now in the United Methodist Church," the new denomination was given birth by two churches that had distinguished histories and influential ministries in various parts of the world.

Theological traditions steeped in the Protestant Reformation, Wesleyanism, similar ecclesiastical structures, and relationships that date back almost 200 years made the union easier and stronger than other mergers might have been. In the Evangelical United Brethren heritage, for example, Philip William Otterbein, the principal founder of the United Brethren in Christ, assisted in the ordination of Francis Asbury to the superintendency of American Methodist worship.

The United Methodist Church refers to the overall denomination, connectional relation, and identity of its many local churches; the various conferences; their respective councils, boards, and agencies; and other church units, all of which collectively constitute the religious system known as United Methodism. United Methodists adhere to a constitution and disciplinary procedures set forth in their Book of Discipline.

The organization of each unit in the church is carefully spelled out in the Book of Discipline. All members are at least acquainted with the local church. It includes those who have professed their belief in Christ, have been baptized, and have taken the vows of membership. The local church is the setting for hearing the Word of God and for receiving the Sacrament. It reaches out in the name of Christ to bring people into its fellowship, to nurture the members in their faith, to witness Christ's love, and to serve the community, both locally and globally. Groups of local churches work together as a district and are supervised by a clergy superintendent. These districts are part of an annual conference, the basic unit of the denomination. Central conferences are regional units outside the United States, whereas conferences within the United States are grouped into five geographic jurisdictions.

The United Methodists have built checks and balances into all aspects of church life. The denomination is organized similarly to that of the U.S.

government. The General Conference is the top legislative body, the nine-member Judicial Council is the "Supreme Court," and the Council of Bishops is similar to the executive branch. Boards of directors, who are composed of lay- and clergypersons, govern agencies within the church and are primarily accountable to the General Conference staff.

Like Christians of other denominations, Methodists proclaim belief in the triune God—Father, Son, and Holy Spirit. This major belief embraces the biblical witness to God's activity in creation, encompasses God's gracious self-involvement in the dramas of history, and anticipates the consummation of God's reign.

The created order of the United Methodist Church was designed for the well-being of all creatures and as a place of human dwelling in covenant with God. As sinful creatures, however, Methodists believe that mankind has broken that covenant, become estranged from God, wounded themselves and one another, and wreaked havoc throughout the natural order. Human beings stand in need of redemption. Methodists believe that because God truly loves men and women in spite of their willful sins, God judges them, summons them to repentance, pardons them, receives them by that grace given to them in Jesus Christ, and gives them hope of life eternal.

The United Methodist Church believes that the sacraments that were ordained by Christ are not only badges or tokens of Christian mankind's profession but rather that they are certain signs of grace and God's good will toward mankind. Sacraments work invisibly in people to strengthen and confirm their faith in Him. Methodists believe that two sacraments were ordained by Christ the Lord in the Gospel, specifically baptism and the Supper of the Lord.

Five other rituals are commonly called sacraments: confirmation, penance, orders, matrimony, and extreme unction (anointing of the sick). These are not to be counted as sacraments of the Gospel because Methodists believe that they have grown out of the corrupt following of the apostles, and are states of life allowed in the Scriptures. Methodists hold that these five do not have the same nature as baptism and the Lord's Supper because they do not have any visible sign or ceremony ordained by God.

The sacraments, according to the United Methodist Church were not ordained by Jesus Christ to be "gazed upon" or to be "carried about" but to be duly used. Methodists also believe that if those who are truly worthy receive them, they have a wholesome effect or operation, but any persons who seek to receive them in an unworthy state, purchases for themselves condemnation, as described by St. Paul.

The United Methodist Church has a long history of concern for human justice. The members of the church have often taken forthright positions on controversial issues involving Christian principles. Early Methodists expressed their opposition to the slave trade, to smuggling, and to the cruel treatment of prisoners.

A social creed was adopted by the Methodist Episcopal Church (North) in 1908. Within the next decade, the Methodist Episcopal Church (South) adopted similar statements and so did the Methodist Protestant Church. The Evangelical United Brethren Church adopted a statement of social principles in 1946 when the United Brethren and the Evangelical Church united. In 1972, four years after the uniting in 1968 of the Methodist Church and the Evangelical United Brethren Church, the General Conference of the United Methodist Church adopted new Social Principles, which were revised in 1976 (and by each successive General Conference).

The Social Principles are a prayerful and thoughtful effort on the part of the General Conference to speak to the human issues in the contemporary world from biblical and theological foundations as historically demonstrated in United Methodist traditions. They are intended to be instructive and persuasive in the best prophetic spirit. The Social Principles are a call to all members of the United Methodist Church to a prayerful, studied dialogue of faith and practice. Excerpts from these Principles follow:

> We, the people called United Methodists, affirm our faith in God our Creator and Father, in Jesus Christ our Savior, and in the Holy Spirit, our Guide and Guard. We acknowledge our complete dependence upon God in birth, in life, in death, and in life eternal. Secure in God's love, we affirm the goodness of life and confess our many sins against God's will for us as we find it in Jesus Christ. We have not always been faithful stewards of all that has been committed to us by God the Creator. We have been reluctant followers of Jesus Christ in his mission to bring all persons into a community of love. Though called by the Holy Spirit to become new creatures in Christ, we have resisted the further call to become the people of God in our dealings with each other and the earth on which we live.

> Grateful for God's forgiving love, in which we live and by which we are judged and affirming our belief in the inestimable worth of each individual, we renew our commitment to become faithful witnesses to the Gospel, not alone to the ends of the earth, but also to the depths of our common life and work.

> All creation is the Lord's, and we are responsible for the ways we use and abuse it. Water, air, soil, minerals, energy resources, plants, animal life, and space are to be valued and conserved because they are God's creation and not solely because they are useful to human beings.

> The community provides the potential for nurturing human beings into the fullness of their humanity. We believe we have a responsibility to innovate, sponsor, and evaluate new forms of

community that will encourage development of the fullest potential in individuals.

The rights and privileges a society bestows upon or withholds from those who comprise it indicate the relative esteem in which that society holds particular persons and groups of persons. We affirm all persons as equally valuable in the sight of God.

We claim all economic systems to be under the judgment of God no less than other facets of the created order.

While our allegiance to God takes precedence over our allegiance to any state, we acknowledge the vital function of government as a principal vehicle for the ordering of society. Because we know ourselves to be responsible to God for social and political life, we declare the following relative to government.

God's world is one world. We commit ourselves to the achievement of a world community that is a fellowship of persons who honestly love one another.

We believe in God, Creator of the world; and in Jesus Christ, the Redeemer of creation. We believe in the Holy Spirit, through whom we acknowledge God's gifts, and we repent of our sin in misusing these gifts to idolatrous ends.

We affirm the natural world as God's handiwork and dedicate ourselves to its preservation, enhancement, and faithful use by humankind.

We joyfully receive for ourselves and others the blessings of community, sexuality, marriage, and the family.

We commit ourselves to the rights of men, women, children, youth, young adults, the aging, and people with disabilities; to improvement of the quality of life; and to the rights and dignity of racial, ethnic, and religious minorities.

We believe in the right and duty of persons to work for the glory of God and the good of themselves and others in the protection of their welfare in so doing; in the rights of property as a trust from God, collective bargaining, and responsible consumption; and in the elimination of economic social distress.

We dedicate ourselves to peace throughout the world, to the rule of justice and law among nations, and to individual freedom for all people of the world.

We believe in the present and final triumph of God's Word in human affairs and gladly accept our commission to manifest the life of the Gospel in the world. Amen. (Social Principles, http://www .umc.org/abouttheumc)

Baptists
Speaking for mainstream Baptists is a hazardous undertaking. We deny that any human understanding of the Bible can be so exhaustive and authorita-

tive as to merit its use as an "instrument of doctrinal accountability." Mainstream Baptists think it more prudent to leave every believer free to interpret the Bible according to the dictates of a conscience guided by the Holy Spirit.

Though Mainstream Baptists insist on thinking for themselves, a broad consensus has been made concerning the scriptures. The Bible is a holy book in that it holds a separate and unique place in their lives. It is the story of God's love. Baptists are part of that story. They identify with this story and it gives meaning and direction to their lives.

Although Baptists love and respect the Bible, they state that they do not worship it. The Bible is believed to be the written Word of God. In and of itself, it is paper and ink, words and sentences, and has no life of its own. The Mainstream Baptist Web site states that the Bible is not the supreme revelation of God. The Bible points to and must be fulfilled and completed by God's Living Word, Jesus Christ. Jesus is believed by Baptists to be the one mediator between God and man. He gives Scriptures life by creating from them a spark of understanding in people's hearts. From that understanding, He calls everyone to a personal relationship with Him. Those who respond in faith to God's call identify with the story of Jesus Christ and commit themselves to a life of discipleship. For them, the Bible becomes more than a reliable record of God's revelation in the past. It is the authoritative tradition from which one must view the horizons of life in both time and eternity.

The story of God's love recorded in the Bible was written by men, but it is God's story. It is the story of the God who created human beings, gave them life, and loved them enough to reveal Himself and die for them. Some of the encounters between God and mankind have been documented in written records. Baptists believe that the spirit of God filled and inspired the writers of the documents collected in the Bible. The language, words, and style in which each author wrote reflect his own individual and unique pattern of thought and understanding. Mainstream Baptists believe that the meaning and significance of what they wrote, however, transcend their own personal purposes and individual intentions. Their writings serve the purposes and intentions of God. Baptists affirm that the entire compiled text, in its parts and as a whole, is the authoritative canon for their beliefs and practices.

Scripture, for Mainstream Baptists, has a surplus of meaning. It always means more than what people can understand or embody. They believe that Jesus alone fully comprehended and perfectly embodied its truth, and that Christ alone has ultimate authority in the life of the believer. No human creed, confession, interpretation, exposition, or application of Scripture has finality, and the Scriptures must always be approached with a sense of humility. Mainstream Baptists believe human minds must be sensitive to the limitations of human understanding, and people's hearts must be open to the guidance of God's spirit.

For Mainstream Baptists, understanding is initially grounded in a straightforward acceptance of the history and truth of the biblical story of God's love. Faith begins as an unquestioning response to the truth of the Gospel. As the "good news" of God's love is presented to them, God's presence appears directly and immediately in their consciousness. They hear God's call individually and feel His claim on their lives personally. Mainstream Baptists are expected to give themselves to God completely and without reservation. This unquestioning, childlike trust and acceptance is the foundation of a Mainstream Baptist's relationship with God. Without it, there is no faith.

Mainstream Baptists' faith and understanding are stretched by struggling through disorientation and doubt. Faith grows in moments of adversity and suffering. During these times, God may seem distant and absent from human beings, but those moments test their convictions, develop their character, and strengthen their faith. Understanding grows when meaning seems distant and people ask probing questions.

Serious questioning requires discipline. Faithful students of the Bible among Mainstream Baptists are developing several disciplines that make careful and deliberate inquiry of the Scriptures. Each discipline looks at the Bible from a different perspective. Like scientific disciplines that make discoveries by developing and utilizing microscopes or telescopes, each biblical discipline is developing methods that are appropriate to its area of specialization. Some focus on its grammar and language, whereas others study the history of the text and the process by which it was transmitted to mankind. Some probe its literary forms and qualities, others examine the literary styles of its authors and editors, and some explore the various responses of its readers.

Disorienting experiences and misunderstandings often leave an emptiness in people's hearts. Individuals want to be "filled" and "called" again. To a Mainstream Baptist, maturing faith moves beyond interpreting Scripture to embodying its truth in daily life. God's presence with individuals becomes most immediate and apparent as they grow to live and love like Christ. His spirit is continually "calling" people and empowering them to put faith and love into action. Only in God's service do human hearts find a measure of completion.

Ultimately truth is personal, and Jesus Christ embodies truth according to Baptist teachings. Scripture points to Him and, according to Mainstream Baptists, that is God's ultimate intention and purpose for Scripture. Jesus is the center that gives unity and meaning to the collection of writings that compose the Bible. Christ is the source of the Scripture's inexhaustible surplus of meaning. He is the one mediator between God and humankind, and He is the Living Word that opens the meaning of Scripture in peoples' hearts and minds. Mainstream Baptists believe that He should be the ultimate authority in people's lives. His spirit should fill them and empower people to live and love like Him.

According to Mainstream Baptists' writings, all lives should point to Him. That is God's ultimate intention and purpose for the church. Christ is the center that gives unity and meaning to the collection of individuals who compose the church. He is the "truth" that each person should know personally. Jesus is the one mediator between God and humanity, and every human being should have direct access to God through Christ.

An important tenet in Baptist belief is that every Christian is his or her own priest. Each person is authorized to go directly to God for the forgiveness of sins and to search the Scriptures with the confidence of being guided by the same spirit that inspired those who wrote the Bible. Every Christian is also a priest to others in that he or she is a member of a royal priesthood and responsible to Christ for ministering to others. "For by grace have you been saved through faith; and that not of yourselves, it is the gift of God; not as a result of works, that no one should boast" (Ephesians 2:8–9 National Association of Southern Baptists).

Baptists believe that God's love and grace are the only basis for any person's relationship with God. Human beings can do nothing to earn or deserve God's love and forgiveness. Faith is not something that individuals "work up." It is not an effort or labor. Faith is receiving God's love with an open heart and finding it transformed by God's grace. George W. Truett expressed Baptist beliefs most succinctly:

> Religious liberty is the nursing mother of all liberty. Without it all other forms of liberty must soon wither and die. The Baptists grasped this conception of liberty in its full-orbed glory, from the very beginning. Their contention has been, is now, and must ever be, that it is the God-given and indefensible right of every human being, to worship God or not, according to the dictates of his conscience; and, as long as he does not infringe on the rights of others, he is to be held accountable to God alone, for all his religious beliefs and practices. (p.)

Mainstream Baptists live to serve and please their Lord. They believe that at the end of their days "we must all appear before the judgment seat of Christ" (2 Cor. 5:9–10). They are socially concerned because they know that the Lord identifies with the hungry, the poor, the sick, and the imprisoned, and they know the rule by which He will judge all:

But when the Son of Man comes in His glory, and all the angels with Him, then He will sit on His glorious throne. And all the nations will be gathered before Him; and He will separate them from one another, as the shepherd separates the sheep from the goats; and He will put the sheep on his right, and the goats on the left. Then the King will say to those on His right, "Come, you who are blessed by My Father, inherit the kingdom prepared for you from the foundation of the world. For I was hungry, and you gave Me something to eat; I was thirsty, and you gave Me drink; I was a stranger and you invited Me in; naked, and you clothed Me; I was sick, and you visited Me; I was in prison, and you came to Me."

Baptists believe that every believer is empowered to be a witness (Acts 1:8) and commissioned to be an ambassador for Christ. Although each of us is responsible to bear witness to Christ in both word and deed in our lives, Baptists recognize that He calls some persons to devote their lives to special ministries. The church supports these persons with its prayers, its encouragement, its labors, and its financial assistance.

Baptists are one branch of the Protestant Reformation that Martin Luther started in 1517. Protestants disagreed with the Roman Catholic Church's understanding of salvation. The reformers declared that people are saved by grace through faith, not by the sacraments of the church. The Catholic Church said Luther's teaching was heresy. Luther quoted the Bible to support his teachings, and Catholic Church leaders claimed to be the official interpreters of Scripture. They told Luther his interpretation was mistaken and held him accountable to teach and preach according to the official Catholic tradition of biblical interpretation. Luther responded:

Unless I am convicted by Scripture and plain reason—I do not accept the authority of popes and councils, for they have contradicted each other—my conscience is captive to the Word of God. I cannot and I will not recant anything, for to go against conscience is neither right nor safe. God help me. Amen.

Luther claimed to be directly accountable to God for how he interpreted Scripture. Then he translated the Bible from Latin into German so others could read the Scriptures and decide for themselves what the Bible said. When the Scriptures were taken from the exclusive domain of church leaders and given to all Christians to read and interpret, the biblical doctrine that all believers are priests was reclaimed.

Luther and most of the other reformers emphasized the priesthood of believers to buttress support for the teaching of salvation by grace. A small group of reformers insisted that the doctrine also had profound implications for the life of the church. This small group of reformers maintained that every believer had the right and responsibility to directly relate to God and to act as a priest. These reformers were labeled "radicals" because they wanted to pattern church life in accordance with the New Testament where every member was commissioned and gifted for service.

Baptists take seriously Christ's command to "love the Lord your God . . . with all your mind" (Matt. 22:37). Each Baptist is supposed to strive to observe the apostle Paul's injunction to "not be conformed to this world, but to be transformed by the renewing of your mind, that you may prove what the will of God is, that which is good and acceptable and perfect" (Romans 12:2 NASB).

Baptists object to being thought of as narrow minded, dogmatic, legalistic, or anti-intellectual. They believe that all truth is God's truth, and people are open to discovering truth by scientific inquiry, philosophic reasoning, and human experience. They humbly recognize that ultimate truth is beyond human conceptualization (Isaiah 55:8), that truth is ultimately personal (John 14:6), and that man must depend on the guidance of God's spirit to discern truth (John 16:13).

In mainstream Baptist churches, every member makes a personal commitment to follow Christ and enter into the fellowship of the church. Unlike churches that baptize infants and incorporate them into the church before they are capable of making a personal response to the Gospel, Baptist churches baptize people only after they make a personal confession of their faith in Christ.

Baptists also practice baptism by totally immersing persons in water, rather than by sprinkling, pouring, or anointing. Baptism by immersion preserves the dramatic imagery of the meaning of baptism as a symbolic death, burial, and resurrection of Christ who died for mankind's sins and the believer's own death to sin, his or her burial of a sinful human nature, and his or her resurrection to a new life in Christ (www.mainstreambaptists.org/mbn).

Presbyterians

The First General Assembly of the Presbyterian Church in America (PCA) took place at the Briarwood Presbyterian Church in Birmingham, Alabama, on December 4–7, 1973. There they adopted the Confession of Faith, the Larger Catechism, and the Shorter Catechism as the doctrinal standards or statements of belief held by Presbyterians of the church. The PCA received the same Confession and Catechisms as those adopted by the first American Presbyterian Assembly of 1789, with two minor exceptions, namely, the deletion of strictures against marrying one's wife's kindred and the reference to the Pope as the antichrist.

Other than these changes and the American amendments of Chapter XXIII on the civil magistrate (adopted in 1789), this formed the Confession and Catechisms as agreed upon by the Assembly of Divines at Westminster, which met from 1643–1647. The Caruthers edition of the Confession and Catechisms, based on the original manuscript written by Cornelius Burgess, is the edition presented to and adopted by the First General Assembly of the PCA.

The Scripture proof texts are essentially those of the Westminster Assembly, which has been approved by the Assembly of the PCA, but which are not a part of the Constitution itself. The King James Version has been used, because this was the English text in use at the time of the Westminster Assembly, the language of which is at times reflected in the Confession and Catechisms. The inclusion of the Ten Commandments, the Lord's Prayer, the Apostle's Creed, and the footnote regarding them with the Shorter Catechism goes back to the Westminster divines, though these are not a formal part of the standards themselves.

The PCA, according to information found at its Web site, has a strong commitment to evangelism, missionary work at home and abroad, and to Christian education. From its inception, the church has determined its purpose to be "faithful to the Scriptures, true to the reformed faith, and obedient to the Great Commission."

A constitutional assembly was held in December 1973 and a new church emerged. This church was first known as the National Presbyterian Church, but changed its name in 1974 to the PCA. It separated from the Presbyterian Church in the United States (Southern) in opposition to the long-developing theological liberalism, which denied the deity of Jesus Christ and the inerrancy and authority of Scripture. Additionally, the PCA held to the traditional position on the role of women in church offices. This was a major controversy for American Presbyterians.

In December 1973, delegates representing some 260 congregations, with a combined communicant membership of over 41,000 that had left the PCUS, gathered at Briarwood Presbyterian Church in Birmingham, Alabama, and organized the National Presbyterian Church, which later became the PCA.

In 1982, the Reformed Presbyterian Church, Evangelical Synod, joined the PCA. This group had been formed in 1965 by a merger of the Evangelical Presbyterian Church and the Reformed Presbyterian Church in North America, General Synod.

The PCA has made a firm commitment to the doctrinal standards that have been significant in Presbyterianism since 1645, namely the Westminster Confession of Faith and Catechisms. These doctrinal standards express the distinctiveness of the Calvinistic or Reformed tradition.

Among the distinctive doctrines of the Westminster Standards and the Reformed tradition is the unique authority of the Bible. The reformers based all their claims on "sola scriptura," the Scriptures alone. This included the doctrine of their inspiration, which is a special act of the Holy Spirit by which He guided the writers of the books of the Scriptures (in their original autographs). Their words should convey the thoughts He wished conveyed, bear a proper relation to the thoughts of other inspired books, and be kept free from errors of fact, of doctrine, and of judgment—all of which were to be an infallible rule of faith and life. Historically, the concept of infallibility has included the idea of inerrancy.

Other distinctive characteristics are the doctrines of grace, which depict what God has done for mankind's salvation:

- *Total depravity of man.* Man is completely incapable within himself to reach out toward God. Man is totally an enmity with God (cf., Romans 3:10–23).
- *Unconditional election by the grace of God.* There is absolutely no condition in any person for which God would save him. As a matter of fact, long before man was created, God chose or predestined some to everlasting life. He did this out of His mere good pleasure (cf., Ephesians 1:4 and 1:5).
- *Particular atonement.* God in His infinite mercy, in order to accomplish the planned redemption, sent His own Son, Jesus Christ, to die as a substitute for the sins of a large but specific number of people (cf., Romans 8:29 and 8:30).
- *The irresistible grace of God.* This is the effectual work of the Holy Spirit moving upon a particular person whom He has called, applying the work of redemption (cf., John 3:5 and 3:6).
- *The perseverance of the saints.* This is that gracious work of God's sanctification whereby He enables a saved person to persevere to the end. Even though the process of sanctification is not complete in this life, from God's perspective it is as good as accomplished (cf., Romans 8:30, 8:38, 8:39, and Philippians 1:6).

The PCA Ministry Buildings in Lawrenceville, Kansas, are where most of the ministries of the Presbyterian denomination are coordinated. Four Program Committees—Mission to the World, Mission to North America, Christian Education and Publication, Reformed University Ministries—and one Service Committee, the Administrative Committee, which is responsible for the administration of the General Assembly, carry on these ministries. Additionally, five agencies also minister to the denomination: the PCA Foundation; the Insurance and Annuities and Relief Board (both of which are located in Lawrenceville); Ridge Haven (the PCA conference center near Rosman, North Carolina); Covenant College in Lookout Mountain, Georgia; and the Covenant Theological Seminary in St. Louis, Missouri (the national education institutions of the PCA).

The PCA is one of the fastest growing denominations in the United States, with over 1,450 churches and missions throughout the United States and Canada. Over 306,000 communicant and noncommunicant members were part of the denomination as of December 2000.

The influence of the PCA extends far beyond the walls of the local church. Mission to the World has 519 career missionaries in almost 60 nations, 169 two-year missionaries, and over 6,500 short-term missionaries. Because of the unique relationship between Mission to the World, an organization of the Presbyterian Church, and over 30 mission organizations, some consider the influence of the missionaries is far greater than size might indicate. Indeed, PCA churches support an additional 690 career missionaries, covering over 130 nations. Further, with more than 100 chaplains in the military, the Veterans Administration, prisons, and hospitals, as well as 45 college and university campus ministers, the Gospel is proclaimed to a rather large audience around the world that would not be reached through usual channels. Because of the emphasis on education, many members of the PCA are teachers and professors at all levels, including a significant number of large universities and theological seminaries.

In this new century, the Presbyterian Church in America continues its commitment to evangelism worldwide and the building up of the church of our Lord Jesus Christ. As one communion in the worldwide church, the Presbyterian Church in America exists to glorify God by extending the kingdom of Jesus Christ over all individual lives through all areas of society and in all nations and cultures. To accomplish this end, the PCA aims to fill the world with churches that are continually growing in vital worship, in theological depth, in true fellowship, in assertive evangelism, and in deeds of compassion.

The distinctiveness of the PCA lies in its emphasis that is both reformation- and revival-oriented. Without an emphasis on revival, "reformation" may become either a mimicking of political ideologies or sterile doctrinalism. Without an emphasis on reformation, "revival" may become a shallow pietism or mysticism. Only reformation and revival together can accomplish the great commission of our Lord.

The Presbyterian Church of America's Web site (http://www.pcanet.org/admin) states:

> We are committed to the Scriptures and the historic Westminster Standards based firmly on a biblical theology that answers the questions and issues of each culture and people to which we minister.

We are committed to worship that practices the presence and power of God within the church to the transformation of the surrounding culture through biblical application in population centers around the world.

We are committed to the winning of new converts and their incorporation into the church through the ministry of the Word and to significant ministry to the needy through deeds of mercy and service.

We are committed to the freedom of every member to minister through spiritual gifts and also to the responsibility to do so under spiritual authority and loving discipline.

We are committed to dynamic, prophetic confrontation on non-Christian thought forms and behavior and also to the demonstration of the church throughout the practice of holiness and love of Christian fellowship.

We are committed to guarding and strengthening the biblical family and also to a ministry to the broken family forms such as the divorced, the widowed, and the unwed parent.

We are committed to teaching and disciplining men and women in the whole counsel of God and also to ministering to the needs of the whole person.

Seventh-day Adventists

Seventh-day Adventists accept the Bible as their only creed and hold certain fundamental beliefs to be the teaching of the Holy Scriptures. These beliefs constitute the church's understanding and expression of the teaching of Scripture. Revision of these statements is undertaken only at a General Conference session when the church is led by the Holy Spirit to a fuller understanding of Bible truth or when it finds better language in which to express the teachings of God's Holy Word.

The Holy Scriptures, the Old and New Testaments, are the written Word of God, given by divine inspiration through holy men of God who spoke and wrote as the Holy Spirit moved them. In this Word, God has committed to man the knowledge necessary for salvation. The Holy Scriptures, according to Seventh-day Adventists, are the infallible revelation of His will. They are the standard of character, the test of experience, the authoritative revealer of doctrines, and the trustworthy record of God's acts in history.

Seventh-day Adventists believe that there is one God—Father, Son, and Holy Spirit—a unity of three co-eternal Persons. God is immortal, all powerful, all knowing, above all, and ever present. He is infinite and beyond human comprehension, yet known through His self-revelation. He is forever worthy of worship, adoration, and service by the whole creation.

According to the teachings of this church, the eternal Father is the creator, source, sustainer, and sovereign of all creation. He is just and holy, merciful and gracious, slow to anger, and abounding in steadfast love and faithfulness. The qualities and powers exhibited in the Son and the Holy Spirit are also believed to be revelations of the Father.

Seventh-day Adventists also believe that God became incarnate in Jesus Christ, the eternal Son. They profess a creed that states that through Him all things were created, the character of God is revealed, the salvation of humanity is accomplished, and the world is judged. Forever truly God, He became also truly man, Jesus Christ. He was conceived of the Holy Spirit and born of the Virgin Mary. He lived and experienced temptation as a human being, but perfectly exemplified the righteousness and love of God. By His miracles, He manifested God's power and was attested as God's promised Messiah. He suffered and died voluntarily on the cross for our sins and in our place, He was raised from the dead, and He ascended to minister in the heavenly sanctuary on our behalf. He will come again in glory for the final deliverance of His people and the restoration of all things. This sums up the major beliefs of the church.

God the eternal spirit was active with the Father and the Son in creation, incarnation, and redemption, and he inspired the writers of Scripture. He filled Christ's life with power and He draws and convicts human beings. To those who respond, He renews and transforms them into the image of God. He was sent by the Father and the Son to always be with God's children, and He extends spiritual gifts to the church, empowers it to bear witness to Christ, and in harmony with the Scriptures leads it into all truth.

A major tenet of this religion is that God is creator of all things and has revealed in Scripture the authentic account of His creative activity. It is believed that in six days the Lord made "the heaven and the earth" and all living things upon the earth, and He rested on the seventh day of that first week. Thus, He established the Sabbath as a perpetual memorial of His completed creative work. The first man and woman were made in the image of God as the crowning work of creation, given dominion over the world, and charged with the responsibility to care for it.

Man and woman were made in the image of God with individuality, the power and freedom to think and act, according to the Seventh-day Adventists. Though created as free beings, each person is an indivisible unity of body, mind, and spirit, dependent upon God for life, breath, and all else. When Adam and Eve, our first parents, disobeyed God, they denied their dependence upon Him and fell from their high position under God. The image of God in them was marred and they became subject to death. Seventh-day Adventists believe that their descendants share this fallen nature and its consequences. Mankind was born with weaknesses and tendencies to evil, but God in Christ reconciled the world to Him and by His spirit restores in penitent mortals the image of their maker. Created for the glory of God, they are called to love Him and one another, and to care for their environment. This emphasis on environmental concerns sets the Seventh-day Adventists apart from other Christians.

The Seventh-day Adventists see Christ's life of perfect obedience to God's will as a model for mankind. God provided the only means of atonement for human sin so that those who, by faith, accept this atonement may have eternal life and the whole creation may better understand the infinite and holy love of the Creator. This perfect atonement vindicates the righteousness of God's law and the graciousness of His character for it both condemns sin and provides for forgiveness. The death of Christ reconciled God and man. The resurrection of Christ proclaimed God's triumph over the forces of evil and, for those who accept the atonement, assures their final victory over sin and death. It declares the Lordship of Jesus Christ, "before whom every knee in heaven and on earth will bow."

Another key Adventist belief is that the universal Church is composed of all who truly believe in Christ, but in the last days, a time of widespread apostasy, a remnant will be called out to keep the commandments of God and the faith of Jesus. This remnant will announce the arrival of the judgment hour, proclaim salvation through Christ, and herald the approach of His second advent. This proclamation will be symbolized by the three angels of Revelation 14, and it will coincide with the work of judgment in heaven and result in a work of repentance and reform on Earth. Every believer will be called to have a personal part in this worldwide witness.

Seventh-day Adventists also believe in baptism as a way to confess their faith in the death and resurrection of Jesus Christ. Baptism testifies to the death of one's sins and of one's purpose to walk in the newness of life. Thus, Seventh-day Adventists acknowledge Christ as Lord and Savior, become His people, and are received as members by His church. Baptism is a symbol of the union with Christ, the forgiveness of sins, and the reception of the Holy Spirit. It is by immersion in water and is contingent on an affirmation of faith in Jesus and evidence of repentance of sin. It follows instruction in the Holy Scriptures and the acceptance of their teachings.

One of the gifts of the Holy Spirit as believed by the Seventh-day Adventists is prophecy. This gift is an identifying mark of the remnant church and was manifested in the ministry of Ellen G. White. As the Lord's messenger, her writings are a continuing and authoritative source of truth for Seventh-day Adventists that provide the church with comfort, guidance, instruction, and correction. They also make clear that the Bible is the standard by which all teaching and experience must be tested.

Seventh-day Adventists keep the Sabbath holy for all people as a memorial of Creation. According to this church, the fourth commandment of God's unchangeable law requires the observance of the seventh-day Sabbath as the day of rest, worship, and ministry in harmony with the teaching and practice of Jesus, the Lord of the Sabbath. The Sabbath is a day of delightful communion with God and one another. It is a symbol of the redemption in Christ, a sign of sanctification, a token of allegiance, and a foretaste of an eternal future in God's kingdom. The Sabbath is God's perpetual sign of His eternal covenant between Him and His people. Joyful observance of this holy time from evening to evening, sunset to sunset, is a celebration of God's creative and redemptive acts.

According to the precepts of the Seventh-day Adventists, marriage was divinely established in Eden and affirmed by Jesus to be a lifelong union between a man and a woman in loving companionship. For the members of the church, a marriage commitment is to God as well as to the spouse, and only partners who share a common faith should enter into it. Mutual love, honor, respect, and responsibility are the fabric of this relationship, which is to reflect the love, sanctity, closeness, and permanence of the relationship between Christ and His church. Regarding divorce, Seventh-day Adventists believe that Jesus taught that the person who divorces a spouse, except for fornication, and marries another, commits adultery. Although some family relationships may fall short of the ideal, marriage partners who fully commit themselves to each other in Christ may achieve loving unity through the guidance of the spirit of the church. God blesses the family and intends that its members shall assist each other toward complete maturity. Parents are to bring up their children to love and obey the Lord. By their example and their words, they are to teach them that Christ is a loving disciplinarian, ever tender and caring, who wants them to become members of His body, the family of God. Increasing family closeness is one of the earmarks of the final gospel message.

The second coming of Christ is the blessed hope of the church, the grand climax of the Gospel. The Seventh-day Adventists believe that the Savior's coming will be literal, personal, visible, and worldwide. When He returns, the righteous dead will be resurrected, and together with the righteous living will be glorified and taken to heaven, but the unrighteous will die. The almost complete fulfillment of most lines of prophecy, together with the present condition of the world, indicates for the members of this church that Christ's coming is imminent. The time of the event has not been revealed, and believers are therefore exhorted to be ready at all times (Source: http://www.watchtower.org/library).

Christian Scientists

Christian Scientists believe that God is an incorporeal spirit—creative principle, supreme, omnipotent father-mother, omnipresent, omniscient—the only intelligence and all that actually exists. God is mind, spirit, soul, principle, life, truth, and love. "God is All-in-all" (Pollock, 2002).

According to this belief system, we are all sons and daughters of God, though not at the level of understanding of Jesus Christ. Jesus was a divine exemplar, and Christ is the divine idea of "sonship," the Master. Jesus showed the way (the "wayshower") for all to realize truth, which is God.

The universe and humans are reflections of God's likeness and image, which is spirit, without beginning or end. Illusions, or delusions, of a material world and material body result from errors in thought and ignorance of the true and only nature of reality, which is spiritual. God is all that truly exists according to these teachings.

Death is the belief in death. According to Christian Scientists' beliefs, there is no death as humans are immortal spirits. After that which humans call "death," spiritual development toward truth continues until all evil, or "error," destroys itself. Heaven and hell are not places, but states of consciousness that continue after death. "Heaven" is the self-made eternal bliss of realizing oneness with God. "Hell" is the self-made anguish of believing in pain and death.

The following are basic truths taught by Christian Scientists. Evil is the belief in evil. God is all that is real, and God is completely good; therefore, good is real and evil is an illusion/delusion. The only power evil has is to destroy itself; attempts to destroy good naturally result in punishment for the evildoer. Sin creates its own hell. Not realizing one's true nature as spirit results in selfishness that can lead to error and disharmony.

Salvation lies in bringing oneself into harmony with one's true nature as God's reflection, through good works, patience, meekness, love, watchfulness, prayerful gratitude, and devout obedience in following Christ's example. According to Christian Scientists, two basic commandments exist: that one turn only to God, the perfect mind, for guidance, and that one "love thy neighbor as thyself." Healing and immortality are realized by becoming conscious that the only true reality is God, which is love, and that one's true and only nature is God's likeness. As one realizes the error of belief in the reality of suffering and evil, these images of thought impressed upon the mortal mind can be altered, thus banishing sickness, death, and sin, while being testimony to the power of faith in God, of mind over matter. This is a belief that Christian Scientists hold dear.

Though appearing real, suffering (and illness) is a false belief or error of mortal thought. Suffering is overcome by asserting the truth of one's being as an idea of God. Often, a trained Christian Science practitioner is called to support the patient's thought through prayerfully "knowing the truth."

The Christian Scientist Church claims no position on abortion, though such a step would clearly not be in harmony with seeing God's child as perfect and divine. A reliance on conventional medicine, though discouraged, is left up to the individual. Physicians are not viewed antagonistically, but their methods are seen as ineffective because they treat disease as originating in the body rather than the mind. Homosexuality is often regarded negatively, a belief that requires healing through Christian Science practices. The Mother Church has not announced opposition to this view (Source: http://www.beliefnet.com/story).

Jehovah's Witnesses

According to the Jehovah's Witness beliefs, there is one God Almighty, a spirit being with a body but not a human body, and no Trinity.

Also contained in the doctrine of the church is the belief that Christ is Lord and Savior, but not God (Jehovah) incarnate, not a God-man but inferior to God, not part of a godhead. He was a created spirit being, God's only begotten son, sent to Earth as a perfect human. His sacrifice became the "ransom" price to redeem mankind from sin and death. God created all in heaven and on Earth through Christ, the "master worker," God's servant. After Christ's resurrection by God, he was "exalted" to a level higher than angels.

Jehovah's Witnesses hold to the belief that God created the heavens and earth in six days, but each "day" is equal to thousands of years. God created and controls all processes and events and "makes all things happen."

No soul remains after death, according to the beliefs of this faith. Soon, Jesus Christ will return to resurrect just the righteous dead, restoring soul and body, and judge who will reign in heaven and who will spend eternity on a restored, paradisiacal earth.

Original sin caused humans to inherit death and sin. Satan and his demons pervade the earth as spirits tempting all to sin, which God allows as a test of faith in Him according to the writings of the Jehovah's Witnesses. Human beings must show faith in God and in Jesus Christ as Lord and Savior. Church members must adhere to the practices, requirements, commandments, laws, and sacraments of the faith. "Witnessing" and active sharing of their faith with others is fundamental. They must avoid behaviors that God dislikes, including the celebration of birthdays and holidays originating from false religions. This sets Jehovah's Witnesses apart from most other Christian faiths.

Jehovah's Witnesses believe that much suffering is caused by the inheritance of mortality from Adam and Eve, which includes vulnerability to illness and disease. Also, those who choose to succumb to Satan's temptations may suffer self-inflicted damage to their health. Satan and his demons cause great misery. God has allowed the situation to continue so that mankind can discover that God's rule is better than independent human rule. He has allowed Satan to cause suffering to challenge Satan's claim that God's creation, humans, would turn from and curse God under pressure.

Members of the Jehovah's Witness faith believe that abortion is wrong. They also believe that homosexuality is a serious sin. Gender roles, for them, are defined: Men are the head of the household and women are loving caretakers who assist the husband in teaching the children. Divorce is permitted under certain circumstances, but Jehovah hates remarriage unless the divorce occurred as a result of adultery. Service in the armed forces or any form of allegiance to government is prohibited; one must show allegiance only to the Kingdom of Christ. Blood transfusions, along with ingesting blood, are considered wrong, as God said the soul is in the blood. Bone marrow transplants are left to the individual conscience, but all other forms of medical treatment are acceptable (Source: http://www.beliefnet .com/story).

Latter-day Saints (Mormons)

Mormons profess belief in a "godhead" of the Father, Son, and Holy Spirit as three separate entities united in purpose. God the Father resides in heaven with His wife, the Heavenly Mother; Christ, their only begotten Son; and "exalted" Mormons, who become God-like in heaven. God, the Incarnate, has a perfect body, which looks like ours.

Jesus Christ is God's firstborn son. Jesus is Lord and Savior, God of this earth, creator of all in heaven and earth as directed by God the Father, one in purpose with the Father and the Holy Spirit—a godhead of three separate members. God created the heavens and Earth in six time periods; the word "day" is not of a specified number of years.

According to the Mormon faith, after death one's spirit immediately joins the spirit world and will be assigned to either paradise or spirit prison. Based on one's record of thoughts, words, and actions, righteous believers will live in a state of paradisiacal happiness. Unbelievers and sinners in spirit prison will live in misery, but they are provided the opportunity to repent, accept the Gospel, receive ordinances performed for them by the living, and thus move to the lowest level of heaven. At the Final Judgment and Resurrection, most will be assigned to one of three kingdoms of heaven where spiritual growth continues. Only a few, the most wicked sinners, will suffer eternal torture in the outer darkness, as most will have accepted the Gospel and suffered for their sins enough by the end of the twentieth century.

Mormon beliefs state that humans did not inherit guilt or a sinful nature from Adam and Eve's original sin. The Fall was a planned blessing from God, enabling people to experience human bodies, procreate, experience the joy of redemption, and to do good (the complement of evil). Satan and his demons pervade the earth as spirits tempting all to sin. God gave people free will, and Satan's temptations are a blessing from God so that people can show their faith by resisting.

According to Mormon doctrines, Adam and Eve disobeyed God; thus, the first humans and their descendants lost their immortality and connection to God, gaining physical bodies that suffer disease and deterioration. Also believed by the faithful is the fact that Satan rules the earth and causes misery to mankind. This was God's design—to bless humans with the ability to enjoy their physical bodies, have free will to choose good over evil, be able to experience pleasure that complements suffering, and to experience the joy of redemption and eternal life through Christ. God allows Satan to cause misery to mankind as an opportunity to strengthen character and faith.

Mormons are expected to show faith in and obedience to God and Jesus Christ as Lord and Savior. They must adhere to the practices, requirements, commandments, laws, and sacraments of the faith as exemplified by Jesus Christ. Good works are integral to the faith through monthly fasts and offerings to the needy to show their obedience and love for God. Baptism at age 8, the age of accountability, is necessary, as is being confirmed as a member of the church. Members are expected to confess all sins to God and major transgressions to a presiding officer as well. Mormons receive the laying on of hands for the gift of the Holy Ghost. Mormons are considered to be married for time and eternity.

Mormons firmly believe that abortion is wrong. They also condemn homosexuality and vehemently oppose rights being given to homosexuals. The divine role of woman is mother and wife, helper to the husband. Men are regarded as the head of the family, provider, leader, and teacher. Marriage is regarded as eternal, but divorce is permitted if necessary. In keeping with the belief that doing good works is essential for salvation and is a Christian act, Mormons have established a "welfare" program (Source: http://www.beliefnet.com/story).

Suggested Approaches

Working with clients who profess to be of a Christian faith tradition may pose many challenges for the practitioner because so many categories of Christianity exist. It is necessary to remain open and mindful that, although clients may have a particular affiliation with a certain Christian sect, they may not necessarily practice that religion. It may be advisable to approach the process by conducting an informal assessment regarding spiritual wellness and determine the place that religion could have within the client's life. Wiggins-Frame (2003) compiled a listing of questions that can be used during the intake session to gain an insight into the client's spiritual and or religious beliefs:

1. If you had to describe in three or four sentences the essence of your religious or spiritual tradition, what would you say?
2. What do you think is the strength of your religious or spiritual tradition?
3. How does your religion view counseling and other mental health services?
4. What do you think counselors need to know about your tradition to better serve clients who share this religious or spiritual tradition? (p. 88)

Exercises

1. Design a support group for Catholic women who may be questioning their faith because of recent discoveries of priests abusing their power in the church. How can women be a part of helping to heal the pain? What role does their spirituality play in this healing?
2. From your perspective, what common spiritual themes do you share with those of the Christian faith? What spiritual themes are different? Write about these in your journal and think about your own spiritual strengths that may need further developing before working with clients.
3. Invite someone whose area of expertise is Christian faith traditions to speak with the group or class.

Dorothy's Case

Dorothy is married to Philip, and they have twin sons. The boys are seniors in high school and are preparing to leave for college. Dorothy is concerned that the boys will not practice their Christian faith and follow the example of Philip who stopped attending services when the boys were young. It was always Dorothy who made sure they attended services together, and within recent years the boys began to resist this practice. Dorothy finds comfort in her devotions and feels guilty her sons are not faithfully practicing their religion. Philip is not sympathetic and at times will make remarks about her religious activities. This, along with other issues, has caused difficulties in their marriage, and Dorothy has sought the services of Jennifer, a counselor who attends Dorothy's church.

Case Discussion

1. What resources regarding Dorothy's religion would be helpful to Jennifer when working with Dorothy?
2. How would you describe Dorothy's presenting concerns?
3. What issues would emerge for you in working with Dorothy?
4. How do you think the issue of religion is affecting Dorothy's relationship with her husband and sons?

References

Barrett, D. B., & Johnson, T. M. (1998). Religion. In *Encyclopedia Britannica Book of the Year*. Chicago: Encyclopedia Britannica.

Esposito, J. L., Fasching, D. J., & Lewis, T. (2002). *World religions today.* New York: Oxford University Press.

Frame, M. W. (2003). *Integrating religion and spirituality into counseling.* United States: Brooks/Cole.

Frankiel, S. S. (1993). Christianity: A way of salvation. In H. B. Earhart (Ed.), *Religious traditions of the world.* San Francisco: Harper San Francisco.

McCullough, M. E., Weaver, A. J., Larson, D. B., & Aay, K. R. (2000). Psychotherapy with mainline protestants: Lutheran, Presbyterian, Episcopal/Anglican, and Methodist. In P. S. Richards & A. E. Bergin (Eds.), *Handbook of psychotherapy and religious diversity* (pp. 105–129). Washington, D.C.: American Psychological Association.

Pelikan, J. (1993–1996). Christianity. In *Encarta 97 Encyclopedia.* Redmond, WA: Microsoft Corporation.

Pollock, R. (2002). *The everything world's religions book.* Avon, MA: Adams Media Corporation.

Thurston, N. S. (2000). Psychotherapy with evangelical and fundamentalist Protestants. In P. S. Richards & A. E. Bergin (Eds.), *Handbook of psychotherapy and religious diversity* (pp. 131–153). Washington, D.C.: American Psychological Association.

Internet Sources
www.beliefnet.com/story
www.watchtower.org/library
www.umc.org
www.mit.edu/~stb/anglican/intro
www.mainstreambaptists.org/mbn
www.lcms.org/president
www.pcanet.org/admin

CHAPTER 15
Islam and Other Eastern Traditions

Islam is a monotheistic religion, civilization, and way of life practiced by 840 million people (Bell, 1994). It is the religion of the majority of citizens in the Near East, Turkey, Saudi Arabia, Iraq, Iran, Pakistan, Afghanistan, and much of Northern Africa. Many people in Indonesia, Malaysia, and China also live in accordance with the traditions of Islam (Ludwig, 1989).

Muslim immigrants to the United States comprise a steadily growing group whose members have come from many different countries with distinct cultural backgrounds. Therefore, it is difficult to make universal statements about Muslims and their attitudes toward life. Local ethnic, social, and historical factors have a major influence on the manner in which the Islamic faith is interpreted in any given place (Daneshpour, 1998).

Although many religious groups in the United States are experiencing a decline in membership, Islam is the nation's fastest growing religion. Banawai and Stockton (1993) estimated that 6 million Muslims live in North America. Because of their increasing numbers, it is essential for counselors to be informed on and sensitive to the culture and values of this population.

The common bond that unites all Muslims is the fact that they recite the Koran in the Arabic language and adhere to the same pillars of faith. These pillars are essential guidelines for Muslim behavior and include a profession of faith, praying five times a day, giving alms, fasting during the month of Ramadan, and taking a pilgrimage to Mecca once in a lifetime, if financially and physically possible. Muslims must have faith in the existence of angels, in prophets and messengers prior to Mohammed, in a day of judgment, in heaven and hell, and in destiny (Banawai & Stockton, 1993). All "graven images" are strictly forbidden to Muslims. You will not find pictures or statues in their mosques; hence, many mosques are decorated with geometric symbols instead.

In the early days of this religious group, Islam became a part of both the spiritual and secular lives of its followers. Islam was a religious institution, but it was also the law, the state, and other government institutions. Islam was not just a religion; it was a way of life.

It was only in the twentieth century that the religious and the secular were somewhat separated. Understanding that the word *Islam* means surrender or submission, one can begin to comprehend the fervor with which Muslims embrace their faith. For Muslims, Islam is the fulfillment and completion of earlier revelations (Exposito, Fasching, & Lewis, 2002, p. 182). Despite the size, global presence, and significant standing of the Islamic community in many areas of the world, myths, stereotypes, and misinformation about Islam and Muslims continues to abound.

Contrary to popular belief, Arabs make up only about 20 percent of the Muslim world; the vast majority of Muslims live in non-Arab societies. Islam has become a very visible presence in the West, especially in Europe and the United States. As such, the followers of Mohammed have struggled with the identity of their religious tradition in the modern world and particularly in the West. What does it mean to live as a Muslim in a non-Muslim majority state in which the Shariah (Islamic law) plays no role? (Fasching, & Lewis, 2002).

Today most Muslim communities reflect both the old and new realities, even though more fundamental members call for a widespread return to older and more traditional forms of dress, dietary laws, worship five times a day, and sexual segregation. Among the Islamic groups, one of the most powerful forces supporting modern changes has been the Muslim woman. In some Muslim communities, women are viewed as being under the strict authority of their husbands and may not appear in public except when wearing garbs that cover the face as well as the body. Other Muslim women have entered professions, run for public office, served in Parliament, conducted women's study groups, and have been active in promoting women's rights among all followers of Islam.

Unique Needs of This Population

The psychosocial needs of the Islamic people are a result of the interaction of religion, family, Muslim culture, and mainstream U.S. culture (Jackson, 1995). The history of Islam in the modern world is one of adapting to dynamic change while attempting to hold fast to traditional beliefs and customs. This is a difficult job for any individual or group.

Muslim families place a high value on education and hold educators in high esteem. Muslim parents would also want counselors and educators to invite them to a conference in order to discuss their children's needs, especially those counselors and educators who proactively express a desire to learn more about Muslim values. Fear of being misunderstood by school officials is a major issue for Muslim families (Jackson, 1995). The more a counselor knows about the Islamic faith, because religion and life are one, the less chance there is for misunderstanding on anyone's part.

Dietary needs for Muslims go beyond physical nutrition to include a person's spiritual dimension. Generally, Muslims eat a diet rich in vegetables and vegetable protein. They are prohibited from eating pork and any meat not killed in a ritualistic manner and cooked with special utensils (Hampton, 1992). Eating in a school cafeteria or at an office function can be difficult for Muslims.

Non-Muslim religious holidays can also be difficult for many Muslims. Overall they support the inclusion of religious holidays, but they have strong feelings that equal coverage should be devoted to all cultures and religions, including Islam (Siraj-Blatchford, 1993). Muslim parents want their children to see their religious beliefs and celebrations revered in the same way that Christians and Jewish holy days are. When one considers the number of Muslims in today's society, this issue becomes even more pressing.

The Koran forbids unmarried men and women to be alone together. This is not a major problem for Muslim men in the United States because Western culture generally gives the males the responsibility for initiating a relationship. Women, however, have to deal with this issue regularly. In some Muslim households, dating can be a major point of controversy (Kelly, Aredi, & Bakhtiar, 1996). Interactions with male teachers or counselors may be more difficult for Muslim females, and greater sensitivity must be used around these issues.

On the other hand, many non-Muslim Americans believe that Muslim women are submissive and subordinate to men. The Muslim religious position, however, holds that women are equal and given the highest respect and honor (Haneef, 1993). Yet because many Muslim men have been reared in countries where male dominance is respected and encouraged, they tend to reflect these traditions. In traditional Muslim roles, married women were in charge of their households and children, and they did not often appear in public. The same is true of Christian or Jewish women in the history of many European countries. In extreme cases, such as the Taliban, Muslim women were treated very harshly, but that should not be considered part of all Muslim communities. Because some Muslim women may be less accustomed to the role of women in western society, the counselor needs to thoroughly explore such a client's perceptions and preferences regarding female customs and social actions.

In the dominant Anglo-American culture, the separateness of the individual takes precedence over connectedness among family members. One criteria of healthy families is the degree of individuation and the autonomy of each individual (Olson, Russell, & Sprenkle, 1989). Because dependency tends to be viewed as a serious problem, a person who cannot function independently by early adulthood is generally seen as maladaptive in the western world (McGoldrick & Preto, 1984). The independence that is deemed necessary and even desirable varies greatly from one culture to another.

Muslims value unity and togetherness more than independence. The preservation of family ties and collective behavior is more highly valued than individualistic orientation and behavior. The Muslim heritage is based on loyalty to family members with strong bonds of kinship (Daneshpour, 1998). This bond involves intensely emotional, intimate relationships, high levels of empathy with family members, and a strong identification with the reputation of the family (Brook, 1995). A common problem for Muslim immigrant families is insufficient connectedness. Counselors and therapists must be aware that to achieve this connectedness in the family, it is important to increase mutual support and maintain group harmony (Daneshpour, 1998).

In Anglo-American culture, overt, explicit, and open communication is highly valued (Tamura & Lau, 1992). In contrast, indirect and implicit expression is common among Muslims (Hang, 1989). This indirect communication includes frequent allusions to proverbs and folk parables, as opposed to making their needs known explicitly. Muslims are expected to be highly sensitive to what other people are thinking despite the minimal use of verbal interactions. Counselors should be aware of this and may need to adjust their techniques accordingly.

To work effectively with American Muslims, counselors must be knowledgeable not only on the diversity within Islam but on what this diversity means when working with individual Muslim clients. Because religion may or may not be important to a particular Muslim client, counselors need to assess religious identity and religiosity (Banawai & Stockton, 1993). Clients who indicate that Muslim and Islamic values guide their lives may need to be assured that the counselor will attempt to understand their perspective and not try to change it (Kelly et al., 1996).

Whether religion is an integral part of a Muslim client's presenting issues depends on the client. Clients who identify strongly with being Muslim may feel that all concerns are potentially religious. The degree of distress or conflict faced by the person depends on the individual's degree of religiosity and adherence to Islamic principles.

An Interview with Inshyra

Inshyra is a 20-year-old college student attending a large state institution in the Midwest. Following the aftermath of September 11, 2001, the author had occasion to speak with her about both her and her family's reactions to the events. Inshyra is a beautiful young woman with large brown eyes and a captivating smile. She was easy to interview and quickly established a rapport with the author. She spoke openly about her beliefs and the role that her religion plays in her life.

Both her parents are professionals; her father is an engineer and her mother is a pediatric surgeon. Both of them are originally from Saudi Arabia and came to America after they married. Inshyra and her brother and sister, however, were born in the United States. They live in a small suburb 15 miles from a major city. She attended public school from kindergarten to sixth grade and then attended a private, Catholic, all-girls school from seventh to twelfth grade. The university she currently attends is coeducational and is very diverse in its student population.

Before Inshyra started kindergarten, she mainly associated with the children of her parents' friends. In her home, Arabic was spoken. Both of her parents were fluent in English, but they felt she would speak English once she started school, and they wanted their children to learn their native language first. Many of her parents' friends felt the same way; therefore, she was not really exposed to English until she began attending public school.

I asked Inshyra what it was like to start kindergarten in an English-speaking school. She described how strange and isolated she felt at first. She talked about how much fear she experienced when she realized no one understood what she was saying and that she couldn't understand even the simplest words that were being spoken. She felt like she was in her own little world and that no one could reach out to her. She did not know how to make friends because she could not communicate with any of the other children. She knew she was intelligent but didn't know how to make others understand what she wanted to say. She related that she often felt completely overwhelmed and cried a lot. She did say her teachers were kind to her, however, and helped her by giving her extra time and attention.

She said that it was not until the end of first grade before she felt really comfortable with English. Her memories of that time when she knew no English yet was thrust into the midst of people who spoke no Arabic are very vivid. She said she would never do the same thing to her own children, were she to have some, because it was too painful. Once she did master English, however, she was an excellent student, making top grades in all subjects.

I asked Inshyra for some other recollections from this period in her life, and she related that the other children in kindergarten made fun of her and would point to her and laugh. "Children can be so cruel," she said. "I was definitely an object of ridicule." Overall, however, she felt it made her stronger, but it definitely affected her self-esteem. She still remembers wanting to run away from all those English-speaking people. She felt helpless, frightened, and alone in their midst. She longed for just one other person with whom to communicate.

I asked Inshyra if she knew where her place was in the world because she comes from two distinct cultures, Arabic and American. She confided that in some ways this is a puzzle to her, because her parents still identify so much with their Middle Eastern roots. "I am an American, however, and while I revere my parents and their ways, I identify more with young Americans my own age. I think the way that they do and I react the way that they do. My parents do not always understand. I grew up in America and I went to American schools. I am an American, much more than I am a Saudi Arabian."

I asked Inshyra about the way she dressed. She wore a traditional Muslim female head covering, but she also wore jeans and a long-sleeved sweater. She explained it was her choice to wear the head covering, which was a decision she had made on her thirteenth birthday. She had thought about it a lot, but her parents did not put pressure on her. She knew that if she adopted the traditional head garb it would call more attention to her as a Muslim, but she felt that by doing so she was acknowledging her heritage. She distinctly remembered the day in the eighth grade when she walked into her classroom with the head garb on. Her classmates were surprised, but they congratulated her for doing so. Inshyra thought that this was rather remarkable, especially because it was a Catholic school. She related that she had never before felt so accepted by her classmates. Many asked her questions about the head garb and wanted to know why she had decided to wear it. Some of the girls wanted to try it on, and many wanted to feel and touch it. After a while, it no longer attracted as much attention from her classmates, and they just accepted the fact that it was now an official part of her everyday dress.

I also asked her about the fact that she wore jeans and sweaters in addition to the traditional head garb. Inshyra answered that nowhere in the Koran does it say that women must wear long dresses. What it mandates is that women must dress modestly and cover most of their body. She felt that her jeans and sweater covered her body completely with only her hands, her face, and parts of her feet showing. She felt that this was as modest as any long dress might be. She also felt that it marks her as an American Muslim.

Inshyra went on to explain that one of the aims of Islam is to protect women as "precious jewels." Therefore, women do not expose themselves to everyone. They keep their eyes downcast as a mark of modesty; to stare someone in the face would be seen as too bold. According to the traditions of Islam, women must conduct themselves in such a way to command respect from everyone. She thought that these traditions were very beautiful, and although it was not always easy to translate them into American life, she was devoted to doing so.

I asked her how this had affected her when she was in high school. Inshyra replied that it was probably easier because she had attended an all-girls school where everyone wore uniforms. She always wore long-sleeved blouses and her uniform shirt was longer that that of her classmates. She fit in, however, and except for her headdress, she did not feel too different.

Because she had attended public school through the sixth grade, however, a Catholic school was an adjustment for her. She explained that many Muslim parents preferred single-sex schools, especially for their daughters. She found the Catholic ceremonies strange at first, but she also described them as being very beautiful and reverent. By studying Catholicism, she came to realize how "alike" most religions are, rather than how different.

At the university she is attending, she took a course in world religions and discovered that all major faiths advocate giving "alms" to the poor. Most of them believe in one God and prescribe ways to venerate Him. Many of the oldest religions have dietary laws, and Judaism, Catholicism, and Islam all have a "holy place" that is sacred to their religious followers. Also, they all trace their roots back to the Middle East. Inshyra felt that her parents' decision to let her learn about other religions was a wise one and a very good one intellectually. It resulted in her strengthening her belief in her own faith.

I asked Inshyra if it was difficult being a Muslim teenager in an American school. She answered by explaining that the customs of American youth in terms of dating are very different from Muslim traditions. Muslim girls do not date in high school and the mingling of the sexes is prohibited at this age. Consequently, the Muslim girls attending her high school did not go to dances, the prom, or parties where boys were present. The commingling of the sexes is seen as dangerous and a source of temptation to most Muslim families. This was hard, she said, because teenagers want to fit in and don't want to be perceived as "different" in any way. She understood what her parents wanted and what her religion demanded, and she tried not to be too upset about missing these things. She stated emphatically, however, that this was extremely difficult.

Inshyra went on to explain that many Muslim families, but not all, still believed in arranged marriages. Parents begin by arranging for introductions between young women and men. It is different, however, from the old days in that either party does have a right of refusal once they meet each other. Because general dating is prohibited among more conservative

Muslims, this is really the only way a couple can be formally introduced. The age at which this occurs is usually 19 or 20, although with so many Muslim women seeking higher education, sometimes it is a little later. In earlier times, the girl may have been as young as 15 or 16 when she was betrothed.

Inshyra stressed the importance that most Muslim families place on education for both women and men. She stated emphatically that it is only the most conservative sects in a few foreign countries who do not see men and women as equal when it comes to receiving an education. Because both of her parents were practicing professionals, she and her siblings had excellent role models. She herself was majoring in business administration and knew of many Muslim women who worked side by side with their husbands in a variety of different businesses.

We spoke about the month of Ramadan, the holiest of Muslim observances. Inshyra said that most Muslim families wake up before dawn, eat a good breakfast, and then fast from sunrise to sunset. At sunset or shortly afterwards, a substantial evening meal is served and the family breaks its fast in this way. Ramadan, according to Inshyra, is a lovely and special time because families take special pains to eat and pray together. She explained that Ramadan and fasting were about sacrifice, humility, and gratitude. Going without food or water from sunrise to sunset is definitely hard to do and requires an enormous sacrifice, especially in a country where food is so available. Inshyra felt that making such sacrifices keeps people humble because they acknowledge the existence of a power higher than themselves in a special way during this holiest of months. Gratitude is felt because one comes to realize how much we take for granted, particularly in America, and the abundance of everything we have. When things like food and water are taken away, even temporarily, we come to realize how awful it would be to have to worry about them on a daily or even an hourly basis. Inshyra stated that God created a beautiful world that he wanted every human being to enjoy, but that overindulgence in the riches of this world causes us to lose a sense of ourselves. Sacrifice, humility, and gratitude restore the proper order to people's lives and to the universe.

Inshyra spoke enthusiastically about the practice of her faith. The mosque was a place to pray and be with people from her ethnic group. The service that took place at noon on Friday was the highlight of her week, which was followed by fellowship. On the final day of Ramadan after a service, worshipers share a large community feast to break the month-long fast. Inshyra, like most faithful Muslims, prayed five times a day, even though she was a busy university student. She abstained from alcohol and followed the dietary prescriptions that excluded the eating of pork and certain other foods. Inshyra remarked that she was still learning about the Muslim laws regarding the paying or receiving of interest payments and did not totally understand them, but she said that the older members of the mosque discussed this frequently.

I asked Inshyra about September 11, 2001 and how it had affected her and her family. She replied that after 9/11 she experienced a lot of anger and distrust aimed at her and other Muslims. It wasn't so much what people said as much as they way they looked at her. "The eyes!" she said with great emotion, "The eyes!" She felt hatred and distrust in every look. She also described how a brick had been hurled through a window at her mosque. Graffiti had been written on the outside walls, other windows were broken by a variety of means, and police security had to be employed to guard the mosque. Inshyra related how difficult it was to feel the emotions any other American citizen would be feeling at this time of tragedy and at the same time to be treated like an enemy. She wanted to cry out to everyone, "I'm an American too! I grieve for my country also! I am one of you!" The doubt and suspicions on the part of others has lessened in the intervening years, but the memory of that time will always stay with her.

Ingersoll (1994) delineated seven different dimensions to the integration of spirituality into one's life:

1. One's conception of the divine, absolute, or "force greater than one's self"
2. One's sense of meaning of what is beautiful or worthwhile
3. One's relationship with the divinity and others
4. One's tolerance or capability for mystery
5. Peak and ordinary experiences that enhance spirituality (which may include rituals or spiritual disciplines)
6. Seeing spirituality as play
7. Viewing spirituality as a systemic force that acts to integrate all the dimensions of one's life (p. 11)

Inshrya was a firm believer in the divine in the person of the God of the Muslim faith. Her life revolved around her religion and its observances. The mystery of a divine being who must be accepted on faith did not pose a problem for Inshyra, and only the rejection of her classmates caused her suffering. Her attitude toward the "differences" that her religion imposed on her as an adolescent was remarkably mature. She saw the rituals and ceremonies of Islam as beautiful and filled with spiritual meaning. They were a guide for her life. She saw religion as a duty, but one that was readily and joyfully performed. The mosque was not only a place of worship but also the center of her social life as well. It pained her immensely when people distrusted and even hated her because of her ethnic origins and religious faith, but she forgave them and also remained true to her religious beliefs.

Religion for her was the source of all life, spiritual and temporal, and it gave meaning to daily life and being.

Suggested Approaches to Working with the Muslim Client

In preparing to work with Muslim clients, counselors may find the following guidelines helpful. Counselors need to (Daneshpour, 1998):

1. Examine their religious values and beliefs relating to Islam and the Muslim culture.
2. Identify any biases, doubts, or resistances that may interfere with the open acceptance of the client.
3. Become familiar with Islam from a comprehensive, open-minded, nonjudgmental viewpoint.
4. Experience Islam in practice and develop a personal sense of the social and cultural dimensions and expressions of the religion.
5. Familiarize themselves with the Islamic community and religious activities that are available and accessible.
6. Be aware that Muslims living in the United States turn to counselors as a last resort because they often do not have extended family members available to them. By the time they come to the counselor, clients are often in a crisis.

Muslim immigrants are reluctant to seek help from health professionals for a number of reasons. First, many westerners label all Muslims with words such as aggressive, militant, and uncivilized (Bell, 1994). Islam is the religion of the sword, and Muslim activists are considered terrorists according to some westerners.

Second, Muslims themselves take issue with these stereotypes and deny them. They maintain they have a different worldview. Muslims see themselves as the afflicted, not as the afflicters; they feel themselves misunderstood about many issues, especially women's rights (Bell, 1994). It is understandable to see why Muslim immigrants hesitate and are reluctant to go to a therapist who is uninformed or has negative views about Islam.

Third, Muslim immigrants usually present problems accompanied by a tremendous sense of failure. Their cultural patterns, intertwined with religious ideology, provide explanations for health and illness, and for normalcy and deviance. Muslims believe that the family is responsible for the degree of deviance of family members (Amini, 1994). Therefore, psychological problems are viewed as a family's lack of responsiveness to its members.

Fourthly, discussing personal problems with someone outside the kinship network brings a deep sense of shame. They believe such problems are private and should be handled within the family. Counselors need to be very sensitive to these needs and take the necessary steps to put the client at ease.

In order for an Anglo-American to be successful with Muslim clients, the following suggestions are presented:

1. Use simple, straightforward language to communicate openly and honestly with the client about both his or her religious values and beliefs, and the counselor's values and beliefs.
2. Invite and encourage the client to describe his or her religious values and beliefs, the religious experiences he or she has had, and how he or she feels about his or her present life, including the goals that are influencing those values and beliefs.
3. Help the client see that religious values and beliefs are a part of the solution to a problem(s) without trying to change those values and beliefs (Georgia, 1994).
4. Make it clear to the client that the counselor is open to any needs and suggestions he or she may have. If the client would like to try an approach to solving the problem(s) that is more in line with ethical Islamic values, be prepared to help him or her with this.
5. It is important to include the clients in finding solutions to their problems. The use of cognitive problem solving is very appropriate.

Working with Families
Because of the emphasis on family life in the Islam religion, counselors need to be particularly well versed in family and couples counseling. Although many of the same general guidelines are appropriate for family work, some specific guidelines should be followed (Daneshpour, 1998):

1. The strong sense of cohesion and interdependency among Muslim families requires a holistic perspective toward family counseling, rather than one that takes only the individual or nuclear family into account. In doing so, the counselor should consider the individual and the nuclear family in addition to the relationship between individuals, their extended families, and others in the cultural context. This is true especially for elderly members whose wisdom is highly respected and valued. Counselors can benefit greatly from the elders' life experiences, their extensive formal and informal ties, and their social status in the family.
2. If counselors encounter a conflict between the interests of the family and the interests of an individual, they must be aware that a

counseling intervention is welcomed by clients as long as it maintains the unity of the family and emphasizes the goals of the family unit, rather than those of individual members.

3. Counselors need to be aware that Muslims may not see the value of resolving problems by verbal communication. Praying is traditionally and religiously considered one of the best ways to heal distress. It is believed that one has these problems because one is struggling against the flow of nature and the will of Allah. By sitting silently, one gets in touch with the true self, which enables a person to accept the pain of the problem as part of the total wholeness of life in relation to Allah.

4. In working with families, the conjoint family session is advised, yet occasions may occur when individual sessions may supplement and complement the therapy. For example, a mother may be able to complain about her husband in an individual session, whereas she would not do so in front of her husband and children. Conversely, a husband may find it difficult to share his feelings for the same reason. Two principles of Muslim culture support this: the values placed on covert communication style and the hierarchical nature of the family structure. An individual session might be particularly useful when trying to engage unmotivated fathers to come to a conjoint session.

5. The use of a genogram at least three generations long is crucial in helping the family understand themselves and their culture. It would be an especially important way to engage the extended family who may live miles away. It would also help them maintain emotional support and be involved in important decisions.

6. Muslim families prefer solutions to problems that are oriented toward the here and now and are more likely to cooperate with counselors who promote these goals. Solutions that overemphasize the historical development of the family or of individuals may be rejected (Saleh, 1989; Ghattas-Soliman, 1991). The goals of the intervention should be practical, immediate, and attainable while remaining consistent with the family values, particularly their religious ideology (Haj-Yahia, 1995).

Working with Children

Because Muslim children adhere strictly to the Islam ideology, counselors and mental health workers need to tailor their interventions to the special needs of these children. The following are some guidelines adapted from Carter (1999):

1. Counselors may need to redefine the traditional concepts of counseling by rethinking the notions of privacy and confidentiality. Because family concerns take precedence over individual concerns, the involvement of family is vital to the counseling relationship. The family is the Muslim child's strongest support.

2. When working with Muslim children, especially in cross-gender situations, it is important that the Muslim child not be placed in a situation that is contrary to his or her culture and religion. Touching, such as handshaking and hugging, is not appropriate, nor is it appropriate for a counselor of the opposite gender to be alone with the child in an isolated room.

3. Individual counseling is more acceptable to Muslims than group counseling because it would be a violation of family privacy to place children in group counseling where family issues would be explored (Kelly et al., 1996).

4. Muslims past the age of puberty must not be expected to participate in coeducational counseling groups. If family issues are to be discussed, family counseling needs to be considered and should involve the father as head of the family.

5. Counselors should discuss their own ignorance of the Muslim culture, should problems arise. By doing this, they display a respect and sensitivity to the Muslim religious dictates and an openness to learning what they need to know to avoid working contrary to a student's religious and cultural needs.

As with other religions, many differences are prominent among Muslim groups, but when studied carefully, one can see that more unites this religious group than divides it. A pressing need exists, however, for counselors to understand both the differences and commonalities of this group. Prior to September 11, 2001, many Americans viewed Muslims as terrorists, fanatics, warriors, and hostage takers (Wormser, 1994). With the impact of America's new war and media coverage, how will Americans view Muslims? Counselors need to be extremely careful to keep their own values and prejudices in check as they work with this diverse ethnic, religious, and cultural group. The importance of developing attitudes of respect, acceptance, nonjudgment, and compassion cannot be overemphasized.

Exercises

1. Design a weekly support group for Muslims who may be having difficulties in daily life as a result of the war in Iraq. Address issues of the prejudice they may encounter and ways that their spirituality might

help them cope with obstacles they encounter. You may also want to address the concerns they have for loved ones who may still be living in their native country.
2. Visit a local mosque and attend a service. What questions arise in your mind about the Muslim faith? Do some research to gain further knowledge of the Muslim faith.
3. Conduct a weekend workshop and invite those of the Muslim faith to attend and discuss the changes in their lives following September 11, 2001. How has their faith helped them through this?

Buddhism

Buddhism has approximately 307 million followers and was founded in the sixth and fifth centuries BCE by Siddhartha Gautama, the Buddha or "Enlightened One." He achieved fame as a charismatic teacher and "wise man," and eventually gathered a community of monks to carry on his teachings. The majority of Buddhists, however, believe that there have been many Buddhas. Some even believe that Jesus Christ was a Buddha, and that Buddhas will continue to arise throughout periods in history.

Siddhartha is the most famous of the Buddhas at this present time, and the central beliefs of Buddhism stem directly from the mind, life, and personality of its founder. He preached a simple path to enlightenment that dealt with an awareness of fundamental realities encompassed in the Four Noble Truths:

1. All life is suffering.
2. Suffering stems from desire.
3. There can be an end to desire.
4. The way is the Eightfold Path.

The process or "path" to end suffering is not easy but requires discipline, both in thought and action, because thought has no value if it is not carried into positive actions. Buddhists believe that in order to obtain purification in life one must follow the Eightfold Path, and because of its difficulty, many Buddhists seek the help of a learned teacher to aid them in this endeavor.

The Eight-Fold Path consists of:

1. Right views—knowledge of the Four Noble Truths
2. Right aspirations—discarding desires and avoiding hurting others
3. Right speech—telling the truth
4. Right conduct—not stealing or cheating
5. Right livelihood—earning a living in a way that does not harm or cause bloodshed to others

6. Right effort—thinking positively in order to follow the path
7. Right mindfulness—being aware of the effects of thoughts and actions
8. Right meditation—attaining a peaceful state of mind

For Buddhists, two manuscripts are revered, the Dhammapada, also known as the Pali canon because of the language in which it was written. Another written work that contains conversations the Buddha had when he was teaching is called the Tripitaka, also known as the Three Baskets or Triple Baskets because the original palm leaf manuscript kept in three woven baskets.

The first basket contained the Sutta Pitaka, the basket of discourse presumed to be written by the Buddha. The second was the Vinaya Pitaka, the basket of discipline, which is the oldest and smallest of the three sections and contained the regulations for monastic life. The third basket, the Abhidhamma Pitaka, was the basket of special doctrine. It is the latest of the three and contained what is referred to as "further knowledge," which is not entirely attributed to the Buddha but highly venerated.

Meditation and chanting are an important part of some Buddhists' devotional practices. Meditation is used to still the distracted and emotional mind, and focus it instead on loftier thoughts and words of wisdom. For most Buddhists, meditation is a daily activity. Chanting is also part of the Buddhist form of prayer and may be done in a temple or in the home. Buddhist scriptures form the basis of what is chanted. Chanting is also a part of most Buddhist ceremonies and festivals.

Meditation as a revered practice is seen in many Eastern religions, but it can also be found in Christian monasteries and convents. To many Buddhists, meditation is the most important aspect of their religion. The Buddha reached his enlightenment through a meditative practice called Samadhi. This is a Sanskrit word meaning "total-self collectedness." It is the highest state of mental concentration that an individual can have while still bound to the body.

Buddhism teaches that meditation and the practice of good religious and moral behavior can lead to Nirvana, the state of enlightenment, although before achieving Nirvana one is subject to repeated lifetimes that are good or bad depending on one's actions (karma). Most non-Buddhists think that Nirvana is some sort of Eastern version of heaven, but it is not. Nirvana simply means cessation. It is the "ceasing" or end of all passion, aggression, and ignorance. It is also the cessation of the struggle to prove one's existence to the world as a means of survival. Nirvana is the proof of one's survival; the struggle was just an extra complication we added to our lives because we lost faith in the way things are. In the state of Nirvana, we no longer need to manipulate things as they are into the things we would like them to be.

Special Needs of the Population

Buddhism appears to many to be a very pragmatic religion. It has no place for metaphysical speculation about first causes and contains no true "theology" or worship of a deity. True Buddhists do not attempt to deify the Buddha but rather see him as an exceptionally wise or holy man who came to deliver a message. Buddhists take a very straightforward look at their human condition. Buddhist parents, for instance, would probably look askance at a counselor who attempts to explain a child's behavior by offering numerous psychological explanations. They would probably prefer a very simple description of what has occurred and what the preferred behavior might be.

Buddhism explains a basic purpose to life; it explains apparent injustice and inequality around the world, and it provides a code of practice or way of life that leads to true happiness. A counselor needs to respect this about the client and not try to impose western values of success, materialism, or aggressiveness on a Buddhist client.

Buddhism is becoming very popular in western countries for a number of reasons, but primarily because it appears to hold answers to many problems of a very materialistic, modern society. Buddhists believe in detachment, simplicity, and a deep inward search for honesty and truth. As such, they may make very good clients because their religious beliefs value a "search for self."

The Buddhist concept of "egolessness" runs counter to the American or Western ideal of the necessity for a strong ego, sense of self, or an extreme sense of self-confidence. Buddhists are self-confident but base it on almost entirely different concepts than westerners do. Buddhists believe more in impermanence, because to their way of thinking most things are temporary at best and imaginary to begin with.

To truly understand the concept of egolessness, as Buddhists subscribe to, we must first grasp that it has a different definition from the Freudian concept of ego with which westerners are most familiar. The Buddhist ego is a collection of mental events classified into different categories that describe the ways in which people try to possess and manipulate the people and objects around them. In doing so, Buddhists believe that people only complicate their lives, causing themselves and others pain and suffering. It is only through the cessation of many chaotic activities and the acquiring of stillness and peace, through a concentration on the present moment, that the ego is brought under control. Westerners, with their emphasis on control of every situation, success in terms of money and worldly possessions, and their glorification of individuals with a "strong ego," may have difficulty understanding these concepts of Buddhist philosophy.

It would be a mistake, however, to regard Buddhists as extremely passive individuals; rather, the term most used today is "engaged Buddhism." At the end of World War II, there was a need to rebuild and renew Buddhism in light of world events. Asian societies also needed to recover from the effects of colonialism and reinvent themselves in light of the ever-spreading Cold War. World War II had forced many Asians to encounter western culture, especially in the religious, scientific, and political domains. In spite of the attempts of some Asian communists to discredit Buddhism doctrines as superstition and the Buddhist institutions as parasites on society, this ancient belief system has seen a global establishment of the faith on a scale that is unprecedented in world history.

Part of the reason for the increased interest in Buddhism can be attributed to the emphasis that Buddhist monks and nuns have placed on the deferment of their usually solitary, individualistic practices in order to stage nonviolent confrontations with the governments and other agencies believed to be the cause of profound suffering. Buddhists are active in causes to stem environmental despoliation, political corruption, and world hunger. Buddhists approach these problems with compassion and conviction, and as an extension of their belief in the sanctity of all living things.

Buddhists believe that in order to travel on the path to holiness or Nirvana, one must first be a moral person, that is, follow the wisdom of cultivating detachment, discernment, and compassion. True Buddhists pass these beliefs on to their children and consequently Buddhist children may appear somewhat passive and "laid back" when compared to their American classmates. Teachers and counselors must learn to appreciate the depth of their feelings about certain, everyday events and cherish the compassion that Buddhists may bring to a situation.

Of the many precepts that most Buddhists believe will help them become a moral person, five central ones are found in almost all Buddhist writings. The five central precepts are presented here with the corresponding positive traits:

1. Not to destroy life intentionally . . . kindness and compassion
2. Not to steal . . . generosity and renunciation
3. Not to have sexual misconduct . . . seeking "joyous satisfaction with one's spouse"
4. Not to lie . . . loving the truth, seeking it, pursuing discernment and insight
5. No intoxication . . . mindfulness, contentment, awareness via meditation (Esposito, Faushing, & Lewis, 2002)

Whether or not religion or spirituality is part of a Buddhist client's presenting problem, or whether or not they seek counseling at all, is very individualistic. It is probably more realistic to think that they would search for a "wise person" within their Buddhist ranks, but with the widening spread of Buddhism into mainstream practice, a counselor may very well have a Buddhist client.

Suggested Approaches to Working with the Buddhist Client
In preparing to work with the Buddhist client, counselors may find the following guidelines helpful. Counselors need to:

1. Examine their religious values and beliefs in light of Buddhist teachings.
2. Identify any biases, doubts, or resistances that may interfere with the open acceptance of the client.
3. Become familiar with Buddhism from a comprehensive, open-minded, nonjudgmental understanding.
4. Make an attempt to experience Buddhism in practice and develop a personal sense of the social and cultural dimensions, as well as the expression, of the religion.
5. Discover how large the Buddhist population is within the immediate geographic area, if possible.
6. Be aware that an Asian Buddhist would probably have trouble seeking out a western counselor, whereas American or western Buddhists may not have quite the same reluctance because of cultural differences.

Buddhists are generally viewed as peaceful, prayerful, and gentle people, in spite of their sometimes forceful actions on behalf of the causes they hold dear (e.g., Buddhist monks setting themselves on fire as a protest or fasting to death to bring attention to a cause). Their reverence for all life is seen as a little extreme but is usually admired by most people. The adherence by most Buddhists to a vegetarian or vegan lifestyle is very popular among some westerners also, but primarily for health reasons.

In dealing with Buddhist adults or children, the country of origin will factor into the equation as much as the Buddhist religion will. However, because of the beliefs that all Buddhists have in common, counselors will be most successful if they follow these steps:

- Use simple, straightforward language to communicate openly and honestly with the client(s) about his or her religious beliefs and values.
- Realize that self-disclosure may be effective on the counselor's part if it is well thought-out, sincere, and appropriate to the situation.

- Encourage the client to describe and elaborate on his or her religious values and beliefs, why they are held, religious experiences the client has had, and how the present is influenced by the religious traditions that guide us as individuals.
- Help the client see that his or her religious values and beliefs are a part of the solution to the problem, without trying to change this belief system.
- Make it clear to the client that the counselor is open to trying an approach to problem-solving that might be more in line with Buddhist thought and practice, with the client's help.

Other Religious Belief Systems

In addition to the religions, mentioned. There are serveral other belief systems that counselors must be aware of.

Hinduism

India today contains approximately 650 million followers of Hinduism, with at least 100 million in the rest of the world. Of this number, approximately 700,000 are in South Africa, nearly 600,000 are in North America, and 500,000 reside in the United Kingdom. A part of the very fabric of India, this religion developed from the indigenous religions there in combination with Aryan religions brought to India about 1500 BCE. It was codified in the Veda and the Upanishads, the sacred scriptures of this faith. Hinduism is a broad term used to describe a vast array of sects to which most Indians belong. Nowadays, many Hindus reject the caste system in which people are born into a particular subgroup that determines their religious, social, and work-related duties. It is, however, still widely accepted in some parts of India and classifies society at large into groups: the Brahmins or priests, the rulers and warriors, the farmers and merchants, and the peasants and laborers.

The goals of Hinduism are for one to be released from repeated reincarnation through the practice of yoga, to adhere to Vedic scriptures, and to be devoted to a personal guru. Various deities are worshipped at shrines; the divine trinities, representing the cyclical nature of the universe, are Brahms the creator, Vishnu the preserver, and Shiva the destroyer.

Although Hindus do not worship one single god, they do believe in a Supreme Being who has unlimited forms. This is not a contradiction of terms, because of the many forms these deities take. For instance, Vishu and Lakshmi have the full powers of a god, but Brahm and Sarasvati have only partial god-like powers. The Hindu approach to all of this is to maintain their philosophy of nonspecific inclusion at its core.

More than almost any other major religion, Hinduism celebrates the breadth and depth of its complex, multileveled spectrum of beliefs. Hinduism encompasses all forms of belief and worship. It has been said that no religious idea in India ever dies; it merely combines with the new ideas that arise in response to it. A popular Hindu prayer states, "May good thoughts come to us from all sides."

Hindus attempt to see the divine in everything. A Hindu may embrace another religion without giving up being a Hindu, because he or she is disposed to regard other forms of worship and different doctrines as inadequate rather than wrong. Hinduism has no beginning, no founder, no central authority, no hierarchy, and no organization (Pollock, 2001).

Hindus believe in the law of karma that states that all actions produce effects in the future. An important part of this belief is that of dharma, one's duty or station in this life. This relationship between karma and dharma is discussed at length in the Bhagavad-Gita, a major text within the Hindu tradition. This holy text has been the exemplary text of Hindu culture for centuries. It is written as a philosophical poem in the form of a dialect. Two of the main characters are Arjuna, the hero preparing to go into battle, and Krishna, his charioteer. They represent aspects of the human and the divine, and the uniting of the two.

Arising from these laws or beliefs is the idea of reincarnation. Hindus accept the doctrine of transmigration and rebirth, and they firmly believe that past acts are the factors that determine the form into which a being is reborn. Reincarnation as a belief is almost universal in India. According to these beliefs, people are born over and over again into a state of suffering, largely because of their inability to become one with true being. A Sanskirt word, *moksha,* reflects the ultimate spiritual goal of the Hindu: the individual soul's release from the bonds of reincarnation or transmigration. What thwarts this release is the presence of bad karma and the attachment to worldly possessions. This obsession with the material is the major obstacle to reaching salvation and eternal peace. The meanings and interpretations of these vary from one Hindu school to another, but in spite of this, most Hindus believe that *moksha* is the highest purpose in life. Hindus also often use the largely Buddhist term Nirvana to express this pinnacle of spiritual attainment.

Hindu worship is filled with bright colors, experiences that tantalize the senses, chanting, and singing. Typical offerings to the various deities might be flowers, fruit, rice, incense, sandalwood paste, and milk water. Hindu worship is called *puja* and encompasses the ceremonial practices that take place in the home or temple. The majority of the worship is carried out in the home because Hinduism is a way of life, so no special days for worship exist. Puja is the daily expression of devotion, and any time is proper for worship. Virtually every Hindu home has a shrine with images of the gods and goddesses. These deities are given a place of honor and accorded the respect that would be given to a royal guest. Their worship can be ordinary or elaborate, depending on the circumstances. If the puja or worship takes place around meal times, food will be placed at the shrine as a means of securing a blessing before it is consumed. It is also a tradition to circumambulate the shrine in the home, walking around the shrine several times, sometimes accompanied by incense, but always with the chanting of the family's or individual's prayers.

A Hindu temple may be a large building that can accompany many hundreds of worshipers or it may be a simple village shrine. Whether large or small, it will contain a ceremonial chariot called a rath, which is like a miniature temple on wheels. A symbol of the main deity will be placed on the rath, which will be used in processions at various festivals. The temple also has a shrine room for one or more deities, where only a Brahmin priest may perform the puja.

Vishnu is one of the principal Hindu deities and illustrates the reverence that Hindus reserve for the many gods they worship. He is often referred to as the "Preserver" and it is believed that if Vishnu somehow departed from the world it would be destroyed. Vishnu has the power to release his worshipers from material desires and bless them with freedom. He has gone through many reincarnations and therefore has reached a state of purity and wisdom that he can impart to those who revere him. Vishnu is thought to be the binding force that holds the universe together. His job is to restore dharma or moral order to society. Vishnu is but one of many very powerful deities in the Hindu religion, which includes Krishna, Radha, Brahma, and Shiva.

Baha'i

Baha'i has more than 5 million followers as of 1996. It was founded by Mirza Husayn 'Ali Nuri, a descendant of Mohammad, who took the name Bahá'u'lláh (Glory of God) while in exile in Baghdad. Bahá'u'lláh's coming was foretold by Mirza Ali Mohammad, known as al-Bab, who founded Babism in 1844, from which the Baha'i faith grew. The central tenets of the Baha'i faith are the oneness of God, the oneness of humanity, and the common foundation of all religion. Bahaists also believe in the equality of men and women, universal education, world peace, and the creation of a world federal system of government.

Baha'i originated in Persia, what is now Iran, in the mid-nineteenth century. Thus, it is a relatively new religious sect and the youngest of the world's independent religions. Bahá'u'lláh's aim was to establish a universal religion that preached peace and harmony. Prejudice, whether based on race, ethnicity, nationality, religion, or class, must be overcome if humanity is to create a peaceful and just global society. Baha'i saw its biggest expansion during the 1960s.

Baha'i also ensures to women full equality with men and strives to eliminate the extremes of poverty and wealth. Followers of Baha'i believe it is the responsibility of each individual to independently search for truth. Bahá'u'lláh advised his followers not to go blindly forward uncritical of traditions, movements, and opinions. The Baha'i believe that harmony exists between science and religion, and that one will strengthen the other.

Confucianism

Confucianism is not officially considered to be a world religion, because it is not organized as such, but it is often grouped with religions because it is a spiritual philosophy, a social ethic, a political ideology, and a scholarly tradition. Confucius started teaching his beliefs in China around the late sixth or early fifth century BCE. Confucianozin places a primary emphasis on learning, and its teachings are a source of values. Confucianism made its mark extensively in Chinese literature, education, and culture, as well as in both spiritual and political life. Confucius lived in a time of political turmoil, so the stage was set for a teacher to emerge who had the ability to dispense a spiritual philosophy. He was among the first to devote his whole life to learning and teaching for the sole purpose of improving the lot of his fellow humans.

Confucius believed that education should be available for all and not just for the rich. During his life, he worked to open the doors of education to all Chinese, and he defined learning as not just the acquisition of knowledge but also the building of character. Another main point of his teaching was that of devotion to one's parents. He considered filial piety to be the foundation of virtue and the root of human character. Proper social behavior and etiquette were considered major components of right living. A set of ethics is contained in his Analects, a collection of moral and social teachings. A famous saying of his was, "One who can bring about the practice of five things everywhere under Heaven has achieved humaneness . . . Courtesy, tolerance, good faith, diligence, and kindness."

The edicts of Confucius did not go without opposition and resistance. Unlike Buddhist beliefs, Confucius said that karma was not a force in the progress of man resulting from moral goodness but rather was to be seen as destiny. He taught that a person should choose what to do in a single-minded manner, without taking into consideration what the outcomes might be. Confucius and his teachings were sometimes in favor and sometimes not, and he spent several years in exile staring at the age of 56. He did, however, return home at the age of 67 and died in his homeland at the age of 72.

Taoism

The Tao in Chinese means path or way. In English, it is pronounced "dow." The Tao is believed to be a natural force that makes the universe the way it is. The foundation or beginning of Taoism is attributed partially to Lao Tzu and his writings, the "Classic Way of Power" (Tao Te Ching). It advocates the philosophy of disharmony or harmony of opposites, meaning that there is no love without hate, no light without darkness, no male without female, and so on. The yin and yang are thought to be the complimentary force that makes up all aspects of life. Yang is considered to be the male source and is seen as light, active, and penetrating; it represents heaven. Yin, on the other hand, is female and is seen as earthy, dark, passive, and absorbing. Yin and yang are often depicted as the light and dark halves of a circle.

Taoist thought was prevalent in China in the same way Confucianism was and the two are often linked. At some point, Taoism became more popular than Confucianism, even though the latter had state support. Taoism focused more on the individual and rejected the organized society of the Confucius's followers. Taoist philosophy, as well as Confucianism, spread beyond China to Vietnam, Japan, Korea, and Taiwan. A westernized version has also been established in Europe and the United States.

When it was first started, Taoism was not conceived of as a religion but rather a philosophy. It later evolved into a sort of religion fostered by some of its followers who worshipped several deities. Lao Tzu was so revered that he was thought of as a deity or a mystical character by many.

A key Taoist concept is that of nonaction or the natural course of things, a direct link to yin and yang. When society gets in the way of man's actions, the balance of yin and yang is disturbed. Yin and yang are said to be identical aspects of the same reality. The basic feature of Taoism is to restore balance in all things and to avoid extremism. The Tao is seen as the principle of creation and the source from which everything emanates.

Taoists have a responsibility to promote good health. Exercises such as tai chi are practiced to help nurture the body. Chi (breath) is seen as energy, spirit, or the life force within everything. The essential belief in Taoism is that the only permanent thing in life is change. Taoists believe that people should not always be trying to look ahead and trying to predict change but rather should live in the present moment and not resist or try to control change. The world is as it is. Accept what is without wanting to change it. Study the natural order and go with it, rather than against it. The philosophy of Taoism is simply "to be."

References

Amini, I. (1994). *Principles of marriage and family ethics*. Tehran, Sepher: Islam Propagation Organization.

Banawai, R., & Stockton, R. (1993). Islamic values relevant to group work with practical applications for the group leader. *Journal of Specialists in Group Work, 18*(3), 151–160.

Bell, J. (1994). Muslims everywhere yet still in chains. *Mabjubeh, 13*(11), 5–6.

Carter, R. B. (1999). Counseling Muslim students in school settings. *Professional School Counseling, 2*(3), 183–189.

Daneshpour, M. (1998). Muslim families and family therapy. *Journal of Marital and Family Therapy, 24*(3), 355–390.

Denny, F. M. (1993). Islam and the Muslim community. In H. B. Earhart (Ed.), *Religions and traditions of the world* (pp. 605–712). New York: Harper.

Esposito, J. L. (2002). *World religions today*. New York: Oxford Press.

Georgia, R. T. (1994). Preparing to counsel clients of different religious backgrounds: A phenomenological approach. In M. T. Burke & J. G. Miranti (Eds.), *Counseling: The spiritual dimension* (pp. 73–81). Alexandria, VA: American Counseling Association.

Ghattas-Soliman, S. (1991). The two-sided image of women in season of migration to the north. In K. W. Harrow (Ed.), *Faces of Islam in African literature* (pp. 91–103). Portsmouth, NH: Heinemann.

Haj-Yahia, M. M. (1995). Toward culturally sensitive intervention with Arab families in Israel. *Contemporary Family Therapy 17*(4), 429–449.

Hang, G. K. (1989). Application of cultural and environmental issues in family therapy with immigrant Chinese Americans. *Journal of Strategic and Systemic Therapies, 8*, 14–21.

Haneef, S. (1993). *What everyone should know about Islam and Muslims*. Des Plaines, Illinois: Library of Islam.

Hampton, J. (Ed.). (1998). *Internally displaced people: A global survey*. Earthscan: London.

Hedayat-Deba, Z. (2000). Psychotherapy with Muslims. In P. S. Richards & A. E. Bergin (Eds.), *Handbook of psychotherapy and religious diversity* (pp. 289–314). Washington, D.C.: American Psychological Association.

Jackson, M. L. (1995). *Counseling youth of Arab ancestry: A guide for school counselors and professionals*. Boston: Ally and Bacon.

Kelly, E. W., Aredi, A., & Bakhtiar, L. (1996). Muslims in the United States: An exploratory study of universal and mental health values. *Counseling and Values, 40*, 206–218.

Ludwig, T. M. (1989). *The sacred paths: Understanding the religions of the world*. New York: Macmillan.

McGoldrick, M., & Preto, N. G. (1984). Ethnic intermarriage: Implications for therapy. *Family Process, 23*, 347–364.

Olson, D. H., Russell, C., & Sprenkle, D. (1989). *Complex model: System assessment and treatment of families*. New York: Hayworth.

Power, C. (1998, March 16). The new Islam. *Newsweek*, 35–37.

Rahman, F. (1993). *Islam Emarta encyclopedia*. Redmond, WA: Microsoft, Inc.

Saleh, M. A. (1989). The cultural milieu of counseling. *International Journal for the Advancement of Counseling, 12*, 3–11.

Siraj-Blatchford, I. (1993). Ethnicity and conflict in physical education: A critique of Carrol and Hollingshead's case study. *British Educational Research Journal, 19*(1), 77–82.

Tamura, T., & Lau, A. (1992). Connectedness versus separateness: Applicability of family therapy to Japanese families. *Family Process, 31*(4), 319–340.

Wormser, R. (1994). *American Islam: Growing up Muslim in America*. New York: Walker.

emuseum.mnsu.edu/cultural/religion/

www.comparativereligion.com/

www.webstationone.com/fecha/religion.htm

www.philtar.ucsm.ac.uk/encyclopedia/

www.sacred-texts.com/world.htm

www.adherents.com/Religions_By_Adherents.html

APPENDIX A

ACA Code of Ethics
   (effective 1995)
   Section A: The Counseling Relationship
   Section B: Confidentiality
   Section C: Professional Responsibility
   Section D: Relationships With Other Professionals
   Section E: Evaluation, Assessment, and Interpretation
   Section F: Teaching, Training, and Supervision
   Section G: Research and Publication
   Section H: Resolving Ethical Issues

Section A: The Counseling Relationship
A.1. Client Welfare
   a. Primary Responsibility. The primary responsibility of counselors is to respect the dignity and to promote the welfare of clients.
   b. Positive Growth and Development. Counselors encourage client growth and development in ways that foster the clients' interest and welfare; counselors avoid fostering dependent counseling relationships.
   c. Counseling Plans. Counselors and their clients work jointly in devising integrated, individual counseling plans that offer reasonable promise of success and are consistent with abilities and circumstances of clients. Counselors and clients regularly review counseling plans to ensure their continued viability and effectiveness, respecting clients' freedom of choice. (See A.3.b.)

    d. Family Involvement. Counselors recognize that families are usually important in clients' lives and strive to enlist family understanding and involvement as a positive resource, when appropriate.

    e. Career and Employment Needs. Counselors work with their clients in considering employment in jobs and circumstances that are consistent with the clients' overall abilities, vocational limitations, physical restrictions, general temperament, interest and aptitude patterns, social skills, education, general qualifications, and other relevant characteristics and needs. Counselors neither place nor participate in placing clients in positions that will result in damaging the interest and the welfare of clients, employers, or the public.

A.2. Respecting Diversity

    a. Nondiscrimination. Counselors do not condone or engage in discrimination based on age, color, culture, disability, ethnic group, gender, race, religion, sexual orientation, marital status, or socioeconomic status. (See C.5.a., C.5.b., and D.1.i.)

    b. Respecting Differences. Counselors will actively attempt to understand the diverse cultural backgrounds of the clients with whom they work. This includes, but is not limited to, learning how the counselor's own cultural/ethnic/racial identity impacts his or her values and beliefs about the counseling process. (See E.8. and F.2.j.)

A.3. Client Rights

    a. Disclosure to Clients. When counseling is initiated, and throughout the counseling process as necessary, counselors inform clients of the purposes, goals, techniques, procedures, limitations, potential risks, and benefits of services to be performed, and other pertinent information. Counselors take steps to ensure that clients understand the implications of diagnosis, the intended use of tests and reports, fees, and billing arrangements. Clients have the right to expect confidentiality and to be provided with an explanation of its limitations, including supervision and/or treatment team professionals; to obtain clear information about their case records; to participate in the ongoing counseling plans; and to refuse any recommended services and be advised of the consequences of such refusal. (See E.5.a. and G.2.)

    b. Freedom of Choice. Counselors offer clients the freedom to choose whether to enter into a counseling relationship and to determine which professional(s) will provide counseling. Restrictions that limit choices of clients are fully explained. (See A.1.c.)

    c. Inability to Give Consent. When counseling minors or persons unable to give voluntary informed consent, counselors act in these clients' best interests. (See B.3.)

A.4. Clients Served by Others   If a client is receiving services from another mental health professional, counselors, with client consent, inform the professional persons already involved and develop clear agreements to avoid confusion and conflict for the client. (See C.6.c.)

A.5. Personal Needs and Values
   a. Personal Needs. In the counseling relationship, counselors are aware of the intimacy and responsibilities inherent in the counseling relationship, maintain respect for clients, and avoid actions that seek to meet their personal needs at the expense of clients.
   b. Personal Values. Counselors are aware of their own values, attitudes, beliefs, and behaviors and how these apply in a diverse society, and avoid imposing their values on clients. (See C.5.a.)

A.6. Dual Relationships
   a. Avoid When Possible. Counselors are aware of their influential positions with respect to clients, and they avoid exploiting the trust and dependency of clients. Counselors make every effort to avoid dual relationships with clients that could impair professional judgment or increase the risk of harm to clients. (Examples of such relationships include, but are not limited to, familial, social, financial, business, or close personal relationships with clients.) When a dual relationship cannot be avoided, counselors take appropriate professional precautions such as informed consent, consultation, supervision, and documentation to ensure that judgment is not impaired and no exploitation occurs. (See F.1.b.)
   b. Superior/Subordinate Relationships. Counselors do not accept as clients superiors or subordinates with whom they have administrative, supervisory, or evaluative relationships.

A.7. Sexual Intimacies With Clients
   a. Current Clients. Counselors do not have any type of sexual intimacies with clients and do not counsel persons with whom they have had a sexual relationship.
   b. Former Clients. Counselors do not engage in sexual intimacies with former clients within a minimum of 2 years after terminating the counseling relationship. Counselors who engage in such relationship after 2 years following termination have the responsibility to examine and document thoroughly that such relations did not have an exploitative nature, based on factors such as duration of counseling, amount of time since counseling, termination circumstances, client's personal history and mental status, adverse impact on the client, and

actions by the counselor suggesting a plan to initiate a sexual relationship with the client after termination.

A.8. Multiple Clients   When counselors agree to provide counseling services to two or more persons who have a relationship (such as husband and wife, or parents and children), counselors clarify at the outset which person or persons are clients and the nature of the relationships they will have with each involved person. If it becomes apparent that counselors may be called upon to perform potentially conflicting roles, they clarify, adjust, or withdraw from roles appropriately. (See B.2. and B.4.d.)

A.9. Group Work
  a. Screening. Counselors screen prospective group counseling/therapy participants. To the extent possible, counselors select members whose needs and goals are compatible with goals of the group, who will not impede the group process, and whose well-being will not be jeopardized by the group experience.
  b. Protecting Clients. In a group setting, counselors take reasonable precautions to protect clients from physical or psychological trauma.

A.10. Fees and Bartering (See D.3.a. and D.3.b.)
  a. Advance Understanding. Counselors clearly explain to clients, prior to entering the counseling relationship, all financial arrangements related to professional services including the use of collection agencies or legal measures for nonpayment. (A.11.c.)
  b. Establishing Fees. In establishing fees for professional counseling services, counselors consider the financial status of clients and locality. In the event that the established fee structure is inappropriate for a client, assistance is provided in attempting to find comparable services of acceptable cost. (See A.10.d., D.3.a., and D.3.b.)
  c. Bartering Discouraged. Counselors ordinarily refrain from accepting goods or services from clients in return for counseling services because such arrangements create inherent potential for conflicts, exploitation, and distortion of the professional relationship. Counselors may participate in bartering only if the relationship is not exploitative, if the client requests it, if a clear written contract is established, and if such arrangements are an accepted practice among professionals in the community. (See A.6.a.)
  d. Pro Bono Service. Counselors contribute to society by devoting a portion of their professional activity to services for which there is little or no financial return (pro bono).

A.11. Termination and Referral

   a. Abandonment Prohibited. Counselors do not abandon or neglect clients in counseling. Counselors assist in making appropriate arrangements for the continuation of treatment, when necessary, during interruptions such as vacations, and following termination.

   b. Inability to Assist Clients. If counselors determine an inability to be of professional assistance to clients, they avoid entering or immediately terminate a counseling relationship. Counselors are knowledgeable about referral resources and suggest appropriate alternatives. If clients decline the suggested referral, counselors should discontinue the relationship.

   c. Appropriate Termination. Counselors terminate a counseling relationship, securing client agreement when possible, when it is reasonably clear that the client is no longer benefiting, when services are no longer required, when counseling no longer serves the client's needs or interests, when clients do not pay fees charged, or when agency or institution limits do not allow provision of further counseling services. (See A.10.b. and C.2.g.)

A.12. Computer Technology

   a. Use of Computers. When computer applications are used in counseling services, counselors ensure that (1) the client is intellectually, emotionally, and physically capable of using the computer application; (2) the computer application is appropriate for the needs of the client; (3) the client understands the purpose and operation of the computer applications; and (4) a follow-up of client use of a computer application is provided to correct possible misconceptions, discover inappropriate use, and assess subsequent needs.

   b. Explanation of Limitations. Counselors ensure that clients are provided information as a part of the counseling relationship that adequately explains the limitations of computer technology.

   c. Access to Computer Applications. Counselors provide for equal access to computer applications in counseling services. (See A.2.a.)

Section B: Confidentiality

B.1. Right to Privacy

   a. Respect for Privacy. Counselors respect their clients right to privacy and avoid illegal and unwarranted disclosures of confidential information. (See A.3.a. and B.6.a.)

   b. Client Waiver. The right to privacy may be waived by the client or his or her legally recognized representative.

c. Exceptions. The general requirement that counselors keep information confidential does not apply when disclosure is required to prevent clear and imminent danger to the client or others or when legal requirements demand that confidential information be revealed. Counselors consult with other professionals when in doubt as to the validity of an exception.

d. Contagious, Fatal Diseases. A counselor who receives information confirming that a client has a disease commonly known to be both communicable and fatal is justified in disclosing information to an identifiable third party, who by his or her relationship with the client is at a high risk of contracting the disease. Prior to making a disclosure the counselor should ascertain that the client has not already informed the third party about his or her disease and that the client is not intending to inform the third party in the immediate future. (See B.1.c and B.1.f.)

e. Court-Ordered Disclosure. When court ordered to release confidential information without a client's permission, counselors request to the court that the disclosure not be required due to potential harm to the client or counseling relationship. (See B.1.c.)

f. Minimal Disclosure. When circumstances require the disclosure of confidential information, only essential information is revealed. To the extent possible, clients are informed before confidential information is disclosed.

g. Explanation of Limitations. When counseling is initiated and throughout the counseling process as necessary, counselors inform clients of the limitations of confidentiality and identify foreseeable situations in which confidentiality must be breached. (See G.2.a.)

h. Subordinates. Counselors make every effort to ensure that privacy and confidentiality of clients are maintained by subordinates including employees, supervisees, clerical assistants, and volunteers. (See B.1.a.)

i. Treatment Teams. If client treatment will involve a continued review by a treatment team, the client will be informed of the team's existence and composition.

B.2. Groups and Families

a. Group Work. In group work, counselors clearly define confidentiality and the parameters for the specific group being entered, explain its importance, and discuss the difficulties related to confidentiality involved in group work. The fact that confidentiality cannot be guaranteed is clearly communicated to group members.

b. Family Counseling. In family counseling, information about one family member cannot be disclosed to another member without permission. Counselors protect the privacy rights of each family member. (See A.8., B.3., and B.4.d.)

B.3. Minor or Incompetent Clients   When counseling clients who are minors or individuals who are unable to give voluntary, informed consent, parents or guardians may be included in the counseling process as appropriate. Counselors act in the best interests of clients and take measures to safeguard confidentiality. (See A.3.c.)

B.4. Records
    a. Requirement of Records. Counselors maintain records necessary for rendering professional services to their clients and as required by laws, regulations, or agency or institution procedures.
    b. Confidentiality of Records. Counselors are responsible for securing the safety and confidentiality of any counseling records they create, maintain, transfer, or destroy whether the records are written, taped, computerized, or stored in any other medium. (See B.1.a.)
    c. Permission to Record or Observe. Counselors obtain permission from clients prior to electronically recording or observing sessions. (See A.3.a.)
    d. Client Access. Counselors recognize that counseling records are kept for the benefit of clients, and therefore provide access to records and copies of records when requested by competent clients, unless the records contain information that may be misleading and detrimental to the client. In situations involving multiple clients, access to records is limited to those parts of records that do not include confidential information related to another client. (See A.8., B.1.a., and B.2.b.)
    e. Disclosure or Transfer. Counselors obtain written permission from clients to disclose or transfer records to legitimate third parties unless exceptions to confidentiality exist as listed in Section B.1. Steps are taken to ensure that receivers of counseling records are sensitive to their confidential nature.

B.5. Research and Training
    a. Data Disguise Required. Use of data derived from counseling relationships for purposes of training, research, or publication is confined to content that is disguised to ensure the anonymity of the individuals involved. (See B.1.g. and G.3.d.)

b. Agreement for Identification. Identification of a client in a presentation or publication is permissible only when the client has reviewed the material and has agreed to its presentation or publication. (See G.3.d.)

B.6. Consultation

a. Respect for Privacy. Information obtained in a consulting relationship is discussed for professional purposes only with persons clearly concerned with the case. Written and oral reports present data germane to the purposes of the consultation, and every effort is made to protect client identity and avoid undue invasion of privacy.

b. Cooperating Agencies. Before sharing information, counselors make efforts to ensure that there are defined policies in other agencies serving the counselor's clients that effectively protect the confidentiality of information.

Section C: Professional Responsibility

C.1. Standards Knowledge Counselors have a responsibility to read, understand, and follow the Code of Ethics and the Standards of Practice.

C.2. Professional Competence

a. Boundaries of Competence. Counselors practice only within the boundaries of their competence, based on their education, training, supervised experience, state and national professional credentials, and appropriate professional experience. Counselors will demonstrate a commitment to gain knowledge, personal awareness, sensitivity, and skills pertinent to working with a diverse client population.

b. New Specialty Areas of Practice. Counselors practice in specialty areas new to them only after appropriate education, training, and supervised experience. While developing skills in new specialty areas, counselors take steps to ensure the competence of their work and to protect others from possible harm.

c. Qualified for Employment. Counselors accept employment only for positions for which they are qualified by education, training, supervised experience, state and national professional credentials, and appropriate professional experience. Counselors hire for professional counseling positions only individuals who are qualified and competent.

d. Monitor Effectiveness. Counselors continually monitor their effectiveness as professionals and take steps to improve when necessary.

Counselors in private practice take reasonable steps to seek out peer supervision to evaluate their efficacy as counselors.

e. Ethical Issues Consultation. Counselors take reasonable steps to consult with other counselors or related professionals when they have questions regarding their ethical obligations or professional practice. (See H.1.)

f. Continuing Education. Counselors recognize the need for continuing education to maintain a reasonable level of awareness of current scientific and professional information in their fields of activity. They take steps to maintain competence in the skills they use, are open to new procedures, and keep current with the diverse and/or special populations with whom they work.

g. Impairment. Counselors refrain from offering or accepting professional services when their physical, mental, or emotional problems are likely to harm a client or others. They are alert to the signs of impairment, seek assistance for problems, and, if necessary, limit, suspend, or terminate their professional responsibilities. (See A.11.c.)

C.3. Advertising and Soliciting Clients

a. Accurate Advertising. There are no restrictions on advertising by counselors except those that can be specifically justified to protect the public from deceptive practices. Counselors advertise or represent their services to the public by identifying their credentials in an accurate manner that is not false, misleading, deceptive, or fraudulent. Counselors may only advertise the highest degree earned which is in counseling or a closely related field from a college or university that was accredited when the degree was awarded by one of the regional accrediting bodies recognized by the Council on Postsecondary Accreditation.

b. Testimonials. Counselors who use testimonials do not solicit them from clients or other persons who, because of their particular circumstances, may be vulnerable to undue influence.

c. Statements by Others. Counselors make reasonable efforts to ensure that statements made by others about them or the profession of counseling are accurate.

d. Recruiting Through Employment. Counselors do not use their places of employment or institutional affiliation to recruit or gain clients, supervisees, or consultees for their private practices. (See C.5.e.)

e. Products and Training Advertisements. Counselors who develop products related to their profession or conduct workshops or training events ensure that the advertisements concerning these products or events are accurate and disclose adequate information for consumers to make informed choices.

    f. Promoting to Those Served. Counselors do not use counseling, teaching, training, or supervisory relationships to promote their products or training events in a manner that is deceptive or would exert undue influence on individuals who may be vulnerable. Counselors may adopt textbooks they have authored for instruction purposes.

    g. Professional Association Involvement. Counselors actively participate in local, state, and national associations that foster the development and improvement of counseling.

C.4. Credentials

    a. Credentials Claimed. Counselors claim or imply only professional credentials possessed and are responsible for correcting any known misrepresentations of their credentials by others. Professional credentials include graduate degrees in counseling or closely related mental health fields, accreditation of graduate programs, national voluntary certifications, government-issued certifications or licenses, ACA professional membership, or any other credential that might indicate to the public specialized knowledge or expertise in counseling.

    b. ACA Professional Membership. ACA professional members may announce to the public their membership status. Regular members may not announce their ACA membership in a manner that might imply they are credentialed counselors.

    c. Credential Guidelines. Counselors follow the guidelines for use of credentials that have been established by the entities that issue the credentials.

    d. Misrepresentation of Credentials. Counselors do not attribute more to their credentials than the credentials represent, and do not imply that other counselors are not qualified because they do not possess certain credentials.

    e. Doctoral Degrees From Other Fields. Counselors who hold a master's degree in counseling or a closely related mental health field, but hold a doctoral degree from other than counseling or a closely related field, do not use the title "Dr." in their practices and do not announce to the public in relation to their practice or status as a counselor that they hold a doctorate.

C.5. Public Responsibility

    a. Nondiscrimination. Counselors do not discriminate against clients, students, or supervisees in a manner that has a negative impact based on their age, color, culture, disability, ethnic group, gender, race, religion, sexual orientation, or socioeconomic status, or for any other reason. (See A.2.a.)

b. Sexual Harassment. Counselors do not engage in sexual harassment. Sexual harassment is defined as sexual solicitation, physical advances, or verbal or nonverbal conduct that is sexual in nature, that occurs in connection with professional activities or roles, and that either (1) is unwelcome, is offensive, or creates a hostile workplace environment, and counselors know or are told this; or (2) is sufficiently severe or intense to be perceived as harassment to a reasonable person in the context. Sexual harassment can consist of a single intense or severe act or multiple persistent or pervasive acts. (See A.2.a., D.1.i)

c. Reports to Third Parties. Counselors are accurate, honest, and unbiased in reporting their professional activities and judgments to appropriate third parties including courts, health insurance companies, those who are the recipients of evaluation reports, and others. (See B.1.g.)

d. Media Presentations. When counselors provide advice or comment by means of public lectures, demonstrations, radio or television programs, prerecorded tapes, printed articles, mailed material, or other media, they take reasonable precautions to ensure that (1) the statements are based on appropriate professional counseling literature and practice; (2) the statements are otherwise consistent with the Code of Ethics and the Standards of Practice; and (3) the recipients of the information are not encouraged to infer that a professional counseling relationship has been established. (See C.6.b.)

e. Unjustified Gains. Counselors do not use their professional positions to seek or receive unjustified personal gains, sexual favors, unfair advantage, or unearned goods or services. (See C.3.d.)

C.6. Responsibility to Other Professionals

a. Different Approaches. Counselors are respectful of approaches to professional counseling that differ from their own. Counselors know and take into account the traditions and practices of other professional groups with which they work.

b. Personal Public Statements. When making personal statements in a public context, counselors clarify that they are speaking from their personal perspectives and that they are not speaking on behalf of all counselors or the profession. (See C.5.d.)

c. Clients Served by Others. When counselors learn that their clients are in a professional relationship with another mental health professional, they request release from clients to inform the other professionals and strive to establish positive and collaborative professional relationships. (See A.4.)

Section D: Relationships With Other Professionals
D.1. Relationships With Employers and Employees
  a. Role Definition. Counselors define and describe for their employers and employees the parameters and levels of their professional roles.
  b. Agreements. Counselors establish working agreements with supervisors, colleagues, and subordinates regarding counseling or clinical relationships, confidentiality, adherence to professional standards, distinction between public and private material, maintenance and dissemination of recorded information, work load, and accountability. Working agreements in each instance are specified and made known to those concerned.
  c. Negative Conditions. Counselors alert their employers to conditions that may be potentially disruptive or damaging to the counselor's professional responsibilities or that may limit their effectiveness.
  d. Evaluation. Counselors submit regularly to professional review and evaluation by their supervisor or the appropriate representative of the employer.
  e. In-Service. Counselors are responsible for in-service development of self and staff.
  f. Goals. Counselors inform their staff of goals and programs.
  g. Practices. Counselors provide personnel and agency practices that respect and enhance the rights and welfare of each employee and recipient of agency services. Counselors strive to maintain the highest levels of professional services.
  h. Personnel Selection and Assignment. Counselors select competent staff and assign responsibilities compatible with their skills and experiences.
  i. Discrimination. Counselors, as either employers or employees, do not engage in or condone practices that are inhumane, illegal, or unjustifiable (such as considerations based on age, color, culture, disability, ethnic group, gender, race, religion, sexual orientation, or socioeconomic status) in hiring, promotion, or training. (See A.2.a. and C.5.b.)
  j. Professional Conduct. Counselors have a responsibility both to clients and to the agency or institution within which services are performed to maintain high standards of professional conduct.
  k. Exploitative Relationships. Counselors do not engage in exploitative relationships with individuals over whom they have supervisory, evaluative, or instructional control or authority.
  l. Employer Policies. The acceptance of employment in an agency or institution implies that counselors are in agreement with its general policies and principles. Counselors strive to reach agreement with

employers as to acceptable standards of conduct that allow for changes in institutional policy conducive to the growth and development of clients.

D.2. Consultation (See B.6.)

a. Consultation as an Option. Counselors may choose to consult with any other professionally competent persons about their clients. In choosing consultants, counselors avoid placing the consultant in a conflict of interest situation that would preclude the consultant being a proper party to the counselor's efforts to help the client. Should counselors be engaged in a work setting that compromises this consultation standard, they consult with other professionals whenever possible to consider justifiable alternatives.

b. Consultant Competency. Counselors are reasonably certain that they have or the organization represented has the necessary competencies and resources for giving the kind of consulting services needed and that appropriate referral resources are available.

c. Understanding With Clients. When providing consultation, counselors attempt to develop with their clients a clear understanding of problem definition, goals for change, and predicted consequences of interventions selected.

d. Consultant Goals. The consulting relationship is one in which client adaptability and growth toward self-direction are consistently encouraged and cultivated. (See A.1.b.)

D.3. Fees for Referral

a. Accepting Fees From Agency Clients. Counselors refuse a private fee or other remuneration for rendering services to persons who are entitled to such services through the counselor's employing agency or institution. The policies of a particular agency may make explicit provisions for agency clients to receive counseling services from members of its staff in private practice. In such instances, the clients must be informed of other options open to them should they seek private counseling services. (See A.10.a., A.11.b., and C.3.d.)

b. Referral Fees. Counselors do not accept a referral fee from other professionals.

D.4. Subcontractor Arrangements

When counselors work as subcontractors for counseling services for a third party, they have a duty to inform clients of the limitations of confidentiality that the organization may place on counselors in providing counseling services to clients. The limits of such confidentiality ordinarily are discussed as part of the intake session. (See B.1.e. and B.1.f.)

Section E: Evaluation, Assessment, and Interpretation
E.1. General
    a. Appraisal Techniques. The primary purpose of educational and psychological assessment is to provide measures that are objective and interpretable in either comparative or absolute terms. Counselors recognize the need to interpret the statements in this section as applying to the whole range of appraisal techniques, including test and nontest data.
    b. Client Welfare. Counselors promote the welfare and best interests of the client in the development, publication, and utilization of educational and psychological assessment techniques. They do not misuse assessment results and interpretations and take reasonable steps to prevent others from misusing the information these techniques provide. They respect the client's right to know the results, the interpretations made, and the bases for their conclusions and recommendations.

E.2. Competence to Use and Interpret Tests
    a. Limits of Competence. Counselors recognize the limits of their competence and perform only those testing and assessment services for which they have been trained. They are familiar with reliability, validity, related standardization, error of measurement, and proper application of any technique utilized. Counselors using computer-based test interpretations are trained in the construct being measured and the specific instrument being used prior to using this type of computer application. Counselors take reasonable measures to ensure the proper use of psychological assessment techniques by persons under their supervision.
    b. Appropriate Use. Counselors are responsible for the appropriate application, scoring, interpretation, and use of assessment instruments, whether they score and interpret such tests themselves or use computerized or other services.
    c. Decisions Based on Results. Counselors responsible for decisions involving individuals or policies that are based on assessment results have a thorough understanding of educational and psychological measurement, including validation criteria, test research, and guidelines for test development and use.
    d. Accurate Information. Counselors provide accurate information and avoid false claims or misconceptions when making statements about

assessment instruments or techniques. Special efforts are made to avoid unwarranted connotations of such terms as IQ and grade equivalent scores. (See C.5.c.)

E.3. Informed Consent
   a. Explanation to Clients. Prior to assessment, counselors explain the nature and purposes of assessment and the specific use of results in language the client (or other legally authorized person on behalf of the client) can understand, unless an explicit exception to this right has been agreed upon in advance. Regardless of whether scoring and interpretation are completed by counselors, by assistants, or by computer or other outside services, counselors take reasonable steps to ensure that appropriate explanations are given to the client.
   b. Recipients of Results. The examinee's welfare, explicit understanding, and prior agreement determine the recipients of test results. Counselors include accurate and appropriate interpretations with any release of individual or group test results. (See B.1.a. and C.5.c.)

E.4. Release of Information to Competent Professionals
   a. Misuse of Results. Counselors do not misuse assessment results, including test results, and interpretations, and take reasonable steps to prevent the misuse of such by others. (See C.5.c.)
   b. Release of Raw Data. Counselors ordinarily release data (e.g., protocols, counseling or interview notes, or questionnaires) in which the client is identified only with the consent of the client or the client's legal representative. Such data are usually released only to persons recognized by counselors as competent to interpret the data. (See B.1.a.)

E.5. Proper Diagnosis of Mental Disorders
   a. Proper Diagnosis. Counselors take special care to provide proper diagnosis of mental disorders. Assessment techniques (including personal interview) used to determine client care (e.g., locus of treatment, type of treatment, or recommended follow-up) are carefully selected and appropriately used. (See A.3.a. and C.5.c.)
   b. Cultural Sensitivity. Counselors recognize that culture affects the manner in which clients' problems are defined. Clients' socioeconomic and cultural experience is considered when diagnosing mental disorders.

E.6. Test Selection
   a. Appropriateness of Instruments. Counselors carefully consider the validity, reliability, psychometric limitations, and appropriateness of

instruments when selecting tests for use in a given situation or with a particular client.

b. Culturally Diverse Populations. Counselors are cautious when selecting tests for culturally diverse populations to avoid inappropriateness of testing that may be outside of socialized behavioral or cognitive patterns.

E.7. Conditions of Test Administration

a. Administration Conditions. Counselors administer tests under the same conditions that were established in their standardization. When tests are not administered under standard conditions or when unusual behavior or irregularities occur during the testing session, those conditions are noted in interpretation, and the results may be designated as invalid or of questionable validity.

b. Computer Administration. Counselors are responsible for ensuring that administration programs function properly to provide clients with accurate results when a computer or other electronic methods are used for test administration. (See A.12.b.)

c. Unsupervised Test Taking. Counselors do not permit unsupervised or inadequately supervised use of tests or assessments unless the tests or assessments are designed, intended, and validated for self-administration and/or scoring.

d. Disclosure of Favorable Conditions. Prior to test administration, conditions that produce most favorable test results are made known to the examinee.

E.8. Diversity in Testing Counselors are cautious in using assessment techniques, making evaluations, and interpreting the performance of populations not represented in the norm group on which an instrument was standardized. They recognize the effects of age, color, culture, disability, ethnic group, gender, race, religion, sexual orientation, and socioeconomic status on test administration and interpretation and place test results in proper perspective with other relevant factors. (See A.2.a.)

E.9. Test Scoring and Interpretation

a. Reporting Reservations. In reporting assessment results, counselors indicate any reservations that exist regarding validity or reliability because of the circumstances of the assessment or the inappropriateness of the norms for the person tested.

b. Research Instruments. Counselors exercise caution when interpreting the results of research instruments possessing insufficient technical data to support respondent results. The specific purposes for the use of such instruments are stated explicitly to the examinee.

c. Testing Services. Counselors who provide test scoring and test interpretation services to support the assessment process confirm the validity of such interpretations. They accurately describe the purpose, norms, validity, reliability, and applications of the procedures and any special qualifications applicable to their use. The public offering of an automated test interpretations service is considered a professional-to-professional consultation. The formal responsibility of the consultant is to the consultee, but the ultimate and overriding responsibility is to the client.

E.10. Test Security Counselors maintain the integrity and security of tests and other assessment techniques consistent with legal and contractual obligations. Counselors do not appropriate, reproduce, or modify published tests or parts thereof without acknowledgment and permission from the publisher.

E.11. Obsolete Tests and Outdated Test Results Counselors do not use data or test results that are obsolete or outdated for the current purpose. Counselors make every effort to prevent the misuse of obsolete measures and test data by others.

E.12. Test Construction Counselors use established scientific procedures, relevant standards, and current professional knowledge for test design in the development, publication, and utilization of educational and psychological assessment techniques.

Section F: Teaching, Training, and Supervision
F.1. Counselor Educators and Trainers
   a. Educators as Teachers and Practitioners. Counselors who are responsible for developing, implementing, and supervising educational programs are skilled as teachers and practitioners. They are knowledgeable regarding the ethical, legal, and regulatory aspects of the profession, are skilled in applying that knowledge, and make students and supervisees aware of their responsibilities. Counselors conduct counselor education and training programs in an ethical manner and serve as role models for professional behavior. Counselor educators should make an effort to infuse material related to human diversity into all courses and/or workshops that are designed to promote the development of professional counselors.

b. Relationship Boundaries With Students and Supervisees. Counselors clearly define and maintain ethical, professional, and social relationship boundaries with their students and supervisees. They are aware of the differential in power that exists and the student's or supervisee's possible incomprehension of that power differential. Counselors explain to students and supervisees the potential for the relationship to become exploitive.

c. Sexual Relationships. Counselors do not engage in sexual relationships with students or supervisees and do not subject them to sexual harassment. (See A.6. and C.5.b)

d. Contributions to Research. Counselors give credit to students or supervisees for their contributions to research and scholarly projects. Credit is given through coauthorship, acknowledgment, footnote statement, or other appropriate means, in accordance with such contributions. (See G.4.b. and G.4.c.)

e. Close Relatives. Counselors do not accept close relatives as students or supervisees.

f. Supervision Preparation. Counselors who offer clinical supervision services are adequately prepared in supervision methods and techniques. Counselors who are doctoral students serving as practicum or internship supervisors to master's level students are adequately prepared and supervised by the training program.

g. Responsibility for Services to Clients. Counselors who supervise the counseling services of others take reasonable measures to ensure that counseling services provided to clients are professional.

h. Endorsement. Counselors do not endorse students or supervisees for certification, licensure, employment, or completion of an academic or training program if they believe students or supervisees are not qualified for the endorsement. Counselors take reasonable steps to assist students or supervisees who are not qualified for endorsement to become qualified.

F.2. Counselor Education and Training Programs

a. Orientation. Prior to admission, counselors orient prospective students to the counselor education or training program's expectations, including but not limited to the following: (1) the type and level of skill acquisition required for successful completion of the training, (2) subject matter to be covered, (3) basis for evaluation, (4) training components that encourage self-growth or self-disclosure as part of the training process, (5) the type of supervision settings and requirements of the sites for required clinical field experiences, (6) student and supervisee evaluation and dismissal policies and procedures, and (7) up-to-date employment prospects for graduates.

b. Integration of Study and Practice. Counselors establish counselor education and training programs that integrate academic study and supervised practice.

c. Evaluation. Counselors clearly state to students and supervisees, in advance of training, the levels of competency expected, appraisal methods, and timing of evaluations for both didactic and experiential components. Counselors provide students and supervisees with periodic performance appraisal and evaluation feedback throughout the training program.

d. Teaching Ethics. Counselors make students and supervisees aware of the ethical responsibilities and standards of the profession and the students' and supervisees' ethical responsibilities to the profession. (See C.1. and F.3.e.)

e. Peer Relationships. When students or supervisees are assigned to lead counseling groups or provide clinical supervision for their peers, counselors take steps to ensure that students and supervisees placed in these roles do not have personal or adverse relationships with peers and that they understand they have the same ethical obligations as counselor educators, trainers, and supervisors. Counselors make every effort to ensure that the rights of peers are not compromised when students or supervisees are assigned to lead counseling groups or provide clinical supervision.

f. Varied Theoretical Positions. Counselors present varied theoretical positions so that students and supervisees may make comparisons and have opportunities to develop their own positions. Counselors provide information concerning the scientific bases of professional practice. (See C.6.a.)

h. Field Placements. Counselors develop clear policies within their training program regarding field placement and other clinical experiences. Counselors provide clearly stated roles and responsibilities for the student or supervisee, the site supervisor, and the program supervisor. They confirm that site supervisors are qualified to provide supervision and are informed of their professional and ethical responsibilities in this role.

i. Dual Relationships as Supervisors. Counselors avoid dual relationships such as performing the role of site supervisor and training program supervisor in the student's or supervisee's training program. Counselors do not accept any form of professional services, fees, commissions, reimbursement, or remuneration from a site for student or supervisee placement.

j. Diversity in Programs. Counselors are responsive to their institution's and program's recruitment and retention needs for training program administrators, faculty, and students with diverse backgrounds and special needs. (See A.2.a.)

F.3. Students and Supervisees

a. Limitations. Counselors, through ongoing evaluation and appraisal, are aware of the academic and personal limitations of students and supervisees that might impede performance. Counselors assist students and supervisees in securing remedial assistance when needed, and dismiss from the training program supervisees who are unable to provide competent service due to academic or personal limitations. Counselors seek professional consultation and document their decision to dismiss or refer students or supervisees for assistance. Counselors ensure that students and supervisees have recourse to address decisions made to require them to seek assistance or to dismiss them.

b. Self-Growth Experiences. Counselors use professional judgment when designing training experiences conducted by the counselors themselves that require student and supervisee self-growth or self-disclosure. Safeguards are provided so that students and supervisees are aware of the ramifications their self-disclosure may have on counselors whose primary role as teacher, trainer, or supervisor requires acting on ethical obligations to the profession. Evaluative components of experiential training experiences explicitly delineate predetermined academic standards that are separate and do not depend on the student's level of self-disclosure. (See A.6.)

c. Counseling for Students and Supervisees. If students or supervisees request counseling, supervisors or counselor educators provide them with acceptable referrals. Supervisors or counselor educators do not serve as counselor to students or supervisees over whom they hold administrative, teaching, or evaluative roles unless this is a brief role associated with a training experience. (See A.6.b.)

d. Clients of Students and Supervisees. Counselors make every effort to ensure that the clients at field placements are aware of the services rendered and the qualifications of the students and supervisees rendering those services. Clients receive professional disclosure information and are informed of the limits of confidentiality. Client permission is obtained in order for the students and supervisees to use any information concerning the counseling relationship in the training process. (See B.1.e.)

e. Standards for Students and Supervisees. Students and supervisees preparing to become counselors adhere to the Code of Ethics and the Standards of Practice. Students and supervisees have the same obligations to clients as those required of counselors. (See H.1.)

Section G: Research and Publication
G.1. Research Responsibilities

a. Use of Human Subjects. Counselors plan, design, conduct, and report research in a manner consistent with pertinent ethical principles, federal and state laws, host institutional regulations, and scientific standards governing research with human subjects. Counselors design and conduct research that reflects cultural sensitivity appropriateness.

b. Deviation From Standard Practices. Counselors seek consultation and observe stringent safeguards to protect the rights of research participants when a research problem suggests a deviation from standard acceptable practices. (See B.6.)

c. Precautions to Avoid Injury. Counselors who conduct research with human subjects are responsible for the subjects' welfare throughout the experiment and take reasonable precautions to avoid causing injurious psychological, physical, or social effects to their subjects.

d. Principal Researcher Responsibility. The ultimate responsibility for ethical research practice lies with the principal researcher. All others involved in the research activities share ethical obligations and full responsibility for their own actions.

e. Minimal Interference. Counselors take reasonable precautions to avoid causing disruptions in subjects' lives due to participation in research.

f. Diversity. Counselors are sensitive to diversity and research issues with special populations. They seek consultation when appropriate. (See A.2.a. and B.6.)

G.2. Informed Consent

a. Topics Disclosed. In obtaining informed consent for research, counselors use language that is understandable to research participants and that (1) accurately explains the purpose and procedures to be followed; (2) identifies any procedures that are experimental or relatively untried; (3) describes the attendant discomforts and risks; (4) describes the benefits or changes in individuals or organizations that might be reasonably expected; (5) discloses appropriate alternative procedures that would be advantageous for subjects; (6) offers to answer any inquiries concerning the procedures; (7) describes any limitations on confidentiality; and (8) instructs that subjects are free to withdraw their consent and to discontinue participation in the project at any time. (See B.1.f.)

b. Deception. Counselors do not conduct research involving deception unless alternative procedures are not feasible and the prospective value of the research justifies the deception. When the methodological requirements of a study necessitate concealment or deception, the investigator is required to explain clearly the reasons for this action as soon as possible.

c. Voluntary Participation. Participation in research is typically voluntary and without any penalty for refusal to participate. Involuntary participation is appropriate only when it can be demonstrated that participation will have no harmful effects on subjects and is essential to the investigation.

d. Confidentiality of Information. Information obtained about research participants during the course of an investigation is confidential. When the possibility exists that others may obtain access to such information, ethical research practice requires that the possibility, together with the plans for protecting confidentiality, be explained to participants as a part of the procedure for obtaining informed consent. (See B.1.e.)

e. Persons Incapable of Giving Informed Consent. When a person is incapable of giving informed consent, counselors provide an appropriate explanation, obtain agreement for participation, and obtain appropriate consent from a legally authorized person.

f. Commitments to Participants. Counselors take reasonable measures to honor all commitments to research participants.

g. Explanations After Data Collection. After data are collected, counselors provide participants with full clarification of the nature of the study to remove any misconceptions. Where scientific or human values justify delaying or withholding information, counselors take reasonable measures to avoid causing harm.

h. Agreements to Cooperate. Counselors who agree to cooperate with another individual in research or publication incur an obligation to cooperate as promised in terms of punctuality of performance and with regard to the completeness and accuracy of the information required.

i. Informed Consent for Sponsors. In the pursuit of research, counselors give sponsors, institutions, and publication channels the same respect and opportunity for giving informed consent that they accord to individual research participants. Counselors are aware of their obligation to future research workers and ensure that host institutions are given feedback information and proper acknowledgment.

G.3. Reporting Results

a. Information Affecting Outcome. When reporting research results, counselors explicitly mention all variables and conditions known to the investigator that may have affected the outcome of a study or the interpretation of data.

b. Accurate Results. Counselors plan, conduct, and report research accurately and in a manner that minimizes the possibility that results will be misleading. They provide thorough discussions of the limitations of their data and alternative hypotheses. Counselors do not engage in fraudulent research, distort data, misrepresent data, or deliberately bias their results.

c. Obligation to Report Unfavorable Results. Counselors communicate to other counselors the results of any research judged to be of professional value. Results that reflect unfavorably on institutions, programs, services, prevailing opinions, or vested interests are not withheld.

d. Identity of Subjects. Counselors who supply data, aid in the research of another person, report research results, or make original data available take due care to disguise the identity of respective subjects in the absence of specific authorization from the subjects to do otherwise. (See B.1.g. and B.5.a.)

e. Replication Studies. Counselors are obligated to make available sufficient original research data to qualified professionals who may wish to replicate the study.

G.4. Publication

a. Recognition of Others. When conducting and reporting research, counselors are familiar with and give recognition to previous work on the topic, observe copyright laws, and give full credit to those to whom credit is due. (See F.1.d. and G.4.c.)

b. Contributors. Counselors give credit through joint authorship, acknowledgment, footnote statements, or other appropriate means to those who have contributed significantly to research or concept development in accordance with such contributions. The principal contributor is listed first and minor technical or professional contributions are acknowledged in notes or introductory statements.

c. Student Research. For an article that is substantially based on a student's dissertation or thesis, the student is listed as the principal author. (See F.1.d. and G.4.a.)

    d. Duplicate Submission. Counselors submit manuscripts for consideration to only one journal at a time. Manuscripts that are published in whole or in substantial part in another journal or published work are not submitted for publication without acknowledgment and permission from the previous publication.

    e. Professional Review. Counselors who review material submitted for publication, research, or other scholarly purposes respect the confidentiality and proprietary rights of those who submitted it.

Section H: Resolving Ethical Issues

H.1. Knowledge of Standards Counselors are familiar with the Code of Ethics and the Standards of Practice and other applicable ethics codes from other professional organizations of which they are member, or from certification and licensure bodies. Lack of knowledge or misunderstanding of an ethical responsibility is not a defense against a charge of unethical conduct. (See F.3.e.)

H.2. Suspected Violations

    a. Ethical Behavior Expected. Counselors expect professional associates to adhere to the Code of Ethics. When counselors possess reasonable cause that raises doubts as to whether a counselor is acting in an ethical manner, they take appropriate action. (See H.2.d. and H.2.e.)

    b. Consultation. When uncertain as to whether a particular situation or course of action may be in violation of the Code of Ethics, counselors consult with other counselors who are knowledgeable about ethics, with colleagues, or with appropriate authorities.

    c. Organization Conflicts. If the demands of an organization with which counselors are affiliated pose a conflict with the Code of Ethics, counselors specify the nature of such conflicts and express to their supervisors or other responsible officials their commitment to the Code of Ethics. When possible, counselors work toward change within the organization to allow full adherence to the Code of Ethics.

    d. Informal Resolution. When counselors have reasonable cause to believe that another counselor is violating an ethical standard, they attempt to first resolve the issue informally with the other counselor if feasible, providing that such action does not violate confidentiality rights that may be involved.

    e. Reporting Suspected Violations. When an informal resolution is not appropriate or feasible, counselors, upon reasonable cause, take action such as reporting the suspected ethical violation to state or national ethics committees, unless this action conflicts with confidentiality rights that cannot be resolved.

f. Unwarranted Complaints. Counselors do not initiate, participate in, or encourage the filing of ethics complaints that are unwarranted or intend to harm a counselor rather than to protect clients or the public.

H.3. Cooperation With Ethics Committees Counselors assist in the process of enforcing the Code of Ethics. Counselors cooperate with investigations, proceedings, and requirements of the ACA Ethics Committee or ethics committees of other duly constituted associations or boards having jurisdiction over those charged with a violation. Counselors are familiar with the ACA Policies and Procedures and use it as a reference in assisting the enforcement of the Code of Ethics.

ACA Standards of Practice
All members of the American Counseling Association (ACA) are required to adhere to the Standards of Practice and the Code of Ethics. The Standards of Practice represent minimal behavioral statements of the Code of Ethics. Members should refer to the applicable section of the Code of Ethics for further interpretation and amplification of the applicable Standard of Practice.

Section A: The Counseling Relationship
Section B: Confidentiality
Section C: Professional Responsibility
Section D: Relationship With Other Professionals
Section E: Evaluation, Assessment and Interpretation
Section F: Teaching, Training, and Supervision
Section G: Research and Publication
Section H: Resolving Ethical Issues

Section A: The Counseling Relationship
Standard of Practice One (SP-1):
Nondiscrimination. Counselors respect diversity and must not discriminate against clients because of age, color, culture, disability, ethnic group, gender, race, religion, sexual orientation, marital status, or socioeconomic status. (See A.2.a.)

Standard of Practice Two (SP-2): Disclosure to Clients. Counselors must adequately inform clients, preferably in writing, regarding the counseling process and counseling relationship at or before the time it begins and throughout the relationship. (See A.3.a.)

Standard of Practice Three (SP-3): Dual Relationships. Counselors must make every effort to avoid dual relationships with clients that could impair their professional judgment or increase the risk of harm to clients. When a dual relationship cannot be avoided, counselors must take appropriate steps to ensure that judgment is not impaired and that no exploitation occurs. (See A.6.a. and A.6.b.)

Standard of Practice Four (SP-4): Sexual Intimacies With Clients. Counselors must not engage in any type of sexual intimacies with current clients and must not engage in sexual intimacies with former clients within a minimum of 2 years after terminating the counseling relationship. Counselors who engage in such relationship after 2 years following termination have the responsibility to examine and document thoroughly that such relations did not have an exploitative nature.

Standard of Practice Five (SP-5): Protecting Clients During Group Work. Counselors must take steps to protect clients from physical or psychological trauma resulting from interactions during group work. (See A.9.b.)

Standard of Practice Six (SP-6): Advance Understanding of Fees. Counselors must explain to clients, prior to their entering the counseling relationship, financial arrangements related to professional services. (See A.10. a.-d. and A.11.c.)

Standard of Practice Seven (SP-7): Termination. Counselors must assist in making appropriate arrangements for the continuation of treatment of clients, when necessary, following termination of counseling relationships. (See A.11.a.)

Standard of Practice Eight (SP-8): Inability to Assist Clients. Counselors must avoid entering or immediately terminate a counseling relationship if it is determined that they are unable to be of professional assistance to a client. The counselor may assist in making an appropriate referral for the client. (See A.11.b.)

Section B: Confidentiality
Standard of Practice Nine (SP-9): Confidentiality Requirement. Counselors must keep information related to counseling services confidential unless disclosure is in the best interest of clients, is required for the welfare of others, or is required by law. When disclosure is required, only information that is essential is revealed and the client is informed of such disclosure. (See B.1. a.+f.)

Standard of Practice Ten (SP-10): Confidentiality Requirements for Subordinates. Counselors must take measures to ensure that privacy and confidentiality of clients are maintained by subordinates. (See B.1.h.)

Standard of Practice Eleven (SP-11): Confidentiality in Group Work. Counselors must clearly communicate to group members that confidentiality cannot be guaranteed in group work. (See B.2.a.)

Standard of Practice Twelve (SP-12): Confidentiality in Family Counseling. Counselors must not disclose information about one family member in counseling to another family member without prior consent. (See B.2.b.)

Standard of Practice Thirteen (SP-13): Confidentiality of Records. Counselors must maintain appropriate confidentiality in creating, storing, accessing, transferring, and disposing of counseling records. (See B.4.b.)

Standard of Practice Fourteen (SP-14): Permission to Record or Observe. Counselors must obtain prior consent from clients in order to record electronically or observe sessions. (See B.4.c.)

Standard of Practice Fifteen (SP-15): Disclosure or Transfer of Records. Counselors must obtain client consent to disclose or transfer records to third parties, unless exceptions listed in SP-9 exist. (See B.4.e.)

Standard of Practice Sixteen (SP-16): Data Disguise Required. Counselors must disguise the identity of the client when using data for training, research, or publication. (See B.5.a.)

Section C: Professional Responsibility
Standard of Practice Seventeen (SP-17): Boundaries of Competence. Counselors must practice only within the boundaries of their competence. (See C.2.a.)

Standard of Practice Eighteen (SP-18): Continuing Education. Counselors must engage in continuing education to maintain their professional competence. (See C.2.f.)

Standard of Practice Nineteen (SP-19): Impairment of Professionals. Counselors must refrain from offering professional services when their personal problems or conflicts may cause harm to a client or others. (See C.2.g.)

Standard of Practice Twenty (SP-20): Accurate Advertising. Counselors must accurately represent their credentials and services when advertising. (See C.3.a.)

Standard of Practice Twenty-One (SP-21): Recruiting Through Employment. Counselors must not use their place of employment or institutional affiliation to recruit clients for their private practices. (See C.3.d.)

Standard of Practice Twenty-Two (SP-22): Credentials Claimed. Counselors must claim or imply only professional credentials possessed and must correct any known misrepresentations of their credentials by others. (See C.4.a.)

Standard of Practice Twenty-Three (SP-23): Sexual Harassment. Counselors must not engage in sexual harassment. (See C.5.b.)

Standard of Practice Twenty-Four (SP-24): Unjustified Gains. Counselors must not use their professional positions to seek or receive unjustified personal gains, sexual favors, unfair advantage, or unearned goods or services. (See C.5.e.)

Standard of Practice Twenty-Five (SP-25): Clients Served by Others. With the consent of the client, counselors must inform other mental health professionals serving the same client that a counseling relationship between the counselor and client exists. (See C.6.c.)

Standard of Practice Twenty-Six (SP-26): Negative Employment Conditions. Counselors must alert their employers to institutional policy or conditions that may be potentially disruptive or damaging to the counselor's professional responsibilities, or that may limit their effectiveness or deny clients' rights. (See D.1.c.)

Standard of Practice Twenty-Seven (SP-27): Personnel Selection and Assignment. Counselors must select competent staff and must assign responsibilities compatible with staff skills and experiences. (See D.1.h.)

Standard of Practice Twenty-Eight (SP-28): Exploitative Relationships With Subordinates. Counselors must not engage in exploitative relationships with individuals over whom they have supervisory, evaluative, or instructional control or authority. (See D.1.k.)

Section D: Relationship With Other Professionals
Standard of Practice Twenty-Nine (SP-29): Accepting Fees From Agency Clients. Counselors must not accept fees or other remuneration for consultation with persons entitled to such services through the counselor's employing agency or institution. (See D.3.a.)

Standard of Practice Thirty (SP-30): Referral Fees. Counselors must not accept referral fees. (See D.3.b.)

Section E: Evaluation, Assesment and Interpretation
Standard of Practice Thirty-One (SP-31): Limits of Competence. Counselors must perform only testing and assessment services for which they are competent. Counselors must not allow the use of psychological assessment techniques by unqualified persons under their supervision. (See E.2.a.)

Standard of Practice Thirty-Two (SP-32): Appropriate Use of Assessment Instruments. Counselors must use assessment instruments in the manner for which they were intended. (See E.2.b.)

Standard of Practice Thirty-Three (SP-33): Assessment Explanations to Clients. Counselors must provide explanations to clients prior to assessment about the nature and purposes of assessment and the specific uses of results. (See E.3.a.)

Standard of Practice Thirty-Four (SP-34): Recipients of Test Results. Counselors must ensure that accurate and appropriate interpretations accompany any release of testing and assessment information. (See E.3.b.)

Standard of Practice Thirty-Five (SP-35): Obsolete Tests and Outdated Test Results. Counselors must not base their assessment or intervention decisions or recommendations on data or test results that are obsolete or outdated for the current purpose. (See E.11.)

Section F: Teaching, Training, and Supervision
Standard of Practice Thirty-Six (SP-36): Sexual Relationships With Students or Supervisees. Counselors must not engage in sexual relationships with their students and supervisees. (See F.1.c.)

Standard of Practice Thirty-Seven (SP-37): Credit for Contributions to Research. Counselors must give credit to students or supervisees for their contributions to research and scholarly projects. (See F.1.d.)

Standard of Practice Thirty-Eight (SP-38): Supervision Preparation. who offer clinical supervision services must be trained and prepared in supervision methods and techniques. (See F.1.f.)

Standard of Practice Thirty-Nine (SP-39): Evaluation Information. Counselors must clearly state to students and supervisees in advance of training

322 • Religious and Spiritual Issues in Counseling

the levels of competency expected, appraisal methods, and timing of evaluations. Counselors must provide students and supervisees with periodic performance appraisal and evaluation feedback throughout the training program. (See F.2.c.)

Standard of Practice Forty (SP-40): Peer Relationships in Training. Counselors must make every effort to ensure that the rights of peers are not violated when students and supervisees are assigned to lead counseling groups or provide clinical supervision. (See F.2.e.)

Standard of Practice Forty-One (SP-41): Limitations of Students and Supervisees. Counselors must assist students and supervisees in securing remedial assistance, when needed, and must dismiss from the training program students and supervisees who are unable to provide competent service due to academic or personal limitations. (See F.3.a.)

Standard of Practice Forty-Two (SP-42): Self-Growth Experiences. Counselors who conduct experiences for students or supervisees that include self-growth or self-disclosure must inform participants of counselors' ethical obligations to the profession and must not grade participants based on their nonacademic performance. (See F.3.b.)

Standard of Practice Forty-Three (SP-43): Standards for Students and Supervisees. Students and supervisees preparing to become counselors must adhere to the Code of Ethics and the Standards of Practice of counselors. (See F.3.e.)

Section G: Research and Publication
Standard of Practice Forty-Four (SP-44): Precautions to Avoid Injury in Research. Counselors must avoid causing physical, social, or psychological harm or injury to subjects in research. (See G.1.c.)

Standard of Practice Forty-Five (SP-45): Confidentiality of Research Information. Counselors must keep confidential information obtained about research participants. (See G.2.d.)

Standard of Practice Forty-Six (SP-46): Information Affecting Research Outcome. Counselors must report all variables and conditions known to the investigator that may have affected research data or outcomes. (See G.3.a.)

Standard of Practice Forty-Seven (SP-47): Accurate Research Results. Counselors must not distort or misrepresent research data, nor fabricate or intentionally bias research results. (See G.3.b.)

Standard of Practice Forty-Eight (SP-48): Publication Contributors. Counselors must give appropriate credit to those who have contributed to research. (See G.4.a. and G.4.b.)

Section H: Resolving Ethical Issues
Standard of Practice Forty-Nine (SP-49): Ethical Behavior Expected. Counselors must take appropriate action when they possess reasonable cause that raises doubts as to whether counselors or other mental health professionals are acting in an ethical manner. (See H.2.a.)

Standard of Practice Fifty (SP-50): Unwarranted Complaints. Counselors must not initiate, participate in, or encourage the filing of ethics complaints that are unwarranted or intended to harm a mental health professional rather than to protect clients or the public. (See H.2.f.)

Standard of Practice Fifty-One (SP-51): Cooperation With Ethics Committees. Counselors must cooperate with investigations, proceedings, and requirements of the ACA Ethics Committee or ethics committees of other duly constituted associations or boards having jurisdiction over those charged with a violation. (See H.3.)

References

The following documents are available to counselors as resources to guide them in their practices. These resources are not a part of the Code of Ethics and the Standards of Practice.

American Association for Counseling and Development/Association for Measurement and Evaluation in Counseling and Development. (1989). The responsibilities of users of standardized tests (rev.). Washington, D.C.: Author.

American Counseling Association. (1995). (Note: This is ACA's previous edition of its ethics code). Ethical standards. Alexandria, VA: Author.

American Psychological Association. (1985). Standards for educational and psychological testing (rev.). Washington, D.C.: Author.

Joint Committee on Testing Practices. (1988). Code of fair testing practices in education. Washington, D.C.: Author.

National Board for Certified Counselors. (1989). National Board for Certified Counselors code of ethics. Alexandria, VA: Author.

Prediger, D. J. (Ed.). (1993, March). Multicultural assessment standards. Alexandria, VA: Association for Assessment in Counseling.

Code of Ethics of the National Association of Social Workers

Approved by the 1996 NASW Delegate Assembly and revised by the 1999 NASW Delegate Assembly

Preamble

The primary mission of the social work profession is to enhance human well-being and help meet the basic human needs of all people, with particular attention to the needs and empowerment of people who are vulnerable, oppressed, and living in poverty. A historic and defining feature of social work is the profession's focus on individual well-being in a social context and the well-being of society. Fundamental to social work is attention to the environmental forces that create, contribute to, and address problems in living.

Social workers promote social justice and social change with and on behalf of clients. "Clients" is used inclusively to refer to individuals, families, groups, organizations, and communities. Social workers are sensitive to cultural and ethnic diversity and strive to end discrimination, oppression, poverty, and other forms of social injustice. These activities may be in the form of direct practice, community organizing, supervision, consultation, administration, advocacy, social and political action, policy development and implementation, education, and research and evaluation. Social workers seek to enhance the capacity of people to address their own needs. Social workers also seek to promote the responsiveness of organizations, communities, and other social institutions to individuals' needs and social problems.

The mission of the social work profession is rooted in a set of core values. These core values, embraced by social workers throughout the profession's history, are the foundation of social work's unique purpose and perspective:
service
social justice
dignity and worth of the person
importance of human relationships
integrity
competence

This constellation of core values reflects what is unique to the social work profession. Core values, and the principles that flow from them, must be balanced within the context and complexity of the human experience.

Purpose of the NASW Code of Ethics
Professional ethics are at the core of social work. The profession has an obligation to articulate its basic values, ethical principles, and ethical standards. The *NASW Code of Ethics* sets forth these values, principles, and standards to guide social workers' conduct. The *Code* is relevant to all social workers and social work students, regardless of their professional functions, the settings in which they work, or the populations they serve.

NASW Code of Ethics
1) The Code identifies core values on which social work's mission is based.
2) The Code summarizes broad ethical principles that reflect the profession's core values and establishes a set of specific ethical standards that should be used to guide social work practice.
3) The Code is designed to help social workers identify relevant considerations when professional obligations conflict or ethical uncertainties arise.
4) The Code provides ethical standards to which the general public can hold the social work profession accountable.
5) The Code socializes practitioners new to the field to social work's mission, values, ethical principles, and ethical standards.
6) The Code articulates standards that the social work profession itself can use to assess whether social workers have engaged in unethical conduct. NASW has formal procedures to adjudicate ethics complaints filed against its members.* In subscribing to this Code, social workers are required to cooperate in its implementation, participate

in NASW adjudication proceedings, and abide by any NASW disciplinary rulings or sanctions based on it.

*For information on NASW adjudication procedures, see *NASW Procedures for the Adjudication of Grievances.*

The *Code* offers a set of values, principles, and standards to guide decision making and conduct when ethical issues arise. It does not provide a set of rules that prescribe how social workers should act in all situations. Specific applications of the *Code* must take into account the context in which it is being considered and the possibility of conflicts among the *Code's* values, principles, and standards. Ethical responsibilities flow from all human relationships, from the personal and familial to the social and professional.

Further, the *NASW Code of Ethics* does not specify which values, principles, and standards are most important and ought to outweigh others in instances when they conflict. Reasonable differences of opinion can and do exist among social workers with respect to the ways in which values, ethical principles, and ethical standards should be rank ordered when they conflict. Ethical decision making in a given situation must apply the informed judgment of the individual social worker and should also consider how the issues would be judged in a peer review process where the ethical standards of the profession would be applied.

Ethical decision making is a process. There are many instances in social work where simple answers are not available to resolve complex ethical issues. Social workers should take into consideration all the values, principles, and standards in this *Code* that are relevant to any situation in which ethical judgment is warranted. Social workers' decisions and actions should be consistent with the spirit as well as the letter of this *Code*.

In addition to this *Code,* there are many other sources of information about ethical thinking that may be useful. Social workers should consider ethical theory and principles generally, social work theory and research, laws, regulations, agency policies, and other relevant codes of ethics, recognizing that among codes of ethics social workers should consider the *NASW Code of Ethics* as their primary source. Social workers also should be aware of the impact on ethical decision making of their clients' and their own personal values and cultural and religious beliefs and practices. They should be aware of any conflicts between personal and professional values and deal with them responsibly. For additional guidance social workers should consult the relevant literature on professional ethics and ethical decision making and seek appropriate consultation when faced with ethical dilemmas. This may involve consultation with an agency-based or social work organization's ethics committee, a regulatory body, knowledgeable colleagues, supervisors, or legal counsel.

Instances may arise when social workers' ethical obligations conflict with agency policies or relevant laws or regulations. When such conflicts occur, social workers must make a responsible effort to resolve the conflict in a manner that is consistent with the values, principles, and standards expressed in this Code. If a reasonable resolution of the conflict does not appear possible, social workers should seek proper consultation before making a decision.

The *NASW Code of Ethics* is to be used by NASW and by individuals, agencies, organizations, and bodies (such as licensing and regulatory boards, professional liability insurance providers, courts of law, agency boards of directors, government agencies, and other professional groups) that choose to adopt it or use it as a frame of reference. Violation of standards in this *Code* does not automatically imply legal liability or violation of the law. Such determination can only be made in the context of legal and judicial proceedings. Alleged violations of the *Code* would be subject to a peer review process. Such processes are generally separate from legal or administrative procedures and insulated from legal review or proceedings to allow the profession to counsel and discipline its own members.

A code of ethics cannot guarantee ethical behavior. Moreover, a code of ethics cannot resolve all ethical issues or disputes or capture the richness and complexity involved in striving to make responsible choices within a moral community. Rather, a code of ethics sets forth values, ethical principles, and ethical standards to which professionals aspire and by which their actions can be judged. Social workers' ethical behavior should result from their personal commitment to engage in ethical practice. The *NASW Code of Ethics* reflects the commitment of all social workers to uphold the profession's values and to act ethically. Principles and standards must be applied by individuals of good character who discern moral questions and, in good faith, seek to make reliable ethical judgments.

Ethical Principles

The following broad ethical principles are based on social work's core values of service, social justice, dignity and worth of the person, importance of human relationships, integrity, and competence. These principles set forth ideals to which all social workers should aspire.

Value: Service

Ethical Principle: Social workers' primary goal is to help people in need and to address social problems.

Social workers elevate service to others above self-interest. Social workers draw on their knowledge, values, and skills to help people in need and to address social problems. Social workers are encouraged to volunteer some portion of their professional skills with no expectation of significant financial return (pro bono service).

Value: Social Justice

Ethical Principle: Social workers challenge social injustice.

Social workers pursue social change, particularly with and on behalf of vulnerable and oppressed individuals and groups of people. Social workers' social change efforts are focused primarily on issues of poverty, unemployment, discrimination, and other forms of social injustice. These activities seek to promote sensitivity to and knowledge about oppression and cultural and ethnic diversity. Social workers strive to ensure access to needed information, services, and resources; equality of opportunity; and meaningful participation in decision making for all people.

Value: Dignity and Worth of the Person

Ethical Principle: Social workers respect the inherent dignity and worth of the person.

Social workers treat each person in a caring and respectful fashion, mindful of individual differences and cultural and ethnic diversity. Social workers promote clients' socially responsible self-determination. Social workers seek to enhance clients' capacity and opportunity to change and to address their own needs. Social workers are cognizant of their dual responsibility to clients and to the broader society. They seek to resolve conflicts between clients' interests and the broader society's interests in a socially responsible manner consistent with the values, ethical principles, and ethical standards of the profession.

Value: Importance of Human Relationships

Ethical Principle: Social workers recognize the central importance of human relationships.

Social workers understand that relationships between and among people are an important vehicle for change. Social workers engage people as partners in the helping process. Social workers seek to strengthen relationships among people in a purposeful effort to promote, restore, maintain, and enhance the well-being of individuals, families, social groups, organizations, and communities.

Value: Integrity

Ethical Principle: Social workers behave in a trustworthy manner.

Social workers are continually aware of the profession's mission, values, ethical principles, and ethical standards and practice in a manner consistent with them. Social workers act honestly and responsibly and promote ethical practices on the part of the organizations with which they are affiliated.

Value: Competence

Ethical Principle: Social workers practice within their areas of competence and develop and enhance their professional expertise.

Social workers continually strive to increase their professional knowledge and skills and to apply them in practice. Social workers should aspire to contribute to the knowledge base of the profession.

Ethical Standards

The following ethical standards are relevant to the professional activities of all social workers. These standards concern (1) social workers' ethical responsibilities to clients, (2) social workers' ethical responsibilities to colleagues, (3) social workers' ethical responsibilities in practice settings, (4) social workers' ethical responsibilities as professionals, (5) social workers' ethical responsibilities to the social work profession, and (6) social workers' ethical responsibilities to the broader society.

Some of the standards that follow are enforceable guidelines for professional conduct, and some are aspirational. The extent to which each standard is enforceable is a matter of professional judgment to be exercised by those responsible for reviewing alleged violations of ethical standards.

1. Social Workers' Ethical Responsibilities to Clients

1.01 Commitment to Clients   Social workers' primary responsibility is to promote the well-being of clients. In general, clients' interests are primary. However, social workers' responsibility to the larger society or specific legal obligations may on limited occasions supersede the loyalty owed clients, and clients should be so advised. (Examples include when a social worker is required by law to report that a client has abused a child or has threatened to harm self or others.)

1.02 Self-Determination   Social workers respect and promote the right of clients to self-determination and assist clients in their efforts to identify and clarify their goals. Social workers may limit clients' right to self-determination when, in the social workers' professional judgment, clients' actions or potential actions pose a serious, foreseeable, and imminent risk to themselves or others.

1.03 Informed Consent
(a) Social workers should provide services to clients only in the context of a professional relationship based, when appropriate, on valid informed consent. Social workers should use clear and understandable language to inform clients of the purpose of the services, risks related to the services, limits to services because of the requirements of a third-party payer, relevant costs, reasonable alternatives, clients' right

to refuse or withdraw consent, and the time frame covered by the consent. Social workers should provide clients with an opportunity to ask questions.

(b) In instances when clients are not literate or have difficulty understanding the primary language used in the practice setting, social workers should take steps to ensure clients' comprehension. This may include providing clients with a detailed verbal explanation or arranging for a qualified interpreter or translator whenever possible.

(c) In instances when clients lack the capacity to provide informed consent, social workers should protect clients' interests by seeking permission from an appropriate third party, informing clients consistent with the clients' level of understanding. In such instances social workers should seek to ensure that the third party acts in a manner consistent with clients' wishes and interests. Social workers should take reasonable steps to enhance such clients' ability to give informed consent.

(d) In instances when clients are receiving services involuntarily, social workers should provide information about the nature and extent of services and about the extent of clients' right to refuse service.

(e) Social workers who provide services via electronic media (such as computer, telephone, radio, and television) should inform recipients of the limitations and risks associated with such services.

(f) Social workers should obtain clients' informed consent before audiotaping or videotaping clients or permitting observation of services to clients by a third party.

1.04 Competence

(a) Social workers should provide services and represent themselves as competent only within the boundaries of their education, training, license, certification, consultation received, supervised experience, or other relevant professional experience.

(b) Social workers should provide services in substantive areas or use intervention techniques or approaches that are new to them only after engaging in appropriate study, training, consultation, and supervision from people who are competent in those interventions or techniques.

(c) When generally recognized standards do not exist with respect to an emerging area of practice, social workers should exercise careful judgment and take responsible steps (including appropriate education, research, training, consultation, and supervision) to ensure the competence of their work and to protect clients from harm.

1.05 Cultural Competence and Social Diversity
  (a) Social workers should understand culture and its function in human behavior and society, recognizing the strengths that exist in all cultures.
  (b) Social workers should have a knowledge base of their clients' cultures and be able to demonstrate competence in the provision of services that are sensitive to clients' cultures and to differences among people and cultural groups.
  (c) Social workers should obtain education about and seek to understand the nature of social diversity and oppression with respect to race, ethnicity, national origin, color, sex, sexual orientation, age, marital status, political belief, religion, and mental or physical disability.

1.06 Conflicts of Interest
  (a) Social workers should be alert to and avoid conflicts of interest that interfere with the exercise of professional discretion and impartial judgment. Social workers should inform clients when a real or potential conflict of interest arises and take reasonable steps to resolve the issue in a manner that makes the clients' interests primary and protects clients' interests to the greatest extent possible. In some cases, protecting clients' interests may require termination of the professional relationship with proper referral of the client.
  (b) Social workers should not take unfair advantage of any professional relationship or exploit others to further their personal, religious, political, or business interests.
  (c) Social workers should not engage in dual or multiple relationships with clients or former clients in which there is a risk of exploitation or potential harm to the client. In instances when dual or multiple relationships are unavoidable, social workers should take steps to protect clients and are responsible for setting clear, appropriate, and culturally sensitive boundaries. (Dual or multiple relationships occur when social workers relate to clients in more than one relationship, whether professional, social, or business. Dual or multiple relationships can occur simultaneously or consecutively.)
  (d) When social workers provide services to two or more people who have a relationship with each other (for example, couples, family members), social workers should clarify with all parties which individuals will be considered clients and the nature of social workers' professional obligations to the various individuals who are receiving services. Social workers who anticipate a conflict of interest among the individuals receiving services or who anticipate having to perform

in potentially conflicting roles (for example, when a social worker is asked to testify in a child custody dispute or divorce proceedings involving clients) should clarify their role with the parties involved and take appropriate action to minimize any conflict of interest.

1.07 Privacy and Confidentiality
  (a) Social workers should respect clients' right to privacy. Social workers should not solicit private information from clients unless it is essential to providing services or conducting social work evaluation or research. Once private information is shared, standards of confidentiality apply.
  (b) Social workers may disclose confidential information when appropriate with valid consent from a client or a person legally authorized to consent on behalf of a client.
  (c) Social workers should protect the confidentiality of all information obtained in the course of professional service, except for compelling professional reasons. The general expectation that social workers will keep information confidential does not apply when disclosure is necessary to prevent serious, foreseeable, and imminent harm to a client or other identifiable person. In all instances, social workers should disclose the least amount of confidential information necessary to achieve the desired purpose; only information that is directly relevant to the purpose for which the disclosure is made should be revealed.
  (d) Social workers should inform clients, to the extent possible, about the disclosure of confidential information and the potential consequences, when feasible before the disclosure is made. This applies whether social workers disclose confidential information on the basis of a legal requirement or client consent.
  (e) Social workers should discuss with clients and other interested parties the nature of confidentiality and limitations of clients' right to confidentiality. Social workers should review with clients circumstances where confidential information may be requested and where disclosure of confidential information may be legally required. This discussion should occur as soon as possible in the social worker-client relationship and as needed throughout the course of the relationship.
  (f) When social workers provide counseling services to families, couples, or groups, social workers should seek agreement among the parties involved concerning each individual's right to confidentiality and obligation to preserve the confidentiality of information shared by others. Social workers should inform participants in family, couples, or group counseling that social workers cannot guarantee that all participants will honor such agreements.

(g) Social workers should inform clients involved in family, couples, marital, or group counseling of the social worker's, employer's, and agency's policy concerning the social worker's disclosure of confidential information among the parties involved in the counseling.

(h) Social workers should not disclose confidential information to third-party payers unless clients have authorized such disclosure.

(i) Social workers should not discuss confidential information in any setting unless privacy can be ensured. Social workers should not discuss confidential information in public or semipublic areas such as hallways, waiting rooms, elevators, and restaurants.

(j) Social workers should protect the confidentiality of clients during legal proceedings to the extent permitted by law. When a court of law or other legally authorized body orders social workers to disclose confidential or privileged information without a client's consent and such disclosure could cause harm to the client, social workers should request that the court withdraw the order or limit the order as narrowly as possible or maintain the records under seal, unavailable for public inspection.

(k) Social workers should protect the confidentiality of clients when responding to requests from members of the media.

(l) Social workers should protect the confidentiality of clients' written and electronic records and other sensitive information. Social workers should take reasonable steps to ensure that clients' records are stored in a secure location and that clients' records are not available to others who are not authorized to have access.

(m) Social workers should take precautions to ensure and maintain the confidentiality of information transmitted to other parties through the use of computers, electronic mail, facsimile machines, telephones and telephone answering machines, and other electronic or computer technology. Disclosure of identifying information should be avoided whenever possible.

(n) Social workers should transfer or dispose of clients' records in a manner that protects clients' confidentiality and is consistent with state statutes governing records and social work licensure.

(o) Social workers should take reasonable precautions to protect client confidentiality in the event of the social worker's termination of practice, incapacitation, or death.

(p) Social workers should not disclose identifying information when discussing clients for teaching or training purposes unless the client has consented to disclosure of confidential information.

(q) Social workers should not disclose identifying information when discussing clients with consultants unless the client has consented to disclosure of confidential information or there is a compelling need for such disclosure.

(r) Social workers should protect the confidentiality of deceased clients consistent with the preceding standards.

1.08 Access to Records

(a) Social workers should provide clients with reasonable access to records concerning the clients. Social workers who are concerned that clients' access to their records could cause serious misunderstanding or harm to the client should provide assistance in interpreting the records and consultation with the client regarding the records. Social workers should limit clients' access to their records, or portions of their records, only in exceptional circumstances when there is compelling evidence that such access would cause serious harm to the client. Both clients' requests and the rationale for withholding some or all of the record should be documented in clients' files.

(b) When providing clients with access to their records, social workers should take steps to protect the confidentiality of other individuals identified or discussed in such records.

1.09 Sexual Relationships

(a) Social workers should under no circumstances engage in sexual activities or sexual contact with current clients, whether such contact is consensual or forced.

(b) Social workers should not engage in sexual activities or sexual contact with clients' relatives or other individuals with whom clients maintain a close personal relationship when there is a risk of exploitation or potential harm to the client. Sexual activity or sexual contact with clients' relatives or other individuals with whom clients maintain a personal relationship has the potential to be harmful to the client and may make it difficult for the social worker and client to maintain appropriate professional boundaries. Social workers— not their clients, their clients' relatives, or other individuals with whom the client maintains a personal relationship—assume the full burden for setting clear, appropriate, and culturally sensitive boundaries.

(c) Social workers should not engage in sexual activities or sexual contact with former clients because of the potential for harm to the client. If social workers engage in conduct contrary to this prohibition or claim that an exception to this prohibition is warranted because of extraordinary circumstances, it is social workers—not their clients—who assume the full burden of demonstrating that the former client has not been exploited, coerced, or manipulated, intentionally or unintentionally.

(d) Social workers should not provide clinical services to individuals with whom they have had a prior sexual relationship. Providing clinical services to a former sexual partner has the potential to be harmful to the individual and is likely to make it difficult for the social worker and individual to maintain appropriate professional boundaries.

1.10 Physical Contact   Social workers should not engage in physical contact with clients when there is a possibility of psychological harm to the client as a result of the contact (such as cradling or caressing clients). Social workers who engage in appropriate physical contact with clients are responsible for setting clear, appropriate, and culturally sensitive boundaries that govern such physical contact.

1.11 Sexual Harassment   Social workers should not sexually harass clients. Sexual harassment includes sexual advances, sexual solicitation, requests for sexual favors, and other verbal or physical conduct of a sexual nature.

1.12 Derogatory Language   Social workers should not use derogatory language in their written or verbal communications to or about clients. Social workers should use accurate and respectful language in all communications to and about clients.

1.13 Payment for Services
(a) When setting fees, social workers should ensure that the fees are fair, reasonable, and commensurate with the services performed. Consideration should be given to clients' ability to pay.

(b) Social workers should avoid accepting goods or services from clients as payment for professional services. Bartering arrangements, particularly involving services, create the potential for conflicts of interest, exploitation, and inappropriate boundaries in social workers' relationships with clients. Social workers should explore and may participate in bartering only in very limited circumstances when it can be demonstrated that such arrangements are an accepted practice among professionals in the local community, considered to be essential for the provision of services, negotiated without coercion, and entered into at the client's initiative and with the client's informed consent. Social workers who accept goods or services from clients as payment for professional services assume the full burden of demonstrating that this arrangement will not be detrimental to the client or the professional relationship.

(c) Social workers should not solicit a private fee or other remuneration for providing services to clients who are entitled to such available services through the social workers' employer or agency.

1.14 Clients Who Lack Decision-Making Capacity   When social workers act on behalf of clients who lack the capacity to make informed decisions, social workers should take reasonable steps to safeguard the interests and rights of those clients.

1.15 Interruption of Services   Social workers should make reasonable efforts to ensure continuity of services in the event that services are interrupted by factors such as unavailability, relocation, illness, disability, or death.

1.16 Termination of Services
(a) Social workers should terminate services to clients and professional relationships with them when such services and relationships are no longer required or no longer serve the clients' needs or interests.
(b) Social workers should take reasonable steps to avoid abandoning clients who are still in need of services. Social workers should withdraw services precipitously only under unusual circumstances, giving careful consideration to all factors in the situation and taking care to minimize possible adverse effects. Social workers should assist in making appropriate arrangements for continuation of services when necessary.
(c) Social workers in fee-for-service settings may terminate services to clients who are not paying an overdue balance if the financial contractual arrangements have been made clear to the client, if the client does not pose an imminent danger to self or others, and if the clinical and other consequences of the current nonpayment have been addressed and discussed with the client.
(d) Social workers should not terminate services to pursue a social, financial, or sexual relationship with a client.
(e) Social workers who anticipate the termination or interruption of services to clients should notify clients promptly and seek the transfer, referral, or continuation of services in relation to the clients' needs and preferences.
(f) Social workers who are leaving an employment setting should inform clients of appropriate options for the continuation of services and of the benefits and risks of the options.

2. Social Workers' Ethical Responsibilities to Colleagues

2.01 Respect

  (a) Social workers should treat colleagues with respect and should represent accurately and fairly the qualifications, views, and obligations of colleagues.
  (b) Social workers should avoid unwarranted negative criticism of colleagues in communications with clients or with other professionals. Unwarranted negative criticism may include demeaning comments that refer to colleagues' level of competence or to individuals' attributes such as race, ethnicity, national origin, color, sex, sexual orientation, age, marital status, political belief, religion, and mental or physical disability.
  (c) Social workers should cooperate with social work colleagues and with colleagues of other professions when such cooperation serves the well-being of clients.

2.02 Confidentiality   Social workers should respect confidential information shared by colleagues in the course of their professional relationships and transactions. Social workers should ensure that such colleagues understand social workers' obligation to respect confidentiality and any exceptions related to it.

2.03 Interdisciplinary Collaboration

  (a) Social workers who are members of an interdisciplinary team should participate in and contribute to decisions that affect the well-being of clients by drawing on the perspectives, values, and experiences of the social work profession. Professional and ethical obligations of the interdisciplinary team as a whole and of its individual members should be clearly established.
  (b) Social workers for whom a team decision raises ethical concerns should attempt to resolve the disagreement through appropriate channels. If the disagreement cannot be resolved, social workers should pursue other avenues to address their concerns consistent with client well-being.

2.04 Disputes Involving Colleagues

  (a) Social workers should not take advantage of a dispute between a colleague and an employer to obtain a position or otherwise advance the social workers' own interests.
  (b) Social workers should not exploit clients in disputes with colleagues or engage clients in any inappropriate discussion of conflicts between social workers and their colleagues.

2.05 Consultation

(a) Social workers should seek the advice and counsel of colleagues whenever such consultation is in the best interests of clients.

(b) Social workers should keep themselves informed about colleagues' areas of expertise and competencies. Social workers should seek consultation only from colleagues who have demonstrated knowledge, expertise, and competence related to the subject of the consultation.

(c) When consulting with colleagues about clients, social workers should disclose the least amount of information necessary to achieve the purposes of the consultation.

2.06 Referral for Services

(a) Social workers should refer clients to other professionals when the other professionals' specialized knowledge or expertise is needed to serve clients fully or when social workers believe that they are not being effective or making reasonable progress with clients and that additional service is required.

(b) Social workers who refer clients to other professionals should take appropriate steps to facilitate an orderly transfer of responsibility. Social workers who refer clients to other professionals should disclose, with clients' consent, all pertinent information to the new service providers.

(c) Social workers are prohibited from giving or receiving payment for a referral when no professional service is provided by the referring social worker.

2.07 Sexual Relationships

(a) Social workers who function as supervisors or educators should not engage in sexual activities or contact with supervisees, students, trainees, or other colleagues over whom they exercise professional authority.

(b) Social workers should avoid engaging in sexual relationships with colleagues when there is potential for a conflict of interest. Social workers who become involved in, or anticipate becoming involved in, a sexual relationship with a colleague have a duty to transfer professional responsibilities, when necessary, to avoid a conflict of interest.

2.08 Sexual Harassment

Social workers should not sexually harass supervisees, students, trainees, or colleagues. Sexual harassment includes sexual advances, sexual solicitation, requests for sexual favors, and other verbal or physical conduct of a sexual nature.

2.09 Impairment of Colleagues

(a) Social workers who have direct knowledge of a social work colleague's impairment that is due to personal problems, psychosocial distress, substance abuse, or mental health difficulties and that interferes with practice effectiveness should consult with that colleague when feasible and assist the colleague in taking remedial action.

(b) Social workers who believe that a social work colleague's impairment interferes with practice effectiveness and that the colleague has not taken adequate steps to address the impairment should take action through appropriate channels established by employers, agencies, NASW, licensing and regulatory bodies, and other professional organizations.

2.10 Incompetence of Colleagues

(a) Social workers who have direct knowledge of a social work colleague's incompetence should consult with that colleague when feasible and assist the colleague in taking remedial action.

(b) Social workers who believe that a social work colleague is incompetent and has not taken adequate steps to address the incompetence should take action through appropriate channels established by employers, agencies, NASW, licensing and regulatory bodies, and other professional organizations.

2.11 Unethical Conduct of Colleagues

(a) Social workers should take adequate measures to discourage, prevent, expose, and correct the unethical conduct of colleagues.

(b) Social workers should be knowledgeable about established policies and procedures for handling concerns about colleagues' unethical behavior. Social workers should be familiar with national, state, and local procedures for handling ethics complaints. These include policies and procedures created by NASW, licensing and regulatory bodies, employers, agencies, and other professional organizations.

(c) Social workers who believe that a colleague has acted unethically should seek resolution by discussing their concerns with the colleague when feasible and when such discussion is likely to be productive.

(d) When necessary, social workers who believe that a colleague has acted unethically should take action through appropriate formal channels (such as contacting a state licensing board or regulatory body, an NASW committee on inquiry, or other professional ethics committees).

(e) Social workers should defend and assist colleagues who are unjustly charged with unethical conduct.

3. Social Workers' Ethical Responsibilities in Practice Settings

3.01 Supervision and Consultation

(a) Social workers who provide supervision or consultation should have the necessary knowledge and skill to supervise or consult appropriately and should do so only within their areas of knowledge and competence.

(b) Social workers who provide supervision or consultation are responsible for setting clear, appropriate, and culturally sensitive boundaries.

(c) Social workers should not engage in any dual or multiple relationships with supervisees in which there is a risk of exploitation of or potential harm to the supervisee.

(d) Social workers who provide supervision should evaluate supervisees' performance in a manner that is fair and respectful.

3.02 Education and Training

(a) Social workers who function as educators, field instructors for students, or trainers should provide instruction only within their areas of knowledge and competence and should provide instruction based on the most current information and knowledge available in the profession.

(b) Social workers who function as educators or field instructors for students should evaluate students' performance in a manner that is fair and respectful.

(c) Social workers who function as educators or field instructors for students should take reasonable steps to ensure that clients are routinely informed when services are being provided by students.

(d) Social workers who function as educators or field instructors for students should not engage in any dual or multiple relationships with students in which there is a risk of exploitation or potential harm to the student. Social work educators and field instructors are responsible for setting clear, appropriate, and culturally sensitive boundaries.

3.03 Performance Evaluation
Social workers who have responsibility for evaluating the performance of others should fulfill such responsibility in a fair and considerate manner and on the basis of clearly stated criteria.

3.04 Client Records

(a) Social workers should take reasonable steps to ensure that documentation in records is accurate and reflects the services provided.

(b) Social workers should include sufficient and timely documentation in records to facilitate the delivery of services and to ensure continuity of services provided to clients in the future.

(c) Social workers' documentation should protect clients' privacy to the extent that is possible and appropriate and should include only information that is directly relevant to the delivery of services.

(d) Social workers should store records following the termination of services to ensure reasonable future access. Records should be maintained for the number of years required by state statutes or relevant contracts.

3.05 Billing   Social workers should establish and maintain billing practices that accurately reflect the nature and extent of services provided and that identify who provided the service in the practice setting.

3.06 Client Transfer

(a) When an individual who is receiving services from another agency or colleague contacts a social worker for services, the social worker should carefully consider the client's needs before agreeing to provide services. To minimize possible confusion and conflict, social workers should discuss with potential clients the nature of the clients' current relationship with other service providers and the implications, including possible benefits or risks, of entering into a relationship with a new service provider.

(b) If a new client has been served by another agency or colleague, social workers should discuss with the client whether consultation with the previous service provider is in the client's best interest.

3.07 Administration

(a) Social work administrators should advocate within and outside their agencies for adequate resources to meet clients' needs.

(b) Social workers should advocate for resource allocation procedures that are open and fair. When not all clients' needs can be met, an allocation procedure should be developed that is nondiscriminatory and based on appropriate and consistently applied principles.

(c) Social workers who are administrators should take reasonable steps to ensure that adequate agency or organizational resources are available to provide appropriate staff supervision.

(d) Social work administrators should take reasonable steps to ensure that the working environment for which they are responsible is consistent with and encourages compliance with the NASW Code of Ethics. Social work administrators should take reasonable steps to eliminate any conditions in their organizations that violate, interfere with, or discourage compliance with the Code.

3.08 Continuing Education and Staff Development Social work administrators and supervisors should take reasonable steps to provide or arrange for continuing education and staff development for all staff for whom they are responsible. Continuing education and staff development should address current knowledge and emerging developments related to social work practice and ethics.

3.09 Commitments to Employers
  (a) Social workers generally should adhere to commitments made to employers and employing organizations.
  (b) Social workers should work to improve employing agencies' policies and procedures and the efficiency and effectiveness of their services.
  (c) Social workers should take reasonable steps to ensure that employers are aware of social workers' ethical obligations as set forth in the NASW Code of Ethics and of the implications of those obligations for social work practice.
  (d) Social workers should not allow an employing organization's policies, procedures, regulations, or administrative orders to interfere with their ethical practice of social work. Social workers should take reasonable steps to ensure that their employing organizations' practices are consistent with the NASW Code of Ethics.
  (e) Social workers should act to prevent and eliminate discrimination in the employing organization's work assignments and in its employment policies and practices.
  (f) Social workers should accept employment or arrange student field placements only in organizations that exercise fair personnel practices.
  (g) Social workers should be diligent stewards of the resources of their employing organizations, wisely conserving funds where appropriate and never misappropriating funds or using them for unintended purposes.

3.10 Labor-Management Disputes
  (a) Social workers may engage in organized action, including the formation of and participation in labor unions, to improve services to clients and working conditions.
  (b) The actions of social workers who are involved in labor-management disputes, job actions, or labor strikes should be guided by the profession's values, ethical principles, and ethical standards. Reasonable differences of opinion exist among social workers concerning their primary obligation as professionals during an actual or threatened

labor strike or job action. Social workers should carefully examine relevant issues and their possible impact on clients before deciding on a course of action.

4. Social Workers' Ethical Responsibilities as Professionals

4.01 Competence

(a) Social workers should accept responsibility or employment only on the basis of existing competence or the intention to acquire the necessary competence.

(b) Social workers should strive to become and remain proficient in professional practice and the performance of professional functions. Social workers should critically examine and keep current with emerging knowledge relevant to social work. Social workers should routinely review the professional literature and participate in continuing education relevant to social work practice and social work ethics.

(c) Social workers should base practice on recognized knowledge, including empirically based knowledge, relevant to social work and social work ethics.

4.02 Discrimination   Social workers should not practice, condone, facilitate, or collaborate with any form of discrimination on the basis of race, ethnicity, national origin, color, sex, sexual orientation, age, marital status, political belief, religion, or mental or physical disability.

4.03 Private Conduct   Social workers should not permit their private conduct to interfere with their ability to fulfill their professional responsibilities.

4.04 Dishonesty, Fraud, and Deception   Social workers should not participate in, condone, or be associated with dishonesty, fraud, or deception.

4.05 Impairment

(a) Social workers should not allow their own personal problems, psychosocial distress, legal problems, substance abuse, or mental health difficulties to interfere with their professional judgment and performance or to jeopardize the best interests of people for whom they have a professional responsibility.

(b) Social workers whose personal problems, psychosocial distress, legal problems, substance abuse, or mental health difficulties interfere with their professional judgment and performance should immediately seek consultation and take appropriate remedial action by seek-

ing professional help, making adjustments in workload, terminating practice, or taking any other steps necessary to protect clients and others.

4.06 Misrepresentation
  (a) Social workers should make clear distinctions between statements made and actions engaged in as a private individual and as a representative of the social work profession, a professional social work organization, or the social worker's employing agency.
  (b) Social workers who speak on behalf of professional social work organizations should accurately represent the official and authorized positions of the organizations.
  (c) Social workers should ensure that their representations to clients, agencies, and the public of professional qualifications, credentials, education, competence, affiliations, services provided, or results to be achieved are accurate. Social workers should claim only those relevant professional credentials they actually possess and take steps to correct any inaccuracies or misrepresentations of their credentials by others.

4.07 Solicitations
  (a) Social workers should not engage in uninvited solicitation of potential clients who, because of their circumstances, are vulnerable to undue influence, manipulation, or coercion.
  (b) Social workers should not engage in solicitation of testimonial endorsements (including solicitation of consent to use a client's prior statement as a testimonial endorsement) from current clients or from other people who, because of their particular circumstances, are vulnerable to undue influence.

4.08 Acknowledging Credit
  (a) Social workers should take responsibility and credit, including authorship credit, only for work they have actually performed and to which they have contributed.
  (b) Social workers should honestly acknowledge the work of and the contributions made by others.

5. Social Workers' Ethical Responsibilities to the Social Work Profession
5.01 Integrity of the Profession
  (a) Social workers should work toward the maintenance and promotion of high standards of practice.

(b) Social workers should uphold and advance the values, ethics, knowledge, and mission of the profession. Social workers should protect, enhance, and improve the integrity of the profession through appropriate study and research, active discussion, and responsible criticism of the profession.

(c) Social workers should contribute time and professional expertise to activities that promote respect for the value, integrity, and competence of the social work profession. These activities may include teaching, research, consultation, service, legislative testimony, presentations in the community, and participation in their professional organizations.

(d) Social workers should contribute to the knowledge base of social work and share with colleagues their knowledge related to practice, research, and ethics. Social workers should seek to contribute to the profession's literature and to share their knowledge at professional meetings and conferences.

(e) Social workers should act to prevent the unauthorized and unqualified practice of social work.

5.02 Evaluation and Research

(a) Social workers should monitor and evaluate policies, the implementation of programs, and practice interventions.

(b) Social workers should promote and facilitate evaluation and research to contribute to the development of knowledge.

(c) Social workers should critically examine and keep current with emerging knowledge relevant to social work and fully use evaluation and research evidence in their professional practice.

(d) Social workers engaged in evaluation or research should carefully consider possible consequences and should follow guidelines developed for the protection of evaluation and research participants. Appropriate institutional review boards should be consulted.

(e) Social workers engaged in evaluation or research should obtain voluntary and written informed consent from participants, when appropriate, without any implied or actual deprivation or penalty for refusal to participate; without undue inducement to participate; and with due regard for participants' well-being, privacy, and dignity. Informed consent should include information about the nature, extent, and duration of the participation requested and disclosure of the risks and benefits of participation in the research.

(f) When evaluation or research participants are incapable of giving informed consent, social workers should provide an appropriate explanation to the participants, obtain the participants' assent to the extent they are able, and obtain written consent from an appropriate proxy.

(g) Social workers should never design or conduct evaluation or research that does not use consent procedures, such as certain forms of naturalistic observation and archival research, unless rigorous and responsible review of the research has found it to be justified because of its prospective scientific, educational, or applied value and unless equally effective alternative procedures that do not involve waiver of consent are not feasible.

(h) Social workers should inform participants of their right to withdraw from evaluation and research at any time without penalty.

(i) Social workers should take appropriate steps to ensure that participants in evaluation and research have access to appropriate supportive services.

(j) Social workers engaged in evaluation or research should protect participants from unwarranted physical or mental distress, harm, danger, or deprivation.

(k) Social workers engaged in the evaluation of services should discuss collected information only for professional purposes and only with people professionally concerned with this information.

(l) Social workers engaged in evaluation or research should ensure the anonymity or confidentiality of participants and of the data obtained from them. Social workers should inform participants of any limits of confidentiality, the measures that will be taken to ensure confidentiality, and when any records containing research data will be destroyed.

(m) Social workers who report evaluation and research results should protect participants' confidentiality by omitting identifying information unless proper consent has been obtained authorizing disclosure.

(n) Social workers should report evaluation and research findings accurately. They should not fabricate or falsify results and should take steps to correct any errors later found in published data using standard publication methods.

(o) Social workers engaged in evaluation or research should be alert to and avoid conflicts of interest and dual relationships with participants, should inform participants when a real or potential conflict of interest arises, and should take steps to resolve the issue in a manner that makes participants' interests primary.

(p) Social workers should educate themselves, their students, and their colleagues about responsible research practices.

6. Social Workers' Ethical Responsibilities to the Broader Society

6.01 Social Welfare   Social workers should promote the general welfare of society, from local to global levels, and the development of people, their communities, and their environments. Social workers should advocate for living conditions conducive to the fulfillment of basic human needs and should promote social, economic, political, and cultural values and institutions that are compatible with the realization of social justice.

6.02 Public Participation   Social workers should facilitate informed participation by the public in shaping social policies and institutions.

6.03 Public Emergencies   Social workers should provide appropriate professional services in public emergencies to the greatest extent possible.

6.04 Social and Political Action
  (a) Social workers should engage in social and political action that seeks to ensure that all people have equal access to the resources, employment, services, and opportunities they require to meet their basic human needs and to develop fully. Social workers should be aware of the impact of the political arena on practice and should advocate for changes in policy and legislation to improve social conditions in order to meet basic human needs and promote social justice.
  (b) Social workers should act to expand choice and opportunity for all people, with special regard for vulnerable, disadvantaged, oppressed, and exploited people and groups.
  (c) Social workers should promote conditions that encourage respect for cultural and social diversity within the United States and globally. Social workers should promote policies and practices that demonstrate respect for difference, support the expansion of cultural knowledge and resources, advocate for programs and institutions that demonstrate cultural competence, and promote policies that safeguard the rights of and confirm equity and social justice for all people.
  (d) Social workers should act to prevent and eliminate domination of, exploitation of, and discrimination against any person, group, or class on the basis of race, ethnicity, national origin, color, sex, sexual orientation, age, marital status, political belief, religion, or mental or physical disability.

APA Ethical Principles

ETHICAL PRINCIPLES OF PSYCHOLOGISTS AND CODE OF CONDUCT

Effective date June 1, 2003.

1.08 Unfair Discrimination Against Complainants and Respondents
2. Competence
    2.01 Boundaries of Competence
    2.02 Providing Services in Emergencies
    2.03 Maintaining Competence
    2.04 Bases for Scientific and Professional Judgments
    2.05 Delegation of Work to Others
    2.06 Personal Problems and Conflicts
3. Human Relations
    3.01 Unfair Discrimination
    3.02 Sexual Harassment
    3.03 Other Harassment
    3.04 Avoiding Harm
    3.05 Multiple Relationships
    3.06 Conflict of Interest
    3.07 Third-Party Requests for Services
    3.08 Exploitative Relationships
    3.09 Cooperation With Other Professionals
    3.10 Informed Consent
    3.11 Psychological Services Delivered To or Through Organizations
    3.12 Interruption of Psychological Services
4. Privacy And Confidentiality
    4.01 Maintaining Confidentiality
    4.02 Discussing the Limits of Confidentiality
    4.03 Recording
    4.04 Minimizing Intrusions on Privacy
    4.05 Disclosures
    4.06 Consultations
    4.07 Use of Confidential Information for Didactic or Other Purposes
5. Advertising and Other Public Statements
    5.01 Avoidance of False or Deceptive Statements
    5.02 Statements by Others
    5.03 Descriptions of Workshops and Non-Degree-Granting Educational Programs
    5.04 Media Presentations
    5.05 Testimonials
    5.06 In-Person Solicitation
6. Record Keeping and Fees
    6.01 Documentation of Professional and Scientific Work and Maintenance of Records

INTRODUCTION AND APPLICABILITY

The American Psychological Association's (APA's) Ethical Principles of Psychologists and Code of Conduct (hereinafter referred to as the Ethics Code) consists of an Introduction, a Preamble, five General Principles (A–E), and specific Ethical Standards. The Introduction discusses the intent, organization, procedural considerations, and scope of application of the Ethics Code. The Preamble and General Principles are aspirational goals to guide psychologists toward the highest ideals of psychology. Although the Preamble and General Principles are not themselves enforceable rules, they should be considered by psychologists in arriving at an ethical course of action. The Ethical Standards set forth enforceable rules for conduct as psychologists. Most of the Ethical Standards are written broadly, in order to apply to psychologists in varied roles, although the application of an Ethical Standard may vary depending on the context. The Ethical Standards are not exhaustive. The fact that a given conduct is not specifically addressed by an Ethical Standard does not mean that it is necessarily either ethical or unethical.

This Ethics Code applies only to psychologists' activities that are part of their scientific, educational, or professional roles as psychologists. Areas covered include but are not limited to the clinical, counseling, and school practice of psychology; research; teaching; supervision of trainees; public service; policy development; social intervention; development of assessment instruments; conducting assessments; educational counseling; organizational consulting; forensic activities; program design and evaluation; and administration. This Ethics Code applies to these activities across a variety of contexts, such as in person, postal, telephone, internet, and other electronic transmissions. These activities shall be distinguished from the purely private conduct of psychologists, which is not within the purview of the Ethics Code.

Membership in the APA commits members and student affiliates to comply with the standards of the APA Ethics Code and to the rules and procedures used to enforce them. Lack of awareness or misunderstanding of an Ethical Standard is not itself a defense to a charge of unethical conduct.

The procedures for filing, investigating, and resolving complaints of unethical conduct are described in the current Rules and Procedures of the APA Ethics Committee. The APA may impose sanctions on its members for violations of the standards of the Ethics Code, including termination of APA membership, and may notify other bodies and individuals of its actions. Actions that violate the standards of the Ethics Code may also lead to the imposition of sanctions on psychologists or students whether or not they are APA members by bodies other than the APA, including state psychological associations, other professional groups, psychology boards, other state or federal agencies, and payors for health services. In addition, the APA may take action against a member after his or her conviction of a felony, expulsion or suspension from an affiliated state psychological association, or suspension or loss of licensure. When the sanction to be imposed by the APA is less than expulsion, the 2001 Rules and Procedures do not guarantee an opportunity for an in-person hearing, but generally provide that complaints will be resolved only on the basis of a submitted record.

The Ethics Code is intended to provide guidance for psychologists and standards of professional conduct that can be applied by the APA and by other bodies that choose to adopt them. The Ethics Code is not intended to be a basis of civil liability. Whether a psychologist has violated the Ethics Code standards does not by itself determine whether the psychologist is legally liable in a court action, whether a contract is enforceable, or whether other legal consequences occur.

The modifiers used in some of the standards of this Ethics Code (e.g., *reasonably, appropriate, potentially*) are included in the standards when they would (1) allow professional judgment on the part of psychologists, (2) eliminate injustice or inequality that would occur without the modifier, (3) ensure applicability across the broad range of activities conducted by psychologists, or (4) guard against a set of rigid rules that might be quickly outdated. As used in this Ethics Code, the term *reasonable* means the prevailing professional judgment of psychologists engaged in similar activities in similar circumstances, given the knowledge the psychologist had or should have had at the time.

In the process of making decisions regarding their professional behavior, psychologists must consider this Ethics Code in addition to applicable laws and psychology board regulations. In applying the Ethics Code to their professional work, psychologists may consider other materials and guidelines that have been adopted or endorsed by scientific and professional psychological organizations and the dictates of their own conscience, as well as consult with others within the field. If this Ethics Code establishes a higher standard of conduct than is required by law, psychologists must meet the higher ethical standard. If psychologists' ethical responsibilities conflict with law, regulations, or other governing legal authority, psychologists make known their commitment to this Ethics Code and take steps to resolve the conflict in a responsible manner. If the conflict is unresolvable via such means, psychologists may adhere to the requirements of the law, regulations, or other governing authority in keeping with basic principles of human rights.

PREAMBLE

Psychologists are committed to increasing scientific and professional knowledge of behavior and people's understanding of themselves and others and to the use of such knowledge to improve the condition of individuals, organizations, and society. Psychologists respect and protect civil and human rights and the central importance of freedom of inquiry and expression in research, teaching, and publication. They strive to help the public in developing informed judgments and choices concerning human behavior. In doing so, they perform many roles, such as researcher, educator, diagnostician, therapist, supervisor, consultant, administrator, social interventionist, and expert witness. This Ethics Code provides a common set of principles and standards upon which psychologists build their professional and scientific work.

This Ethics Code is intended to provide specific standards to cover most situations encountered by psychologists. It has as its goals the welfare and protection of the individuals and groups with whom psychologists work and the education of members, students, and the public regarding ethical standards of the discipline.

The development of a dynamic set of ethical standards for psychologists' work-related conduct requires a personal commitment and lifelong effort to act ethically; to encourage ethical behavior by students, supervisees, employees, and colleagues; and to consult with others concerning ethical problems.

GENERAL PRINCIPLES

This section consists of General Principles. General Principles, as opposed to Ethical Standards, are aspirational in nature. Their intent is to guide and inspire psychologists toward the very highest ethical ideals of the profession. General Principles, in contrast to Ethical Standards, do not represent obligations and should not form the basis for imposing sanctions. Relying upon General Principles for either of these reasons distorts both their meaning and purpose.

Principle A: Beneficence and Nonmaleficence
Psychologists strive to benefit those with whom they work and take care to do no harm. In their professional actions, psychologists seek to safeguard the welfare and rights of those with whom they interact professionally and other affected persons, and the welfare of animal subjects of research. When conflicts occur among psychologists' obligations or concerns, they attempt to resolve these conflicts in a responsible fashion that avoids or minimizes harm. Because psychologists' scientific and professional judgments and actions may affect the lives of others, they are alert to and guard against personal, financial, social, organizational, or political factors that might lead to misuse of their influence. Psychologists strive to be aware of the possible effect of their own physical and mental health on their ability to help those with whom they work.

Principle B: Fidelity and Responsibility
Psychologists establish relationships of trust with those with whom they work. They are aware of their professional and scientific responsibilities to society and to the specific communities in which they work. Psychologists uphold professional standards of conduct, clarify their professional roles and obligations, accept appropriate responsibility for their behavior, and seek to manage conflicts of interest that could lead to exploitation or harm. Psychologists consult with, refer to, or cooperate with other professionals and institutions to the extent needed to serve the best interests of those with whom they work. They are concerned about the ethical compliance of their colleagues' scientific and professional conduct. Psychologists strive to contribute a portion of their professional time for little or no compensation or personal advantage.

Principle C: Integrity
Psychologists seek to promote accuracy, honesty, and truthfulness in the science, teaching, and practice of psychology. In these activities psychologists do not steal, cheat, or engage in fraud, subterfuge, or intentional misrepresentation of fact. Psychologists strive to keep their promises and to avoid unwise or unclear commitments. In situations in which deception may be ethically justifiable to maximize benefits and minimize harm,

psychologists have a serious obligation to consider the need for, the possible consequences of, and their responsibility to correct any resulting mistrust or other harmful effects that arise from the use of such techniques.

Principle D: Justice

Psychologists recognize that fairness and justice entitle all persons to access to and benefit from the contributions of psychology and to equal quality in the processes, procedures, and services being conducted by psychologists. Psychologists exercise reasonable judgment and take precautions to ensure that their potential biases, the boundaries of their competence, and the limitations of their expertise do not lead to or condone unjust practices.

Principle E: Respect for People's Rights and Dignity

Psychologists respect the dignity and worth of all people, and the rights of individuals to privacy, confidentiality, and self-determination. Psychologists are aware that special safeguards may be necessary to protect the rights and welfare of persons or communities whose vulnerabilities impair autonomous decision making. Psychologists are aware of and respect cultural, individual, and role differences, including those based on age, gender, gender identity, race, ethnicity, culture, national origin, religion, sexual orientation, disability, language, and socioeconomic status and consider these factors when working with members of such groups. Psychologists try to eliminate the effect on their work of biases based on those factors, and they do not knowingly participate in or condone activities of others based upon such prejudices.

ETHICAL STANDARDS

1. Resolving Ethical Issues

1.01 Misuse of Psychologists' Work　If psychologists learn of misuse or misrepresentation of their work, they take reasonable steps to correct or minimize the misuse or misrepresentation.

1.02 Conflicts Between Ethics and Law, Regulations, or Other Governing Legal Authority　If psychologists' ethical responsibilities conflict with law, regulations, or other governing legal authority, psychologists make known their commitment to the Ethics Code and take steps to resolve the conflict. If the conflict is unresolvable via such means, psychologists may adhere to the requirements of the law, regulations, or other governing legal authority.

1.03 Conflicts Between Ethics and Organizational Demands　If the demands of an organization with which psychologists are affiliated or for whom they are working conflict with this Ethics Code, psychologists clarify the nature of the conflict, make known their commitment to the Ethics Code, and to the extent feasible, resolve the conflict in a way that permits adherence to the Ethics Code.

1.04 Informal Resolution of Ethical Violations When psychologists believe that there may have been an ethical violation by another psychologist, they attempt to resolve the issue by bringing it to the attention of that individual, if an informal resolution appears appropriate and the intervention does not violate any confidentiality rights that may be involved. (See also Standards 1.02, Conflicts Between Ethics and Law, Regulations, or Other Governing Legal Authority, and 1.03, Conflicts Between Ethics and Organizational Demands.)

1.05 Reporting Ethical Violations If an apparent ethical violation has substantially harmed or is likely to substantially harm a person or organization and is not appropriate for informal resolution under Standard 1.04, Informal Resolution of Ethical Violations, or is not resolved properly in that fashion, psychologists take further action appropriate to the situation. Such action might include referral to state or national committees on professional ethics, to state licensing boards, or to the appropriate institutional authorities. This standard does not apply when an intervention would violate confidentiality rights or when psychologists have been retained to review the work of another psychologist whose professional conduct is in question. (See also Standard 1.02, Conflicts Between Ethics and Law, Regulations, or Other Governing Legal Authority.)

1.06 Cooperating With Ethics Committees Psychologists cooperate in ethics investigations, proceedings, and resulting requirements of the APA or any affiliated state psychological association to which they belong. In doing so, they address any confidentiality issues. Failure to cooperate is itself an ethics violation. However, making a request for deferment of adjudication of an ethics complaint pending the outcome of litigation does not alone constitute noncooperation.

1.07 Improper Complaints Psychologists do not file or encourage the filing of ethics complaints that are made with reckless disregard for or willful ignorance of facts that would disprove the allegation.

1.08 Unfair Discrimination Against Complainants and Respondents Psychologists do not deny persons employment, advancement, admissions to academic or other programs, tenure, or promotion, based solely upon their having made or their being the subject of an ethics complaint. This does not preclude taking action based upon the outcome of such proceedings or considering other appropriate information.

2. Competence
2.01 Boundaries of Competence

(a) Psychologists provide services, teach, and conduct research with populations and in areas only within the boundaries of their competence, based on their education, training, supervised experience, consultation, study, or professional experience.

(b) Where scientific or professional knowledge in the discipline of psychology establishes that an understanding of factors associated with age, gender, gender identity, race, ethnicity, culture, national origin, religion, sexual orientation, disability, language, or socioeconomic status is essential for effective implementation of their services or research, psychologists have or obtain the training, experience, consultation, or supervision necessary to ensure the competence of their services, or they make appropriate referrals, except as provided in Standard 2.02, Providing Services in Emergencies.

(c) Psychologists planning to provide services, teach, or conduct research involving populations, areas, techniques, or technologies new to them undertake relevant education, training, supervised experience, consultation, or study.

(d) When psychologists are asked to provide services to individuals for whom appropriate mental health services are not available and for which psychologists have not obtained the competence necessary, psychologists with closely related prior training or experience may provide such services in order to ensure that services are not denied if they make a reasonable effort to obtain the competence required by using relevant research, training, consultation, or study.

(e) In those emerging areas in which generally recognized standards for preparatory training do not yet exist, psychologists nevertheless take reasonable steps to ensure the competence of their work and to protect clients/patients, students, supervisees, research participants, organizational clients, and others from harm.

(f) When assuming forensic roles, psychologists are or become reasonably familiar with the judicial or administrative rules governing their roles.

2.02 Providing Services in Emergencies
In emergencies, when psychologists provide services to individuals for whom other mental health services are not available and for which psychologists have not obtained the neces-

sary training, psychologists may provide such services in order to ensure that services are not denied. The services are discontinued as soon as the emergency has ended or appropriate services are available.

2.03 Maintaining Competence   Psychologists undertake ongoing efforts to develop and maintain their competence.

2.04 Bases for Scientific and Professional Judgments   Psychologists' work is based upon established scientific and professional knowledge of the discipline. (See also Standards 2.01e, Boundaries of Competence, and 10.01b, Informed Consent to Therapy.)

2.05 Delegation of Work to Others   Psychologists who delegate work to employees, supervisees, or research or teaching assistants or who use the services of others, such as interpreters, take reasonable steps to (1) avoid delegating such work to persons who have a multiple relationship with those being served that would likely lead to exploitation or loss of objectivity; (2) authorize only those responsibilities that such persons can be expected to perform competently on the basis of their education, training, or experience, either independently or with the level of supervision being provided; and (3) see that such persons perform these services competently. (See also Standards 2.02, Providing Services in Emergencies; 3.05, Multiple Relationships; 4.01, Maintaining Confidentiality; 9.01, Bases for Assessments; 9.02, Use of Assessments; 9.03, Informed Consent in Assessments; and 9.07, Assessment by Unqualified Persons.)

2.06 Personal Problems and Conflicts
   (a) Psychologists refrain from initiating an activity when they know or should know that there is a substantial likelihood that their personal problems will prevent them from performing their work-related activities in a competent manner.
   (b) When psychologists become aware of personal problems that may interfere with their performing work-related duties adequately, they take appropriate measures, such as obtaining professional consultation or assistance, and determine whether they should limit, suspend, or terminate their work-related duties. (See also Standard 10.10, Terminating Therapy.)

3. Human Relations
3.01 Unfair Discrimination   In their work-related activities, psychologists do not engage in unfair discrimination based on age, gender, gender identity,

race, ethnicity, culture, national origin, religion, sexual orientation, disability, socioeconomic status, or any basis proscribed by law.

3.02 Sexual Harassment Psychologists do not engage in sexual harassment. Sexual harassment is sexual solicitation, physical advances, or verbal or nonverbal conduct that is sexual in nature, that occurs in connection with the psychologist's activities or roles as a psychologist, and that either (1) is unwelcome, is offensive, or creates a hostile workplace or educational environment, and the psychologist knows or is told this or (2) is sufficiently severe or intense to be abusive to a reasonable person in the context. Sexual harassment can consist of a single intense or severe act or of multiple persistent or pervasive acts. (See also Standard 1.08, Unfair Discrimination Against Complainants and Respondents.)

3.03 Other Harassment Psychologists do not knowingly engage in behavior that is harassing or demeaning to persons with whom they interact in their work based on factors such as those persons' age, gender, gender identity, race, ethnicity, culture, national origin, religion, sexual orientation, disability, language, or socioeconomic status.

3.04 Avoiding Harm Psychologists take reasonable steps to avoid harming their clients/patients, students, supervisees, research participants, organizational clients, and others with whom they work, and to minimize harm where it is foreseeable and unavoidable.

3.05 Multiple Relationships
   (a) A multiple relationship occurs when a psychologist is in a professional role with a person and (1) at the same time is in another role with the same person, (2) at the same time is in a relationship with a person closely associated with or related to the person with whom the psychologist has the professional relationship, or (3) promises to enter into another relationship in the future with the person or a person closely associated with or related to the person.
   A psychologist refrains from entering into a multiple relationship if the multiple relationship could reasonably be expected to impair the psychologist's objectivity, competence, or effectiveness in performing his or her functions as a psychologist, or otherwise risks exploitation or harm to the person with whom the professional relationship exists.
   Multiple relationships that would not reasonably be expected to cause impairment or risk exploitation or harm are not unethical.
   (b) If a psychologist finds that, due to unforeseen factors, a potentially harmful multiple relationship has arisen, the psychologist takes rea-

sonable steps to resolve it with due regard for the best interests of the affected person and maximal compliance with the Ethics Code.

(c)   When psychologists are required by law, institutional policy, or extraordinary circumstances to serve in more than one role in judicial or administrative proceedings, at the outset they clarify role expectations and the extent of confidentiality and thereafter as changes occur. (See also Standards 3.04, Avoiding Harm, and 3.07, Third-Party Requests for Services.)

3.06 Conflict of Interest   Psychologists refrain from taking on a professional role when personal, scientific, professional, legal, financial, or other interests or relationships could reasonably be expected to (1) impair their objectivity, competence, or effectiveness in performing their functions as psychologists or (2) expose the person or organization with whom the professional relationship exists to harm or exploitation.

3.07 Third-Party Requests for Services   When psychologists agree to provide services to a person or entity at the request of a third party, psychologists attempt to clarify at the outset of the service the nature of the relationship with all individuals or organizations involved. This clarification includes the role of the psychologist (e.g., therapist, consultant, diagnostician, or expert witness), an identification of who is the client, the probable uses of the services provided or the information obtained, and the fact that there may be limits to confidentiality. (See also Standards 3.05, Multiple Relationships, and 4.02, Discussing the Limits of Confidentiality.)

3.08 Exploitative Relationships   Psychologists do not exploit persons over whom they have supervisory, evaluative, or other authority such as clients/patients, students, supervisees, research participants, and employees. (See also Standards 3.05, Multiple Relationships; 6.04, Fees and Financial Arrangements; 6.05, Barter With Clients/Patients; 7.07, Sexual Relationships With Students and Supervisees; 10.05, Sexual Intimacies With Current Therapy Clients/Patients; 10.06, Sexual Intimacies With Relatives or Significant Others of Current Therapy Clients/Patients; 10.07, Therapy With Former Sexual Partners; and 10.08, Sexual Intimacies With Former Therapy Clients/Patients.)

3.09 Cooperation With Other Professionals   When indicated and professionally appropriate, psychologists cooperate with other professionals in order to serve their clients/patients effectively and appropriately. (See also Standard 4.05, Disclosures.)

3.10 Informed Consent

(a) When psychologists conduct research or provide assessment, therapy, counseling, or consulting services in person or via electronic transmission or other forms of communication, they obtain the informed consent of the individual or individuals using language that is reasonably understandable to that person or persons except when conducting such activities without consent is mandated by law or governmental regulation or as otherwise provided in this Ethics Code. (See also Standards 8.02, Informed Consent to Research; 9.03, Informed Consent in Assessments; and 10.01, Informed Consent to Therapy.)

(b) For persons who are legally incapable of giving informed consent, psychologists nevertheless (1) provide an appropriate explanation, (2) seek the individual's assent, (3) consider such persons' preferences and best interests, and (4) obtain appropriate permission from a legally authorized person, if such substitute consent is permitted or required by law. When consent by a legally authorized person is not permitted or required by law, psychologists take reasonable steps to protect the individual's rights and welfare.

(c) When psychological services are court ordered or otherwise mandated, psychologists inform the individual of the nature of the anticipated services, including whether the services are court ordered or mandated and any limits of confidentiality, before proceeding.

(d) Psychologists appropriately document written or oral consent, permission, and assent. (See also Standards 8.02, Informed Consent to Research; 9.03, Informed Consent in Assessments; and 10.01, Informed Consent to Therapy.)

3.11 Psychological Services Delivered To or Through Organizations

(a) Psychologists delivering services to or through organizations provide information beforehand to clients and when appropriate those directly affected by the services about (1) the nature and objectives of the services, (2) the intended recipients, (3) which of the individuals are clients, (4) the relationship the psychologist will have with each person and the organization, (5) the probable uses of services provided and information obtained, (6) who will have access to the information, and (7) limits of confidentiality. As soon as feasible, they provide information about the results and conclusions of such services to appropriate persons.

(b) If psychologists will be precluded by law or by organizational roles from providing such information to particular individuals or groups, they so inform those individuals or groups at the outset of the service.

3.12 Interruption of Psychological Services Unless otherwise covered by contract, psychologists make reasonable efforts to plan for facilitating services in the event that psychological services are interrupted by factors such as the psychologist's illness, death, unavailability, relocation, or retirement or by the client's/patient's relocation or financial limitations. (See also Standard 6.02c, Maintenance, Dissemination, and Disposal of Confidential Records of Professional and Scientific Work.)

4. Privacy And Confidentiality

4.01 Maintaining Confidentiality Psychologists have a primary obligation and take reasonable precautions to protect confidential information obtained through or stored in any medium, recognizing that the extent and limits of confidentiality may be regulated by law or established by institutional rules or professional or scientific relationship. (See also Standard 2.05, Delegation of Work to Others.)

4.02 Discussing the Limits of Confidentiality
  (a) Psychologists discuss with persons (including, to the extent feasible, persons who are legally incapable of giving informed consent and their legal representatives) and organizations with whom they establish a scientific or professional relationship (1) the relevant limits of confidentiality and (2) the foreseeable uses of the information generated through their psychological activities. (See also Standard 3.10, Informed Consent.)
  (b) Unless it is not feasible or is contraindicated, the discussion of confidentiality occurs at the outset of the relationship and thereafter as new circumstances may warrant.
  (c) Psychologists who offer services, products, or information via electronic transmission inform clients/patients of the risks to privacy and limits of confidentiality.

4.03 Recording Before recording the voices or images of individuals to whom they provide services, psychologists obtain permission from all such persons or their legal representatives. (See also Standards 8.03, Informed Consent for Recording Voices and Images in Research; 8.05, Dispensing With Informed Consent for Research; and 8.07, Deception in Research.)

4.04 Minimizing Intrusions on Privacy
  (a) Psychologists include in written and oral reports and consultations, only information germane to the purpose for which the communication is made.

(b) Psychologists discuss confidential information obtained in their work only for appropriate scientific or professional purposes and only with persons clearly concerned with such matters.

4.05 Disclosures
  (a) Psychologists may disclose confidential information with the appropriate consent of the organizational client, the individual client/patient, or another legally authorized person on behalf of the client/patient unless prohibited by law.
  (b) Psychologists disclose confidential information without the consent of the individual only as mandated by law, or where permitted by law for a valid purpose such as to (1) provide needed professional services; (2) obtain appropriate professional consultations; (3) protect the client/patient, psychologist, or others from harm; or (4) obtain payment for services from a client/patient, in which instance disclosure is limited to the minimum that is necessary to achieve the purpose. (See also Standard 6.04e, Fees and Financial Arrangements.)

4.06 Consultations   When consulting with colleagues, (1) psychologists do not disclose confidential information that reasonably could lead to the identification of a client/patient, research participant, or other person or organization with whom they have a confidential relationship unless they have obtained the prior consent of the person or organization or the disclosure cannot be avoided, and (2) they disclose information only to the extent necessary to achieve the purposes of the consultation. (See also Standard 4.01, Maintaining Confidentiality.)

4.07 Use of Confidential Information for Didactic or Other Purposes
Psychologists do not disclose in their writings, lectures, or other public media, confidential, personally identifiable information concerning their clients/patients, students, research participants, organizational clients, or other recipients of their services that they obtained during the course of their work, unless (1) they take reasonable steps to disguise the person or organization, (2) the person or organization has consented in writing, or (3) there is legal authorization for doing so.

5. Advertising and Other Public Statements
5.01 Avoidance of False or Deceptive Statements
  (a) Public statements include but are not limited to paid or unpaid advertising, product endorsements, grant applications, licensing applications, other credentialing applications, brochures, printed matter,

directory listings, personal resumes or curricula vitae, or comments for use in media such as print or electronic transmission, statements in legal proceedings, lectures and public oral presentations, and published materials. Psychologists do not knowingly make public statements that are false, deceptive, or fraudulent concerning their research, practice, or other work activities or those of persons or organizations with which they are affiliated.

(b) Psychologists do not make false, deceptive, or fraudulent statements concerning (1) their training, experience, or competence; (2) their academic degrees; (3) their credentials; (4) their institutional or association affiliations; (5) their services; (6) the scientific or clinical basis for, or results or degree of success of, their services; (7) their fees; or (8) their publications or research findings.

(c) Psychologists claim degrees as credentials for their health services only if those degrees (1) were earned from a regionally accredited educational institution or (2) were the basis for psychology licensure by the state in which they practice.

5.02 Statements by Others

(a) Psychologists who engage others to create or place public statements that promote their professional practice, products, or activities retain professional responsibility for such statements.

(b) Psychologists do not compensate employees of press, radio, television, or other communication media in return for publicity in a news item. (See also Standard 1.01, Misuse of Psychologists' Work.)

(c) A paid advertisement relating to psychologists' activities must be identified or clearly recognizable as such.

5.03 Descriptions of Workshops and Non-Degree-Granting Educational Programs   To the degree to which they exercise control, psychologists responsible for announcements, catalogs, brochures, or advertisements describing workshops, seminars, or other non-degree-granting educational programs ensure that they accurately describe the audience for which the program is intended, the educational objectives, the presenters, and the fees involved.

5.04 Media Presentations   When psychologists provide public advice or comment via print, Internet, or other electronic transmission, they take precautions to ensure that statements (1) are based on their professional knowledge, training, or experience in accord with appropriate psychological literature and practice; (2) are otherwise consistent with this Ethics Code; and (3) do not indicate that a professional relationship has been established with the recipient. (See also Standard 2.04, Bases for Scientific and Professional Judgments.)

5.05 Testimonials Psychologists do not solicit testimonials from current therapy clients/patients or other persons who because of their particular circumstances are vulnerable to undue influence.

5.06 In-Person Solicitation Psychologists do not engage, directly or through agents, in uninvited in-person solicitation of business from actual or potential therapy clients/patients or other persons who because of their particular circumstances are vulnerable to undue influence. However, this prohibition does not preclude (1) attempting to implement appropriate collateral contacts for the purpose of benefiting an already engaged therapy client/patient or (2) providing disaster or community outreach services.

6. Record Keeping and Fees

6.01 Documentation of Professional and Scientific Work and Maintenance of Records Psychologists create, and to the extent the records are under their control, maintain, disseminate, store, retain, and dispose of records and data relating to their professional and scientific work in order to (1) facilitate provision of services later by them or by other professionals, (2) allow for replication of research design and analyses, (3) meet institutional requirements, (4) ensure accuracy of billing and payments, and (5) ensure compliance with law. (See also Standard 4.01, Maintaining Confidentiality.)

6.02 Maintenance, Dissemination, and Disposal of Confidential Records of Professional and Scientific Work
  (a) Psychologists maintain confidentiality in creating, storing, accessing, transferring, and disposing of records under their control, whether these are written, automated, or in any other medium. (See also Standards 4.01, Maintaining Confidentiality, and 6.01, Documentation of Professional and Scientific Work and Maintenance of Records.)
  (b) If confidential information concerning recipients of psychological services is entered into databases or systems of records available to persons whose access has not been consented to by the recipient, psychologists use coding or other techniques to avoid the inclusion of personal identifiers.
  (c) Psychologists make plans in advance to facilitate the appropriate transfer and to protect the confidentiality of records and data in the event of psychologists' withdrawal from positions or practice. (See also Standards 3.12, Interruption of Psychological Services, and 10.09, Interruption of Therapy.)

6.03 Withholding Records for Nonpayment   Psychologists may not with-hold records under their control that are requested and needed for a client's/patient's emergency treatment solely because payment has not been received.

6.04 Fees and Financial Arrangements
  (a) As early as is feasible in a professional or scientific relationship, psy-chologists and recipients of psychological services reach an agree-ment specifying compensation and billing arrangements.
  (b) Psychologists' fee practices are consistent with law.
  (c) Psychologists do not misrepresent their fees.
  (d) If limitations to services can be anticipated because of limitations in financing, this is discussed with the recipient of services as early as is feasible. (See also Standards 10.09, Interruption of Therapy, and 10.10, Terminating Therapy.)
  (e) If the recipient of services does not pay for services as agreed, and if psychologists intend to use collection agencies or legal measures to collect the fees, psychologists first inform the person that such meas-ures will be taken and provide that person an opportunity to make prompt payment. (See also Standards 4.05, Disclosures; 6.03, With-holding Records for Nonpayment; and 10.01, Informed Consent to Therapy.)

6.05 Barter With Clients/Patients   Barter is the acceptance of goods, serv-ices, or other nonmonetary remuneration from clients/patients in return for psychological services. Psychologists may barter only if (1) it is not clin-ically contraindicated, and (2) the resulting arrangement is not exploita-tive. (See also Standards 3.05, Multiple Relationships, and 6.04, Fees and Financial Arrangements.)

6.06 Accuracy in Reports to Payors and Funding Sources   In their reports to payors for services or sources of research funding, psychologists take rea-sonable steps to ensure the accurate reporting of the nature of the service provided or research conducted, the fees, charges, or payments, and where applicable, the identity of the provider, the findings, and the diagnosis. (See also Standards 4.01, Maintaining Confidentiality; 4.04, Minimizing Intrusions on Privacy; and 4.05, Disclosures.)

6.07 Referrals and Fees   When psychologists pay, receive payment from, or divide fees with another professional, other than in an employer-employee relationship, the payment to each is based on the services provided (clini-cal, consultative, administrative, or other) and is not based on the referral itself. (See also Standard 3.09, Cooperation With Other Professionals.)

7. Education and Training

7.01 Design of Education and Training Programs   Psychologists responsible for education and training programs take reasonable steps to ensure that the programs are designed to provide the appropriate knowledge and proper experiences, and to meet the requirements for licensure, certification, or other goals for which claims are made by the program. (See also Standard 5.03, Descriptions of Workshops and Non-Degree-Granting Educational Programs.)

7.02 Descriptions of Education and Training Programs   Psychologists responsible for education and training programs take reasonable steps to ensure that there is a current and accurate description of the program content (including participation in required course- or program-related counseling, psychotherapy, experiential groups, consulting projects, or community service), training goals and objectives, stipends and benefits, and requirements that must be met for satisfactory completion of the program. This information must be made readily available to all interested parties.

7.03 Accuracy in Teaching
  (a) Psychologists take reasonable steps to ensure that course syllabi are accurate regarding the subject matter to be covered, bases for evaluating progress, and the nature of course experiences. This standard does not preclude an instructor from modifying course content or requirements when the instructor considers it pedagogically necessary or desirable, so long as students are made aware of these modifications in a manner that enables them to fulfill course requirements. (See also Standard 5.01, Avoidance of False or Deceptive Statements.)
  (b) When engaged in teaching or training, psychologists present psychological information accurately. (See also Standard 2.03, Maintaining Competence.)

7.04 Student Disclosure of Personal Information   Psychologists do not require students or supervisees to disclose personal information in course- or program-related activities, either orally or in writing, regarding sexual history, history of abuse and neglect, psychological treatment, and relationships with parents, peers, and spouses or significant others except if (1) the program or training facility has clearly identified this requirement in its admissions and program materials or (2) the information is necessary to evaluate or obtain assistance for students whose personal problems could reasonably be judged to be preventing them from performing their training or professionally related activities in a competent manner or posing a threat to the students or others.

7.05 Mandatory Individual or Group Therapy
  (a) When individual or group therapy is a program or course require-
      ment, psychologists responsible for that program allow students in
      undergraduate and graduate programs the option of selecting such
      therapy from practitioners unaffiliated with the program. (See also
      Standard 7.02, Descriptions of Education and Training Programs.)
  (b) Faculty who are or are likely to be responsible for evaluating stu-
      dents' academic performance do not themselves provide that ther-
      apy. (See also Standard 3.05, Multiple Relationships.)

7.06 Assessing Student and Supervisee Performance
  (a) In academic and supervisory relationships, psychologists establish a
      timely and specific process for providing feedback to students and
      supervisees. Information regarding the process is provided to the
      student at the beginning of supervision.
  (b) Psychologists evaluate students and supervisees on the basis of their
      actual performance on relevant and established program require-
      ments.

7.07 Sexual Relationships With Students and Supervisees   Psychologists do
not engage in sexual relationships with students or supervisees who are in
their department, agency, or training center or over whom psychologists
have or are likely to have evaluative authority. (See also Standard 3.05,
Multiple Relationships.)

8. Research and Publication
8.01 Institutional Approval   When institutional approval is required, psychologists provide accurate information about their research proposals and
obtain approval prior to conducting the research. They conduct the research in accordance with the approved research protocol.

8.02 Informed Consent to Research
  (a) When obtaining informed consent as required in Standard 3.10,
      Informed Consent, psychologists inform participants about (1) the
      purpose of the research, expected duration, and procedures; (2) their
      right to decline to participate and to withdraw from the research
      once participation has begun; (3) the foreseeable consequences of
      declining or withdrawing; (4) reasonably foreseeable factors that
      may be expected to influence their willingness to participate such as
      potential risks, discomfort, or adverse effects; (5) any prospective re-
      search benefits; (6) limits of confidentiality; (7) incentives for partic-
      ipation; and (8) whom to contact for questions about the research

and research participants' rights. They provide opportunity for the prospective participants to ask questions and receive answers. (See also Standards 8.03, Informed Consent for Recording Voices and Images in Research; 8.05, Dispensing With Informed Consent for Research; and 8.07, Deception in Research.)

(b) Psychologists conducting intervention research involving the use of experimental treatments clarify to participants at the outset of the research (1) the experimental nature of the treatment; (2) the services that will or will not be available to the control group(s) if appropriate; (3) the means by which assignment to treatment and control groups will be made; (4) available treatment alternatives if an individual does not wish to participate in the research or wishes to withdraw once a study has begun; and (5) compensation for or monetary costs of participating including, if appropriate, whether reimbursement from the participant or a third-party payor will be sought. (See also Standard 8.02a, Informed Consent to Research.)

8.03 Informed Consent for Recording Voices and Images in Research Psychologists obtain informed consent from research participants prior to recording their voices or images for data collection unless (1) the research consists solely of naturalistic observations in public places, and it is not anticipated that the recording will be used in a manner that could cause personal identification or harm, or (2) the research design includes deception, and consent for the use of the recording is obtained during debriefing. (See also Standard 8.07, Deception in Research.)

8.04 Client/Patient, Student, and Subordinate Research Participants
(a) When psychologists conduct research with clients/patients, students, or subordinates as participants, psychologists take steps to protect the prospective participants from adverse consequences of declining or withdrawing from participation.
(b) When research participation is a course requirement or an opportunity for extra credit, the prospective participant is given the choice of equitable alternative activities.

8.05 Dispensing With Informed Consent for Research Psychologists may dispense with informed consent only (1) where research would not reasonably be assumed to create distress or harm and involves (a) the study of normal educational practices, curricula, or classroom management methods conducted in educational settings; (b) only anonymous questionnaires, naturalistic observations, or archival research for which disclosure of responses would not place participants at risk of criminal or civil liability or damage their financial standing, employability, or reputation, and confidentiality is protected; or (c) the study of factors related to job or organization effectiveness conducted in organizational settings for which there is no risk to participants' employability, and confidentiality is protected or (2) where otherwise permitted by law or federal or institutional regulations.

8.06 Offering Inducements for Research Participation
   (a) Psychologists make reasonable efforts to avoid offering excessive or inappropriate financial or other inducements for research participation when such inducements are likely to coerce participation.
   (b) When offering professional services as an inducement for research participation, psychologists clarify the nature of the services, as well as the risks, obligations, and limitations. (See also Standard 6.05, Barter With Clients/Patients.)

8.07 Deception in Research
   (a) Psychologists do not conduct a study involving deception unless they have determined that the use of deceptive techniques is justified by the study's significant prospective scientific, educational, or applied value and that effective nondeceptive alternative procedures are not feasible.
   (b) Psychologists do not deceive prospective participants about research that is reasonably expected to cause physical pain or severe emotional distress.
   (c) Psychologists explain any deception that is an integral feature of the design and conduct of an experiment to participants as early as is feasible, preferably at the conclusion of their participation, but no later than at the conclusion of the data collection, and permit participants to withdraw their data. (See also Standard 8.08, Debriefing.)

8.08 Debriefing
   (a) Psychologists provide a prompt opportunity for participants to obtain appropriate information about the nature, results, and conclusions of the research, and they take reasonable steps to correct any misconceptions that participants may have of which the psychologists are aware.
   (b) If scientific or humane values justify delaying or withholding this information, psychologists take reasonable measures to reduce the risk of harm.
   (c) When psychologists become aware that research procedures have harmed a participant, they take reasonable steps to minimize the harm.

8.09 Humane Care and Use of Animals in Research
  (a) Psychologists acquire, care for, use, and dispose of animals in compliance with current federal, state, and local laws and regulations, and with professional standards.
  (b) Psychologists trained in research methods and experienced in the care of laboratory animals supervise all procedures involving animals and are responsible for ensuring appropriate consideration of their comfort, health, and humane treatment.
  (c) Psychologists ensure that all individuals under their supervision who are using animals have received instruction in research methods and in the care, maintenance, and handling of the species being used, to the extent appropriate to their role. (See also Standard 2.05, Delegation of Work to Others.)
  (d) Psychologists make reasonable efforts to minimize the discomfort, infection, illness, and pain of animal subjects.
  (e) Psychologists use a procedure subjecting animals to pain, stress, or privation only when an alternative procedure is unavailable and the goal is justified by its prospective scientific, educational, or applied value.
  (f) Psychologists perform surgical procedures under appropriate anesthesia and follow techniques to avoid infection and minimize pain during and after surgery.
  (g) When it is appropriate that an animal's life be terminated, psychologists proceed rapidly, with an effort to minimize pain and in accordance with accepted procedures.

8.10 Reporting Research Results
  (a) Psychologists do not fabricate data. (See also Standard 5.01a, Avoidance of False or Deceptive Statements.)
  (b) If psychologists discover significant errors in their published data, they take reasonable steps to correct such errors in a correction, retraction, erratum, or other appropriate publication means.

8.11 Plagiarism   Psychologists do not present portions of another's work or data as their own, even if the other work or data source is cited occasionally.

8.12 Publication Credit
  (a) Psychologists take responsibility and credit, including authorship credit, only for work they have actually performed or to which they have substantially contributed. (See also Standard 8.12b, Publication Credit.)

(b) Principal authorship and other publication credits accurately reflect the relative scientific or professional contributions of the individuals involved, regardless of their relative status. Mere possession of an institutional position, such as department chair, does not justify authorship credit. Minor contributions to the research or to the writing for publications are acknowledged appropriately, such as in footnotes or in an introductory statement.

(c) Except under exceptional circumstances, a student is listed as principal author on any multiple-authored article that is substantially based on the student's doctoral dissertation. Faculty advisors discuss publication credit with students as early as feasible and throughout the research and publication process as appropriate. (See also Standard 8.12b, Publication Credit.)

8.13 Duplicate Publication of Data   Psychologists do not publish, as original data, data that have been previously published. This does not preclude republishing data when they are accompanied by proper acknowledgment.

8.14 Sharing Research Data for Verification
(a) After research results are published, psychologists do not withhold the data on which their conclusions are based from other competent professionals who seek to verify the substantive claims through reanalysis and who intend to use such data only for that purpose, provided that the confidentiality of the participants can be protected and unless legal rights concerning proprietary data preclude their release. This does not preclude psychologists from requiring that such individuals or groups be responsible for costs associated with the provision of such information.

(b) Psychologists who request data from other psychologists to verify the substantive claims through reanalysis may use shared data only for the declared purpose. Requesting psychologists obtain prior written agreement for all other uses of the data.

8.15 Reviewers   Psychologists who review material submitted for presentation, publication, grant, or research proposal review respect the confidentiality of and the proprietary rights in such information of those who submitted it.

9. Assessment
9.01 Bases for Assessments
(a) Psychologists base the opinions contained in their recommendations, reports, and diagnostic or evaluative statements, including

374 • Religious and Spiritual Issues in Counseling

forensic testimony, on information and techniques sufficient to sub-
stantiate their findings. (See also Standard 2.04, Bases for Scientific
and Professional Judgments.)

(b) Except as noted in 9.01c, psychologists provide opinions of the psychological characteristics of individuals only after they have conducted an examination of the individuals adequate to support their
statements or conclusions. When, despite reasonable efforts, such an
examination is not practical, psychologists document the efforts they
made and the result of those efforts, clarify the probable impact of
their limited information on the reliability and validity of their opinions, and appropriately limit the nature and extent of their conclusions or recommendations. (See also Standards 2.01, Boundaries of
Competence, and 9.06, Interpreting Assessment Results.)

(c) When psychologists conduct a record review or provide consultation or supervision and an individual examination is not warranted
or necessary for the opinion, psychologists explain this and the
sources of information on which they based their conclusions and
recommendations.

9.02 Use of Assessments

(a) Psychologists administer, adapt, score, interpret, or use assessment
techniques, interviews, tests, or instruments in a manner and for
purposes that are appropriate in light of the research on or evidence
of the usefulness and proper application of the techniques.

(b) Psychologists use assessment instruments whose validity and reliability have been established for use with members of the population
tested. When such validity or reliability has not been established, psychologists describe the strengths and limitations of test results and
interpretation.

(c) Psychologists use assessment methods that are appropriate to an individual's language preference and competence, unless the use of an
alternative language is relevant to the assessment issues.

9.03 Informed Consent in Assessments

(a) Psychologists obtain informed consent for assessments, evaluations,
or diagnostic services, as described in Standard 3.10, Informed
Consent, except when (1) testing is mandated by law or governmental regulations; (2) informed consent is implied because testing is
conducted as a routine educational, institutional, or organizational
activity (e.g., when participants voluntarily agree to assessment
when applying for a job); or (3) one purpose of the testing is to evaluate decisional capacity. Informed consent includes an explanation

of the nature and purpose of the assessment, fees, involvement of third parties, and limits of confidentiality and sufficient opportunity for the client/patient to ask questions and receive answers.

(b) Psychologists inform persons with questionable capacity to consent or for whom testing is mandated by law or governmental regulations about the nature and purpose of the proposed assessment services, using language that is reasonably understandable to the person being assessed.

(c) Psychologists using the services of an interpreter obtain informed consent from the client/patient to use that interpreter, ensure that confidentiality of test results and test security are maintained, and include in their recommendations, reports, and diagnostic or evaluative statements, including forensic testimony, discussion of any limitations on the data obtained. (See also Standards 2.05, Delegation of Work to Others; 4.01, Maintaining Confidentiality; 9.01, Bases for Assessments; 9.06, Interpreting Assessment Results; and 9.07, Assessment by Unqualified Persons.)

9.04 Release of Test Data

(a) The term test data refers to raw and scaled scores, client/patient responses to test questions or stimuli, and psychologists' notes and recordings concerning client/patient statements and behavior during an examination. Those portions of test materials that include client/patient responses are included in the definition of test data. Pursuant to a client/patient release, psychologists provide test data to the client/patient or other persons identified in the release. Psychologists may refrain from releasing test data to protect a client/patient or others from substantial harm or misuse or misrepresentation of the data or the test, recognizing that in many instances release of confidential information under these circumstances is regulated by law. (See also Standard 9.11, Maintaining Test Security.)

(b) In the absence of a client/patient release, psychologists provide test data only as required by law or court order.

9.05 Test Construction   Psychologists who develop tests and other assessment techniques use appropriate psychometric procedures and current scientific or professional knowledge for test design, standardization, validation, reduction or elimination of bias, and recommendations for use.

9.06 Interpreting Assessment Results   When interpreting assessment results, including automated interpretations, psychologists take into account the purpose of the assessment as well as the various test factors, test-taking abilities, and other characteristics of the person being assessed, such as situational, personal, linguistic, and cultural differences, that might affect psychologists' judgments or reduce the accuracy of their interpretations. They indicate any significant limitations of their interpretations. (See also Standards 2.01b and c, Boundaries of Competence, and 3.01, Unfair Discrimination.)

9.07 Assessment by Unqualified Persons   Psychologists do not promote the use of psychological assessment techniques by unqualified persons, except when such use is conducted for training purposes with appropriate supervision. (See also Standard 2.05, Delegation of Work to Others.)

9.08 Obsolete Tests and Outdated Test Results
  (a) Psychologists do not base their assessment or intervention decisions or recommendations on data or test results that are outdated for the current purpose.
  (b) Psychologists do not base such decisions or recommendations on tests and measures that are obsolete and not useful for the current purpose.

9.09 Test Scoring and Interpretation Services
  (a) Psychologists who offer assessment or scoring services to other professionals accurately describe the purpose, norms, validity, reliability, and applications of the procedures and any special qualifications applicable to their use.
  (b) Psychologists select scoring and interpretation services (including automated services) on the basis of evidence of the validity of the program and procedures as well as on other appropriate considerations. (See also Standard 2.01b and c, Boundaries of Competence.)
  (c) Psychologists retain responsibility for the appropriate application, interpretation, and use of assessment instruments, whether they score and interpret such tests themselves or use automated or other services.

9.10 Explaining Assessment Results   Regardless of whether the scoring and interpretation are done by psychologists, by employees or assistants, or by automated or other outside services, psychologists take reasonable steps to ensure that explanations of results are given to the individual or designated representative unless the nature of the relationship precludes provision of an explanation of results (such as in some organizational consulting, pre-employment or security screenings, and forensic evaluations), and this fact has been clearly explained to the person being assessed in advance.

9.11. Maintaining Test Security   The term *test materials* refers to manuals, instruments, protocols, and test questions or stimuli and does not include *test data* as defined in Standard 9.04, Release of Test Data. Psychologists make reasonable efforts to maintain the integrity and security of test materials and other assessment techniques consistent with law and contractual obligations, and in a manner that permits adherence to this Ethics Code.

10. Therapy
10.01 Informed Consent to Therapy

(a) When obtaining informed consent to therapy as required in Standard 3.10, Informed Consent, psychologists inform clients/patients as early as is feasible in the therapeutic relationship about the nature and anticipated course of therapy, fees, involvement of third parties, and limits of confidentiality and provide sufficient opportunity for the client/patient to ask questions and receive answers. (See also Standards 4.02, Discussing the Limits of Confidentiality, and 6.04, Fees and Financial Arrangements.)

(b) When obtaining informed consent for treatment for which generally recognized techniques and procedures have not been established, psychologists inform their clients/patients of the developing nature of the treatment, the potential risks involved, alternative treatments that may be available, and the voluntary nature of their participation. (See also Standards 2.01e, Boundaries of Competence, and 3.10, Informed Consent.)

(c) When the therapist is a trainee and the legal responsibility for the treatment provided resides with the supervisor, the client/patient, as part of the informed consent procedure, is informed that the therapist is in training and is being supervised and is given the name of the supervisor.

10.02 Therapy Involving Couples or Families

(a) When psychologists agree to provide services to several persons who have a relationship (such as spouses, significant others, or parents and children), they take reasonable steps to clarify at the outset (1) which of the individuals are clients/patients and (2) the relationship the psychologist will have with each person. This clarification includes the psychologist's role and the probable uses of the services provided or the information obtained. (See also Standard 4.02, Discussing the Limits of Confidentiality.)

(b) If it becomes apparent that psychologists may be called on to perform potentially conflicting roles (such as family therapist and then witness for one party in divorce proceedings), psychologists take reasonable steps to clarify and modify, or withdraw from, roles appropriately. (See also Standard 3.05c, Multiple Relationships.)

10.03 Group Therapy   When psychologists provide services to several persons in a group setting, they describe at the outset the roles and responsibilities of all parties and the limits of confidentiality.

10.04 Providing Therapy to Those Served by Others   In deciding whether to offer or provide services to those already receiving mental health services elsewhere, psychologists carefully consider the treatment issues and the potential client's/patient's welfare. Psychologists discuss these issues with the client/patient or another legally authorized person on behalf of the client/patient in order to minimize the risk of confusion and conflict, consult with the other service providers when appropriate, and proceed with caution and sensitivity to the therapeutic issues.

10.05 Sexual Intimacies With Current Therapy Clients/Patients   Psychologists do not engage in sexual intimacies with current therapy clients/patients.

10.06 Sexual Intimacies With Relatives or Significant Others of Current Therapy Clients/Patients   Psychologists do not engage in sexual intimacies with individuals they know to be close relatives, guardians, or significant others of current clients/patients. Psychologists do not terminate therapy to circumvent this standard.

10.07 Therapy With Former Sexual Partners   Psychologists do not accept as therapy clients/patients persons with whom they have engaged in sexual intimacies.

10.08 Sexual Intimacies With Former Therapy Clients/Patients
  (a) Psychologists do not engage in sexual intimacies with former clients/patients for at least two years after cessation or termination of therapy.
  (b) Psychologists do not engage in sexual intimacies with former clients/patients even after a two-year interval except in the most unusual circumstances. Psychologists who engage in such activity after the two years following cessation or termination of therapy and of having no sexual contact with the former client/patient bear the burden of demonstrating that there has been no exploitation, in light of all relevant factors, including (1) the amount of time that has passed since therapy terminated; (2) the nature, duration, and intensity of

the therapy; (3) the circumstances of termination; (4) the client's/patient's personal history; (5) the client's/patient's current mental status; (6) the likelihood of adverse impact on the client/patient; and (7) any statements or actions made by the therapist during the course of therapy suggesting or inviting the possibility of a posttermination sexual or romantic relationship with the client/patient. (See also Standard 3.05, Multiple Relationships.)

10.09 Interruption of Therapy   When entering into employment or contractual relationships, psychologists make reasonable efforts to provide for orderly and appropriate resolution of responsibility for client/patient care in the event that the employment or contractual relationship ends, with paramount consideration given to the welfare of the client/patient. (See also Standard 3.12, Interruption of Psychological Services.)

10.10 Terminating Therapy
   (a) Psychologists terminate therapy when it becomes reasonably clear that the client/patient no longer needs the service, is not likely to benefit, or is being harmed by continued service.
   (b) Psychologists may terminate therapy when threatened or otherwise endangered by the client/patient or another person with whom the client/patient has a relationship.
   (c) Except where precluded by the actions of clients/patients or third-party payors, prior to termination psychologists provide pretermination counseling and suggest alternative service providers as appropriate.

HISTORY AND EFFECTIVE DATE
This version of the APA Ethics Code was adopted by the American Psychological Association's Council of Representatives during its meeting, August 21, 2002, and is effective beginning June 1, 2003. Inquiries concerning the substance or interpretation of the APA Ethics Code should be addressed to the Director, Office of Ethics, American Psychological Association, 750 First Street, NE, Washington, D.C. 20002-4242. The Ethics Code and information regarding the Code can be found on the APA web site, http://www.apa.org/ethics. The standards in this Ethics Code will be used to adjudicate complaints brought concerning alleged conduct occurring on or after the effective date. Complaints regarding conduct occurring prior to the effective date will be adjudicated on the basis of the version of the Ethics Code that was in effect at the time the conduct occurred.

The APA has previously published its Ethics Code as follows:

American Psychological Association. (1953). Ethical standards of psychologists. Washington, D.C.: Author.

American Psychological Association. (1959). Ethical standards of psychologists. American Psychologist, 14, 279-282.

American Psychological Association. (1963). Ethical standards of psychologists. American Psychologist, 18, 56-60.

American Psychological Association. (1968). Ethical standards of psychologists. American Psychologist, 23, 357-361.

American Psychological Association. (1977, March). Ethical standards of psychologists. APA Monitor, 22-23.

American Psychological Association. (1979). Ethical standards of psychologists. Washington, D.C.: Author.

American Psychological Association. (1981). Ethical principles of psychologists. American Psychologist, 36, 633-638.

American Psychological Association. (1990). Ethical principles of psychologists (Amended June 2, 1989). American Psychologist, 45, 390-395.

American Psychological Association. (1992). Ethical principles of psychologists and code of conduct. American Psychologist, 47, 1597-1611.

Request copies of the APA's Ethical Principles of Psychologists and Code of Conduct from the APA Order Department, 750 First Street, NE, Washington, D.C. 20002-4242, or phone (202) 336-5510.

APPENDIX **D**

AAMFT Code of Ethics
Effective July 1, 2001

Preamble

The Board of Directors of the American Association for Marriage and Family Therapy (AAMFT) hereby promulgates, pursuant to Article 2, Section 2.013 of the Association's Bylaws, the Revised AAMFT Code of Ethics, effective July 1, 2001.

The AAMFT strives to honor the public trust in marriage and family therapists by setting standards for ethical practice as described in this Code. The ethical standards define professional expectations and are enforced by the AAMFT Ethics Committee. The absence of an explicit reference to a specific behavior or situation in the Code does not mean that the behavior is ethical or unethical. The standards are not exhaustive. Marriage and family therapists who are uncertain about the ethics of a particular course of action are encouraged to seek counsel from consultants, attorneys, supervisors, colleagues, or other appropriate authorities.

Both law and ethics govern the practice of marriage and family therapy. When making decisions regarding professional behavior, marriage and family therapists must consider the AAMFT Code of Ethics and applicable laws and regulations. If the AAMFT Code of Ethics prescribes a standard higher than that required by law, marriage and family therapists must meet the higher standard of the AAMFT Code of Ethics. Marriage and family therapists comply with the mandates of law, but make known their commitment to the AAMFT Code of Ethics and take steps to resolve the conflict in a responsible manner. The AAMFT supports legal mandates for reporting of alleged unethical conduct.

The AAMFT Code of Ethics is binding on Members of AAMFT in all membership categories, AAMFT-Approved Supervisors, and applicants for membership and the Approved Supervisor designation (hereafter, AAMFT Member). AAMFT members have an obligation to be familiar with the AAMFT Code of Ethics and its application to their professional services. Lack of awareness or misunderstanding of an ethical standard is not a defense to a charge of unethical conduct.

The process for filing, investigating, and resolving complaints of unethical conduct is described in the current Procedures for Handling Ethical Matters of the AAMFT Ethics Committee. Persons accused are considered innocent by the Ethics Committee until proven guilty, except as otherwise provided, and are entitled to due process. If an AAMFT Member resigns in anticipation of, or during the course of, an ethics investigation, the Ethics Committee will complete its investigation. Any publication of action taken by the Association will include the fact that the Member attempted to resign during the investigation.

Contents
1. Responsibility to clients
2. Confidentiality
3. Professional competence and integrity
4. Responsibility to students and supervisees
5. Responsibility to research participants
6. Responsibility to the profession
7. Financial arrangements
8. Advertising

Principle I

Responsibility to Clients
Marriage and family therapists advance the welfare of families and individuals. They respect the rights of those persons seeking their assistance, and make reasonable efforts to ensure that their services are used appropriately.

1.1. Marriage and family therapists provide professional assistance to persons without discrimination on the basis of race, age, ethnicity, socioeconomic status, disability, gender, health status, religion, national origin, or sexual orientation.

1.2 Marriage and family therapists obtain appropriate informed consent to therapy or related procedures as early as feasible in the therapeutic relationship, and use language that is reasonably understandable to clients. The content of informed consent may vary depending upon the client and treatment plan; however, informed consent generally necessitates that the client: (a) has the capacity to consent; (b) has been adequately informed of significant information concerning treatment processes and procedures; (c) has been adequately informed of potential risks and benefits of treatments for which generally recognized standards do not yet exist; (d) has freely and without undue influence expressed consent; and (e) has provided consent that is appropriately documented. When persons, due to age or mental status, are legally incapable of giving informed consent, marriage and family therapists obtain informed permission from a legally authorized person, if such substitute consent is legally permissible.

1.3 Marriage and family therapists are aware of their influential positions with respect to clients, and they avoid exploiting the trust and dependency of such persons. Therapists, therefore, make every effort to avoid conditions and multiple relationships with clients that could impair professional judgment or increase the risk of exploitation. Such relationships include, but are not limited to, business or close personal relationships with a client or the client's immediate family. When the risk of impairment or exploitation exists due to conditions or multiple roles, therapists take appropriate precautions.

1.4 Sexual intimacy with clients is prohibited.

1.5 Sexual intimacy with former clients is likely to be harmful and is therefore prohibited for two years following the termination of therapy or last professional contact. In an effort to avoid exploiting the trust and dependency of clients, marriage and family therapists should not engage in sexual intimacy with former clients after the two years following termination or last professional contact. Should therapists engage in sexual intimacy with former clients following two years after termination or last professional contact, the burden shifts to the therapist to demonstrate that there has been no exploitation or injury to the former client or to the client's immediate family.

1.6 Marriage and family therapists comply with applicable laws regarding the reporting of alleged unethical conduct.

1.7 Marriage and family therapists do not use their professional relationships with clients to further their own interests.

1.8 Marriage and family therapists respect the rights of clients to make decisions and help them to understand the consequences of these decisions. Therapists clearly advise the clients that they have the responsibility to make decisions regarding relationships such as cohabitation, marriage, divorce, separation, reconciliation, custody, and visitation.

1.9 Marriage and family therapists continue therapeutic relationships only so long as it is reasonably clear that clients are benefiting from the relationship.

1.10 Marriage and family therapists assist persons in obtaining other therapeutic services if the therapist is unable or unwilling, for appropriate reasons, to provide professional help.

1.11 Marriage and family therapists do not abandon or neglect clients in treatment without making reasonable arrangements for the continuation of such treatment.

1.12 Marriage and family therapists obtain written informed consent from clients before videotaping, audio recording, or permitting third-party observation.

1.13 Marriage and family therapists, upon agreeing to provide services to a person or entity at the request of a third party, clarify, to the extent feasible and at the outset of the service, the nature of the relationship with each party and the limits of confidentiality.

Principle II

Confidentiality

Marriage and family therapists have unique confidentiality concerns because the client in a therapeutic relationship may be more than one person. Therapists respect and guard the confidences of each individual client.

2.1 Marriage and family therapists disclose to clients and other interested parties, as early as feasible in their professional contacts, the nature of confidentiality and possible limitations of the clients' right to confidentiality. Therapists review with clients the circumstances where confidential information may be requested and where disclosure of confidential information may be legally required. Circumstances may necessitate repeated disclosures.

2.2 Marriage and family therapists do not disclose client confidences except by written authorization or waiver, or where mandated or permitted by law. Verbal authorization will not be sufficient except in emergency situations, unless prohibited by law. When providing couple, family or group treatment, the therapist does not disclose information outside the treatment context without a written authorization from each individual competent to execute a waiver. In the context of couple, family or group treatment, the therapist may not reveal any individual's confidences to others in the client unit without the prior written permission of that individual.

2.3 Marriage and family therapists use client and/or clinical materials in teaching, writing, consulting, research, and public presentations only if a written waiver has been obtained in accordance with Subprinciple 2.2, or when appropriate steps have been taken to protect client identity and confidentiality.

2.4 Marriage and family therapists store, safeguard, and dispose of client records in ways that maintain confidentiality and in accord with applicable laws and professional standards.

2.5 Subsequent to the therapist moving from the area, closing the practice, or upon the death of the therapist, a marriage and family therapist arranges for the storage, transfer, or disposal of client records in ways that maintain confidentiality and safeguard the welfare of clients.

2.6 Marriage and family therapists, when consulting with colleagues or referral sources, do not share confidential information that could reasonably lead to the identification of a client, research participant, supervisee, or other person with whom they have a confidential relationship unless they have obtained the prior written consent of the client, research participant, supervisee, or other person with whom they have a confidential relationship. Information may be shared only to the extent necessary to achieve the purposes of the consultation.

Principle III

Professional Competence and Integrity
Marriage and family therapists maintain high standards of professional competence and integrity.

3.1 Marriage and family therapists pursue knowledge of new developments and maintain competence in marriage and family therapy through education, training, or supervised experience.

3.2 Marriage and family therapists maintain adequate knowledge of and adhere to applicable laws, ethics, and professional standards.

3.3 Marriage and family therapists seek appropriate professional assistance for their personal problems or conflicts that may impair work performance or clinical judgment.

3.4 Marriage and family therapists do not provide services that create a conflict of interest that may impair work performance or clinical judgment.

3.5 Marriage and family therapists, as presenters, teachers, supervisors, consultants and researchers, are dedicated to high standards of scholarship, present accurate information, and disclose potential conflicts of interest.

3.6 Marriage and family therapists maintain accurate and adequate clinical and financial records.

3.7 While developing new skills in specialty areas, marriage and family therapists take steps to ensure the competence of their work and to protect clients from possible harm. Marriage and family therapists practice in specialty areas new to them only after appropriate education, training, or supervised experience.

3.8 Marriage and family therapists do not engage in sexual or other forms of harassment of clients, students, trainees, supervisees, employees, colleagues, or research subjects.

3.9 Marriage and family therapists do not engage in the exploitation of clients, students, trainees, supervisees, employees, colleagues, or research subjects.

3.10 Marriage and family therapists do not give to or receive from clients (a) gifts of substantial value or (b) gifts that impair the integrity or efficacy of the therapeutic relationship.

3.11 Marriage and family therapists do not diagnose, treat, or advise on problems outside the recognized boundaries of their competencies.

3.12 Marriage and family therapists make efforts to prevent the distortion or misuse of their clinical and research findings.

3.13 Marriage and family therapists, because of their ability to influence and alter the lives of others, exercise special care when making public their professional recommendations and opinions through testimony or other public statements.

3.14 To avoid a conflict of interests, marriage and family therapists who treat minors or adults involved in custody or visitation actions may not also perform forensic evaluations for custody, residence, or visitation of the minor. The marriage and family therapist who treats the minor may provide the court or mental health professional performing the evaluation with information about the minor from the marriage and family therapist's perspective as a treating marriage and family therapist, so long as the marriage and family therapist does not violate confidentiality.

3.15 Marriage and family therapists are in violation of this Code and subject to termination of membership or other appropriate action if they: (a) are convicted of any felony; (b) are convicted of a misdemeanor related to their qualifications or functions; (c) engage in conduct which could lead to conviction of a felony, or a misdemeanor related to their qualifications or functions; (d) are expelled from or disciplined by other professional organizations; (e) have their licenses or certificates suspended or revoked or are otherwise disciplined by regulatory bodies; (f) continue to practice marriage and family therapy while no longer competent to do so because they are impaired by physical or mental causes or the abuse of alcohol or other substances; or (g) fail to cooperate with the Association at any point from the inception of an ethical complaint through the completion of all proceedings regarding that complaint.

Principle IV

Responsibility to Students and Supervisees
Marriage and family therapists do not exploit the trust and dependency of students and supervisees.

4.1 Marriage and family therapists are aware of their influential positions with respect to students and supervisees, and they avoid exploiting the trust and dependency of such persons. Therapists, therefore, make every effort to avoid conditions and multiple relationships that could impair professional objectivity or increase the risk of exploitation. When the risk of impairment or exploitation exists due to conditions or multiple roles, therapists take appropriate precautions.

4.2 Marriage and family therapists do not provide therapy to current students or supervisees.

4.3 Marriage and family therapists do not engage in sexual intimacy with students or supervisees during the evaluative or training relationship between the therapist and student or supervisee. Should a supervisor engage in sexual activity with a former supervisee, the burden of proof shifts to the supervisor to demonstrate that there has been no exploitation or injury to the supervisee.

4.4 Marriage and family therapists do not permit students or supervisees to perform or to hold themselves out as competent to perform professional services beyond their training, level of experience, and competence.

4.5 Marriage and family therapists take reasonable measures to ensure that services provided by supervisees are professional.

4.6 Marriage and family therapists avoid accepting as supervisees or students those individuals with whom a prior or existing relationship could compromise the therapist's objectivity. When such situations cannot be avoided, therapists take appropriate precautions to maintain objectivity. Examples of such relationships include, but are not limited to, those individuals with whom the therapist has a current or prior sexual, close personal, immediate familial, or therapeutic relationship.

4.7 Marriage and family therapists do not disclose supervisee confidences except by written authorization or waiver, or when mandated or permitted by law. In educational or training settings where there are multiple supervisors, disclosures are permitted only to other professional colleagues, administrators, or employers who share responsibility for training of the supervisee. Verbal authorization will not be sufficient except in emergency situations, unless prohibited by law.

Principle V

Responsibility to Research Participants
Investigators respect the dignity and protect the welfare of research participants, and are aware of applicable laws and regulations and professional standards governing the conduct of research.

5.1 Investigators are responsible for making careful examinations of ethical acceptability in planning studies. To the extent that services to research participants may be compromised by participation in research, investigators seek the ethical advice of qualified professionals not directly involved in the investigation and observe safeguards to protect the rights of research participants.

5. 2 Investigators requesting participant involvement in research inform participants of the aspects of the research that might reasonably be expected to influence willingness to participate. Investigators are especially sensitive to the possibility of diminished consent when participants are also receiving clinical services, or have impairments which limit understanding and/or communication, or when participants are children.

5.3 Investigators respect each participant's freedom to decline participation in or to withdraw from a research study at any time. This obligation requires special thought and consideration when investigators or other members of the research team are in positions of authority or influence over participants. Marriage and family therapists, therefore, make every effort to avoid multiple relationships with research participants that could impair professional judgment or increase the risk of exploitation.

5.4 Information obtained about a research participant during the course of an investigation is confidential unless there is a waiver previously obtained in writing. When the possibility exists that others, including family members, may obtain access to such information, this possibility, together with the plan for protecting confidentiality, is explained as part of the procedure for obtaining informed consent.

Principle VI

Responsibility to the Profession
Marriage and family therapists respect the rights and responsibilities of professional colleagues and participate in activities that advance the goals of the profession.

6.1 Marriage and family therapists remain accountable to the standards of the profession when acting as members or employees of organizations. If the mandates of an organization with which a marriage and family therapist is affiliated, through employment, contract or otherwise, conflict with the AAMFT Code of Ethics, marriage and family therapists make known to the organization their commitment to the AAMFT Code of Ethics and attempt to resolve the conflict in a way that allows the fullest adherence to the Code of Ethics.

6.2 Marriage and family therapists assign publication credit to those who have contributed to a publication in proportion to their contributions and in accordance with customary professional publication practices.

6.3 Marriage and family therapists do not accept or require authorship credit for a publication based on research from a student's program, unless the therapist made a substantial contribution beyond being a faculty advisor or research committee member. Coauthorship on a student thesis, dissertation, or project should be determined in accordance with principles of fairness and justice.

6.4 Marriage and family therapists who are the authors of books or other materials that are published or distributed do not plagiarize or fail to cite persons to whom credit for original ideas or work is due.

6.5 Marriage and family therapists who are the authors of books or other materials published or distributed by an organization take reasonable precautions to ensure that the organization promotes and advertises the materials accurately and factually.

6.6 Marriage and family therapists participate in activities that contribute to a better community and society, including devoting a portion of their professional activity to services for which there is little or no financial return.

6.7 Marriage and family therapists are concerned with developing laws and regulations pertaining to marriage and family therapy that serve the public interest, and with altering such laws and regulations that are not in the public interest.

6.8 Marriage and family therapists encourage public participation in the design and delivery of professional services and in the regulation of practitioners.

Principle VII

Financial Arrangements
Marriage and family therapists make financial arrangements with clients, third-party payors, and supervisees that are reasonably understandable and conform to accepted professional practices.

7.1 Marriage and family therapists do not offer or accept kickbacks, rebates, bonuses, or other remuneration for referrals; fee-for-service arrangements are not prohibited.

7.2 Prior to entering into the therapeutic or supervisory relationship, marriage and family therapists clearly disclose and explain to clients and supervisees: (a) all financial arrangements and fees related to professional services, including charges for canceled or missed appointments; (b) the use of collection agencies or legal measures for nonpayment; and (c) the procedure for obtaining payment from the client, to the extent allowed by law, if payment is denied by the third-party payor. Once services have begun, therapists provide reasonable notice of any changes in fees or other charges.

7.3 Marriage and family therapists give reasonable notice to clients with unpaid balances of their intent to seek collection by agency or legal recourse. When such action is taken, therapists will not disclose clinical information.

7.4 Marriage and family therapists represent facts truthfully to clients, third-party payors, and supervisees regarding services rendered.

7.5 Marriage and family therapists ordinarily refrain from accepting goods and services from clients in return for services rendered. Bartering for professional services may be conducted only if: (a) the supervisee or client requests it, (b) the relationship is not exploitative, (c) the professional relationship is not distorted, and (d) a clear written contract is established.

7.6 Marriage and family therapists may not withhold records under their immediate control that are requested and needed for a client's treatment solely because payment has not been received for past services, except as otherwise provided by law.

Principle VIII

Advertising

Marriage and family therapists engage in appropriate informational activities, including those that enable the public, referral sources, or others to choose professional services on an informed basis.

8.1 Marriage and family therapists accurately represent their competencies, education, training, and experience relevant to their practice of marriage and family therapy.

8.2 Marriage and family therapists ensure that advertisements and publications in any media (such as directories, announcements, business cards, newspapers, radio, television, Internet, and facsimiles) convey information that is necessary for the public to make an appropriate selection of professional services. Information could include: (a) office information, such as name, address, telephone number, credit card acceptability, fees, languages spoken, and office hours; (b) qualifying clinical degree (see subprinciple 8.5); (c) other earned degrees (see subprinciple 8.5) and state or provincial licensures and/or certifications; (d) AAMFT clinical member status; and (e) description of practice.

8.3 Marriage and family therapists do not use names that could mislead the public concerning the identity, responsibility, source, and status of those practicing under that name, and do not hold themselves out as being partners or associates of a firm if they are not.

8.4 Marriage and family therapists do not use any professional identification (such as a business card, office sign, letterhead, Internet, or telephone or association directory listing) if it includes a statement or claim that is false, fraudulent, misleading, or deceptive.

8.5 In representing their educational qualifications, marriage and family therapists list and claim as evidence only those earned degrees: (a) from institutions accredited by regional accreditation sources recognized by the United States Department of Education, (b) from institutions recognized by states or provinces that license or certify marriage and family therapists, or (c) from equivalent foreign institutions.

8.6 Marriage and family therapists correct, wherever possible, false, misleading, or inaccurate information and representations made by others concerning the therapist's qualifications, services, or products.

8.7 Marriage and family therapists make certain that the qualifications of their employees or supervisees are represented in a manner that is not false, misleading, or deceptive.

8.8 Marriage and family therapists do not represent themselves as providing specialized services unless they have the appropriate education, training, or supervised experience.

This Code is published by:
American Association for Marriage and Family Therapy
112 South Alfred Street, Alexandria, VA 22314
Phone: (703) 838-9808 - Fax: (703) 838-9805
www.aamft.org
Violations of this Code should be brought in writing to the attention of:
AAMFT Ethics Committee
112 South Alfred Street, Alexandria, VA 22314
Phone: (703) 838-9808 - Fax: (703) 838-9805
email: ethics@aamft.org

Index

Date Due

AUG 1 3 2008		
JUN 2 6 2008		
JUN 0 1 2009		
JUN 09 2010		

BRODART, CO.   Cat. No. 23-233-003   Printed in U.S.A.